African Legal Theory and Contemporary Problems

IUS GENTIUM

COMPARATIVE PERSPECTIVES ON LAW AND JUSTICE

VOLUME 29

For further volumes:
http://www.springer.com/series/7888

Oche Onazi
Editor

African Legal Theory and Contemporary Problems

Critical Essays

Springer

Editor
Oche Onazi
Lecturer in Law
University of Dundee
Dundee, UK

ISBN 978-94-007-7536-7 ISBN 978-94-007-7537-4 (eBook)
DOI 10.1007/978-94-007-7537-4
Springer Dordrecht Heidelberg New York London

Library of Congress Control Number: 2013955026

Printed on acid-free paper

Springer is part of Springer Science+Business Media (www.springer.com)

Acknowledgements

An earlier version of Chap. 3 – 'When British Justice (in African Colonies) Points Two Ways: On Dualism, Hybridity, and the Genealogy of Juridical Negritude in Taslim Olawale Elias' – was published in slightly different form as part of a special issue in the 'International Law and the Periphery' series dedicated to the work and thought of Taslim O. Elias in 2008 in the *Leiden Journal of International Law* (21, 377–410. Reprinted with the kind permission of Cambridge University Press).

An earlier version of Chap. 6 – 'The Legal Subject in Modern African Law: A Nigerian Report' – was published in slightly different form as part of a special issue on 'Economic, Social, and Cultural Rights' in 2002 in the *Human Rights Review* (7/2, 17–34. Reprinted with the kind permission of Springer-Verlag).

An earlier version of Chap. 11 – 'Legal Empowerment of the Poor: Does Political Participation Matter?' – was previously published as part of a special issue on 'Contemporary African Jurisprudence' in 2012 in *The Journal Jurisprudence* (14, 201–224. Reprinted with the kind permission of The Elias Clark Group).

Contents

1 **Introduction** ... 1
Oche Onazi

Part I Law

2 **On 'African' Legal Theory: A Possibility, an Impossibility or Mere Conundrum?** ... 17
Chikosa Mozesi Silungwe

3 **When British Justice (in African Colonies) Points Two Ways: On Dualism, Hybridity, and the Genealogy of Juridical Negritude in Taslim Olawale Elias** ... 31
Mark Toufayan

4 **Decoding Afrocentrism: Decolonizing Legal Theory** ... 71
Dan Kuwali

5 **Connecting African Jurisprudence to Universal Jurisprudence Through a Shared Understanding of Contract** ... 93
Dominic Burbidge

6 **The Legal Subject in Modern African Law: A Nigerian Report** ... 109
Olúfẹ́mi Táíwò

Part II Rights

7 **African Values, Human Rights and Group Rights: A Philosophical Foundation for the Banjul Charter** ... 131
Thaddeus Metz

8 **Before Rights and Responsibilities: An African Ethos of Citizenship** ... 153
Oche Onazi

9 The Practice and the Promise of Making Rights Claims: Lessons from the South African Treatment Access Campaign 173
Karen Zivi

10 Unpacking the Universal: African Human Rights Philosophy in Chinua Achebe's *Things Fall Apart* 199
Basil Ugochukwu

Part III Society

11 Legal Empowerment of the Poor: Does Political Participation Matter? 221
Oche Onazi

12 The Humanist Basis of African Communitarianism as Viable Third Alternative Theory of Developmentalism 241
Adebisi Arewa

13 Crime Detection and the *Psychic Witness* in America: An Allegory for Re-appraising Indigenous African Criminology 265
Babafemi Odunsi

Index 289

Contributors

Adebisi Arewa Fellow Nigerian Institute of Advanced Legal Studies (NIALS) Lagos, Nigeria; Head Editorial & External Linkages Department, Nigerian Institute of Advanced Legal Studies, Nigeria; Executive Director, NIALS Justice E. Ayoola, CON, JSC (Rtd.) Centre for Transnational Legal Practice and Cross-Border Criminality, Nigeria.

Dominic Burbidge D.Phil. candidate at the University of Oxford, Oxford, UK and researcher for Strathmore University, Nairobi, Kenya.

Dan Kuwali Post-Doctoral Fellow, Centre for Human Rights, Faculty of Law, University of Pretoria, Pretoria, South Africa.

Associate Professor of Law, Centre for Security Studies, Mzuzu University, Malawi.

Thaddeus Metz Professor of Philosophy, University of Johannesburg, Johannesburg, South Africa.

Babafemi Odunsi Lecturer, Faculty of Law, Obafemi Awolowo Unversity, Ile-Ife, Nigeria; MacArthur Fellow, Faculty of Law, University of Toronto, Toronto, Canada.

Oche Onazi Lecturer in Law, University of Dundee, Dundee, UK.

Chikosa Mozesi Silungwe Legal Consultant at The Mizumali Foundation, Malawi.

Olúfémi Táíwò Professor, Africana Studies and Research Center, Cornell University, Ithaca, USA.

Mark Toufayan Assistant Professor, Faculty of Law, University of Ottawa, Canada.

Basil Ugochukwu Legal Process Instructor and Ph.D. candidate at Osgoode Hall Law School, York University, Toronto, Canada.

Karen Zivi Assistant Professor of Political Science, Grand Valley University, Michigan, USA.

Chapter 1
Introduction

Oche Onazi

This book aims to situate, at a general level of abstraction, African legal theory in the context of contemporary problems of war, crimes against humanity, the misery of poverty, hunger, disease and the crises of the environment, among many other pressing problems, which affect African and non-African societies alike. While the global or specific nature of these problems is debatable, given the disparity of experiences between African and non-African societies, what is less arguable is the absence of African approaches or responses to such questions, an issue that extends beyond legal theory.

In response to this shortcoming, this book not only seeks to provide African solutions to contemporary problems, but also provide an *African* contribution to the understanding of legal theory. Under the aegis of African legal theory, therefore, the contributors in this book explore the promise of the African philosophical, cultural and social experience and understanding of law in relation to contemporary problems. Although what is called African legal theory is still up for debate, what the contributors generally explore are the ways in which law, legal concepts and institutions embody or reflect the most salient and common attributes of life in sub-Saharan Africa, attributes which are most often called Afro-communitarian (Metz 2012, pp. 22–23). Indeed, what is significantly articulated in this book is not just what is 'African' in legal theory, but also what is attractive in the African tradition.[1] In doing so, the contributors by no means claim that the Afro-communitarian characteristics of law, legal concepts and institutions are present in all sub-Saharan societies or that everything African is philosophically plausible. Rather, the contributors interpret and draw from the African tradition in a way that leads to philosophically attractive ideas about what law, legal concepts and institutions ought to be in all sub-Saharan societies.

[1] I owe this point to Thaddeus Metz. I thank him for drawing my attention to it.

O. Onazi (✉)
Lecturer in Law, University of Dundee, Dundee, UK
e-mail: o.onazi@dundee.ac.uk

O. Onazi (ed.), *African Legal Theory and Contemporary Problems: Critical Essays*, Ius Gentium: Comparative Perspectives on Law and Justice 29,
DOI 10.1007/978-94-007-7537-4_1, © Springer Science+Business Media Dordrecht 2014

Notwithstanding, the objective of this book might invite some scepticism, especially because the connection between legal theory and practical contemporary problems is not always obvious, and also, because of the already mentioned issue of the unsettled meaning of African legal theory itself. This scepticism is not by any means misplaced. Indeed, even the contributors do not agree on what African legal theory means, let alone on its relevance to contemporary problems.

For a moment, part of the scepticism about the relationship between legal theory and contemporary problems can, at least, be placated by understanding the intricate relationship between legal theory, legal philosophy and sociology of law. A valuable way to respond to this scepticism is by clarifying the methodological nature, scope or boundaries of the discipline of legal theory. Generally speaking, legal theory is quite narrow or specific in its scope; even though opinions vary on how restrictive or expansive it can or should be (see, for example, Friedmann 1967, p. 3). Nevertheless, it can be argued that, although legal theory typically refers to systematic or scientific inquiries into the nature of law, laws in general and legal institutions; it is not concerned, but does not necessarily exclude, philosophical, moral or sociological enquiries (Cotterrell 2003, p. 3). Although legal theory is ambiguous about questions relating to the nature of justice or the moral justifications of laws and legal institutions, it provides an opportunity to address some of these concerns through theories of natural law (2003).

In another sense, although legal theory does not directly address the problems of concern of this book, it, nevertheless, provides a window of opportunity for the type of investigations in this context through its interaction with legal philosophy and sociology of law. Legal theory, as such, is not far removed from concerns of legal philosophy or sociology of law, a relationship which is made more apparent under the umbrella subject of jurisprudence. The relevance of legal theory to contemporary problems is, therefore, dependent upon grasping the nature of contributions of legal philosophy and sociology of law to legal theory. Legal philosophy and sociology of law impact upon legal theory, and, thereby, on contemporary problems, by grounding normative and empirical inquiries into the nature of concepts of law, justice, responsibility, obligation, rights, duties, property, land, ownership, ethics, person, identity, citizenship, community, state, market, crime, punishment and other important concepts. Very few would disagree that the ability to evaluate and develop legally-based practical solutions to many problems of the world today depend on a proper understanding of these concepts. Legal theory, as such, has a pivotal role to play in relation to contemporary problems around the globe.

Looked at this way, the essays in this book, through the critical lens of African legal theory, collectively seek to rejuvenate the discipline of legal theory in a way that reinforces its concern for contemporary problems. This is achieved, not only by challenging dominant perceptions of legal theory, but also by establishing its foundational concepts on a different (African) theoretical basis. This is more so because – and another common theme among the essays in this book – the contemporary problems of concern have an indelible African mark on them. Wars, famine, hunger, disease, poverty, and other symptoms of injustice, are endemic in Africa, apart from being problems that have failed to attract African approaches or responses. The popular, very often, negative image of Africa as a continent of enormous catastrophes has, among other reasons, accounted for the lack of interest, appreciation and analysis of different forms of indigenous African thought, especially how these forms of thought may be relevant to addressing contemporary problems. Indeed, a common argument among the essays in this book is particularly that African legal theoretical, philosophical, jurisprudential or other forms of thought have been excluded, under-explored or under-theorised in relation to many contemporary African problems, not least problems outside Africa.

The lack of knowledge, interest or simply the neglect of African legal theory in intellectual circles can, among other things, directly be traced to the central controversy surrounding the subject. This controversy is simply about the existence of African legal theory; in other words, whether anything like African legal theory exists, a question that is related to an earlier scepticism about the existence of African philosophical knowledge. African legal theory invites a similar sort of scepticism, especially when it is exclusively defined or established, as often the case, from African philosophy.

The source of this controversy appears to be epistemological, particularly because of the obvious long-standing methodological question about the disciplinary parameters of African philosophy. The controversy is that, if legal theory, in the general sense of the term, is the scientific analysis of laws, legal concepts and institutions, then positing the existence of African legal theory is also a matter of debate simply because of the unorthodox, unscientific or unsystematic method of analysis it derives from African philosophy. It is not so much, a controversy about the existence of African law, a question which is controversial in its own right; rather it is a question about the existence of African knowledge. More specifically, it is a question of whether African philosophical knowledge, which forms the basis of claims of the existence of African legal theory, allows for scientific reasoning, analysis, deduction or speculation about African law. After all, African philosophy is commonly unwritten and established from customs, culture, tradition, religion, moral values, folklore, stories, proverbs, parables and art, among other things. In spite of this, it must be recognised that African philosophy, in its recent history, continues to benefit from an increasing volume of textual sources, which are relied upon by many contributors in this book.

A first type of response to the scepticism above is to argue that African philosophy offers a different approach to legal theory, and this does not mean it is not legal theory at all. To be specific, African philosophy offers a different method of scientific reasoning or analysis, which yields to a different technique or approach to legal theory. After all, other philosophical traditions do not solely depend on textual forms of reasoning, analysis, deduction or speculation about law, so why should African philosophy be different in this respect? For example, there appears to be some new research interest in understanding law beyond textual forms of analysis (Del Mar and Bankowski 2013). Although African thought is yet to be explored, it provides an appropriate context to investigate such non-textual understandings of law.

A second kind of response can be made, through Boaventura de Sousa Santos (2007), which challenges dominant perceptions of knowledge, especially the monopoly assumed by modern knowledge and law. According to this view, there are other forms of knowledge and modern knowledge is only a species. In assuming dominance over other forms of knowledge, modern knowledge contributes or concretises the anonymity of other forms of knowledge. Modern knowledge is discernible, while other forms of knowledge are not.

The dominance of modern knowledge is affirmed through the distinction between scientific truth and falsehood. Only modern science, not theology or philosophy, can generate ascertainable and universal truths about the world. The dominance of modern knowledge lies behind the distinction between scientific and non-scientific truth, something that contributes to the unrecognisable nature of indigenous knowledge. Modern knowledge discounts other techniques of establishing universal truth simply because they do not conform to its methods. Indigenous knowledge, on this account, is simply beyond comprehension; it is incapable of establishing either universal truth or falsehood. Indigenous knowledge is nothing short of a belief, myth, opinion or intuition, a basis for further investigation and subjugation by modern scientific knowledge. This is the same, Santos says, with modern law. Legality is determined by state or international law. The legal and illegal are the only ways of thinking of law. The a-legal and non-legal or legal or illegal according to non-state law is beyond comprehension. This thesis conforms to Santos's (2002, pp. 12–14) seminal work on the exhaustive nature or inability of modern knowledge to offer solutions to contemporary problems in ways that can ground some of the inquiries in this book.

There is a further epistemological point that stems from the above, one which may point to the limitations or incompleteness of aligning African legal theory so close to, or establishing it only from African philosophy. The point is that if it was, for whatever reason, ever valid to dismiss the existence of African legal theoretical, philosophical or jurisprudential knowledge, it is no longer tenable to continue to do so today. There has been so much legal experimentation and transformation in postcolonial African societies, which more than anything point in the direction of a nascent legal theory or legal theories. Although the full ramifications of these developments are not exactly clear or conclusive, the important epistemological point is that they require us to study them both philosophically and sociologically, to determine what exactly is unfolding, and also, the ways in which these developments can be understood and described.

The point being made is not only that defining African legal theory on the basis of African philosophy alone discounts the possibility of more descriptive, empirical-driven or sociological accounts of law, but also that it exposes African legal theory to the criticism of being backward-looking, nostalgic or static. African legal theory, from this standpoint, will fail to account for the evolutionary and asymptotic nature of African law and the society to which it is most relevant. While thinking of African legal theory sociologically does have to rely heavily on Western influenced methods, the advantage it offers, however, is that it allows us to study the impact or otherwise of African legal theory and philosophical concepts under the continuous and changing nature of the African environment.

Thinking of African legal theory sociologically can help shed light on how African concepts of law and philosophy have intermingled, transformed or taken up new forms or how entirely new concepts have emerged or simply how old concepts have lost their significance. More importantly, it may help shed light on how African concepts have interlocked and transformed received or colonial concepts of law into something else. For instance, a reference to modern Africa can be a good way to elaborate on this point. Indeed, modern Africa is not modern in the Western sense of the term. Modern Africa retains something from the past and the present. It is a fusion of both worlds; it is at best a combination of the traditional and modern.

The opportunity for studying legal theory in contemporary settings is provided by sociological and anthropological studies on African urban cities (see, for example, Hetch and Simone 1994; Simone 2001). More recently, such studies have pioneered explorations into new forms of collaboration and co-operation that have emerged as a result of exclusion from formal economic and political systems. Without overstating or failing to acknowledge the endemic nature of poverty across Africa, the studies on urban cities importantly underscore the degree of creativity, solidarity, trust, reciprocity and cooperation among those excluded from the formal institutions, including formal institutions of law. It would be interesting to explore what African legal theory would mean in the light of these emerging organisational forms; in other words, it would be fascinating to explore how these developments impact upon sociologically informed theories of African law, laws in general and legal institutions.

The essays in this book do not claim to definitively settle all the issues highlighted above; rather they introduce readers to some of the key issues, questions, concepts, impulses and problems that underpin the idea of African legal theory. They outline the potential offered by African legal theory and open up its key concepts and impulses for critical scrutiny. This is done in order to develop a better understanding of the extent to which African legal theory can contribute to discourses seeking to address some of the challenges that confront African and non-African societies alike.

Although the essays in this book have a common aim, they, however, vary on the degree of emphasis given to either the question of African legal theory or to its potential or to its degree of application to contemporary problems. Understandably, given the controversy that has surrounded the existence of African legal theory, there is a genuine attempt to strike the difficult balance between expanding on its meaning on the one hand and its application to contemporary problems on the other. Similarly, because of the controversial nature of the subject of the book, the style – even though each essay varies considerably – is polemic. Some essays, however, are more polemic than others, just as some are more critical than others. Differences in terminology are noticeable. African legal theory, African jurisprudence and African legal philosophy are given different level of emphasis and they are used interchangeably in the essays to refer to the same thing.

The book is structured in three main parts, with each covering similar themes. In the first part, the essays consider questions relating to the definition of African legal theory, and to a certain extent, questions of its application. Chikosa Silungwe provides an appropriate point of departure into some of these issues; he touches on the nuances surrounding the definition of African legal theory, a term used interchangeably with African jurisprudence and African philosophy. For him, it is farfetched to relate African legal theory to contemporary problems without, first of all, clarifying the nature of this theory. He argues against, and points to the flaws, of a purist concept of African legal theory, synonymous with what he describes as sentimentalist and legal pluralist approaches. Similarly, both approaches seek to show the continuity of African norms in contemporary settings, a point that makes them susceptible to criticisms from a third approach – the revisionist perspective on African legal theory. The revisionist approach, unlike the others, is sensitive to the distorting nature of the Enlightenment movement, colonial and capitalist projects on African legal theory. The debate at the heart of all approaches, however, is the question of culture, in particular, whether the African legal culture exists in a pure form. In contrast to these, Silungwe articulates a non-purist form of African legal theory inspired by Homi Bhabha's idea of culture's-in between, an approach that denies the purity of culture thereby recognising the 'convoluted socio–political environment of "law" or the "legal" in Africa (or in the African) which permeates into its theory, jurisprudence or philosophy'. The in-betweenness of cultures is evident from contemporary migrations, where cultures transform but retain something from their ancestral origins. Culture's-in between favours hybridity and infusion, not duality. It is a dialectic phenomenon that transcends, not into a Hegelian synthesis, but rather into a third space, a space of unequal power relations, which articulate, negotiate and contradict each other. Silungwe illustrates how this conception of African legal theory provides a better explanation for Anti-Witchcraft Laws, Anti-Homosexual Laws and the much talked about relationship between the Southern African concept of ubuntu and human rights norms. In all instances, African and Western norms – some more positively than others – intermingle or interlock confusingly, without necessarily becoming 'transmogrified'.

If hybridity and convolution are hallmarks of African legal theory, Mark Toufayan's rich contribution to this book demonstrates how this is achieved in a different way through the seminal writings of the late Nigerian Jurist Taslim Elias. This is part of Toufayan's broader aim of understanding how international law was appropriated by local intellectuals as a bargaining tool for local decolonisation struggles. Elias was one such intellectual. Elias spoke of the hybridity or the interaction between African customary law and English law, something which could only be achieved by properly maintaining the purity of the former in order to interact with the later. For Elias, it is the framework for various laws, not necessarily the African cultural norm, that should be considered as hybrid. In other words, Elias therefore sought to maintain the authenticity of African customary law as a way of interacting with English or other received laws. Toufayan argues that Elias placed African and Western laws on equal footing, that is, 'side by side'. He emphasised hybridity and duality at the same time. African humanism was the hallmark of the authenticity of African customary law. Elias, in Toufayan's words, 'succeeded remarkably in retrieving African humanism as the genus of the hybridity of its Western and indigenous influences'. Elias was well aware of the convoluted African legal environment and his aim was to try and map out or encourage the harmonious growth and interaction of the various norms in this heavily complex setting. In doing so, as Toufayan argues, Elias presented a form of Negritude, a much wider term for political projects and the production of African consciousness to compensate and respond to the reception of imposed colonial laws. Elias's judicial Negritude was different, but not independent from the more popular use of the term by the inter-war movement in Franco-phone Africa. In the end, Elias gives us a different perspective of '– a law in-between'. For him, it was 'the conditions of a discourse working *between...*' African and English law. Like Silungwe the question of defining Africa is ultimately an enquiry into the nature of African law. Elias, however, had a different view on the question of African law. For him, it was necessary to uncover the purity or authenticity of African law, not by defining it in opposition, but rather by showing it could contribute and benefit from received laws. Indeed, Elias writings, as we learn from Toufayan, provide the foundations for the kind of investigations in this book, given that he strongly argued against 'isolating African ideas about law and government from general problems of political and legal theory'. It follows that this can only be achieved through a proper understanding and articulation of African law.

Dan Kuwali's contribution seeks to distinguish African legal theory from the mainstream legal theory, to make it more accessible to problems affecting contemporary African societies. He attributes the inadequate knowledge or relevance of African legal theory to domestic affairs and problems across the continent to the deleterious effects of colonial rule. Inadvertently, and although not seeking to engage in the debate about authenticity of African legal theory, Kuwali seems to subscribe to purity by seeking to decipher African characteristics in legal theory. The features can be deciphered, he suggests, by philosophical speculation of the visual and oral practices and customs of indigenous societies, and also, by extrapolating African legal theory from the work of the African jurist, among other people. Apart from arguing that international legal theoretical traditions have failed Africans at crucial moments, it is commonplace to argue that the laws of every society must be representative of its fundamental values. African societies cannot be different, if their laws are to have any legitimacy, acceptance or effectiveness. Kuwali puts the African characteristics of legal theory as follows: that it is rooted in culture, something which is derived from proverbs; that it seeks to maintain equilibrium in society; that it provides the foundations for a theory of restorative and reconciliatory justice; that it honours interdependence and collective responsibility, and finally, that it yields to a consensus-based theory of decision-making.

Dominic Burbidge moves the focus of this book beyond questions of the authenticity of African law and legal theory. He argues that African jurisprudence together with deductions from relational contract theory present an African perspective of the person, which not only is universalisable, but can also ground studies of culture, society and trust. The uniqueness of the African concept of person has been overlooked by Africanist political science discourse, which has almost exclusively focused on the lack of, or the degradation of institutions as the primary source of African problems. In doing so, they have excluded 'moral deliberation', including an understanding of the richness of the social and rational person regarding African problems. Africanist political science discourse is particularistic in another sense; it fails to provide a continent-wide explanatory model for African problems, something which even the much celebrated political theories of pan-Africanism and ujamaa either distorted or failed to do. Burbidge argues that the explanatory model lies in the focus on the person, 'the person with Africa, not in Africa'. Burbidge finds support for this objective from African jurisprudence, especially a definition of the concept espoused by John Murungi. Burbidge's interpretation of Murungi's work is that African jurisprudence is likened to human dialogue, one that seeks to unite African human experiences with those across the world. In Burbidge's view, this notion of jurisprudence excludes theoretical distinctions between African jurisprudence and general jurisprudence. Burbidge's aim, not only is to show the similarity between both jurisprudential accounts, but also to show how African jurisprudence can contribute to general jurisprudence, something which has been overlooked by practitioners of the latter. African jurisprudence achieves this through its focus on the richness of human solidarity and the norms of social cooperation present in Africa. Burbidge goes on to unite the African account of the person with relational contract theory, to provide a better foundation for studies into the nature of society in general. This is because contracts are, in essence, a basis of formalising interpersonal promise-making; thereby (together with African jurisprudence) provide a stable foundation for economic and political life in the societies concerned.

Olúfémi Táíwò's contribution considers the common phenomenon of the violation of individual rights, a problem that can be generalised across legal systems in Africa. Although it is a well-documented issue, it does not feature prominently in scholarship related to African law and African legal theory. Táíwò argues that a proper understanding of why the violation of individual rights continues to persist rests on our grasp of the raison d'être of the modern legal system. And to effectively grasp the workings of the modern legal system is dependent upon an understanding of the metaphysical template of the individual. Indeed, unlike the African worldview of personality, communalism or collectivism, what rarely features in African legal or legal theoretical scholarship is the account of what he calls the 'metaphysics of the self that yields to the legal subject'. The fabric of the modern legal system is built on the primacy of the individual. The individual, amongst other things, is constituted centrally by reason and is guaranteed certain rights, which protects him or her from unnecessary interference from the state or state agents. The ability to reason is not the only feature of the individual, but it is arguably the most important one. Reason is necessary to determine life choices. Reason is an indication of freedom, something which is expressed through the capacity to function in the world. Overall, Táíwò is arguing for a modern African legal system that gives primacy to the liberty of the individual, something which should be built on legal systems in Euro-American legal discourse. He charges scholars of African legal theory to embrace modernity discourse as well as 'overcome their aversion of the self at the base of modernity'. Táíwò is not suggesting that there is nothing to be gained from the rich African philosophical heritage, rather that we must recognise the modern legal system exists almost exclusively as a received one. Unless we get rid of the existing modern legal system, we must become students of it and carefully decipher how its central philosophical underpinnings can help secure human dignity, no matter how minimal its prospect of achieving this might be.

The essays in the second part of the book consider questions related to the significance of rights, including how they are established from African legal theoretical or philosophical approaches. Thaddeus Metz explores the extent to which human rights have a place in African legal and political philosophy, something which is achieved through the lens of Claude Ake's seminal essay, 'The African Context of Human Rights'. Metz argues against Ake's preference for group rights and economic and social rights by showing that individual rights and civil liberties are consistent with Afro-communitarian values. While accepting that Ake was accurate about the importance of communal relationships in Africa, he was wrong to say that those relationships negated the importance of human rights. In rejecting these claims, Metz responds by constructing a unified philosophy of rights based on important and common values in sub-Saharan African moral philosophy. Metz's philosophy of rights not only provides the foundation for the most central human rights and group rights, but also for the rights contained in the African Charter on Human and Peoples Rights. He achieves this by reconciling two important African values – the value of community and the value of human dignity. Living a dignified life depends on the capacity to commune with others, something which demands respect, especially the respect for the rights of others. The capacity to commune is simply 'the biological capacity to think of *oneself* as bound up with others and to act for their sake, i.e., *to be friendly or to love*, in a broad sense'. From this standpoint, a human right must be protected by the state and respected by others, because it contributes to a person's capacity to commune with others. In the end, Metz's demonstrates the application of this philosophy of rights to a range of rights, including civil liberties, due process rights, rights to political participation and rights to socio-economic goods.

Consistent with the overall objective of the book, my chapter considers what citizenship means today, what this definition overlooks and how this can be remedied by restating it from an African jurisprudential standpoint. My concern is that the basic set of ethical and moral values that are associated with citizenship (those that should encourage individuals to treat each other with dignity and respect) is taken for granted by both rights-based and duty-based definitions of the concept. Regarding rights, I question their capacity for integration, that is, whether they can offer more than just the protections of individuals against the state and other individuals. For instance, do rights encourage community, societal coexistence or social cohesion? Does the emphasis on autonomy, freedoms or liberation synonymous with rights necessary translate into relatedness, connectedness, integration or community? Duties otherwise referred to as responsibilities offer more in this respect, since they imply a sort of virtue and character. Nevertheless, they also crucially fail, at the moment, when individuals need to act morally or responsibly towards each other. This is because responsibilities are defined almost exclusively in vertical terms, in terms of the duties to the state, such as voting, compulsory military service, the payment of taxes and the obligation to obey the law. It is much easier, for lack of a better term, to show allegiance to the state by performing responsibilities while neglecting obligations to each other. Influenced by John

Murungi's seminal definition of African jurisprudence, which gives primacy to human ontology, I argue that it can help remedy these short comings by yielding to an ethical and morally embedded concept of citizenship. I argue that the kind of moral obligations demanded by the African jurisprudential concept of citizenship is first directed to humanity; it precedes and does not depend on rights and responsibilities.

Karen Zivi's chapter focuses on the contemporary problem of access to HIV and other health related treatment rights. She seeks to show the subtleties involved in making treatment rights claims in South Africa, including the role ubuntu, among other sources, play in articulating those claims. In doing so, she interprets and rejects two dominant interpretations of the novel legal discourse in South Africa in favour of her own account. What is missing from both accounts, she argues, is the articulation of the variety of sources of rights claims in a way that reveal the formation of new identities or the political subjectivies implicated in social struggles. Zivi offers a performative perspective on rights as a conceptual medium for a better appreciation and articulation of those nuances. With a focus on the campaign for HIV treatment access rights, she explains how the performative perspective provides a better way of grasping the 'varied roots of rights discourses' involved in the struggle for access to treatment. This is because the performative perspective 'is a complex linguistic practice the outcomes of which often exceed our complete control'. It comes into force 'through speech acts – understood expansively to include utterances as well as actions – that we often bring into existence the very things which we presume or are presumed to reference'. In other words, certain ends are brought into existence by utterances and actions among other things through a non-referential theory of language. The advantage of the performative perspective becomes apparent through a process of sedimentation. Sedimentation, in turn, implies using familiar norms, customs and gestures in novel contexts, or using them in familiar situations anticipating that they will generate new meanings. For instance, and what Zivi is ultimately suggesting in practical terms, is that the codification of a right does not sufficiently explain the effect of having that right. Indeed, what she shows is how the effect of a right claim '…occurs in practices beyond legal argumentation or traditional acts of speaking'. The advantage of the performative approach, then, not only rests on appreciating the intricacies of a rights claim, it also explains the diversity of the sources of those claims. In conclusion, Zivi's chapter demonstrates the diversity of sources of rights claims in South Africa. They include the constitution, international human rights documents, Marxism, liberalism, international feminist discourse, and particularly important, for present purposes, the South African concept of ubuntu. Part of her argument, then, is that a deeper appreciation of the role ubuntu plays, especially how it contributes to the treatment access rights campaigns can be valued by adopting a performative perspective.

Basil Ugochukwu importantly contributes to the understanding of how African literature or the arts more generally can serve as a source of an African philosophy or theory of law. He explores this through Chinua Achebe's *Things Fall Apart*, a novel not famous for its human rights credentials. Ugochukwu's overall aim, then, is, first, to reconstruct this popular, but negative image of *Things Fall Apart* in relation to human rights. Contingent on the success of the first objective, Ugochukwu's second aim is to use *Things Fall Apart* to decrypt certain practices in pre-colonial African societies that are equivalent of human rights practices. Although they may not have been practiced in the form of human rights today, Ugochukwu argues that this does not mean they were not human rights practices at all. Ugochukwu argues that these pre-colonial practices yield to what can be called an Igbo philosophy of human rights, a philosophy with distinct Afro-communitarian characteristics. It is a similar type of philosophy that grounds the African Charter on Human and Peoples Rights, the novelty of which is the introduction of duties to international human rights law discourse. In exploring these themes, Ugochukwu is mindful of the difficulties of generalising the experiences of a particular ethnic group across the continent, and also, that of ascertaining the validity of a particular account of those practices. These difficulties more generally raise question marks about the plausibility of relying on literary works or the arts more generally as a normative framework for the regulation of any given society. Notwithstanding, Ugochukwu proceeds to carry out a discursive exercise of teasing out the narrative of *Things Fall Apart* in relation to women's rights, the right to life and the right to fair hearing. Regarding women's rights, *Things Fall Apart* was more of a reflection of the practices of many societies at that time than something specific to the Umuofia community. That is, the fact that women lived as second class citizens in the Umuofia community is not conclusive enough to suggest that they had no rights protections at all. Umuofia culture also recognised the right to life, even though this was sometimes 'ambivalent or inadequate'. *Things Fall Apart* also presents evidence of the existence of the right to fair hearing; it showed how parties to disputes had equal procedural rights.

The essays that make up the third part of the book also have a common theme; they address more societal questions, especially the place of law in the context of poverty and development. In the next chapter, I focus on some general themes relating to poverty and development. The chapter offers a critique of a report on Legal Empowerment of the Poor, a poverty eradication initiative of the United Nations Development Programme (UNDP). The chapter responds to the generalisation by the legal empowerment of the poor initiative on the benefits of the formalisation of certain legal rights, especially on the perceived benefits of legal formalisation of rights on poverty alleviation. While problems with the formalisation thesis have been addressed in relation to property, business and labour rights, very little has been said in relation to how the approach deals with the value of political participation. While responding to this oversight by the legal empowerment of the poor initiative, the chapter shows that activities of contemporary poor Africans in the informal sphere have a better grasp of the value of political participation to the extent that they point to how to ground new thinking in this respect. Informal political participation, something which reflects the spirit of Africa, 'covers grounds that even the best-intentioned, planned and supported formal initiative can only aspire'. Informal political participation assumes the following characteristics: it refers to organisational forms and networks of groups attempting to escape the harshness and rigidity of formal systems, especially formal systems of law. Informal political participation is directed at seizing political controls for the allocation of public goods and services. Informal political participation not only gives the poor autonomy over important decisions that affect their lives, but also the ability to live dignified lives, whether it is through the distribution of public goods or the formation of non-state physical planning settlements. Informal political participation is relational; it cuts across kinship, family, religious and ethnic ties. In conclusion, I suggest that the advantage informal political participation holds over the human right to political participation is that it is not defined by a radical separation between the economic and political sphere. Informal political participation firmly grasps the correlation between economic and political exclusion, thereby opening up the possibility for the much needed democratisation of the economic sphere.

Adebisi Arewa's contribution postulates African humanist egalitarianism, described as the philosophical basis of all socio-economic and political African institutions, as the alternative to received and failed paradigms of capitalist and socialist development instantiated through theories of modernisation and dependency respectively. Both paradigms, according to Arewa, have crucially failed in improving the human condition, as evident from the spiraling levels of poverty, hunger, disease, homelessness, unemployment, inequality, lack of access to healthcare, and also the unequal distribution of resources across the African continent. African egalitarianism is underpinned by a 'metaphysical notion of sociability', that is, the biological interdependency between each human being, something which is important for 'growth, development, security and well-being'. What is fundamental to every African socio-economic and political institution is this notion of sociability. Arewa provides a practical example of African egalitarianism from African customary land law and property rights. African theories of land and property rights provide the foundation for networks of ownership patterns ranging from private to family, kinship to communal holding schemes, which are in turn used to secure the use of land for all the members of a given community and beyond. With the emphasis of the connectedness between the individual and community, African egalitarianism – as reflected by the different property owning relationships – offers a more robust model of development to meet the challenges of poverty and inequality, among other things, across the African continent.

In the final chapter, Babafemi Odunsi makes a case for the relevance of indigenous African criminal law (a pre-colonial system of criminology) in response to contemporary problems of crime detection, resolution and prevention. Starting from colonial rule, he argues that there has been a tendency to dismiss African criminal law, a tendency which still exists in many postcolonial African countries today. Through reform, the introduction of Western education, religious missionary activities, and public policy, African criminal law has been rejected and dismissed as barbaric. This is primarily because the practice of African criminal law depends on the invocation of the supernatural. Although there is a physical and supernatural element to African criminal law, the former and latter are indivisible. Odunsi encourages us to rethink the negative perceptions of African criminal law. After all, he argues that, despite sustained efforts to discourage African criminal law some of its practices still remain popular in many contemporary African societies. At another level, Odunsi draws parallels between certain practices of African criminal law and

'Psychic Witness' – an approach to crime detection in the United States of America that depends on the invocation of the supernatural. Odunsi uses 'Psychic Witness' as a heuristic device to question the wholesale dismissal of African criminal law. Odunsi does more than this; he illustrates the effectiveness of African criminal law system, especially in relation to the inadequacies of the modern criminal law system. African criminal law system offers a different way of understanding the purposes of criminal law system – the goals of rehabilitation, retribution and deterrence. African criminal law is rehabilitative in the sense that it places emphasis on restitution and reconciliation. Indeed, even though capital punishment exists, it is used as a last resort under African criminal law. In terms of retribution, vengeance is not the primary aim of punishment; rather the aim is to collectively denounce individual crime. Deterrence is achieved through supernatural sanctions, such as demonstrated through his detailed discussion of oath-taking. In conclusion, Odunsi outlines other advantages of the African criminal law, especially its participatory nature, as it demands an engagement of individuals at community level. African criminal law, he argues, is also cheaper and faster than modern criminal law systems.

References

Cotterrell R (2003) The politics of jurisprudence: a critical introduction to legal philosophy. Oxford University Press, Oxford

Del Mar M, Bankowski Z (2013) The moral imagination and legal life: beyond text in legal education. Ashgate, Surrey

Friedmann W (1967) Legal theory. Stevens & Sons, London

Hetch D, Simone M (1994) Invisible governance: the art of African micropolitics. Automedia, New York

Metz T (2012) African conceptions of human dignity: vitality and community as the grounds of human rights. Hum Rights Rev 13:19–37

Santos B (2002) Towards a new legal commonsense: law, globalisation and emancipation. Butterworths LexisNexis, London

Santos B (2007) Beyond abyssal thinking: from global lines to ecologies of knowledges. Review XXX(1):45

Simone A (2001) Straddling the divides: remaking associational life in the informal African city. Int J Urban Reg Res 25(1):103

Part I
Law

Chapter 2
On 'African' Legal Theory: A Possibility, an Impossibility or Mere Conundrum?

Chikosa Mozesi Silungwe

2.1 Introduction

Does an identifiable body of African legal theoretical or philosophical scholarship exist? If such scholarship exists, what is its nature or form? Is it folly for (mainstream) discourse to confront the global phenomena without any consideration of the African legal theoretical or philosophical scholarship? While these are important queries, however, I suggest that the inquiry ought to move a number of steps backwards. Before we advocate the reflection of 'African' legal theory, jurisprudence or philosophy in resolving 'contemporary global challenges', we must ask this question: Is the conception of 'African' legal theory, jurisprudence or philosophy a possibility, an impossibility or a mere conundrum? In this Chapter, I argue that if the descriptor 'African legal theory, jurisprudence or philosophy' suggests a purist conception of 'African' legal theory, jurisprudence or philosophy then the intellectual enterprise so undertaken is futile and impossible.[1] In the context of the creation of 'knowledge' under the Enlightenment period and indeed in light of the capitalism and the colonialism projects that underpinned modernity, there has been a pervasive process of 'othering'; of declarations of 'not-knowledge'. A related point here is that the human as a social being constructs a 'reality' she responds to. This construction of reality is influenced by what is presented as 'memory'. Given how pregnant 'reality' and 'memory' are, I contend that it is more plausible to envision 'African' legal theory, jurisprudence or philosophy under Homi Bhabha's idea of 'culture's in-between' (Bhabha 1996, pp. 53–60); which denies a purist conception of 'culture' and emphasizes the diversity of influence (1996). This interpretation is pertinent since in the

[1] See also Woodman and Obilade (1995, pp. xxiv–xxvi).

C.M. Silungwe, Ph.D. (✉)
The Mizumali Foundation, Lilongwe, Malawi
e-mail: c.m.silungwe@gmail.com

O. Onazi (ed.), *African Legal Theory and Contemporary Problems: Critical Essays*, Ius Gentium: Comparative Perspectives on Law and Justice 29,
DOI 10.1007/978-94-007-7537-4_2,

consideration of 'Africa' as a space and the received-ness of 'law' and 'the legal' in that space, the understanding of any phenomenon as 'African' ought to be a nuanced engagement. I am not denying the ability of the constituency re-identified as 'African' to *know* or to *think*. I am suggesting that scholarship must, first, acknowledge that the violence of modernity on 'knowledge' or 'thought' has been far-reaching and deep-rooted. Second, the de-Europeanization or de-Americanization among the authorship of (supposedly) 'African' legal theory, jurisprudence or philosophy does not necessarily imply that the underlying conceptions of the resultant scholarship are not rooted in modernity. An approach to what may be called 'African' legal theory, jurisprudence or philosophy based on the idea of 'culture's in-between' acknowledges two things: First, the convoluted socio-political environment of 'law' or the 'legal' in Africa (or in the African) which permeates into its theory, jurisprudence or philosophy. Second, the diversity of influence that underlies the 'culture's in-between' thesis presents a window for the consideration of what is being termed 'African' in theory, jurisprudence or philosophy in confronting global phenomena.

2.2 The Thesis on African Legal Theory

It is more precise to talk of the theses on African legal theory. I identify at least three here. The first one – what I call the sentimentalist approach – states that African legal theory is a pre-colonial repertoire of 'norms' with historical continuity (for example, Elias 1962, 1971; Okoth–Ogendo 1989). The second one – what I call the revisionist approach – states that African legal theory is a colonial invention with a historical specificity and whose core purpose was to entrench colonial capitalism and late imperialism (Snyder 1981, pp. 90–121, 1984, p. 34; Fitzpatrick 1984, p. 20; Seidman and Seidman 1984, p. 44; Chanock 1985; Ranger 1983, pp. 211–262; Mamdani 1996). The third one is the legal pluralist approach. Here, the proponents argue that the analysis of the lived reality of the 'indigene' society is critical; whereby State or lawyers' (customary) law may be recreated and re-interpreted to serve interests of the 'indigene' society (Benda–Beckmann 1984, p. 28; Woodman and Obilade 1995, pp. xi–xxvi).

The conception of African 'customary' law, for example, assists to elaborate upon the three approaches: Under the sentimentalist approach, the extent of the survival, transformation and historical continuity of the norms are often taken for granted. In relation to land, 'customary' (land) tenure has a communitarian *ethos*. Indeed, once colonial rule got entrenched, the communitarian *ethos* of 'customary' (land) tenure was 'profoundly shaped' and often served the interests of the colonial State, private Europeans and an African elite comprising mostly of male, African chiefs and an emergent male-dominated entrepreneurial class (Peters 2009). Peters (2009, p. 1317) has observed that this communitarian *ethos* to 'customary' land tenure stemmed from a patronizing, imperial attitude amongst the early colonial administrators and missionaries who viewed 'communal' tenure as inferior to individual, private landholding that was pervasive, for example, under the English landholding system. This process of 'shaping' often led to a restatement of 'customary' law of a colony.[2]

Some of the most prolific proponents of the revisionist approach include Francis Snyder, Peter Fitzpatrick, Martin Chanock, Mahmood Mamdani, Anne and Robert Seidman, Terence Ranger and VY Mudimbe (2004). These proponents have criticized the sentimentalist approach on the grounds that it reifies a normative continuity from pre-colonial to colonial (African) society; they also raise methodological concerns relating to the ascertainment of the 'norms'; and more critically, they argue that the interface between the colonial ruler and the male, African elite has produced that which has been called 'customary' law and has been applied in the colonial, 'native' courts (for example, Roberts 1984). They also argue that the violence occasioned by the incidence of colonialism in Africa, for example, entails that the erstwhile 'acephalous' African groups were, in the words of Roberts, subjected to 'discontinuities, abrupt transition and coercive domination' (Roberts 1984, p. 3). Fitzpatrick (1984, p. 20) and Snyder (1984, p. 34) have gone on to argue that this 'shaping' is generally imbricated in the capitalist mode of production. Economic and political interests have greatly influenced the interpretation and re-interpretation of the 'customary' space (Fitzpatrick above; Snyder above). The 'myth' of the 'customary' space, it has been argued, was a necessary 'totem' for colonial capitalism to flourish (Fitzpatrick 2001; Paliwala 2003).

The legal pluralist approach acknowledges the effect of colonial capitalism and late imperialism on 'Africa' and the 'African'. However, this approach suggests that the existence of an African legal theory 'may be distinguished by a predominant concern with characteristic features of African law' (Woodman and Obilade 1995, p. xi). In any event, the sentimentalist and legal pluralist approaches are complementary. In this case, the proponents of the legal pluralist approach argue that it is perilous to differentiate an 'understanding' of the norms of African legal theory that have been passed down generations of State agents or intra-community from the 'lived' reality of the 'indigene' society (Snyder 1981, 1984).

However, reality raises its own conceptual challenges. It has been argued that reality is a mosaic that is subjective and, among other things, it is prone to the complexities of perception, depth of knowledge, and interpretation (Bless 2004; Bourdieu 1990). Hence, to the extent that 'reality' – as lived or otherwise – is prone to construction, the legal pluralist approach to the African legal theory is tenuous.

The three theses to African legal theory revolve around the existence or lack of a particular, purist conception of 'culture'. I return to the point under Sect. 2.4 below. Suffice it to say that, indeed, the debate that ensues here raises question in relation to what constitutes 'Africa'. Is it merely a space, a body of *gnosis* or both? I proceed on the basis that any discussion of African legal theory must acknowledge that 'Africa' may be conceptualized as a space and not an exclusive and purist body of knowledge. In this way, it is possible for scholarship to acknowledge that the violence of modernity on 'knowledge' or 'thought' has been far-reaching and deep-rooted.

[2] In the case of the Malawi, for instance, one finds a restatement of customary land law under the Restatement of African Law Project that was done by the School of Oriental and African Studies of the University of London: see Ibik (1971).

2.3 The Creation of 'Knowledge': The Legacy of Modernity

I propose two flaws with a purist African legal theory in light of the creation of 'knowledge' under the Enlightenment and the legacy of modernity. This is the first flaw: In the context of the creation of 'knowledge' under the Enlightenment period and indeed in light of the capitalism and the colonialism projects that underpinned modernity, there has been a pervasive process of 'othering'; of declarations of 'not-knowledge'. I reiterate the views of Boaventura de Sousa Santos in 'Beyond Abyssal Thinking' here (Santos 2007). 'Beyond Abyssal Thinking' is a biting polemic on the creation of 'knowledge' and the attendant processes of 'othering'. Santos demonstrates that a harsh process of 'othering' through the making of the 'visible' and the making of the 'invisible' has always been the foundation of modernity. He contends that, in fact, the 'greatest manifestations of abyssal thinking' are modern knowledge and modern law on the back of their claim to scientific truth. Santos states,

> Modern knowledge and modern law represent the most accomplished manifestations of abyssal thinking. They account for the two major global lines of modern times, which, though being different and operating differently, are mutually interdependent. Each one creates a sub-system of visible and invisible distinctions in such a way that the invisible ones become the foundation of the visible ones. In the field of knowledge, abyssal thinking consists in granting to modern science the monopoly of the universal distinction between true and false, to the detriment of two alternative bodies of knowledge: philosophy and theology. The exclusionary character of this monopoly is at the core of the modern epistemological disputes between scientific and nonscientific forms of truth.[3]

But is this surprising? Modernity has been driven by a triumvirate of Enlightenment-based knowledge, colonialism and the capitalism project. Indeed, modernity when envisaged as a value system that puts at its core reason, the individual, and social progress, the creation of 'knowledge' may be easier to comprehend (Comeliau 2002). First, reason involves the explanation of 'matter' that originally was understood in the context of a divine authority. Hence, the nature of 'knowledge' that was made visible has a predominantly European tradition. The arts and humanities, the social sciences, and the natural sciences in the academy have a distinct Enlightenment origin. Anything else outside the Enlightenment is 'not-knowledge' and immediately invisible (Santos 2007). Second, the individual is the main driver. The centrality of the individual is based on the myth of equality of footing in terms of choice, access, principle, resources and opportunity (Comeliau 2002, p. 24). Third, social progress is defined under an economic prism of prosperity, growth or poverty. It becomes the sole goal of the livelihood of the individual. Comeliau observes,

> Beginning with the Enlightenment, this individual rationality is applied to the *goal of social progress*, a concept we have now integrated so deeply that we are scarcely capable of understanding its radical novelty [.][4]

---

[3] Santos (2007, p. 3).

[4] Comeliau (2002, p. 24) [emphasis in the original].

The flipside is Mudimbe's conception of 'Africa' and 'identity'. He begins with an unswerving probe as follows,

> The question of African identities generally imposes itself as obvious and rarely interrogates its two components, 'Africa' and 'identity.' What do they mean and since when, exactly? Moreover, and more importantly, there is always, implicit, another question: Who's speaking, and from which intellectual background, and in order to produce what and communicate a knowledge to whom?[5]

On account of the Enlightenment, Mudimbe argues that 'Africa' as a space – certainly sub-Saharan Africa – has been a victim, at best, or a mimic at worst, of the 'colonial library'. It is impossible, in his view, to conceive of a purist, body of knowledge that is 'Africa' or 'African'. This then leads to yet another perspective of an understanding of the legacy of modernity: The Enlightenment discovered disciplines and valorized salvation, power-knowledge and education conceived as *doxa* as opposed to *epistème* (Carmen 1996, p. 60).[6] The most poignant exposition of the disciplines is through what Homi Bhabha calls mimicry. He states,

> The discourse of post-Enlightenment English colonialism often speaks in a tongue that is forked, not false. If colonialism takes power in the name of history, it repeatedly exercises its authority through the figures of farce. For the epic intention of the civilizing mission, 'human and not wholly human' [...] often produces a text rich in the traditions of *trompe l'oeil*, irony, mimicry, and repetition. In this comic turn from the high ideals of the colonial imagination to its low mimetic literary effects, mimicry emerges as one of the most elusive and effective strategies of colonial power and knowledge.[7]

Bhabha then concludes thus,

> The success of colonial appropriation depends on a proliferation of inappropriate objects that ensure its strategic failure, so that mimicry is at once resemblance and menace.[8]

The second flaw with a purist conception of African legal theory is this: Beyond the gloom arising out of the legacy of modernity in the context of knowledge-production, an agitation for a purist African legal theory, jurisprudence or philosophy is tenuous on the basis of two other limbs: reality and memory. The human as a social being constructs a reality she responds to. Social constructionism scholars such as Peter Berger and Thomas Luckmann have argued that while social practices of human beings shape or construct the 'reality', at the same time these human beings may experience (or seek to experience) this 'reality' as if it is fixed or pre-ordered (Berger and Luckmann 1971).[9] In other words, human beings construct their (social) world which then becomes the 'reality' (Berger and Luckmann above; Burr 2003, pp. 185–190). Within these parameters, 'reality' is a 'contested space'. These then resonates with Mudimbe's colonial library or Bhabha's query on mimicry. In relation to memory, I will reiterate Zygmunt Bauman's observations.

[5] Mudimbe (2004).

[6] On the disciplines: See Foucault (1991).

[7] Bhabha (1984, p. 126) [internal citation omitted].

[8] Bhabha (1984, p. 127).

[9] See also Burr (2003), especially Chap. 9.

He has argued that in the post-Enlightenment period, memory – or more precisely, 'collective memory' – is intimately tied with the colonial encounter (Bauman 2009). Indeed, the traditions, narratives and practices produce a group psychology that is (often) contradictory.

Finally, how do we conceive of the de-Europeanization or de-Americanization among the authorship of African legal theory? I assert as follows: mere de-Europeanization or de-Americanization among the authorship of 'African' legal theory, jurisprudence or philosophy should not quickly presuppose a 'purist' African legal theory. What ought to be crucial here is the violence and indeed the ring fencing modernity has had on 'knowledge-production' (Santos 2007; Comeliau 2002). Hence, the fact that the authorship of 'African' legal theory has been de-Europeanized or de-Americanized does not mean the scholarship is not rooted in modernity. I dare say, of course, it is. This is the case given the receivedness of 'law' or the 'legal' in Africa the space. The 'African' law school is at once Anglo-, Franco-, or Lusophone-based. Ahiauzu, for instance, acknowledges this dilemma that comes with mere de-Europeanization or de-Americanization among the authorship of African legal theory in the following manner,

> An obvious problem could however be that having been trained in the Western tradition of legal theory [...] we are ill-equipped to tackle the project. Our thinking with relation to law is fundamentally Western and in order to successfully accomplish tasks in African legal theory we would have to, as it were 'think outside the box'. We would have to create a new box to think in. In order to think differently we would require a different 'frame' from which to think. But even that would still require us to set out what it means to be African. However, herein could lay our special advantage – that we are able to explore two traditions and thereby get a better understanding of law. In trying to break out of the box we would be challenging the presumptions on which the box is founded. We would be able to discover another world in legal theory that is not Western. We would also be able to engage in comparative studies and better explore all the possible ramifications of legal concepts that the limits of boxes may deny us.[10]

2.4 What 'Culture's In-between' Offers

'African' legal theory, jurisprudence or philosophy may be conceptualized under Bhabha's idea of 'culture's in-between'. My proposition is as follows: An approach to what may be called 'African' legal theory, jurisprudence or philosophy based on the idea of 'culture's in-between' acknowledges two things: First, the convoluted socio-political environment of 'law' or the 'legal' in Africa (or in the African) which permeates into its theory, jurisprudence or philosophy. Second, the diversity of influence that underlies the 'culture's in-between' thesis presents a window for the consideration of what is being termed 'African' in theory, jurisprudence or philosophy in confronting global phenomena.

[10] Ahiauzu (2006).

What then is the conception of 'culture's in-between'? In a few paragraphs it is a daunting task to do justice to Homi Bhabha's conception of 'culture's in-between'. Bhabha's starting point is that there is no 'pure culture'. In other words, Bhabha forcefully argues that the notion of 'pure culture' is a myth. Bhabha begins from T.S. Eliot and observes,

> What is at issue today is not the essentialized or idealized Arnoldian notion of 'culture' as an architectonic assemblage of the Hebraic and the Hellenic. In the midst of the multicultural wars we are surprisingly closer to an insight from T. S. Eliot's *Notes towards the Definition of Culture,* where Eliot demonstrates a certain incommensurability, a necessary impossibility, in *thinking* culture. Faced with the fatal notion of a self-contained European culture and the absurd notion of an uncontaminated culture in a single country, he writes, 'We are therefore pressed to maintain the ideal of a world culture, while admitting it is something we cannot *imagine.* We can only conceive it as the logical term of the relations between cultures.' The fatality of thinking of 'local' cultures as uncontaminated or self-contained forces us to conceive of 'global' cultures, which itself remains unimaginable. What kind of logic is this?[11]

Bhabha points out that while Eliot made his point in the context of the colonial encounter; the assertion remains valid in the 'contemporary condition of third world migration'.[12] Bhabha quotes Eliot extensively as follows,

> The migrations of modern times [...] have transplanted themselves according to some social, religious, economic or political determination, or some peculiar mixture of these. There has therefore been something in the removements analogous in nature to religious schism. The people have taken with them only a part of the total culture. [...] The culture which develops on the new soil must therefore be bafflingly alike and different from the parent culture: it will be complicated sometimes by whatever relations are established with some native race and further by immigration from other than the original source. In this way, peculiar types of culture-sympathy and culture-clash appear.[13]

Hence, on the basis of the 'part culture', 'culture-sympathy' and 'culture-clash', Bhabha argues for the conception of 'culture's in-between'. He states,

> This 'part' culture, this *partial* culture, is the contaminated yet connective tissue between cultures – at once the impossibility of culture's containedness and the boundary between. It is indeed something like culture's 'in-between', bafflingly both alike and different. To *enlist* in the defence of this 'unhomely', migratory, partial nature of culture we must revive that archaic meaning of 'list' as 'limit' or 'boundary' Having done so, we introduce into the polarizations of liberals and liberationists the sense that the translation of cultures, whether assimilative or agonistic, is a complex act that generates borderline affects and identifications, 'peculiar types of culture-sympathy and culture-clash'. The peculiarity of cultures' partial, even metonymic presence lies in articulating those social divisions and unequal developments that disturb the self-recognition of the national culture, its anointed horizons of territory and tradition. The discourse of minorities, spoken for and against in the multicultural wars, proposes a social subject constituted through cultural hybridization, the overdetermination of communal or group differences, the articulation of baffling alikeness and banal divergence.[14]

---

[11] Bhabha (1996, pp. 53–54) [internal citations omitted].

[12] Bhabha (1996, p. 54).

[13] Eliot in Bhabha (1996, p. 54).

[14] Bhabha (1996, p. 54).

Bhabha contends that an understanding of 'culture' as precisely 'culture's in-between' ought to be based on what he calls 'discursive doubleness' (Bhabha 1996, p. 58). Discursive doubleness is not based on duality or binarism. It is based on hybridity; on strategies of hybridization. Bhabha states,

> Strategies of hybridization reveal an estranging movement in the 'authoritative', even authoritarian inscription of the cultural sign. At the point at which the precept attempts to objectify itself as a generalized knowledge or a normalizing, hegemonic practice, the hybrid strategy or discourse opens up a space of negotiation where power is unequal but its articulation may be equivocal. Such negotiation is neither assimilation nor collaboration. It makes possible the emergence of an 'interstitial' agency that refuses the binary representation of social antagonism. Hybrid agencies find their voice in a dialectic that does not seek cultural supremacy or sovereignty. They deploy the partial culture from which they emerge to construct visions of community, and versions of historic memory, that give narrative form to the minority positions they occupy; the outside of the inside: the part in the whole.[15]

In this way, I interpret Bhabha's account of 'culture's in-between' as inherently wary of binaries; or being dialectical. It is possible however to suggest that 'culture's in-between' is a 'dialectic' phenomenon that does not necessarily lead to a Hegelian concrete – the synthesis – but to a uniquely Bhabhaian 'third space' (Bhabha 1995). In fact, in an interview with WJT Mitchell, Bhabha has said,

> I'm looking for a form of the dialectic without transcendence, as you put it. But you are also right when you say that there are certain dialectical structures, certain conceptual pairings, that you can live neither within nor without. To write contra Hegel requires that you 'work through' Hegel toward other 'supplemental' concepts of dialectical thinking. You do not surpass or bypass Hegel just because you contest the process of sublation. The lesson lies, I think, in learning how to conceptualize 'contradiction' or the dialectic as that state of being or thinking that is 'neither the one nor the other, but something else besides, Abseits,' as I've described it in *The Location Of Culture*.
>
> This is where the influence of Walter Benjamin has been formative for me. His meditations on the disjunctive temporalities of the historical 'event' are quite indispensable to thinking the cultural problems of late modernity. His vision of the Angel of History haunts my work as I attempt to grasp, for the purposes of cultural analysis, what he describes as the condition of translation: the 'continua of transformation, not abstract ideas of identity and similarity.' His work has led me to speculate on differential temporal movements within the process of dialectical thinking and the supplementary or interstitial 'conditionality' that opens up alongside the transcendent tendency of dialectical contradiction – I have called this a 'third space,' or a 'time lag.' To think of these temporalities in the context of historical events has led me to explore notions of causality that are not expressive of the contradiction 'itself,' but are contingently effected by it and allow for other translational moves of resistance, and for the establishment of other terms of generality.[16]

Bhabha here asserts that the 'third space' resides within the contradiction and it is in this space of contradiction that 'culture's in-between' thrives. Within the 'third space', other norms or 'other terms of generality' emerge. I will discuss three examples to make the point: anti-witchcraft laws in Africa; anti-homosexuality laws in Africa; and *ubuntu* as a human rights norm.

---

[15] Bhabha (1996, p. 58).

[16] Bhabha (1995).

2.4.1 On Anti-witchcraft Laws

Witchcraft, as a belief system, typically entails that a person has the power to inflict (usually) an injury through supernatural means. The belief in witchcraft is pervasive in Africa (for example Quarmyne 2011, p. 478). Anti-witchcraft laws are colonial constructs meant to assimilate the native African into a 'civilized' form of belief based primarily on Christian doctrine. These laws proscribe – through criminal law – the native African's quest for the metaphysical *why* to an 'occurrence'; which can be 'a misfortune, disease, accident, natural disaster and death' (Byrne 2011). Hence, in a number of English common law jurisdictions in Africa, the typical criminal law on witchcraft makes it an offence to accuse another person of witchcraft or indeed to profess the belief in witchcraft. For example, under the Malawian Witchcraft Act of 1911, witchcraft is not recognized at law. It is an offence to allege that someone practices witchcraft. Section 4 of the Act provides,

> Any person who, otherwise than in laying information before a court, a police officer, a Chief, or other proper authority, accuses any person with being a witch or with practising witchcraft or names or indicates any person as being a witch or wizard shall be liable to a fine of [...] and to imprisonment for five years.

It is also an offence for one to claim that he practices witchcraft. Section 6 of the Act provides,

> Any person who by his statements or actions represents himself to be a wizard or witch or as having or exercising the power of witchcraft shall be liable to a fine of [...] and to imprisonment for ten years.

In the latter case, a person is charged with pretending witchcraft. Section 5 of the Malawian Witchcraft Act also criminalizes the employment or solicitation of a witchfinder. In practice, it is often the 'accused witch' who often faces the wrath of the anti-witchcraft laws (Byrne 2011). The law enforcers in Malawi seem to implicitly recognize the existence of witchcraft.

Further, in the post-Cold War period, most African countries have adopted largely, liberal democratic constitutions. These constitutions provide, among others, the right to the enjoyment of one's culture, and the freedom of expression including belief. The constitutions also typically have a proscription against statutory laws or 'customary' laws or practices that are inconsistent with the constitutions themselves.

Indeed, the Malawian example I have highlighted above reveals a delicate balancing act between the constitutional provisions on the right to culture and freedom of expression on the one hand and the criminalization of witchcraft as a belief system on the other. Similar tensions emerge in South Africa, Zimbabwe, Tanzania and Zambia, for example, where the law does not recognize witchcraft as a belief system and criminalizes the system accordingly. Cameroon presents a unique case where the State legal system recognizes witchcraft as a belief system but still criminalizes it (see Quarmyne 2011). Either way, the interface between a purported 'indigene' 'culture'–norm and a norm of received law results in the transmogrification of the former. The received legal norm is defining the ('cultural') status quo.

2.4.2 On Anti-homosexuality Laws

Here, I will not go into a detailed discussion of the homosexuality debate in Africa. I simply point out that the global North-global South 'cultural' linkages underpinning the debate have made it the most polarized and emotive. In a number of English common law jurisdictions, the provisions in a criminal code that deal with 'carnal knowledge against the order of nature' or those on 'gross indecency' have been used against persons that engage in 'homosexual' practices. Indeed the provisions under these criminal codes were largely influenced by the morality of Victorian England and spread throughout the British Empire as part of the colonizing and civilizing project (see for example Read 1963). Hence, the period between the mid-nineteenth century CE and the end of the First World War must have witnessed plenty an encounter of a British colonizer telling the colonized local what sexual intercourse according to the order of nature was, or indeed, what ('acceptable') decency was. There were consequences for engaging in carnal knowledge against the order of nature, or engaging in acts of gross indecency. At the turn of the twenty-first century CE, we witness a predominantly indigene African religious right wing that is vehemently opposed to lesbian, gay, bisexual and transgender rights on account of 'culture'. The 'culture' argument has also meant that any suggestions to repeal the laws on sodomy based on the morality of Victorian England are met with even more vehemence. Unlike the case with anti-witchcraft laws, here we have a situation where a norm of received law and morality is actually appropriated as an indigenous one. The received legal and moral norm is appropriated as the ('cultural') status quo.

Again, some largely, liberal democratic constitutions recognize lesbian, gay, bisexual and transgender rights through the proscription of discrimination on account of a person's sexual orientation. Notable among these is the Constitution of South Africa. Section 9 of the South African Constitution provides,

(1) Everyone is equal before the law and has the right to equal protection and benefit of the law.
(2) Equality includes the full and equal enjoyment of all rights and freedoms to promote the achievement of equality, legislative and other measures designed to protect or advance persons, or categories of persons, disadvantaged by unfair discrimination may be taken.
(3) The state may not unfairly discriminate directly or indirectly against anyone on one or more grounds, including race, gender, sex, pregnancy, marital status, ethnic or social origin, colour, **sexual orientation**, age, disability, religion, conscience, belief, culture, language and birth.
(4) No person may unfairly discriminate directly or indirectly against anyone on one or more grounds in terms of subsection (3). National legislation must be enacted to prevent or prohibit unfair discrimination.
(5) Discrimination on one or more of the grounds listed in subsection (3) is unfair unless it is established that the discrimination is fair.

However, the recognition of the legal norm on sexuality in a constitution as text has not meant that incidents of homophobia are inexistent. In the case of South Africa, despite a clear provision on non-discrimination on the basis of sexual orientation, cases of homophobic violence have been reported in the country.

In Malawi, Section 20 of the Constitution provides,

(1) Discrimination of persons in any form is prohibited and all persons are, under any law, guaranteed equal and effective protection against discrimination on grounds of race, colour, sex, language, religion, political or other opinion, national, ethnic or social origin, disability, property, birth or **other status** or condition.
(2) Legislation may be passed addressing inequalities in society and prohibiting discriminatory practices and the propagation of such practices and may render such practices criminally punishable by the courts.

It is possible to interpret 'other status' under subsection (1) of section 20 of the Malawian Constitution more expansively to include the recognition of lesbian, gay, bisexual and transgender rights. The matter has not benefitted from judicial interpretation. Suffice it to say that the debate on homosexuality in Malawi proceeds on the basis that the Constitution or statutory laws do not recognise non-heterosexual orientation. In sum, from a comparative constitutional perspective, what the positions under the South African and Malawian constitutions confirm is that the recognition of a legal or moral norm under a ('cultural') status quo is not necessarily dependent on the constitution as the text.

2.4.3 On **Ubuntu** *as a Human Rights Norm*

The discussion on *ubuntu* seeks to highlight the problems of precision of language when an indigenous norm is appropriated into (mainstream) discourse. The discussion also demonstrates an instance where an indigene African norm has a positive complementary interface with mainstream discourse. Indeed, in the latter case, the uniqueness of the positive complementarity lies in the fact that it is based solely on the conceptual properties of the indigene African norm.

The term *ubuntu* is *Nguni* which may be loosely translated as 'personhood, humanity, humanness and morality' (Mokgoro 1998; Nkhata 2010, p. 31). Scholars do concede that the term is elusive to define with precision. Mokgoro, for example, notes,

> The concept *ubuntu*, like many African concepts, is not easily definable. To define an African notion in a foreign language and from an abstract as opposed to a concrete approach to defy [sic] the very essence of the African world-view and [sic] can also be particularly elusive. I will therefore not in the least attempt to define the concept with precision. That would in any case be unattainable. In one's own experience, *ubuntu* it seems, is one of those things that you recognise when you see it. I will therefore only put forward some views which relate to the concept itself and like many who wrote on the subject, I can never claim the last word. In an attempt to define it, the concept has generally been described as a world-view of African societies and a determining factor in the formation of perceptions which influence social conduct.[17]

While, Mokgoro proffers a way of translating *ubuntu* as a 'world-view', other scholars have also conceived of the norm as 'a philosophy of life' or 'a social value'. The depiction of *ubuntu* as a philosophy of life stems from its full *Nguni* expression

[17] Mokgoro (1998, p. 2).

umuntu ngumuntu ngabantu; which is literally translated as 'a person is a person through others' (Nkhata 2010, p. 34). Nkhata (2010, pp. 36–37) has argued that *ubuntu* as a philosophy of life must be understood as interdependence and not communalism or communitarianism. *Ubuntu* here is almost akin or in fact central to the state of human being-ness. The other case where *ubuntu* is conceptualized as a social value is understood as 'group solidarity, conformity, compassion, respect, human dignity, humanistic orientation and collective unity' (Mokgoro 1998, p. 3). Indeed, *ubuntu* has traversed all aspects of life including religion, politics, law, business, social security, education, healthcare, gender and globalization (Nkhata 2010, p. 38).

Ubuntu as the social value of *human dignity* is the most visible in human rights discourse. The link between *ubuntu* and human dignity is in recognition at international law of the 'inherent worth' of every human being (Kamchedzera and Banda 2009, pp. 76–81). Human rights discourse recognize that human dignity cannot be lost (for example, Kamchedzera and Banda, above). Perhaps the link between *ubuntu* and human dignity may also be discerned from the Kantian notion of dignity; a human being is not a means but an end in himself or herself (Kant in Kamchedzera and Banda 2009, p. 77). If *ubuntu* and Kantian dignity define human being-ness, it follows that the parallels are swiftly made at international law. Hence, *ubuntu* as a norm in human rights discourse represents an instance where an 'African' norm and a norm rooted in modernity are complementary. There is no transmogrification. There is no appropriation of one over the other.

2.4.4 Convolution, Socio-political Environments, Diversity of Influence

With the three examples above, I have endeavoured to demonstrate in graphic terms the futility of a purist notion of African legal theory. The stories on anti-witchcraft laws and anti-homosexuality laws seek to demonstrate the internal contradictions that arise from monocultural reification of legal (or even moral) norms. The inconsistencies in the treatment of the same norms under a constitutional order on the one hand and a statutory setting on the other reveal the socio-political factors that may underwrite a legal framework. A number of personas have played lead acting roles in the historical narrative of 'knowledge', and the legacy of modernity in Africa as the space. The persona include the European missionary, the European colonizer, the European entrepreneur, the indigene African male, and the nascent indigene African right wing religious leader. These leading actors, however, thrive with a supporting cast – a 'vagabond population' – which instrumentally leads to the Foucauldian subjectification of the vagabond population as the 'uncivilized' or 'marginalized' or 'minority' (Rabinow 1984, pp. 3–29). It is possible to argue that a universal narrative of 'culture' becomes of a form of discipline. Indeed, this has been the critic of liberalism which, as it were, emphasized the universality of 'culture'; read 'western culture'. Similarly, agitations for a 'purist' African legal theory, jurisprudence or philosophy falls within the same trappings of a universalizing narrative of 'culture'.

2.5 Conclusion

The central point I am making is this: A purist conception of 'African' legal theory, jurisprudence or philosophy is an intellectual enterprise that is futile and impossible. An approach to what may be called 'African' legal theory, jurisprudence or philosophy based on the idea of 'culture's in-between' acknowledges two things: First, the convoluted socio-political environment of 'law' or the 'legal' in Africa (or in the African) which permeates into its theory, jurisprudence or philosophy. Second, the diversity of influence that underlies the 'culture in-between' thesis presents a window for the consideration of what is being termed 'African' in theory, jurisprudence or philosophy in confronting global phenomena. Hence, a purist conception of 'African' legal theory, jurisprudence or philosophy assumes a perilous monolithic, homogenous and universal interpretation of a much more nuanced territory.

References

Ahiauzu N (2006) Ubuntu and the obligation to obey the law. Camb Law Rev 37:17

Bauman Z (2009) Memories of class: the prehistory and after life of class. Taylor & Francis Abingdon, Oxford

Benda–Beckmann Fv (1984) Law out of context: a comment on the creation of tradition law discussion. J Afr Law 28

Berger P, Luckmann T (1971) The social construction of reality: a treatise in the sociology of knowledge. Penguin, Harmondsworth

Bhabha H (1984) Of mimicry and man: the ambivalence of colonial discourse. October 28:125

Bhabha H (1995) Interview with W.J.T. Mitchell. Artforum 33(7):80

Bhabha H (1996) Culture's in-between. In: Hall S, Du Gay P (eds) Questions of cultural identity, Sage, London pp. 53–60

Bless H (2004) Social cognition: how individuals construct reality. Psychology Press, Hove

Bourdieu P (1990) In other words: essays towards a reflexive sociology. Country Press, Cambridge

Burr V (2003) Social constructionism. Routledge, London

Byrne C (2011) Hunting the vulnerable: witchcraft and the law in Malawi. Available at www.consultancyafrica.com Accessed on 11 Feb 2013

Carmen R (1996) Autonomous development: humanizing the landscape: an excursion into radical thinking and practice. Zed Books, London

Chanock M (1985) Law, custom and social order. Cambridge University Press, Cambridge

Comeliau C (2002) The impasse of modernity: debating the future of the global market economy. Zed Books, London

Elias TO (1962) British colonial law: a comparative study of the interaction between English and local laws in British dependencies. Stevens & Sons, London

Elias TO (1971) Nigerian land law. Sweet & Maxwell, London

Fitzpatrick P (1984) Traditionalism and tradition law. J Afr Law 28(1/2):20
Fitzpatrick P (2001) Modernism and grounds of law. Cambridge University Press, Cambridge
Foucault M (1991) Discipline and punish: the birth of a prison (trans: Sheridan A). Penguin, Hamondsworth
Ibik JO (1971) Restatement of African law, vol 4, Malawi II, the law of land, succession, movable property, agreements and civil wrongs. Sweet & Maxwell, London
Kamchedzera G, Banda CU (2009) Dignified rural living, the right to development, multiparty politics and legislation in Malawi. S A J Hum Right 25:73
Mamdani M (1996) Citizen and subject: contemporary Africa and the legacy of late colonialism. Princeton University Press, Princeton, NJ
Mokgoro JY (1998) Ubuntu and the law in South Africa. Available at http://web.archive.org/web/20040928041520/www.puk.ac.za/law/per/documents/98v1mokg.doc. Accessed on 11 Feb 2013
Mudimbe VY (2004) African identity and globalization. Available at http://muse.jhu.edu. Accessed on 11 Feb 2013
Nkhata MJ (2010) Rethinking governance and constitutionalism in Africa: the relevance and viability of social trust-based governance and constitutionalism in Malawi. Unpublished LLD thesis, University of Pretoria
Okoth–Ogendo HWO (1989) Some issues of theory in the study of tenure relations in African agriculture. Afr J Int Afr Inst 59(1):6
Paliwala A (2003) Irresolutions of modernity, law, nation and empire: a reading of Fitzpatrick's modernism and the grounds of law in conjunction with Hardt and Negri's empire. Law Soc Just Glob Dev J 1. Available at http://www2.warwick.ac.uk/fac/soc/law/elj/lgd/2003_1/paliwala/. Accessed on 11 Feb 2013
Peters PE (2009) Challenges in land tenure and land reform in Africa: anthropological contributions. World Dev 37(8):1317
Quarmyne M (2011) Witchcraft: a human rights conflict between customary/traditional laws and the legal protection of women in: contemporary Sub-Saharan Africa. William Mary J Wom Law 17:475
Rabinow P (ed) (1984) The Foucault reader. Pantheon Books, New York
Ranger T (1983) The invention of tradition in colonial Africa. In: Hobsbawm E, Ranger T (eds) The invention of tradition. Cambridge University Press, Cambridge, p 211
Read J (1963) Criminal law in the Africa of today and tomorrow. J Afr Law 7:5
Roberts S (1984) Some notes on the "African Customary Law". J Afr Law 28(1/2)
Santos BS (2007) Beyond abyssal thinking: from global lines to ecologies knowledge. XXX Review 1:45
Seidman A, Seidman RB (1984) The political economy of the customary law in the former British territories of Africa' law. J Afr Law 28(1/2):44
Snyder F (1981) Colonialism and legal form: the creation of "customary" law in Senegal. In: Sumner C (ed) Crime, justice and underdevelopment. Heinemann, London, p 90
Snyder F (1984) Customary law and the economy. J Afr Law 28(1/2):34
Woodman G, Obilade A (1995) African law and legal theory. Darthmouth Publishing Co Ltd, England

Chapter 3
When British Justice (in African Colonies) Points Two Ways: On Dualism, Hybridity, and the Genealogy of Juridical Negritude in Taslim Olawale Elias

Mark Toufayan

3.1 Introduction

The ills and challenges wrought by colonialism on the peoples brought within its whim have generated constant demands and conflicts over the status of indigenous subjects and cultural others in relation to metropolitan laws, institutions, and practices. These developments have led to a recrudescence of attention of late both at the 'centre' and the 'periphery'.[1] The political struggles and resistance projects fashioned by non-European intellectuals have hardly been quaint and have, of necessity, been mounted on two related fronts. On the international plane, they have fiercely indicted colonial international law for legitimizing the subjugation and oppression of Third World peoples and sought to transform international law from a language of domination and oppression to one of emancipation embodying their manifold struggles and aspirations.[2] At home, they have resisted entrenched modes of

This chapter is a reprint of an article first published as "When British Justice (in African Colonies) Points Two Ways: On Dualism, Hibridity and the Genealogy of Juridical Negritude in Taslim Olawale Elias", 21 *Leiden Journal of International Law* 377–410 (2008), as part of a special issue in the "International Law and the Periphery" series dedicated to the work and thought of Taslim O. Elias. I thank the publisher, Cambridge University Press, for permission to reproduce it in this thought-provoking collection of essays. I dedicate this work to the memory of Aimé Césaire, whose passing contemporaneous with this essay's original publication renders renewal of thinking on African Legal Theory that this books represents all the more pressing and necessary.

[1] For an excellent study of the claims and strategies deployed by colonizers and indigenous peoples alike in negotiating the intersection between normative orders, see L. Benton, *Law and Local Cultures. Legal Regimes in World History 1400–1900* (2002).

[2] A. Anghie and B. S. Chimni, 'Third World Approaches to International Law and Individual Responsibility in Internal Conflicts', (2003) 2 *Chinese Journal of International Law* 77, at 80–2.

M. Toufayan (✉)
University of Ottawa, Ottawa, Canada
e-mail: Mark.Toufayan@uottawa.ca

O. Onazi (ed.), *African Legal Theory and Contemporary Problems: Critical Essays*, Ius Gentium: Comparative Perspectives on Law and Justice 29,
DOI 10.1007/978-94-007-7537-4_3, © Springer Science+Business Media Dordrecht 2014

representation and complexes of norms and rules and have articulated ways of engaging the universal and pragmatic claims of the colonizer and its laws.[3] This parallelism, whereby non-Western scholars have asserted claims on behalf of and, fundamentally, within their own locality to a place in law's historical construction of its own narrative, has also meant engagement in a series of obfuscated comparative moves and tropes which can be read as 'a symptom of the global (sic local) intellectual's strategy of identity formation and stabilization'.[4] Work exploring the extent to which comparativism in national, regional, or local traditions has been a tool of nation-building or modernization alongside its overt concern with intercultural understanding and the mapping of similarities and differences has barely begun.[5] Nor has there been much in the form of serious and sustained analyses of how international law may have been strategically appropriated domestically by legal intellectuals on the periphery to increase bargaining power vis-à-vis Europe and challenge the legitimacy of the 'standard of civilization'.

The intellectual portrait of Taslim Olawale Elias, a renowned Nigerian Third World scholar of the first generation, is in this respect illuminating, if not unique, given his versatility and multifacetedness as teacher, scholar, politician, diplomat, and judge.[6] It aptly demonstrates his commitment at various stages of his long and prolific career to rewriting the narrative of international law's development and the positioning of Africa within its reach.[7] His pioneering work on African customary law can, similarly, be understood in part as an attempt to decentre hegemonic relationships in the world system and foreground the legal alongside the geopolitical map of contemporary Africa drawn along lines determined by a 400-year history of the continent's relationship to its metropolis. The two projects are intimately connected. Elias continued to write tirelessly on African customary law while contemplating other pursuits prompted by the economic, social, and political upheavals

[3] A good example of this trend are the works on Algeria by Mohammed Bedjaoui. See notably his *La révolution algérienne et le droit* (1961).

[4] D. Kennedy, 'New Approaches to Comparative Law: Comparativism and International Governance', (1997a) 2 *Utah Law Review* 545, at 621.

[5] David Kennedy describes internationalists' and comparativists' mutual apprehension and distrust thus: 'From the comparativist perspective, the public internationalist seems philistine, crassly preoccupied with enlisting participation in new-fangled governance structures built on the flimsiest base of cross-cultural understanding. To the internationalist, the comparativist can seem quaint, elitist, irrelevant.' Ibid., at 588.

[6] I have been able to locate three biographies of Elias: I. O. Smith and C. A. Alade, *Taslim Elias: A Jurist of Distinction* (1991); F. A. Kuti, *Elias: A Man of His Time* (1991); and A. Thompson, *Favored by the Gods* (1991). These have been out of stock with major distributors, and thus any biographical references have had to rely on individual contributions, where available.

[7] See by T. O. Elias, *Africa and the Development of International Law* (1972; 1988); *Africa before the World Court* (1981); *The United Nations Charter and the World Court* (1989a); *The International Court of Justice and Some Contemporary Problems: Essays on International Law* (1983); and 'The Role of the International Court of Justice in Africa', (1989b) 1 *African Journal of International and Comparative Law* 1.

in newly independent states.[8] It is possible to read his later work as having in a sense been foreshadowed by his voluminous scholarship on the impact of English law on the growth of African law. Many of the insights he had developed were later deployed regarding a new subject to which he inevitably came as a second-life personal and professional project.[9] Even so, there has been a marked reluctance to receiving the latter beyond African – and Africanist – intellectual circles. Elias has been fetishized and revered as having set the yardstick against which all subsequent references to African customary law had to be measured, but there have been few attempts to connect this work to broader efforts at transforming the international law traditions discovered at the 'centre'.[10] Internationalists, conversely, have for the most part remained oblivious to the significance of this vast body of work for contemporary debates on international human rights law.[11]

European expansion and trade with its colonies has brought about many changes in their social and economic as well as legal structures. As the first chief justice of the Federal Republic of Nigeria and a scholar widely commanding authority and

[8] Elias was, for example, instrumental in organizing a major workshop in August 1974 under the aegis of the Institute of African Studies of the University of Nigeria, Nsukka, followed by publication of the proceedings as an edited volume: T. O. Elias, S. N. Nwabara, and C. O. Akpamgbo (eds.), *African Indigenous Laws* (1975).

[9] The best example remains Elias's approximation of African customary law to customary international law, as both were 'law' although they did not share the criteria imposed by Western conceptions and theories of law and sovereignty. See T. O. Elias, 'African Law', in A. Larson and C. W. Jenks (eds.), *Sovereignty within the Law* (1965), at 220, 222. Just as he dedicated his life to developing African customary law, he would spend many years in such august international institutions as the United Nations, the International Law Commission and the International Court of Justice to break the Manichaeism surrounding General Assembly resolutions and declarations and customary law as sources of law-making in the international community as a means to furthering Third World nations' emancipatory projects. See also A. Anghie, *Imperialism, Sovereignty and the Making of International Law* (2005), pp. 7, 20 (citing Elias as one of many Third World jurists who 'attempted to demonstrate that some of the fundamental principles of international law – relating, for example, to treaties and to equity – were also to be found in African or Eastern systems of thinking and statecraft and indeed, originated not in the West, but the colonial world itself'). This argumentative strategy is all too reminiscent of Elias's work on African customary law.

[10] Nowhere is this more aptly epitomized than in the essays collected in the Festschrift dedicated to Elias himself: E. G. Bello and B. A. Ajibola (eds.), *Essays in Honour of Judge Taslim Olawale Elias*, 2 vols. (1992). Contributions were organized around two themes that permeated his work: public international law, and African law and comparative public law. The editors were at pains to emphasize that 'The framework of the essays suggest that they are designed to overlap both in the well-tested and established fields of law and those branches of law dealing with development and change in the "peripheral areas". It is not unlikely, *grosso modo*, that either side will draw from and upon the richness of the whole exercise in a mutually reinforcing manner' (xi), but a glimpse of the various contributions confirms that there is little such cross-breeding taking place. The present essay makes no pretence of faring any better on this score.

[11] In the post-colonial era the human rights movement has provided a similar supervening code of values to the general idea underlying colonial policy that the fundamental rights and freedoms of Europe were the basis of the colonial legal order. For some interesting insights drawing on anthropological work and connecting human rights to customary law, see T. W. Bennett, *Human Rights and African Customary Law* (1995); S. E. Merry, *Human Rights and Gender Violence: Translating International Law into Local Justice* (2006).

repute in a field which he dominated throughout his life, Taslim Elias was at the forefront of many significant legal developments in the colonies and was thus 'central' to the development of 'British colonial law'.[12] He remained acutely aware of the need to preserve indigenous customs and traditions, which in some cases would have significantly hampered efforts to assimilate. He also happened to be a Nigerian lawyer educated in Britain, where he gained several degrees, including his Ph.D. in 1949 at the University of London, and a staunch admirer of the British, their peculiarities, their system of legal education, and legal and particularly sharp-witted judicial profession, as well as English law's reputation for liberalism, adaptability, sense of justice, and fair play.[13] Should we interpret his work and life, then, like so many of his contemporaries, as a 'peripheral' attempt to trace the influence of political and intellectual developments at the centre upon law at the periphery? What does he mean by 'Africa'? Is it a useful category to think about in terms of legal phenomena or sites of production of a legal consciousness? Does his map of the development of African customary law have a sense of direction or stability, a narrative of progress, a geography? Does his work, in the end, merely replicate the positioning – already encountered in international law, comparative law, and postcolonial scholarship – of the West as the source of theoretical models and constructs and the Third World as the gaping receptacle and substratum of evidence and raw material supplied for theoretical study and confirming images of the 'other' already projected at the margins, the only available alternatives oscillating between assimilation and a robust cultural nativism?

The present essay uses a selection of Elias's key writings as a heuristic device to retrieve the discursive maps coalescing around the positioning of Africa alongside frames of production and reception. The focus is not, however, on tracing patterns of influence or the transplantation of British legal ideas to the colonies and the corresponding elaboration of maps of ensuing similarities and differences, which are at best of descriptive value. Rather, the historical project I have in mind seeks to explore, through a contextual re- (and de)construction of Elias's leading texts, the relationship between the rise of legal thought in Africa and political projects of unity, domination, and reform in cross-cultural settings. The general relationship between the appropriation and reinvention of law from the 'centre' of the world system in the 'periphery' is usually all we have by way of a conceptual vocabulary to think about law in terms of its development in Africa; we lack 'thicker' analytical and methodological devices to identify local institutional designs and native legal creativity.

[12] Elias defines this expression broadly, as encompassing 'the body of principles consisting partly of Imperial legislation and colonial enactments and partly of all applicable English law and local customary law throughout the British colonies'. T. O. Elias, *British Colonial Law: A Comparative Study of the Interaction between English and Local Laws in British Dependencies* (1962), p. 6.

[13] 'Judge Elias appreciated the British; their peculiar characteristics, and their system of education. He has an extremely high opinion of Lord Denning. He also admires the game of cricket, and often uses the language of this sport to describe everyday events'. E. Bello, 'Preface', in Bello and Ajibola, *supra* note 10, at x.

Elias befriended a generation of more sociologically informed and anti-formalist figures and approaches to legal thought to give their respective countries or regions a say in the legal tradition in a way which would acknowledge but could also bypass the European legacy. His work subverts more mainstream accounts of the stability of 'centres' and 'peripheries'. My intuition is that his scholarship typically exemplifies the production of an African legal consciousness which I call 'juridical Negritude', home to a variety of political projects, and which became associated at various moments with a more limited project, both through reception (at what is traditionally depicted as the 'centre') and through its displacement by a new avatar of that consciousness as it became habitually 'spoken' at the site of its production.[14] My use of the term 'Negritude' departs from, while dovetailing to some extent with, the intellectual movement emerging in inter-war francophone Africa bearing the same name, which celebrated Negro culture and pride as a necessary counterpoint to discursive reason as an instrument of understanding the distinctive attributes of African culture. While there are no explicit references to the ideas championed by the movement's founders in any of his works, I argue that Elias's thinking and scholarship in the years of struggle leading to Nigerian independence (1954–1960)

[14]As for others whose work has been analysing the rise of legal consciousness in geographical locales traditionally ascribed to the 'periphery', my understanding of the concept is indebted to the legal-historical work of Duncan Kennedy: 'Consciousness refers to the total contents of a mind, including images of the external world, images of the self, of emotions, goals and values and theories about the world and self ... The main peculiarity of this [legal] consciousness is that it contains a vast number of legal rules, arguments, and theories, a great deal of information about the institutional workings of the legal process and the constellation of ideals and goals current in the profession at a given moment'. D. Kennedy, 'Toward an Historical Understanding of Legal Consciousness: The Case of Classical Legal Thought in America 1850–1940', (1980) 3 *Research in Law and Sociology* 3, at 23. The difficulties of gesturing at an 'African legal consciousness' as an essentializing frame become evident when what is sought to be embodied is not merely legal thought in one country (the United States) and a relatively fixed period (the nineteenth century) but a regional consciousness across an entire continent riven by ethnic strife and social and political turmoil, given the, one would surmise, different conceptualizations and understandings of their national legal regimes during colonial and post-colonial times. Part of the perils and predilections of engaging in historically informed work on legal thought in Africa is to verify whether a prior sense of 'Africanness' or 'pan-African solidarity' can be located as the set of shared discourses and practices across a wide range of groups and peoples concerning their explicit or implicit awareness of regional unity and identity. My understanding of juridical Negritude is much more limited, however, and confined to the retrieval from the works and thought of one leading figure on the African legal scene (Taslim Elias) of what Kwame Nkrumah (the first president of independent Ghana) called 'consciencism', as a way of incorporating in traditional African humanism principles borrowed from European and Islamic models which, Nkrumah felt, had also become part of Africa's cultural heritage. See K. Nkrumah, *Consciencism: Philosophy and Ideology for Decolonization and Development with Particular Reference to the African Revolution* (1964), pp. 68–70. This consciousness is understood as a vocabulary (or *langue*) within which its specific avatars in the form of positively enacted rules, or legal regimes (*subsystems* or structures or *paroles*) take hold along a wide spectrum of historical events. On 'langue' and 'parole', see D. Kennedy, 'A Semiotics of Critique', (2001) 22 *Cardozo Law Review* 1147, at 1175. On 'subsystems', see Kennedy, 'Toward an Historical Understanding of Legal Consciousness', *supra*. My integrative reading of the structure of legal discourse and elements in legal consciousness draws on D. Kennedy, *A Critique of Adjudication (Fin de Siècle)* (1997b), pp. 133–134.

must be understood against the context of ascendance of Negritude, but that his consciousness about law in Africa and the positioning of Africa in a global history of legal philosophy transcends it and cannot be reducible to it. Thus it is more appropriate to conceptualize the scheme of periods, modes, and narratives of production and reception in the English law/African customary law nexus elaborated in this article as 'a set of boxes for the organization of facts and factoids, a structure within which to propose low-level hypotheses, and the locale of a narrative'.[15]

Why focus on the writings of a scholar from the 'periphery' in this way? The heuristic usefulness of Taslim Elias's intellectual portrait is the situatedness of his narrative of Africa at the intersection of analyses of world history, legal consciousness, and legal pluralism. Africa appears as a disputed territory in what Ali Mazrui calls an ongoing war of 'its own changing gods'[16] – indigenous and Islamic legal traditions constantly vying for hegemony over British positivism in a 'quest for a new civilizational synthesis'.[17] The ideology of Elias's juridical Negritude needed to foster harmonious growth and development is one which would emerge from the productive encounter, *within* African consciousness, of Africa's triple heritage; it finds expression in his lifelong project of developing a common law for Nigeria modelled on, and thus in strategic alliance with, English common law. Elias embraced hybridity and eschewed assimilation. It is not so much that he seemed to be writing *about* Africa and the West as he was foregrounding through and through the conditions of a discourse working *between* them – a law in-between.

Methodologically, I believe that it is more useful to engage with his work by juxtapositions and comparative readings of his leading texts through the bearings of what Marie-Claire Belleau calls an 'intersectionalité stratégique'[18] (strategic identitarian intersectionality). Belleau's own work examines the impact of the intersectionality between political struggles of national and cultural identity and feminism in relation to the dichotomy of public law and private law in Quebec. Her approach seeks to substitute differences grounded in political and cultural contextualizations for those based on essentializations, thus creating opportunities for a deeper mutual understanding of emancipatory projects and the fostering of strategic alliances between sites of cultural practices, dominant and marginal.[19] I argue that Elias's

[15] D. Kennedy, 'Three Globalizations of Law and Legal Thought: 1850–2000', in D. Trubek and A. Santos (eds.), *The New Law and Economic Development. A Critical Appraisal* (2006), p. 24.

[16] A. A. Mazrui, 'Cultural Forces in African Politics: In Search of a Synthesis', in I. J. Mowoe and R. Bjornson (eds.), *Africa and the West. The Legacies of Empire* (1986), p. 33.

[17] Ibid., at 33–4.

[18] M.-C. Belleau, 'La dichotomie droit privé/droit public dans le contexte québécois et canadien et l'intersectionnalité identitaire', (1998) 39 *Cahiers de droit* 177.

[19] Belleau explains the methodological *démarche* undergirding her approach thus: 'Strategic intersectionality consists in imagining strategies that take into account experiences rendered invisible when we consider separately feminism and political struggles of national and cultural identity. Imagining spare intersectional strategies presupposes disclosing hidden differences and similarities, deconstructing myths, revealing processes of projection and dissociation, as well as promoting the emergence of new coalitions.' Ibid., at 181 (my translation). Elsewhere, Belleau has engaged in comparative reading of sociologically oriented French and Quebecois legal scholars in an attempt

obsessive yearnings for the uniform development of a 'common law of the realm' reveals a complex picture of mediating between simultaneous participation in various struggles and projects within African humanism which may at times have appeared contradictory, without subordinating any one of them to the others.[20] This impels us to appreciate the rich and multifarious significations and consequences of the interplay between identitarian struggles and the different legal manifestations unfolding in Africa at the time he was writing, which an analysis structured around the centre–periphery divide distorts, rather than imagining them as being locked into a single matrix of assimilation or rejection.

The periodization followed in this article roughly spans two decades and cuts across different facets of African colonial and post-colonial history. The various sections emulate this structure and expose different aspects of Elias's intellectual trajectory without, however, suggesting, for reasons it is hoped will become obvious, that this necessarily followed a linear progressive narrative. The first (1954–1960) situates Elias's interventions in the socio-historical context of the extension of British rule over dependent territories in west and east Africa and the introduction of English law in what was known in 1863 as the Lagos settlement and which was later to become contemporary Nigeria. I begin Sect. 3.2 by introducing briefly the African socio-political and cultural landscape, ranging from the end of the nineteenth century, when British administration of justice in the colonies was carried over from the Royal Niger Company to the British crown, to the middle of the twentieth century, which immediately preceded Elias's interventions on the legal scene. Faced with the apparent hegemony of an outside determinant that seemed all-encompassing, non-European intellectuals were hard put to make Africa understood on its own terms, freed from Western ethnocentric conceptions and values. During this period of heightened arrogance and paternalistic pronouncements, transcending the question of what is 'African' necessarily meant answering the question, 'What is law, and how do we enforce it?' I argue that Elias's strategy of engagement with English law during these formative years was as ambitious as it was Herculean: exposing Africa's relevance to the West and those seeking to understand the lived realities of its people without, in the process, reducing it to a cog in the Western knowledge wheel, and, at the same time, establishing that 'nearly all ideology in contemporary Africa reflects the fusion of humanistic ideals drawn from Western and indigenous sources'.[21] Connecting law to the social consciousness and lived realities of a people was a modernist attempt to subvert the region's marginal

to explicate the invention and loss of a critical jurisprudential tradition or consciousness which would have facilitated understanding the civil law as a social/political institution, much like the critiques of American legal realists have succeeded in doing. See M.-C. Belleau, 'The "Juristes Inquiets": Legal Classicism and Criticism in Early Twentieth-Century France', (1997) 2 *Utah Law Review* 379.

[20] For the 'mediating' function of 'contradictions of experience' in consciousness (arising, for example, from 'inconsistent facts, conflicting emotions, or operative abstractions') in ways which make the contradiction less striking, see Kennedy, 'Toward an Historical Understanding of Legal Consciousness', *supra* note 14, at 24.

[21] R. Bjornson and I. J. Mowoe, 'Introduction', in Mowoe and Bjornson (1986), *supra* note 16, at 4.

position and elevate it to the same status as that enjoyed by the colonizer. I read Elias's efforts against the currents of a regional intellectual trend represented by the works of the poetics of Negritude to show their participation in an African philosophy in the making as well as the precariousness of defending both the rise of cultural nationalism and a viable sense of identity under the centripetal pressures of British law and the looming perils and predilections of independence.

The second period (1960 to the 1970s) which I analyse, in Sect. 3.3 of the article, places Elias in the context of decolonization, which witnessed at once the dislocation of the social formations inherited from the colonial period and the transformations wrought by modernization. The British colonial policy of indirect rule under Fredrick (later Lord) Lugard's administration, through the agency of a literate elite capable of performing subordinate but necessary functions in colonial administration, had secured African customary law's 'relevance' to English law through the enactment of local ordinances and legislation and jurisprudential developments.[22] Retrieving and asserting a unified consciousness of the self, under which tended to be subsumed all other concrete issues making up the objective reality of a people under subjugation and oppression, became in the circumstances far less important and, in fact, counterproductive. I illustrate in this part how confidence in customary law's 'presence' in the colonial and post-colonial eras allowed Elias to build on the insights he had already developed and downplay fears over the progressive absorption of customary law into the all-pervading English system in order to harness the positive integrative force of British law as a means of advancing the project of greater harmonization and uniformity based on 'ordered reason', 'social progress', and 'development'. The ability of Africans to synthesize fragmented elements from seemingly opposed cultures had allowed them to live through a turbulent history without contradiction or schizophrenia, yet the divisiveness of the continent post-independence along federal lines threatened unity; it required both an inward- and outward-looking continental cultural synthesis through law's agency during this early phase of nation-building in order to negotiate customary law's critical engagement with English law on equal terms. Finally, I examine Elias's specific intervention in the debate on legal reform over codification of customary law as the hybrid site of contestation and intersection between the various political projects of nation-building, African cultural liberation, and development, in which the evolution of a common law of Nigeria was to become the accessory to and frame for (re)writing the history of African humanism.

[22] For a fascinating study on how court assessors of customary law and clerks were routinely complicit in consolidating colonial rule, sometimes unbeknown to themselves, see B. N. Lawrance, E. L. Osborn, and R. L. Roberts (eds.), *Intermediaries, Interpreters, and Clerks. African Employees in the Making of Colonial Africa* (2006). See also Elias's admonishment of the 'arming of such subordinate officials of the statutory court with the new magic wand of the record book and of spoken English' in T. O. Elias, *The Nature of African Customary Law* (1956a), p. 275.

3.2 Taslim Elias Situated: The Rise and Retrieval of an African Humanist Tradition (*C.*1954–1960)

Elias's initial legal interventions on the African scene coincided with the populist inquiry as to whether there was anything like African customary law – whether it was law at all or just a hotchpotch of desultory, discordant, and ever-changing customs. Understanding the challenges he was facing and the background theories against which he was writing is crucial to the hybridity of his narrative. Accordingly, I begin this part by sketching a very brief history of the evolution of African law and institutions arising from the colonial encounter and, particularly, of the role and place of customary law administered in British dependencies and, specifically, Nigeria, since this was the context most familiar to Elias and on which he wrote most extensively. There are obvious risks in such oversimplified framing, but it will suffice for the purposes of grounding the broader argument. I then turn to explicate the vicissitudes of Elias's emancipatory 'programme' of African cultural liberation as elaborated in his seminal work *The Nature of African Customary Law*, making extensive references to his text in order to retrieve the politics of an African socio-legal consciousness in the making.

3.2.1 Out of Eden? Interrogating Africa

As the various European powers established their rule over African territories, whether by annexation, conquest, or cession, and were confronted with the problem of governing their possessions and administering justice therein, their attention was invariably drawn to indigenous laws and customs when 'either the pressure of culture contact or the necessities of trade made it no longer possible to ignore what goes on among the "natives"'.[23] In the former colony, protectorate, and mandated territory of what was to become Nigeria, the bulk of the country was first administered by the Royal Niger Company under a charter granted to it in 1886. The company established a system of courts, and its charter contained a provision ensuring that in administering justice due regard was to be had to the customs and laws of the class, tribe, or nation that came under their sway.[24] There took place between 1886 and 1900 further extension of British power inland, largely through the

[23] Elias, *supra* note 12, at 102. For an excellent survey of how cross-cultural trade has influenced the migration of behavioural norms, ideas, and institutions during imperial and colonial rule, see P. D. Curtin, *Cross-Cultural Trade in World History* (1984).

[24] For a personal recollection of the leading jurists and publicists that influenced the making of Nigerian law, see T. O. Elias, *Makers of Nigerian Law* (1956b), a series of studies commissioned in 1956 by the editor of the journal *West Africa* and reproduced in T. O. Elias, *Law in a Developing Society* (1973a), pp. 11–75. For a brief historical exposition of the impact of the Royal Niger Company on acquisition of territory and conclusion of treaties with tribal leaders, see T. O. Elias, *Nigerian Land Law* (1971), pp. 17–33.

company's administration, but native resistance to its virtual trade monopoly and the need to strengthen the western border against the French, coupled with the necessity for the suppression of the internal slave trade in the north, proved too much for a commercial venture. The British government eventually took over the administration of the territory in 1900, while in theory maintaining the company's policy regarding native laws and customs.[25] References to how private corporate power influenced law-making and the administration of justice within colonies, rather than merely the acquisition of territories through negotiated treaty arrangements or coercion and consolidation of sovereign rule,[26] are belittled in the history of international law, which constructs disciplinary narratives of origin around the distinction between 'civilized'/'uncivilized' whose relationships become further structured and regulated around the municipal/international, public/private divides. This dual exclusionary move renders invisible a range of local governance issues which are parasitic on the colonial and imperial policies of great powers and accordingly blur the distinction.[27]

There were obvious differences as regards both the manner of introducing Western legal systems and ideas and the subject matter of the law thus introduced. For example, the way in which English law was operative in its overseas dependencies differed according to whether they fell into the category of colonies, protectorates, or mandated territories. As far as French, Portuguese, and Spanish African territories were concerned, problems of conflict of laws were epitomized in the idea of 'citizenship' and confined to status-bearing groups (*evolués* or *assimilados*) on the one hand, who were 'deserving' of being assimilated into the imported European legal order, and to the ordinary unsophisticated Africans on the other, who, paradoxically, came under a watered-down version of that system which provided a measure of protection to their differences by way of some admixture of acceptable local usages. The British, on the other hand,

[25] For extensive treatment of how British rule impacted on the development of laws in Nigeria, one is invariably referred to T. O. Elias, *Nigeria. The Development of its Laws and Constitution* (1967).

[26] M. F. Lindley, *The Acquisition and Government of Backward Territory in International Law* (1969), pp. 91–108.

[27] The typical discursive moves within the disciplinary narratives of its own construction as regards chartered corporations were essentially twofold: either they were not 'subjects' of international law and thus were removed from the reach of international law in their relationships with native peoples; or they were considered to be subjects and, hence, sovereign in relation to the natives, who, however, looked at them from a position of subordination and delight as to their majesty and ability to administer order and justice in their territories. The former can be traced, for example, in Henry Wheaton's *Elements of International Law* (1866), p. 30, §17. For the latter see T. J. Lawrence, *The Principles of International Law* (1900), p. 79, §54 ('It is easy to see how the natives must regard a body of men armed with such authority as that granted to the British South Africa Company, and possessed of skill, energy, scientific machinery, and weapons of precision. To them the company must be all-powerful. They know little or nothing of the Imperial Government … He is thousands of miles from the scene of action … Practically the company rules its territories in so far as they are ruled at all. It legislates, it administers, it punishes, it negotiates, it makes war, and it concludes peace … They are sovereign in relation to the barbarous or semi-barbarous inhabitants of the districts in which they bear sway'.

lacked the resources needed to impose their laws on large and potentially hostile populations and were interested instead in preserving African institutions in order to use them as intermediaries and thus minimize the cost of administering the territories that would have resulted from direct utilization of British labour; they were thus forced to compromise and recognize the operation and applicability of indigenous laws, provided, however, that they were suitably 'civilized', or, as it was then understood, not 'repugnant to natural justice, equity or good conscience, or incompatible' with English law. I explore in the third part of this essay the way in which this 'repugnancy doctrine', which was born out of the colonial encounter to structure a legal system that would account for the relationship between subaltern and metropolitan laws and institutions, in fact served the interests of both colonizer and colonized by ensuring the reinforcing mutuality of law's function as a tool both of development, national-building, and social legitimacy, and of resistance. In practice, however, despite the differences in philosophy and method of governance in the colonies, the colonial 'masters' and their judicial acolytes all over Africa exhibited a blatant contempt for the values of traditional African society.[28] A central corollary 'at home', as it were, to Tony Anghie's provocative thesis on the colonial origins of international law thus became implacably obvious: because the decentralized polities of Africa did not comply with European ideas of statehood, they could not be considered sovereign, and, consequently, could have no 'law'.[29] Colonialism firmly imprinted its values on custom, which was derided and consigned to the study of anthropologists whose interests lay in whatever was alien or secondary. But what counted as 'indigenous' or 'foreign' was often a matter of the level of cohesion of an imagined body or institution and the feeling or fear of, or desire for, or seduction of, its importation, penetration and influence.[30]

[28] A classical example of the prevailing state of mind are these words of a famous colonial judge: '"How do you justify the application of English principles of justice to so many different peoples whose outlook and mentality vary so much from our own, especially when English ideas pass their understanding?" We believe that these ideas are the best that can regulate our administration of justice, and an Englishman, because he is an Englishman and not someone quite different, cannot adopt other persons' conception of justice. Whether there is really much difference and whether our ideas are not understandable to others, I will not stay to discuss, because if they are not understandable it is a pity, but it must not be allowed to stand in the way of doing what we believe to be right since in the last resort we govern other peoples by our conscience and not by their understanding.' Sir S. Abrahams, 'The Colonial Legal Service and the Administration of Justice in Colonial Dependencies', (1948) 30 *Journal of Comparative Legislation and International Law* (3rd Series) 1, at 10.

[29] A. Anghie, 'Finding the Peripheries: Sovereignty and Colonialism in Nineteenth-Century International Law', (1999) 40 *Harvard International Law Journal* 1, at 29–30.

[30] My idea of a customary law as a weaker and underdeveloped geographical space inviting foreign, namely Western, interest, penetration, insemination, in short colonization, borrows from Edward Said's reference to how 'Oriental sexuality' was depicted in Orientalist literature, the supine feminine Orient suggesting not only fecundity but sexual promise (and threat) as well, and thus portrayed as both dangerous and threatening, in need of control and regulation. E. W. Said, *Orientalism* (1979), p. 190, 218.

3.2.2 Negritude in Ascendancy

Implicit in this view was, of course, a particular conception of the 'primitive' mind: spontaneous, traditional, personal, commonly known, corporate, relatively unchanging, and so on. These, alongside other more derogatory epithets, have strongly influenced the production of classical works on customary law, which were as much responsible for data-gathering as for producing theory.[31] The quest for an original integrity of 'being' gradually came to dominate African thinking as it fulfilled a therapeutic need to resist the dislocation of social structures and cultural life that colonial domination had engendered and that were reflected in the tensions assaulting the consciousness of the self. To be sure, writing against the colonial policy of the administration of justice in British dependencies instilled with this covert racial stigma carried bewildering difficulties that 'beset the path of the writer on African laws and customs'.[32] Elias was no doubt aware of his leadership role in these dire times and of the need to confront these attitudes with the 'African awakening' and '*prise de conscience*'[33] about its leading position in world history and human life:

> The increasing economic and social importance of the Continent for our time, the emergence of political consciousness among the indigenous peoples in various parts of the Continent, and their aspirations towards recognition in the various fields of human endeavour, make it all the more urgent that an attempt should be made to give expression to the immanent ideas of the African peoples in the rapidly changing circumstances of their modern life.[34]

The *Nature of African Customary Law* was a child of necessity. In an earlier work, published in 1954, Elias had expressed no intention of being embroiled in the theoretical controversy as to whether or not rules of customary observance were by positivist (or other) standards law, but simply assumed this to be the case and proceeded to demonstrate 'what it is in the Nigerian customary law that entitles it to the name of enforceable legal rules'.[35] His *Native Land Law and Custom*, which was a slightly revised version of his doctoral dissertation first published in 1951, was groundbreaking, not least because of a change in nomenclature in the expression 'native law and custom' – where 'native' was typically associated with something

---

[31] It is generally accepted that Hegel's *Philosophy of World History* (1837), in its general reference to non-Western peoples and its particular bearing on Africa, provides the most important intellectual foundation for the colonial ideology. It was on this foundation that classical anthropology sought to rationalize European domination of other races by presenting them as inherently inferior to the white race. This ideological thrust of classical anthropology found its culmination in Lucien Lévy-Bruhl's *La Mentalité primitive* (1922) and marked the development of proto-Negritude thought in the Caribbean, particularly Haiti, in the nineteenth century.

[32] Elias, *supra* note 22, at 1.

[33] I borrow the expression from J.-P. Sartre, 'Orphée noire', in L.-Sédar Senghor, *Anthologie de la nouvelle poésie nègre et malgache de langue française* (1948), pp. XI–XV, who sees it in the passage from an unreflected to a reflected mode of experience.

[34] Elias, *supra* note 22, at 4.

[35] T. O. Elias, *The Nigerian Legal System* (1963), p. 12 (first published in 1954 under the title: Groundwork of Nigerian Law).

uncivilized or barbaric – to 'customary law'. Ethnographers fashionably used the terms 'law' and 'culture' on the one hand, and 'law', 'custom', and 'tradition' on the other, interchangeably; whereas laws were deemed coextensive with cultures which were conceived as bounded and static, custom implied a normative order legitimated by tradition which was understood as being apolitical and socially, but not legally (as understood through a Western lens), sanctioned.[36] Considering that such misconceptions continue today to plague the disciplines of social and legal anthropology, Elias's reshuffling of these concepts in what appeared to the casual onlooker to be a mere cosmetic change had profound implications not only for understanding custom and its position in modern legal systems, but also for Africa in a global history of (legal) philosophy.

In *The Nigerian Legal System* (originally published in 1954 as *Groundwork of Nigerian Law*), a book he wrote while Simon Fraser Research Fellow at the University of Manchester, Elias was quintessentially pragmatic, if not comically ironic, about the effects of the colonial encounter on law in Africa. Custom was not 'peripheral' to the Nigerian legal system as it was in England, but, in the context of the history of Nigeria's development, was one of its main sources of law.[37] Precisely because it already existed when the country came under British rule, courts had recognized it, and colonial administrators had done as much, and it was regularly being enforced.[38] His task thus became to study it painstakingly, and to ascertain it or create an environment conducive to its ascertainment.[39] As the British accorded it recognition, while fatally ignoring its content and how they could apply it in their

[36] See the insightful discussion on the reification in mainstream property relations scholarship of the dichotomy between formal law and custom in connection to gender and property relations in Kenya by C. I. Nyamu, 'Achieving Gender Equality in a Plural Legal Context: Custom and Women's Access to and Control of Land in Kenya', (1998–99) *Third World Legal Studies* 21.

[37] Elias, *supra* note 35, at 12, 14.

[38] Ibid., at 13.

[39] Ibid., at 14 ('The problem here is largely one of finding out what the true indigenous rule is and whether and how far, when one has been discovered, it can be said to have originated or to have been adopted'). In many of his works (almost all with the exception of *The Nature of African Customary Law*), there is in Elias's narrative a sense of a self-appointed, almost messianic, role, catering to the needs of lawyers, judges, administrators, and all concerned by his endeavour and exhibiting a heroic urge to revamp the academic discipline of African customary law and rescue it from indifference, ineptitude, placidity, and bewilderment. For example, in the preface to the fourth edition of *Nigerian Land Law and Custom*, *supra* note 24, he candidly states: 'The received English law on these subjects has been carefully blended with Nigerian law wherever necessary, the aim throughout being to present the living law of land tenure as it is practised and applied in Nigeria today … This edition should, accordingly, meet the new demands of the revised syllabuses of all the Faculties of Law in Nigeria, while the long felt needs of the members of the Nigerian Bar should now be better served. The requirements of the administrator and the investor should also be largely met. In short, all those interested in comparative law, especially in the study of the interaction between English law and indigenous African customary law in a dynamic society, should find this book a reliable and stimulating guide.' While this is testimony to his staggering erudition and learning, it also exemplifies the attitude of certain pioneers of a legal discipline to make their task a 'personal quest' on a long journey towards a better tomorrow. On the 'personal quest' device in international legal scholarship, although in a different context, see D.Z. Cass, 'Navigating the

own courts, they had to learn about or find out what African customary law in Nigeria was! While Elias did not explain why customary law was 'law' from the vantage point of legal theory, he did lay out the 'groundwork', as it were, of his vision of law:

> But the wise policy of not ignoring the customary law of dependent peoples has been based upon a realization of the sound legal fact that law as an expression of the social consciousness of every people subject to its authority cannot always be judged by purely exotic standards. What is by one people regarded as possessing the attributes of law may not impress another people as such, if the rules of social behaviour and the juridical sentiment of the latter are different from those of the former. This is not to say that 'reception' of the law of the former by the latter is impossible; it is only to emphasise that law is a relative phenomenon and any attempt to judge its validity by absolute canons is doomed to failure. The important thing is its acceptance and recognition by the particular people whose conduct it is deemed to regulate.[40]

Whatever explains this self-imposed restraint, the question could no longer be avoided. Yet there was a significant shift in tone and posture in *The Nature of African Customary Law*, where the entire enterprise took on the rather austere allure of dealing with 'the whole problem of the African in contact with white man's law'.[41] This behavioural shift was hardly innocent. There needed to be a 'change of heart and of attitude on the part of Western jurists towards indigenous laws and customs in Africa',[42] for isolating African ideas about law and government from general problems of political and legal theory would 'fall … into the kind of error … that "political theory and political practice (including colonial administration) have often suffered by reason of this type of system being set up, consciously or unconsciously, as a norm"'.[43] Whereas Africa had been read from the perspective of 'law' (Europe), 'law', in turn, had failed to be interrogated by Africa. 'An intellectual adventure into African legal conceptions', in his view, 'should enlarge our horizon, if it does not enrich our knowledge, of the function and purpose of law in the modern world.'[44] It would then become clear that 'African law, when once its essential characteristics are fully appreciated, forms part and parcel of law in general. It is thus no longer to be set in opposition to what is frequently but loosely termed "European law", and this notwithstanding a number of admitted differences of content and of method'.[45]

What is remarkable in these two juxtaposed sentences lies in what they adroitly conceal: the ingredients of an African legal consciousness defined both against and in conjunction with Europe as an aspect of African humanism. 'African law' was

---

Newstream: Recent Critical Scholarship in International Law', (1997) 65 *Nordic Journal of International Law* 341, at 365–9.

[40] Elias, *supra* note 35, at 5–6.

[41] Elias, *supra* note 22, at 5.

[42] Ibid.

[43] Ibid., at 17.

[44] Ibid., at 6.

[45] Ibid., at v. The expression 'European law' may appear to be a misnomer, for it was hardly disputed that 'law' was 'European'. Nonetheless, it could be argued that this was deliberate, for the entire debate on whether African law was law turned on what differentiated 'Africa' from 'Europe'.

'not law' because of what made it distinctly 'African', its Africanness. Yet answering the question 'What is 'African?' had been collapsed into the question 'What is law?' and measured against criteria prevalent in Western societies. There was no independent source for assessing either; they defined themselves against each other, as each other's opposites. It thus became necessary to probe the inner selves of Africans, to retrieve their 'essential characteristics', for only then would it become possible to position Africa in relation to law in general. By expressing the distinctive attributes of African culture (e.g. the nature of African societies in terms of political organization and their theories of government), Elias was necessarily differentiating it from Europe and asserting its position in world history. But this was only an accessory to his overall project, for despite differences, both shared similar legal ideas, which was testimony to 'the unity of all human knowledge and experience', and were accordingly brought together under law's soothing yoke; for 'law, apart from differences in social environment, is no respecter of race or tribe, and the problems it has to solve are everywhere the same, namely the resolution of conflicts in human society and the maintenance of peace and order'.[46] Once 'law' was stripped of its Western garb and made 'relevant' and palatable to the needs of African and European peoples alike, there could be no doubt that African customary law, no less than English law, drew from the same abundant well.

Elias's reference to African law's 'essential characteristics' was a rhetorical move, part of his goal of African empowerment. It paralleled, and therefore must be set against the background of, the rise of Negritude as a full-fledged cultural ideology in the early post-Second World War era and the wider shift in black intellectual and literary circles during the inter-war years, although the movement's tenets seemingly percolated only modestly outside francophone Africa. There were, however, marked differences in the strategies deployed by Elias on the one hand, and the leaders of Negritude on the other. The former, while perhaps not as polemical in tone and posture, were no less a counter-thesis to the scheme of ideas, systems of meaning, and representations by which the colonial system was sustained.[47]

The term 'Negritude', first used by the Martinican poet Aimé Césaire in his 1939 poem 'Cahier d'un retour au pays natal' (Notebook of a return to my native land),[48] refers in its Césairian acceptation to a collective identity of the African diaspora born of a common historico-cultural experience of subjugation. Both the term and the subsequent literary and cultural movement that developed emphasized the possible negation of that subjugation via concerted actions of racial cultural affirmation. In succeeding decades the term became a focus for ideological

---

[46] Ibid., at 6.

[47] See C. Mwalimu, *The Nigerian Legal System, Volume 1: Public Law* (2005), p. 121 ('Elias was also one of the distinguished freedom fighters who used law, just as Sarbah had done in 1898 to advance the cause of freedom and independence for the new and emerging African state ….').

[48] For a useful introduction to Césaire's poem and the context of its conception, composition, and publication, see M. Rosello, 'Introduction', in *Aimé Césaire: 'Notebook of a Return to My Native Land/Cahier d'un retour au pays natal'*, trans. and ed. M. Rosello, with A. Pritchard (1995), pp. 9–68.

disputes among the black intelligentsia of a francophone world in the process of decolonization. Negritude as a concept encompassed and distilled a wide range of previous historical moments, in turn generating a diverse field of debate that has, in its use of the term, extended, and at times even contradicted, Césaire's original intervention. It is not necessary to enter the debate here; suffice it to say that there were essentially two opposing lines of interpretation around which all critiques could be organized. The first, associated with Césaire, sustained the notion as a cultural, historically developing process with a political dimension of resistance to the politics of assimilation.[49] In his usage, an alienated black identity is forced to confront itself as a reified object. This conception postulated Negritude as self-estrangement, a fact or quality that confronts the black subject as an object. Such a gesture initiates an aesthetic movement in Césaire's poem, through an intense symbolism of aggression and complexity of imagery involving a drama of consciousness, towards a self-consciousness that breaks the bonds of subjugation through a grappling with negativity in the form of self-alienation. Césaire applied to the realm of black subjectivity Hegel's insight that 'alienation' is in fact a transformational process in which the individual's so-called 'natural' existence, in this case the ideological subjugation of blacks, is concretely negated for an artificial, self-created one. He thus produced the material, textual objectification of black self-consciousness, a programme for self-understanding and liberation.[50] In contrast, Léopold Sédar Senghor's notion of Negritude and the general reception and critique of the concept in west Africa following Senghor (a poet and later the first president of independent Senegal) focused on the putatively 'African' characteristics of emotion, intuition, artistic creativity, and 'anthropopsychism', by which he referred to the unmediated relation of the 'black soul' to the phenomenological world, its 'eternal' characteristic,[51] as opposed to a Western, or 'Hellenic', rationality. The quintessential African civilization emphasized the group over the individual, race and culture over class, the irrational and mythical over the conscious and rational, images over concepts, and art and religion over science and technology. The very process of delineation between Africa and Europe was itself 'part of the organicist, antimodern tradition of European thought that sought to retrieve what had allegedly been lost with the triumph of modernity'.[52] In short, Senghor's Negritude was, to use his own vocable, a revisionist 'ontology', or study of 'black being' in the world, a fundamentally ahistorical, transcultural determination and celebration of the constituents and commonalities of 'blackness' in African diasporic societies.

At almost the same time as these views confronted each other in a clash at the First International Congress of Negro Writers and Artists, held at the Sorbonne, Paris, in September 1956, Elias's *The Nature of African Customary Law* gave a modernist turn to the debate on whether African law was really 'law', by making use of European anti-modernist thought against Europe through a set of typically

[49] Ibid., at 125.

[50] J. G. Vaillant, *Black, French and African: A Life of Leopold Sedar Senghor* (1990), p. 244.

[51] L. Sédar Senghor, *Liberté I: Négritude et humanisme* (1964), pp. 71–4.

[52] R. H. King, *Race, Culture, and the Intellectuals 1940–1970* (2004), p. 241.

modernist moves (not in the sense of the system of ideas and thought of the Enlightenment, but the cultural and aesthetic experiment and innovation of the early twentieth-century avant-garde). Whereas Senghor assumed the objective existence of the 'African personality' as it had been accepted in years of ethnological and sociological investigation, Elias's juridical Negritude instead defined 'African' in African law by precisely what it was not, by what Ernesto Laclau calls its 'lack' or 'absent totality' as marking the 'emptiness' of signifiers, the non-'purely differential space of an objective identity'[53]: irrational, primitive, communal,[54] mystical, conservative, static,[55] yet 'boastful, arrogant and self-assertive'[56]; in other words, everything for which previous generations of writers on customary law had argued and which tainted their analysis with racial prejudice.[57] The move was significant, since it departed from other influential scholarly accounts. For example, Elias's contemporary, Kéba M'Baye from Senegal, has argued in a typically Senghorian vein that African law has its own special characteristics, which are the result of 'the African idea of law itself, and its finality, and also of the dimensions of Negro African civilization'.[58] Elias faulted missionaries, who 'are accustomed to regard African law and custom as merely detestable aspects of paganism which it is their duty to wipe out in the name of Christian civilization'.[59] The district officer, whose policy was 'the sublimation of native custom so that it may approximate more nearly' to what he believed to be a 'higher standard',[60] was no more enlightened on this score. While the anthropologists, because of their training, had a better understanding of African material, their views were flawed; those of the older generation saw little or no law in African societies and were emphatic that 'custom is king',[61] whereas the younger ones were prepared to concede that African law was indeed law but, due to the social environment and economic milieu in which it had to operate, was nonetheless somehow 'different' from other forms of law.[62] As for the judiciary, they recognized the fact that African law was law, but felt that it had nothing in common with European conceptions of law and justice, which could not therefore be used 'to explain the basis of primitive legal theory'.[63]

[53] E. Laclau, *Emancipation(s)* (1996), p. 42. For Laclau, the empty signifier stands for the universal, the *impossible* fullness of the community. It is a particular 'which has divested itself of its particularity' or 'which overflows its particularity' to stand for the universal. Ibid., at 22.

[54] Elias, *supra* note 22, at 98.

[55] Ibid., at 80.

[56] Ibid., at 93.

[57] Elias's main antagonist was Sir Henry Maine and the views on evolutionism he had expressed in his *Ancient Law* (1906).

[58] K. M'Baye, 'The African Conception of Law', in *International Encyclopedia of Comparative Law* (1973), I, 148 ff.

[59] Elias, *supra* note 22, at 25.

[60] Ibid., at 26.

[61] Ibid., at 92–3, also 160.

[62] Ibid., at 29.

[63] Ibid., at 36.

Elias dismantled the civilized/barbarous distinction on which each of these theories rested, not by showing and glorifying Africa's cultural distinctiveness or 'essence' but by revealing the region's similitude with all human societies, its participation in humanity, in one and the same civilization. The uniqueness of African law lay not so much in the rules or legal ideas applicable in the region (which were no different from those in England,[64] where differences were 'of degree and not of kind',[65] where 'while institutions may differ, processes tend to be everywhere the same'[66]) but in the historical, economic, and, especially, social conditions that these rules and norms were to embody and mark out.[67] He then internalized differences as marking different levels of legal development and social cohesion, rather than as constitutive of the organic character of 'human law'[68] and thus reconfigured the distinction along development lines *internal* to the legal system.[69] But Elias's genius unquestionably lay in the fact that by rejecting the stigma of the 'primitive mind' or what he called the 'inferiority complex',[70] he did not confront himself or Africa, for that matter, as a reified object as Césaire had contemplated. As Arnulf Becker notes in relation to the Chilean jurist Alejandro Álvarez, 'Overcoming the civilized/barbarian boundary did not mean the exaltation of a reified local identity (as *criollismo* or *indigenismo* [or *nègre*]) but the juxtaposition of the elements of the dichotomy',[71] the marking out of a space between Africa and Europe where there would subsist something which was neither one nor the other.[72]

[64] Elias's main examples of areas where African law and British law were in unison were the distinction between civil and criminal law (ibid., at 110–29), principles of liability for legal wrongs (criminal, contract, and tort) (ibid., at 130–61), concepts of ownership and possession (ibid., at 162–75), resort to legal fictions (ibid., at 176–86), modern and customary legislation (where British influence was palatable) (ibid., at 187–211), and the judicial process (ibid., at 212–72). For each item, he masterfully refuted all detractors of African customary law, demonstrating how their objections were all predicated on misconceptions, ignorance, and racial bias against African societies and the all-too-ready desire to assume that African law in general must, by the very fact of being African, be irreconcilably different from English and, broadly, European law.

[65] Ibid., at 36.

[66] Ibid., at 31.

[67] Ibid., at 121–2 ('we are not by any means suggesting that there is, therefore, no difference between the African and a more developed legal system like the English ... It would be not only foolish but also absurd to ignore the obvious fact that the legal, no less than the other, arrangements of a society, are affected by their sociological context ... such notions will vary as much, or as little, with the *mores* and the *ethos* of particular communities as with their historical and geographical conditions').

[68] Ibid., at 34. See also Elias, *supra* note 35, at 8.

[69] References are numerous in his work on the different levels of development of African societies. See, for example, Elias, *supra* note 35, at 9 ('Of course, the areas are not all at the same level of development and there are hierarchies of courts corresponding to the particular stage of advancement attained by the community concerned').

[70] Ibid., at 376.

[71] A. Becker Lorca, 'Alejandro Álvarez Situated: Subaltern Modernities and Modernisms that Subvert', (2006) 19 LJIL 879, at 915.

[72] For an illustration of this hybridity, see Elias, *supra* note 22, at 213 ('We need not emphasize that this synthesis of the two English and African legal ideas is a curious amalgam partaking of the nature of neither pure common law arbitration nor customary law arbitrament').

Clearing up the question of civilization by collapsing the civilized/primitive distinction and disentangling it from the question of what is 'law' allowed Elias to rest Africa and Europe side by side and include them in the same grouping of human societies, thus expressing a will to power and influence and securing a pre-eminent place for the region. But a further inclusionary move was necessary to substantiate the claim that African customary law was law. If 'The question whether African customary law is law or not, can best be answered only when we know what law is'[73] and not what we mean by 'Africa', then the elements of Africanness were no more relevant to making this determination than were Western criteria of society and government. Only a unified theory of law that was not discriminatory could legitimately account for both, while variations would be accommodated within a single frame of reference. Recall that in his earlier work Elias had already demonstrated strong modernist affinities with an anti-formalist legal consciousness and the turn to the 'social' whose influence could be felt on the continent, at least insofar as French anti-formalist social ideas in the French African colonies were concerned. Of all the extant theories considered, he appears to have been most seduced by Pound's suggestive metaphor of law's 'social engineering' function, Ehrlich's 'living law' idea, and Savigny's concept chiding at the 'inner consciousness' of the people (*Weltanschauung*) as the true foundation of law (although he was also known as a formalist, hence the more appropriate denomination of the 'social associated with tradition' to characterize his work). But Savigny's nationalist bent crucially failed to explain 'why its reception by these alien peoples can ever make the French Code an expression of *their* popular consciousness'[74] or, as Duncan Kennedy puts it, 'why, at the moment of discovering national particularity, *each nation discovered the same thing*'.[75] Ultimately Elias found all of them wanting, and no more convincing on this score[76] than they were in explaining (along with social contract models of a Western pedigree) why law was habitually obeyed[77]: the law of a given community was 'the body of rules which are recognized as obligatory by its members',[78] a tailor-made definition that ensured that the determinant of 'the *ethos* of the community is its social imperative', which 'does not assume a particular type of political organization or a special brand of social philosophy'[79] and which is applied equally to Africa and Europe. For 'order, regularity and a sense of social obligation

[73] Ibid., at 37.

[74] Ibid., at 44.

[75] D. Kennedy, 'Two Globalizations of Law and Legal Thought: 1850–1968', (2003) 36 *Suffolk University Law Review* 631, at 661 (emphasis in original). Kennedy's hypothesis that 'The ideology of The Social was (perhaps) not a reflection of national particularity, but an instrument in the "imagining" of presently non existent national communities', is not implausible for colonies, given the fact that they are stripped of their capacity to make a claim based on nationalistic consciousness, hence the paradox of defining (or imagining) the 'social' through 'lack'.

[76] Elias, *supra* note 22, at 53.

[77] Ibid., at 73.

[78] Ibid., at 55.

[79] Ibid.

are essential attributes of law, in Western no less than in non-Western societies'.[80] His was an attempt to distinguish African customary law from Western conceptions and theories of law (differentiation) while defining it from the perspective of both (sameness),[81] and not from a romanticized and reified 'African' perspective which was less of a localized trope with a placid signifier than a rhetorical device.[82] In positioning African law on a par with English law, Elias was able to locate Africa at the centre of legal developments in the colonies and succeeded remarkably in retrieving African humanism as the genus of the hybridity of its Western and indigenous influences, both of which were required for the development of African states on the brink of imminent independence.[83]

3.3 Strategizing Fringes in Search of Synthesis: Constructing the African (Nation-) State in the Shadow Of Dualism (1960–1970s)

The previous section has argued that the first wave of legal consciousness in Africa during British colonial rule as retrieved from the work of Elias coincided with the rise of African humanist thought marked by a self-assertion of an African consciousness about its place and role in world history and the inscription of the double heritage of Africa as the site of Western and indigenous cultures, laws, and politics. With the independence in 1960 of many African states, energies came to be directed away from ontological and philosophical questions towards pragmatism – that is, managing conflicts and the harmonization of African indigenous laws and received Western legal ideas. In this period of resurgence of nationalist sentiments and militant ethnocentrism within a fledgling Africa coping with modernity, it became necessary to give more assertiveness and clarification to African customary law in a movement towards fashioning a cultural continental convergence (pan-African culture) so as to prevent it from being swallowed up by the 'exotic other', and, at the

[80] Ibid. See also ibid., at 131, 268.

[81] Such a reading seems to be doing more justice to Elias's feat than the following comments, which do little more than confuse the reader because of a certain circularity in reasoning: 'Rather, he combined the views or attributes of a future definition of African law to the fundamental elements that go in defining law in general in western societies. However, he specifically omitted certain factors, primarily because none of them would adequately describe the nature of African customary law.' Mwalimu, *supra* note 47, at 125.

[82] For a contrary view, see ibid., at 128–9 ('Indeed Elias did not per se define customary law, but rather defined law in general from an African perspective to which we have subscribed and attributed the ingredients for a definition of African customary law.').

[83] Kéba M'Baye, a prominent African scholar as well as the first president of the Supreme Court of Senegal and a former judge of the International Court of Justice, has rather spoken of a 'stratification' of African law, African society having been transformed by contact with the monotheist religions and the influence of colonization, with the successive contributions being superimposed on one another without really becoming unified. See M'Baye, *supra* note 58, at 151.

same time, to weld the two into a unified legal system which was thought to be the only road to modernization's salvation. Rather than tracing patterns of norm diffusion and reception widely emerging in the works of Elias during this period, particularly in his *British Colonial Law* (which was partly written during the previous era and published in 1962), and the anxieties of influence, I examine in this section the politics of his narratives of 'uniformity' and 'progress' in his quest for an ever-greater amalgamation of the legal legacies bestowed by the multiple influences in the region.[84] Two distinctive elements whose combination would mediate between seemingly conflicting projects of cultural nationalism, ethnic particularism, and development-oriented 'ordered reason and progress' were to emerge: the heroic figure of the enlightened judge as the guarantor of the social equilibrium against a rigidified dualism, and the instrumentality of the 'repugnancy' doctrine as catalyst for law's growth negotiated *between* assimilation and resistance, tradition and modernity.

The question of how much of African customary law was still 'relevant' and what were its prospects for survival, given its contact with English law, had already been considered, albeit under different socioeconomic conditions, under British colonial rule. In 1954 Elias had noted the inevitability of this dualism: 'the tempo of life is already quickening fast in many rural communities and the infiltration of new ideas into these goes on apace; the people are learning rapidly and are imbibing many alien notions of law which the new civilization is making familiar day by day'.[85] '[N]ew legal situations naturally follow in the wake of modern transactions between the two, and as these are often foreign to traditional legal ideas English law has to be adopted by the local people.'[86] But whether such trends in the progressive absorption of customary law into the all-pervading English system would result in the 'total or partial extinction' of the former was too early to gauge, although this would be unlikely, especially in those personal aspects of indigenous law relating to marriage and the family, land tenure, and succession and inheritance where English law's application was virtually excluded by legislation. In *The Nature of African Customary Law*, however, a rather mixed picture was given. On the one hand, English law's 'creative role of supplying the deficiencies of the traditional law and usage brought about by the new commercial and economic values',[87] such as the loosening up of kinship ties and obligations, the widening of the ambit of customary rights, and the narrowing of the extent of the traditional duties of individuals, as well as the self-sufficiency of a reconfigured *Homo economicus*, was seen to be 'a

[84] One cannot help notice the enduring paradox in Elias's efforts to employ the formalist medium of the treatise or textbook to write about and advance his project of developing African customary law. If we readily concede that customary law is 'living law', which is the law in fact being observed by its subjects, it must also be the case that law is not directly available to outsiders. Surely the mere fact of writing about what the customary law in Africa is constitutes in some ways the creation of a new and somewhat artificial distillation of that body of law to make it 'ascertainable' and 'known'. For the virtues of the legal textbook, see Elias, *supra* note 12, at 283.

[85] Elias, *supra* note 35, at 7.

[86] Ibid., at 5. See also ibid., at 7.

[87] Elias, *supra* note 22, at 273.

logical development of the traditional African conception that a person should be free to do what he likes with his own so long as social solidarity is not thereby endangered'.[88] At other times, it was hastened by his daily contact with European habits and ideas, 'which seem to be bringing out of him the less sociable traits in his indigenous culture but which he is powerless to resist in modern world conditions'.[89] On the other hand, the process of such assimilation was often subtle and imperceptible, such that it was not always possible to tell whether a particular rule was adopted through 'conscious' incorporation.[90] On the civil and criminal sides of African law, 'For better or for worse, British Colonial Africa is bound to tread a path of legal and administrative development which may be very similar to, if not always identical with, that already trodden by Great Britain.'[91] The overall effect of the contact, however, would not be complete uniformity, but '[a] kind of legal *tertium quid*'.[92]

Elias's 1956 prognosis may have had far-reaching implications which have transcended its importance for anglophone Africa. The book was translated into Russian and French and published in 1961, under the editorship of Alioune Diop, in *Présence Africaine*, which became the chief forum in which issues of Negritude were aired. At the First International Congress of Negro Writers and Artists in Paris in September 1956, a crucial event in the cultural politics of the Third World which was seen by many as the cultural counterpart to the Bandung conference held the previous year in Indonesia, and which was organized under the aegis of Diop's journal, one of the tasks was to explore the possibilities of African cultural independence from, but coexistence with, the West. The contributions of Césaire and Senghor, who were at odds on their understanding of Negritude, are instructive, as both seem to have envisioned ultimately the conditions for a cultural synthesis within African humanism. Senghor came to see the ultimate goal as one of 'reconciliation' between Negritude and Western culture and the realization of a universal humanism, a new world cultural order which he dubbed 'la civilisation de l'universel',[93] in which each culture would be respected and allowed to contribute its characteristic virtues to the rest, although the terms of assimilation had to be set by people of African descent, not by Europeans.[94] Césaire also imagined a condition in which a 'new civilization' was possible that would 'owe something both to Europe and to the native civilization'.[95] He thus recognized that whatever cultural synthesis might emerge in the future, it would look different from the pure, ideal type of either culture: not quite the one nor the other. But Césaire also insisted on

[88] Ibid., at 281.

[89] Ibid., at 282.

[90] Ibid., at 278–9. See also ibid., at 280.

[91] Ibid., at 292.

[92] Ibid., at 274.

[93] L. Sédar Senghor, *Liberté III: Civilisation de l'universel* (1977).

[94] L. Sédar Senghor, 'The Spirit of Civilization, or the Laws of African Negro Culture', (June–November 1956) 8–10 *Présence Africaine* 51, at 52, and his comments during the Discussion Session on 20 September 1956, ibid., at 219.

[95] A. Césaire, 'Culture and Colonization', (June–November 1956) 8–10 *Présence Africaine* 193, at 202.

a complex kind of coherence in which the disparate materials making up the new culture had to be experienced as a cultural unity or, as he put it, 'lived internally as homogeneity'.[96] A leading figure in the Negritude movement, Cheikh Anta Diop of Senegal, also aired his idea of 'pan-Africanism', the goal of which was the development of a complex political and cultural unity.[97] One could speculate as to the extent to which Elias, on the one hand, and Césaire, Senghor, and Diop, on the other, were influenced by each other's ideas,[98] but the parallelism is nonetheless striking. Yet Elias's work seems to have had a more 'visible' connection to the broader political events taking place at the time when, 2 years before *The Nature of African Customary Law* was published in French, his remark that 'there are surprising similarities, at least in important essentials, in bodies of African customary laws as divergent as those of the Yorubas, the Bantus, the Sudanese, the Ashantis and the Congolese'[99] was cited with approval in favour of the African 'unity of law' thesis – a central pillar of African humanist thought post-independence – in a report which was presented at the Second Congress of Negro Writers and Artists held in Rome in March and April 1959.[100] Incidentally, the congress would also turn out to be the occasion when Frantz Fanon would definitely abandon cultural pan-Africanism and Negritude and enlist the ideology of national liberation as the basis for a national culture.[101] The point here is not to debate the congruity of these various prescriptive views or intimate that Elias was endorsing any one or more of these positions, nor that his work was directly connected to the Negritude movement; rather, it is to highlight that pan-Africanism (however understood), cultural nationalism, and split ethnic identity politics were as many political projects and elements (subsystems or *paroles*) of an African legal consciousness (*langue*) as

---

[96] Ibid., at 204.

[97] C. Anta Diop, 'The Cultural Contributions and Prospects of Africa', (June–November 1956) 8–10 *Présence Africaine* 347, at 350–3. It is not clear, however, whether Diop was a historical particularist, who saw the future of Africa as separate from the rest of humanity, or a universalist who hoped for a historical and cultural convergence between Africa and Europe. On the ambivalence of his narrative, see M. Diouf and M. Mbodj, 'The Shadow of Cheikh Anta Diop', in V. Y. Mudimbe (ed.), *The Surreptitious Speech:* Présence Africaine *and the Politics of Otherness 1947–1987* (1992), pp. 118–35.

[98] It is not entirely clear, for example, whether Elias attended the two congresses of Negro Writers and Artists, given that his work and ideas about the unity of African law were to be presented in Rome in 1959, or what to make of his contribution to a collection of essays (T. O. Elias, 'Judicial process and legal development in Africa', in Bjornson and Mowoe (1986), *Legacies of Empire*, pp. 189–210, supra note 16) presented in late May 1982 at the conference 'Africa and the West: The Challenge of African Humanism' in Columbus, Ohio, where the tenets of the Negritude movement were discussed. It was attended by Senghor, but it is unclear whether Elias participated at all or was merely solicited to contribute an additional essay 'in areas of specialization that had not been fully represented in the conference sessions.' See Bjornson and Mowoe, 'Introduction', ibid., at 6.

[99] Elias, *supra* note 22, at 3.

[100] The report, which was published in the *Présence Africaine* congress proceedings, is reproduced in A. Allott, *Essays in African Law* (1960), pp. 55–71.

[101] F. Fanon, 'The Reciprocal Basis of National Cultures and the Struggles for Liberation', (February–May 1959) *Présence Africaine* 89.

would intersect, rather than subordinate one another, in the complex and hybrid site of negotiation of the trajectories of English law and African customary law in an emerging post-independence Africa.

3.3.1 Repugnancy: The Politics and Fashions of Inclusion–Exclusion

In spite of having rediscovered a sense of pride and self-confidence depicted in Elias's *The Nature of African Customary Law*, newly independent states resisted an Africanism resolutely turned towards the past. The singular concern of the previous generation with the problem of identity had given way to a complete rethinking and redefinition of what one might call the 'African problematic'. One can also trace this shift in the thought of Elias, who was appointed the first Attorney General of the Federal Republic of Nigeria in October 1960. It resonates, too, in the works of the so-called 'new philosophers' such as Marcien Towa, whose call for the renunciation of the self constituted by the African past that the protagonists of Negritude had championed, in his *Essai sur la problématique philosophique dans l'Afrique actuelle* (1971), represented a restorative move for African philosophy towards new perspectives of thought and action in the modern world through, invariably, Western rationalism and philosophy as an agent of development and accession to modernity.[102] Because custom stood for ethnic pluralism and rural conservatism, it was all too often seen as an obstacle to the realization of the two great imperatives of the time of national unity and modernization. Some states, especially those which had inherited a civil law regime, responded either by excluding customary law from the national legal system or restricting its scope of operation. T. W. Bennett refers to René David, the great twentieth-century comparatist and universal taxonomist, as an illustration of the former.[103] David, who drafted the Ethiopian civil code, thought that custom was too fluid and unstable and lacked a true juridical character, and that Ethiopian society based on custom was not satisfactorily developed; thus Ethiopians could not wait for centuries until their legal system had evolved to the appropriate level of maturity: a 'revolution' was necessary.[104]

David, of course, was hardly known as a staunch sympathizer of African societies and traditions.[105] I refer to his work here only in sharp contradistinction to the policy which prevailed in former British colonies, where English law would be

[102] A. Irele, 'Contemporary Thought in French Speaking Africa', in Mowoe and Bjornson (1986), *supra* note 16, at 144–6, 154–5.

[103] T. W. Bennett, 'Comparative Law and African Customary Law', in M. Reimann and R. Zimmermann (eds.), *The Oxford Handbook of Comparative Law* (2006), p. 662.

[104] R. David, 'La Refonte du Code Civil dans les états africains', (1962) 1 *Annales Africaines* 160, at 162.

[105] David subsumed custom under civil, common, and socialist law, systems which he regarded as the world's main legal families. Only as an afterthought did he add an assorted group of exotic

introduced and, where necessary, moulded to fit the contours of traditional customary law. British colonial administrators knew all too well that the sudden imposition of an entire body of 'alien' rules on indigenous peoples, particularly on the illiterate in rural areas, would cause social upheaval. With the spectre of the 'return to the primitive' looming large in the minds of African elites all too eager to enlist their system of law in the service of a 'law of decolonization', cultural unity, and, later, a 'law of development', the social and economic conditions of their new lived reality made them increasingly aware of the need to break with the 'backward' aspects of the past and carry out legislative reforms through the dictates of modern law. The way to achieve this compromise was through the fashioning of the 'repugnancy' doctrine, which implied that those customary practices that were found by judges to be 'repugnant to national justice, equity and good conscience' should be disallowed. I consider in the next section Elias's misgivings about the direct implications of 'repugnancy rule' and legal dualism, and the discursive strategies or tropes he strategically deployed to contain its deleterious effects and further his overall project for Africa.

Elias first considered the ramifications of the doctrine in his 1958 Lugard Lectures commissioned by the federal government of Nigeria and entitled 'The Impact of English Law upon Nigerian Customary law', noting that its actual application had proved difficult. Yet his messianic faith in the judiciary as vital in the maintenance of the social equilibrium at a crucial stage of transition through which the country was passing, sometimes by offering a sober dose of legal conservatism, made him rather apologetic: how could they, after all, be blamed for sometimes applying 'exotic' standards (or those based on judges' professional training, social background, or personal predilections) to situations for which there were no exact precedents as to what the 'social' (the common ethos of the people of Nigeria) commanded in the circumstances?[106] Writing contemporaneously in his first work after Nigerian independence, *British Colonial Law: A Comparative Study of the Interaction between English and Local Laws in British Dependencies,* in which he masterfully undertook a systematization of the various ways in which customary laws differed from each other on the one hand, and from the imported English law on the other, Elias resurrected the civilized/barbarous distinction, in relation to particular rules of customary law, which he had so cleverly dissolved to rehabilitate African law as a whole at a par with English law. He used the terms 'barbarous', 'obnoxious', 'obsolete', and 'contrary to natural justice and good conscience' interchangeably: 'the many approaches to the unvarying ideal of justice, which the components varying local laws represent, should conform to the modern standards of civilized values'[107] or 'the canons of decency and humanity considered appropriate to the situation at hand.'[108] These were not necessarily English but 'the average

'other' laws – Jewish, Hindu, Asian, and African. See R. David, *Les grands systèmes de droit contemporains* (1973), pp. 571–602.

[106] T. O. Elias, 'The Impact of English Law upon Nigerian Customary Law', reproduced in Elias, *Law in a Developing Society*, *supra* note 24, at 3, 83–4.

[107] Elias, *supra* note 12, at 17.

[108] Ibid., at 104.

good sense and good taste of all decent men and women of every clime'.[109] Judges were faced with the difficult task of 'striking a balance between what is reasonably tolerable and what is essentially below the minimum standard of civilized values in the contemporary world'[110]; this was compounded by the fact that these criteria of validity were themselves subject to modifications and amplifications. Yet Elias was at pains to downplay the considerable influence exerted by British notions of morality and justice: although difficult to define, these standards were 'an essential attribute of British justice' and were 'for that reason if no other, the yardstick of the fundamental aim and purpose of all colonial legal systems'.[111] He did not deny that there were, on occasion, wrongful applications of English legal ideas in the determination of 'alien' issues which had resulted in injustice, but, on the whole, 'the judicial attitude to colonial customary law has always been more liberal [one could say 'liberating'] than such isolated instances of prejudice'.[112]

Despite the radical reforms wrought by the application of the doctrine and aimed ostensibly at 'reforming' Africans to resist a return to those aspects of the 'dark' past that would inhibit the task of facing the challenges of modernization, it was widely perceived that its emergence, itself a product of colonialism which now, paradoxically, provided a tool of resistance against its effects in the post-colonial era, perpetuated the contempt or ignorance (or both) of former colonial masters towards 'native law and custom', who would thus be enabled to reject a rule which they believed was contrary to British ideas of civilized behaviour.[113] These critics considered the role the doctrine had to play in creating the boundaries, distinctions, and practices that produced, organized, and sustained conditions of subjugation and domination. Since the application of Nigerian or, more broadly, African conceptions would have made British justice look both ways, the British system, backed by all the force of a judiciary trained in the finest crafts of British justice and the legal profession, would be in a position in which it would gradually swallow up the indigenous system. Given the weight of the views of the detractors of the doctrine and the anxieties about a return to the stigma of civilization which Elias had so relentlessly struggled to break, what, then, explains his extolling of the doctrine's virtues and marginalization of its vices?

Custom, like tradition, is a tool which can be resorted to in struggles for power. As Bennett explains,

> Colonial, and then post-colonial, governments reconstituted existing institutions to achieve new policies, but then returned these same institutions to the people as if they were unchanged. In this process, 'history was denied and tradition created instead'. The people subjected to these changes also invoked tradition, however, partly to resist the imposition of new laws and partly to make sense of new situations.[114]

---

[109] Ibid., at 17.

[110] Ibid., at 104.

[111] Ibid., at 17.

[112] Ibid., at 106.

[113] See P. Nnaemeka-Agu, 'The Contribution of Judge Elias to African Customary Law', in Bello and Ajibola, *supra* note 10, at 518, 526; E. K. M. Yakpo, 'The Public Policy Doctrine in African Interlocal Conflict of Laws', in ibid., at 864–7.

[114] Bennett, *supra* note 103, at 665.

Elias understood that human agency participated in the creation of culture and tradition,[115] just as it did in negotiating its ever-shifting boundaries with the received legal system following culture contact, and that this had a profound effect on Africans' understanding of the ideological function of customary law. Clearly, barbarous customs such as witchcraft, the killing of twins, and trials by ordeal had to be (and were) ruled out (though, even here, it was not always easy to define what actually constituted these often imprecise and amorphous notions of customary practice),[116] as this would influence the future development of the law along progressive lines towards forging a cultural continental unity.[117] It would thus become necessary to decide which particular local customs should be diffused and adopted throughout the continent in a movement towards pan-Africanism.[118] Whereas in 1956 Elias had eschewed fashionable attempts to distinguish in *négro-africanité*, behind the diversity of traditional practices, a family likeness (a particular vocabulary, methods, feeling, and intuition) which was the manifestation of the values of black civilization and allowed to maintain that there was a distinctive African conception of law, his embrace and externalization of the unity thesis on similar grounds was here resolutely strategic[119]: a repugnancy doctrine, sparingly applied, could be valuable in a federal state such as Nigeria to protect and unify the basic principles of the various customary systems as a tool of nation-building against the threatening imposition of an 'alien' system. Elias reconfigured the mission of the legal elites of the newly formed states as the development of African law in a world of formally equal nation-states, rather than in the outer darkness of 'barbarism'. Any greater powers of modification possessed by judges over customary laws than over English law would therefore be 'a matter of degree and not of kind'.[120] Receiving the doctrine through legislation permitted a gesture of striking liberal cosmopolitanism in furtherance of a nationalist project based on the notion of national particularity as a

[115] See also J. Ngugi, 'Re-examining the Role of Private Property in Market Democracies: Problematic Ideological Issues Raised by Land Registration', (2004) 25 *Michigan Journal of International Law* 467 (arguing that certain sectors in Kenyan society, who refused to accept the full range of implications of land registration such as near-absolute powers of the individual registered owner, organized, invented, and mobilized customary norms to frustrate the complete operationalization of the new 'formal' regime of tenurial arrangements).

[116] Elias, 'Impact of English Law', *supra* note 106, at 81.

[117] Ibid., at 109.

[118] Elias observed that this was already taking place in large areas of Africa where there had emerged broadly similar political and economic conditions and, therefore, similar rules of customary law, 'which makes it possible to speak of the existence of a universal body of principles of African customary law that is not essentially dissimilar to the broad principles of European law.' Elias, *supra* note 9, at 220.

[119] M'Baye, although inclined to recognize the unity of African law as being bound up with the assertion of the Negro-African disposition towards the world, nonetheless recognized that this had often been raised to the level of a matter of doctrine and that 'This attitude, although flattering to African pride, is not realistic; those who adopt it immediately realize this and do not hesitate to abandon it, turning firmly towards modernity'. M'Baye, *supra* note 58, at 155.

[120] Elias, *supra* note 12, at 119.

secular force, against both the old colonial power and the fragmenting elements in the local situation, thus not sacrificing, but rather reinforcing, local autonomy.

There was, for Elias, another important function for the doctrine which arose in the context of discussing situations of incompatibility or conflicts between indigenous customs and English laws. There were 'borderline' cases that neither offended against the judges' enlightened sense of morality and fairness nor affronted the indigenous code of ethics. What should be made of those instances? Not any incompatibility would disqualify the local rule, just as not all rules that were 'not repugnant to principles of natural law, equity and good conscience' would be retained; in such cases, or whenever there was no precise rule either of English law or of native law and custom applicable to a case, judges had discretion to decide them according to principles of natural law, equity, and good conscience or through an appeal to 'natural justice and "sweet reasonableness" – a mixture of *jus gentium* and *jus naturale*'.[121] These were largely pragmatic indicators of 'progress' and grounded in 'naturalizing', 'dichotomizing', and 'dissimulating'[122] effects of categories and ideas of 'native welfare'[123] versus backwardness, or 'orderly development and social welfare'[124] versus underdevelopment, or of bringing the body of law 'up to date' in the light of modern-day economic conditions of commerce and industrialization versus regression.[125] Here, the question of community versus individual system of land tenure and the former's suitability for modern economic development projects becomes paradigmatic as the site where particular techniques and progress vocabularies help to shape the conditions in the colonies that are sympathetic to receiving

[121] Ibid., at 213, 222.

[122] I usefully derive these notions from their borrowing from ideology critique scholarship and application to the work of Stelios Seferiades by Thomas Skouteris in developing the analytical sketch of 'vocabularies of progress' in international law, namely 'discursive strategies with which arguments buttress their power over others and seek to distinguish themselves from their ideological opponents'. T. Skouteris, 'The Vocabulary of Progress in Interwar International Law: An Intellectual Portrait of Stelios Seferiades', (2005) 19 EJIL 823, at 824, 837–40. I argue that Elias's work can be seen as another scholarly endeavour shaping the face of 'progress' as a narrative straddling different ideological struggles and personal/professional projects, making the relationship between progress and African customary law central to the renewal of the discipline.

[123] Kennedy, *supra* note 75, at 659.

[124] Elias, *supra* note 12, at 241. Francescakis suggests the concept of 'ordre public du développement' as a way to assuage fears over the arbitrary application of the repugnancy doctrine, based on the idea that local rules that are detrimental to social development should be discounted. See P. Francescakis, 'Problèmes de droit international privé de l'Afrique noire indépendante', (1964-II) 112 RCADI 269, at 305. It is not entirely clear in what sense 'social development', a political policy goal, would be a more useful device and applied with a greater degree of certitude, or be purged of an ethnocentric bias. Both the social development and repugnancy doctrines, however, seem to share the same function of contributing towards the unification of the local legal systems and a unified society run, to paraphrase Senghor, on the principles of universal civilization (*civilisation de type universel*).

[125] Elias, *supra* note 12, at 142. See also Elias, 'Impact of English Law', *supra* note 106, at 107 ('Under any progressive legal system most of the alterations would have had to be carried out if orderly development in social and economic life were to be at all ensured').

such a renewalist political ethos.[126] Whenever it was in their 'interests' (as they would understand or be made to understand it), the operation of English law through the applications of such notions would be ratified by local elites, sometimes with necessary transformations; but when it reflected peculiarities of English law that it would be unjust to impose on the local peoples, or when it confronted racial and ethnic idiosyncrasies, they would compromise with the local forces that identified with tradition and resist it. Still, on some occasions custom was upheld but reinterpreted such as to make it appear as conforming to principles of development, equality, and progress.[127] Duncan Kennedy explains thus the effect of post-colonial appropriation of formalism through experiences of strategic selection in reconciling various, and at times conflicting, political projects:

> [I]t offered peripheral elites the categorization of their family law as popular, political, religious, cultural and particular, and therefore as eminently *national*. In exchange, they accepted (usually with alacrity) that the law of the market would be, not positively and in every detail, but generally and 'essentially', the property and contract-based law of a national 'free' market.[128]

This is identitarian intersectionality thinking through and through, alternating between essentializing a particular trait (tradition or 'Africanness') that sets its possessors apart in furtherance and legitimation of legal claims (custom), and trying to reconcile these claims when they conflict with each other (cultural synthesis) and with claims from other identity-based narratives (development). Repugnancy doctrine and its corollaries were well received because both former colonial administrators and local elites could live with it. The doctrine framed what we could perceive as resistance and domination and provided an effective mode of assimilation and resistance. It helped both to preserve the neo-feudal institutions and to sustain ethnic nationalism and thus served as the hybrid site of negotiations of a law between tradition and modernity.

3.3.2 Against Dualism! Mimicry in Defence of Hybridity

The previous sections of this article have suggested how African legal systems, following the introduction of English law in colonial dependencies, became the product of Westernization, by transplantation on the one hand and as containing pockets of pre-modern customs or informal practices on the other. Throughout his life Elias waged an uncompromising crusade against the sometimes uncomfortable and uncanny dualism between received English law and indigenous customary law. Occasional frictions and conflicts occurred from the competitive coexistence of the two bodies of law with different systems of courts not always hierarchically

[126] Elias, *supra* note 12, at 223–44.

[127] Bennett, *supra* note 103, at 662–3.

[128] Kennedy, *supra* note 75, at 646.

integrated.[129] In *The Nature of African Customary Law*, he noted that there was 'no intrinsic opposition between the two and that the extrinsic divergencies of form and content of some basic principles have been occasioned as much by historical and geographical factors as by commercial and technological considerations', but also grudgingly acknowledged that 'given its specific context, each system is valid for the type of society and the species of task for which it is designed, at least so long as the process of acculturation has not resulted in a disruption of the African society by the European impact'.[130] While there has been recognition of the diversity of forces – British and indigenous – active in the creation of African customary law, it could not always be ascertained and distinguished clearly between the substratum and the borrowed, whether the telling blend between tradition and modernity had been a Westernization of African law, or whether British law had, in fact, been 'Africanized', thus unsettling fringes. How could one address the duality of operating in alternative and at times incommensurate discourses?

There is certainly a progressive movement in Elias's narrative, from the assertion of an African consciousness in the development of law's identity to the realization of a pan-African cultural unity of law as a tool for nation-building, both set up against the imperial domination of the West, to the need for 'the existence of conditions which would ensure the stimulation of common purposes and loyalties in the legal, no less than in the national, fields of our endeavour',[131] for developing the law along a 'common path' guided by and modelled on 'the unifying force of English law'. The latter's own development as the 'common custom of the realm' had been 'evolutionary' rather than 'revolutionary'[132] in adapting itself to changing social and economic circumstances; it had proved 'capable of absorbing the shock due to alien contacts and new ideas and of meeting the ever-present challenge of rapidly changing social needs'.[133] It thus offered to Nigerian law 'an example of flexible and pragmatic legal development in a relatively dynamic society'.[134] But this could not sustain deriving from an 'is' the 'ought' claim that African customary law *should* evolve along the lines of British common law in substantive and procedural terms. Here, Elias was emphatic: 'English law had supplied the framework' within which indigenous laws could 'flourish in an atmosphere of ordered freedom and rational progress'.[135] Since a closer degree of assimilation with English law could be forecast, an ultimate 'amalgam' of elements from both was desirable and would be 'the best bulwark against tribal cant and ethnocentric prejudices' in the search for unity and uniformity in the 'conscious striving after the worthwhile ideals of social justice and national solidarity'.[136] The

[129] T. O. Elias, 'The Commonwealth in Africa', (1968) 31 *Modern Law Review* 284, at 301; Elias, 'Impact of English Law', *supra* note 106, at 106.

[130] Elias, *supra* note 22, at 299.

[131] Elias, 'Impact of English Law', *supra* note 106, at 110–11.

[132] Elias, *supra* note 22, at 301, also 274.

[133] Elias, *supra* note 22, at 301, also 274.

[134] Elias, 'Impact of English Law', *supra* note 106, at 108.

[135] Ibid., at 111.

[136] Ibid.

judiciary would emerge as the hero figure that would, through rational thought and scientific study, supply 'the necessary *esprit de corps* for the achievement of the symbiosis, if not an initial synthesis',[137] and would therefore not be so preoccupied with the charge of doing 'politics by other means'.[138] It was unclear, however, what this mishmash of rules and legal ideas would ultimately look like. Such, then, was Elias's broad vision for constructing the post-colonial African state already legally and constitutionally fissured by regionalization and federalism – his background story about Africa which the discursive tropes of 'the unifying force of English common law' and 'rational order and progress' aligned on the unity (reform)/tribal ethnocentricity (regression) dichotomy were going to assist in sustaining.[139]

Discussion on how best to achieve the harmonious synthesis of British law and indigenous law – the classical tropes of monism and dualism – itself becomes a discourse that plays a role in critiquing or sustaining various political projects. These can be informed, for example, by newly fashioned theories of race (answering the question 'Who is a native?' takes centre stage when one seriously considers monism a judicial policy option[140]) and models of post-colonial or neo-colonial governance. Through their deployment, various elites and subalterns would be produced and reproduced, always negotiating, marking, and disciplining the shifting boundary between centre and periphery, and playing defining although varying roles (to civilize, restrain, develop, manage, protect, or dominate) in the decolonization movement. Elias (writing prior to independence but meaning to apply his words in the post-colonial context) considered that the inquiry raised the further problem of

> the proper aim of English law in a colony's legal development. Should it merely help the indigenous law to develop itself into a vital instrument of social control in the evolving colonial society, without claiming a share in whatever the finished product might be? Or is it eventually to replace the indigenous law after an evolutionary adaptation of it to English law and ideas has fully prepared the way?[141]

The truth, once again, lay somewhere in between: neither one nor the other, 'at once various and unitary', 'unity in diversity'.[142] 'The mixing of English and indigenous ideas of law must be so proportioned as to make each supplement the other by supplying deficiencies and removing excrescences, with the avowed aim of producing a truly *native* body of law in each colony.'[143]

---

[137] T. O. Elias, 'Towards a Common Law in Nigeria', in T. O. Elias (ed.), *Law and Social Change in Nigeria* (1972), p. 271.

[138] T. O. Elias, 'Judicial Process and Legal Development in Africa', in Mowoe and Bjornson (1986), *supra* note 16, at 208 ('On the whole, it can be said that the application of the judicial technique of the English common law to our customary laws has often resulted in the remoulding of the traditional rules and concepts along lines of rational development to suit our economic and social characteristics').

[139] Elias, *supra* note 12, at 288.

[140] Ibid., at 102–3, 130–1.

[141] Ibid., at 287.

[142] Ibid., at 9.

[143] Ibid., at 289 (emphasis in original).

There is, however, one sense in which 'mimicry' becomes significant for retrieving the *langue* of Elias's juridical Negritude. I argue that Elias's narrative of 'uniform amalgam' or *tertium quid* impels us to re-imagine normative developments in the English law/African customary law nexus as the institutional matrix constructed out of the 'mimicry' of cultural practices and local conflicts. My understanding of this concept is informed by the distinct usage of the term by post-colonial critical scholar Homi Bhabha in his critique of metropolitan literature: as an elusive and effective strategy of colonial power and knowledge which, however, in its 'double vision' of the Other inscribed in its enunciatory act – 'almost the same but not quite' – menaces the colonial mode of representation and mocks the power that supposedly makes it imitable by disclosing the ambivalence within colonial discourse,[144] thus disrupting its cultural authority without, however, destroying it entirely.[145] Bhabha offers such a reading of Fanon's *Black Skin, White Masks/Peau noire, masques blancs* (1952), where the latter undertook a phenomenology of black existence. In psychoanalytical terms, Fanon investigates the way in which the introjection of social values is disturbed in the case of the black subject placed within a socio-psychological field dominated by the white paradigm. The conflict between the external 'fact of his blackness' and his internalization of a highly valorized symbolism of whiteness creates a distortion of his self-image and installs within him a profound 'neurosis', with repercussions upon his total mode of being. Bhabha explains,

> The ambivalence of mimicry – almost but not quite – suggests that the fetishized colonial culture is potentially and strategically an insurgent counter-appeal. What I have called its 'identity-effects' are always crucially *split*. Under cover of camouflage, mimicry, like the fetish, is a part-object that radically revalues the normative knowledges of the priority of race, writing, history. For the fetish mimes the forms of authority at the point at which it deauthorizes them. Similarly, mimicry rearticulates presence in terms of its 'otherness', that which it disavows.[146]

[144] Bhabha explains the colonial presence in its enunciative act as 'always ambivalent, split between its appearance as original and authoritative and its articulation as repetition and difference. It is a disjunction produced within the act of enunciation as a specifically colonial articulation of those two disproportionate sites of colonial discourse and power: the colonial scene as the invention of historicity, mastery, mimesis or as the 'other scene' of *Entstellung*, displacement, fantasy, psychic defence, and an 'open' textuality. Such a display of difference produces a mode of authority that is agonistic (rather than antagonistic)', i.e. 'within the terms of a negotiation (rather than negation) of oppositional and antagonistic elements.' H. K. Bhabha, *The Location of Culture* (2004), p. 153.

[145] Bhabha thus explains, 'the discourse of mimicry is constructed around an *ambivalence*; in order to be effective, mimicry must continually produce its slippage, its excess, its difference. The authority of that mode of colonial discourse that I have called mimicry is therefore stricken by an indeterminacy: mimicry emerges as the representation of a difference that is itself a process of disavowal. Mimicry is thus the sign of a double articulation; a complex strategy of reform, regulation and discipline, which "appropriates" the Other as it visualizes power. Mimicry is also the sign of the inappropriate, however, a difference or recalcitrance which coheres the dominant strategic function of colonial power, intensifies surveillance, and poses an immanent threat to both "normalized" knowledges and disciplinary powers.' Ibid., at 122–3.

[146] Ibid., at 129–30 (emphasis in original).

The signifier of colonial mimicry is produced as an 'affect of hybridity – at once a mode of appropriation and of resistance, from the disciplined to the desiring'.[147] This is 'the more ambivalent, third choice ... black skins/white masks'.[148] 'Black skin splits under the racist gaze, displaced into signs of bestiality, genitalia, grotesquerie, which reveal the phobic myth of the undifferentiated whole white body.'[149] Thus

> hybridity is not a *problem* of genealogy or identity between two *different* cultures which can then be resolved as an issue of cultural relativism. Hybridity is a problematic of colonial representation and individuation that reverses the effects of the colonialist disavowal, so that other 'denied' knowledges enter upon the dominant discourse and estrange the basis of its authority – its rules of recognition.[150]

The paranoid threat from the hybrid is finally uncontainable because it breaks down the symmetry and duality of self/other, inside/outside, familiar/foreign.

I suggest that the introduction of English law in former British African dependencies can be seen as the production of hybridization within Africa as well as Elias's narrative that subverts imageries of indigenous culture as sites of reception in a dialectic of influence or assimilation and resistance, or a more amorphously aesthetic process of structural transformation. The turn to hybridity characterizing Elias's work means that comparativists and local intellectuals at the core and the periphery do not necessarily come to produce and understand similar maps of what are assimilable and inassimilable legal cultures. In his narrative African law is portrayed as both sufficiently unique, distinct, and insulated to support nationalist projects of decolonization and pan-Africanism, and sufficiently resilient, already assimilated, and permeable to outside influences (Western and Islamic) to support assimilation. In this story of the rise of African legal consciousness, it is, however, not a matter of choosing between alternatives (which dualism implies),[151] but of an intersectionality between political struggles of national cultural identity and ethnocentric particularisms in relation to broader ideological projects of legal unity and pluralism structured around the development paradigm of modernization in an era of decolonization. Asserting a strong cultural nativism through the diffusion of particular customary rules can be inscribed in alliance with Western law as an attempt to break away from those elements of the past that hamper progress and develop-

[147] Ibid., at 172.

[148] Ibid.

[149] Ibid., at 131.

[150] Ibid., at 162 (emphasis in original).

[151] David Kennedy reads M'Baye, *supra* note 58, at 155–6 ('The African continent is a world of contradictions: subjected to a variety of frequently contradictory forces, it is ever hesitating between them'), as assisting local intellectuals and elites in making such a 'choice' between assimilation and exceptionalism, noting that 'a postcolonial African law will involve each country choosing the legal models and rules, whether Western or African, best suited to achieve the national priorities of development and modernization in its particular circumstances.' Kennedy, *supra* note 4, at 619–20, n. 104. My reading of Elias's scholarship as signalling a turn to hybridity of an African law always already reflecting the double heritage of African humanism indicates otherwise.

ment, just as it can easily be mounted as a 'racial front' (unity of law through diffusionism of certain 'traditional' rules) to resist receiving Western ideas and institutions about development. Coalitions are thus formed between European and indigenous laws strategically within patterns of production and reception of imageries of Africa that are not settled but constantly shifting and being negotiated.[152] This means that images of what are 'Africa' and the 'West' are only partial and tendentious and 'the presence of the first world in the third and the third world in the first'[153] challenges those narratives that make only some development strategies seem available and foregrounds that they, too, just like those seeking to disrupt the frames within which such strategies are articulated, are engaged in the pursuit of ideological and political projects.

3.3.3 Repetition as Renewal: Anti-formalism as Reform

The previous sections of Sect. 3.3 have highlighted that the most important task in the field of African law after independence was to carry out codification and structural reforms.[154] Changes through the decolonization of the legal system led to the adoption of a development-oriented model. There were imitations, adaptations, inventions, and, occasionally, resistance. The unification of law (internal, regional, and 'continental') became a subject of particular importance. The question was how to achieve synthesis into 'a common law for the country'. In francophone Africa newly independent states began to codify their customary laws mainly in order to stave off neo-colonization by France. Elias desired not only the modernization of African law, but the harmonization and, ultimately, unification of the emerging modern system.[155] Yet unlike most of his peers he eschewed codification and the importation of legal orthodoxies to sustain a new stream of legal reform, and refashioned those 'at home' to tackle the pressing social issues. What were the forces behind his extreme faith in anti-formalist legal reform and how were they to affect African societies?

---

[152] Belleau, *supra* note 18.

[153] Kennedy cites the work of Lama Abu Odeh on Islamic legal culture and 'honour killings' as eschewing the alternatives of exotism and assimilation and embracing hybridity ('She does so by insisting on the presence within the subjective identity of those brought up there of both traditional and modern elements, of assimilation and exotism, confounding efforts to categorize Islam from the centre as either one or the other'). Kennedy, *supra* note 4, at 622.

[154] Two of the 'structural' reforms proposed by Elias were the reorganization of courts to avoid the parallelism of jurisdiction as between those administering English law or some modified versions of it and those administering customary or other traditional law, and the simplification of English law so as to make easy the work of integrating it with customary law and social patterns of the local communities. See Elias, *supra* note 12, at 288.

[155] Elias, *Law in a Developing Society*, *supra* note 24, at 139.

Elias believed that the overall effects of developing customary law along similar lines as the British common law had been 'salutary and enlightening'.[156] Where there had been difficulties, it was due to neglect of scientific and systematic study of the problems of culture contact and of adaptation to the local environment of alien ideas and institutions. Much work could be and needed to be done. There was 'the need to examine the role of law in the new society for which the traditional methods of legal education of would-be lawyers and the administration of justice were no longer adequate or even relevant'.[157] Anthropological fieldwork was no doubt necessary.[158] But there was 'a crying need for the early introduction of an enlightened system of legal education and legal research which would be designed to produce future lawyers imbued with a new sense of social purpose and moral responsibility'.[159] The judiciary, too, had to be trained and to 'emulate all the great virtues of the Bench and Bar' to 'return well-fitted to discharge properly their obligations to their communities'.[160] Elias had no doubt that 'Given the will and a conscious national direction, eventual unification … is only a question of time.'[161] But the method of achieving it was for him crucially important too. Elias had an almost fetishist admiration for the judiciary, which had succeeded remarkably (no doubt due to his own involvement in these formative years (1972–1975) as chief justice of Nigeria) in ensuring the coalescing of English law and African customary laws and 'to introduce order into chaos by the rational application of the judicial process'[162] without there having been resort to codification.[163] Customary law was adaptable and situational, qualities which contributed to a sense of process and transaction, and hence progress, whereas codification would render customary law artificial, a set of irrevocable acts and events, far removed from the experience and comprehension of the people, while encouraging ethnocentric prejudices.[164] For Elias, the anti-formalist 'social' was thus a positive ideological programme which had a symbolic effect in a period of transition.[165] The drive for formalist legal reforms would overlook both

---

[156] Elias, 'Towards a Common Law in Nigeria', *supra* note 137, at 266–7.

[157] Elias, *Law in a Developing Society*, *supra* note 24, at 5.

[158] Elias, *supra* note 12, at 276–7.

[159] Ibid., at 299. See also Elias, *Law in a Developing Society*, *supra* note 24, at 141. Elias was instrumental in establishing the Nigerian Institute of Advanced Legal Studies, with a robust research agenda through which he was to contribute further to the development of customary law in Nigeria. See Nnaemeka-Agu, *supra* note 113, at 528–9.

[160] Elias, *supra* note 12, at 290.

[161] Elias, *Law in a Developing Society*, *supra* note 24, at 140.

[162] Elias, *supra* note 138, at 208–9. See also Elias, *supra* note 35, at 375–6.

[163] Elias's first-hand account of the judicial delineation of analysis of thought and reasoning underlying the articulation and objectivity of principles as well as practice in the 'Newer Commonwealth' (Commonwealth countries of Africa, the Caribbean, and Asia) of many strands in African law dealt with by judges trained in English law and usage is distilled in a collection of lectures and papers he gave between 1975 and 1985. See T. O. Elias, *Judicial Process in the Newer Commonwealth* (1990).

[164] Elias, *supra* note 138, at 205. See also Elias, *supra* note 12, at 299.

[165] Elias, *supra* note 12, at 280.

the legitimating and demobilizing effects of political emancipation causes won elsewhere as legal victories. I have argued in the previous section that anti-formalism was an element in a post-identity politics of hybridization in Elias's scholarship. While codification could represent resistance to universal claims of English law, it could also be the instrument of Western resistance to Africans' claims for sovereignty or redistribution. The development of a common law for Nigeria through case law as the hybrid site of contestation and negotiation, on the other hand, would harness Western law as an instrument of development and social change and resist unnecessary local divergences not rooted in the ethos of the people, just as it would support nationalist resistance to Western legal science and conceptions of development.

3.4 Conclusion

Taslim Elias's work and life display a complex map of receptions and misreadings of 'foreign' legal ideas, of strategic appropriations and alliances and rebellious cultural nativism: a map of alternative images of law in Africa and Africa in law, one that effaces the borders of legal thinking and disrupts imageries of allegiances of scholars from the 'periphery' with dominant modes, canons, and practices at the 'centre'. This article is a modest attempt to rethink the history of legal influences in Africa alongside the history of political, economic, and cultural hegemonies of various kinds through the thought and writings of such a scholar. Specifically, I have asked what role legal intellectuals such as Taslim Elias have played in resisting or entrenching hegemonic relationships in the world system. What has emerged is an unsettling picture, where it is less a different or distinctive theoretical voice hailing from Africa on legal ideas that was produced than a legal consciousness which I have called juridical Negritude and within which projects of national cultural integration or fragmentation on a local basis, cultural convergence or drift at the continental level, and a developmental ideology compatible with or resisted by African culture became nested and found expression in their unstable relationship to law and Western culture.[166] I have introduced the notion of the production of hybridization or hybridity in legal discourse and in Elias's project of a uniform common law for Nigeria as a way to explicate the workings of this relationship and how African law is inscribed in the interplay of cultural forces constantly negotiating the boundaries of their engagement with one another, and noted that it must be read on that level to be fully understood. How much of this is a never-ending search by Third World intellectuals for the right proportions of each, for finding their own place as 'global intellectuals' locally situated, and how much of it is an alert attempt strategically to use just about enough of each side to satisfy the elite role of the intellectual with his or her personal and ideological goals and objectives (nationalist, pan-nationalist, internationalist, etc.) remains uncertain. The practical effects a

[166] Kennedy, *supra* note 75, at 675.

distinction between 'conscious hybridity' and 'unconscious working through a law-in-between' oscillating between the native and the other would have on the work of a historian of (international) law are potentially considerable and worth considering further.

Africa has tried to build national systems of law and legislation heavily affected by 'legal transplants'. There are many ways of understanding this phenomenon, and the article has touched upon some of these: the way in which law is taught and understood as a discipline, the prevailing status of the legal and judicial profession, history, cultural bias, and, of course, grounds of political and social realities. Elias's scholarship illustrates well the controversies in colonial and independent Africa over identity, legal theory, political perspective, legal education, and so on, in which he occupied the privileged status of an observer-participant. Yet he did not refrain from debunking myths and forming coalitions with the dominant currents in African society. He made sense of the confused and racist approach of many anthropologists and legal scholars who concerned themselves with the legal problems in African customary law, and in the process firmly positioned Africa in world history and a global history of legal philosophy. He also engaged in modernist moves to professionalize legal studies and the legal and judicial profession, and constructed a narrative of progress as a discursive strategy through which he sought to update and reform law to tackle the social and economic problems resulting from modernization by means of a strategic alliance with English law.[167] But it is his confidence and faith in the judiciary which he had helped to train and equip and whose ultimate aim was 'to effect a dynamic compromise between law and society, between the technicalities of legal science and the requirements of social justice'[168] that, in the end, truly remains crucial to understanding the hybridity of his narrative about African humanist thought, to which his work stands out as vintage contribution.

References

Allott A (1960) Essays in African law. Butterworths, London

Anghie A (1999) Finding the peripheries: sovereignty and colonialism in nineteenth-century international law. Harv Int Law J 40(1):1–80

Anghie A (2005) Imperialism, sovereignty and the making of international law. Cambridge University Press, Cambridge

Anghie A, Chimni BS (2003) Third world approaches to international law and individual responsibility in internal conflicts. Chin J Int Law 2:77

Anta Diop C (1956) The cultural contributions and prospects of Africa. Présence Africaine 347:8–10

Becker Lorca A (2006) Alejandro Alvarez situated: subaltern modernities and modernisms that subvert. Leiden J Int Law 19:879

Bedjaoui M (1961) La révolution algérienne et le droit. Association internationale des juristes démocrates, Bruxelles

[167] Elias, *Law in a Developing Society*, *supra* note 24, at 141.

[168] Elias, *supra* note 138, at 121.

Belleau MC (1997) The “Juristes Inquiets”: legal classicism and criticism in early twentieth-century France. Utah Law Rev 2:379
Belleau MC (1998) La dichotomie droit privé/droit public dans le contexte québécois et canadien et l’intersectionnalité identitaire. Cah de droit 39:177
Bello EG, Ajibola BA (1992) Preface. In: Bello EG, Ajibola BA (eds) Essays in honour of judge Taslim Olawale Elias. Martinus Nijhoff Publishers, Dordrecht/Boston/London, 2 vols
Bennett TW (1995) Human rights and African customary law. Juta, Cape Town
Bennett TW (2006) Comparative law and African customary law. In: Reimann M, Zimmermann R (eds) The Oxford handbook of comparative law. Oxford University Press, Oxford
Benton L (2002) Law and local cultures, legal regimes in world history 1400–1900. Cambridge University Press, Cambridge
Bhabha HK (2004) The location of culture. Routledge, London/New York
Cass DZ (1997) Navigating the newstream: recent critical scholarship in international law. Nordic J Int Law 65:341
Césaire A (1956) Culture and colonization, Présence Africaine 193:8–10
Curtin PD (1984) Cross-cultural trade in world history. Cambridge University Press, Cambridge (Cambridgeshire)/New York
David R (1962) La Refonte du Code Civil dans les états africains. Ann Afr 1:160
David R (1973) Les grands systémes de droit contemporains. Dalloz, Paris
Diouf M, Mbodj M (1992) The shadow of Cheikh Anta Diop. In: Mudimbe VY (ed) The surreptitious speech: Présence Africaine and the politics of otherness. University of Chicago Press, Chicago, pp 1947–1987
Elias TO (1954) Groundwork of Nigerian law. Routledge & Paul, London
Elias TO (1956a) The nature of African customary law. Manchester University Press, Manchester
Elias TO (1956b) Makers of Nigerian law. Hazell Watson & Viney, Surrey
Elias TO (1961) La nature du droit coutumier africain (trans: Découfle et Dessau). Présence africaine, Paris
Elias TO (1962) British colonial law: a comparative study of the interaction between English and local laws in British dependencies. Stevens, London
Elias TO (1963) The Nigerian legal system. Routledge, London
Elias TO (1965) African law. In: Larson A, Jenks CW (eds) Sovereignty within the law. Oceana Publications, New York
Elias TO (1967) Nigeria: the development of its laws and constitution. Stevens, London
Elias TO (1968) The commonwealth in Africa. Mod Law Rev 31:284
Elias TO (1971) Nigerian land law. Routledge and Kegan Paul, London
Elias TO (1972a) Towards a common law in Nigeria. In: Elias TO (ed) Law and social change in Nigeria. University of Lagos/Evans Bros, Lagos
Elias TO (1972; 1988) Africa and the development of international law. A W Sijthoff/Oceana Publications, Leiden/Dobbs Ferry
Elias TO (1973a) Law in a developing society. Inaugural Lecture Series, Lagos
Elias TO (1973b) The impact of English law upon Nigerian customary law. Reproduced in Elias TO, Law in a developing society. Inaugural lecture series, Lagos
Elias TO (1981) Africa before the world court. University of Nairobi, Nairobi
Elias TO (1983) The international court of justice and some contemporary problems: essays on international law. Martinus Nijhoff Publishers, The Hague/London
Elias TO (1986) Judicial process and legal development in Africa. In: Mowoe IJ, Bjornson R (eds) Africa and the West: the legacies of empire. Greenwood Press, New York
Elias TO (1989a) The United Nations charter and the world court. Nigerian Institute of Advanced Legal Studies, Lagos
Elias TO (1989b) The role of the international court of justice in Africa. Afr J Int Comp Law 1:1
Elias TO (1990) Judicial process in the newer commonwealth. University of Lagos Press, Lagos
Elias TO, Nwabara SN, Akpamgbo CO (eds) (1975) African indigenous laws. Government Printer, Enugu
Fanon F (1952) Peau noire, masques blancs. Éditions du Seuil, Paris

Fanon F (1959) The reciprocal basis of national cultures and the struggles for liberation. Présence Africaine 89:24–25
Francescakis P (1964–II) Problèmes de droit international privé de l'Afrique noire indépendante. 112 RCADI 269
Hegel GWF (1837) In: Gans E (ed) The philosophy of history (trans: Sibree J, 1857). Bohn, London
Irele A (1986) Contemporary thought in French speaking Africa. In: Mowoe IJ, Bjornson R (eds) Africa and the West: the legacies of empire. Greenwood Press, New York
Kennedy D (1980) Toward an historical understanding of legal consciousness: the case of classical legal thought in America 1850–1940. Res Law Sociol 3:3
Kennedy D (1997a) New approaches to comparative law: comparativism and international governance. Utah Law Rev 2:545
Kennedy D (1997b) A critique of adjudication (Fin de Siècle). Harvard University Press, Cambridge
Kennedy D (2001) A semiotics of critique. Cardozo Law Rev 22:1147
Kennedy D (2003) Two globalizations of law and legal thought: 1850–1968. Suffolk Univ Law Rev 36:631
Kennedy D (2006) Three globalizations of law and legal thought: 1850–2000. In: Santos A, Trubek D (eds) The new law and economic development. A critical appraisal. Cambridge University Press, Cambridge
King RH (2004) Race, culture and the intellectuals 1940–1970. Woodrow Wilson Center Press/ Johns Hopkins University Press, Washington, DC/Baltimore
Kuti FA (1991) Elias: a man of his time. Patrac, Benin City
Laclau E (1996) Emancipation(s). Verso, London
Lawrence TJ (1900) The principles of international law. DC Heath, Boston
Lawrence BN, Osborn EL, Roberts RL (eds) (2006) Intermediaries, interpreters, and clerks: African employees in the making of Colonial Africa. University of Wisconsin Press, Madison
Lévy-Bruhl L (1922) La Mentalité primitive. Presses universitaires de France, Paris
Lindley MF (1969) The acquisition and government of backward territory in international law. Negro Universities, New York
M'Baye K (1973) The African conception of law. In: Zweigert K, Drobnig U (eds) International encyclopaedia of comparative law, vol II, Ch 1, 138
Maine H (1906) Ancient law: its connection with the early history of society and its relation to modern ideas. H. Holt, New York
Mazrui AA (1986) Cultural forces in African politics: in search of a synthesis. In: Mowoe IJ, Bjornson R (eds) Africa and the West: the legacies of empire. Greenwood Press, New York
Merry SE (2006) Human rights and gender violence: translating international law into local justice. University of Chicago Press, Chicago
Mowoe IJ, Bjornson R (1986) Introduction. In: Mowoe IJ, Bjornson R (eds) Africa and the West: the legacies of empire. Greenwood Press, New York
Mwalimu C (2005) The Nigerian legal system, vol 1, Public law. P Lang, New York
Ngugi J (2004) Re-examining the role of private property in market democracies: problematic ideological issues raised by land registration. MIJ Int Law 25:467
Nkrumah K (1964) Consciencism: philosophy and ideology for decolonization and development with particular reference to the African revolution. Heinemann, London
Nnaemeka-Agu P The contribution of judge Elias to African customary law. In: Bello EG, Ajibola BA (eds) Essays in honour of judge Taslim Olawale Elias, 2 vols. Martinus Nijhoff Publishers, Dordrecht/Boston/London
Nyamu CI (1998–99) Achieving gender equality in a plural legal context: custom and women's access to and control of land in Kenya. Third World Legal Studies 15:21
Rosello M (1995) Introduction. In: Rosello M, Pritchard A (trans & eds) Aimé Césaire: notebook of a return to my native land/Cahier d'un retour au pays natal. Bloodaxe Books
Said EW (1979) Orientalism. Vintage Books/Random House, New York/Toronto

Sartre JP (1948) Orphée noire. In: Sédar Senghor L (ed) Anthologie de la nouvelle poésie nègre et malgache de langue française. Presses universitaires de France, Paris

Sédar Senghor L (1956) The spirit of civilization, or the laws of African Negro culture. Présence Africaine 51:8–10

Sédar Senghor L (1964) Liberté I: Négritude et humanisme. Éditions du Seuil, Paris

Sédar Senghor L (1977) Liberté III: civilisation de l'universel. Éditions du Seuil, Paris

Sir Abrahams S (1948) The colonial legal service and the administration of justice in colonial dependencies. J Comp Legis Int Law (3rd Series) 30(1):1–11

Skouteris T (2005) The vocabulary of progress in interwar international law: an intellectual portrait of Stelios Seferiades. Eur J Int Law 19:823

Smith IO, Alade CA (1991) Taslim Elias: a jurist of distinction. Lagos State University, Lagos

Thompson A (1991) Favored by the gods. Kolapo Standard Press, Ibadan

Towa M (1971) Essai sur la problématique philosophique dans l'Afrique actuelle. Éditions CLE, Yaoundé

Vaillant JG (1990) Black, French and African: a life of Leopold Sédar Senghor. Harvard University Press, Cambridge, MA

Wheaton H (1866) Elements of international law. Stevens and Sons, London

Yakpo EKM (1992) The public policy doctrine in African interlocal conflict of laws. In Bello EG, Ajibola BA (eds) Essays in honour of judge Taslim Olawale Elias, 2 vols. Martinus Nijhoff Publishers, Dordrecht/Boston/London

Chapter 4
Decoding Afrocentrism: Decolonizing Legal Theory

Dan Kuwali

4.1 Introduction

Broadly speaking, the term 'theory' is defined as a "supposition or system of ideas explaining something" (Allen 1989, p. 801). Put differently, Okafor (2008, pp. 372–373) views a theory as a systematic and formalized expression of all previous observations, and is predictive, logical, and testable. Thus, 'theory' refers to a proposed explanation of empirical phenomena, made in a way consistent with scientific method. What this means is that a theory is employed as a framework for describing the behavior of a related set of natural or social phenomena. In this sense, the task of 'legal theory' – which is also known as 'jurisprudence' or 'legal philosophy' – is the "clarification of legal values and postulates up to their ultimate philosophical foundations" (Friedmann 1969, p. 449).

The philosophy of law is commonly known as 'jurisprudence', which can further be broken down into analytical and normative jurisprudence. Normative jurisprudence is essentially political philosophy, and poses the question: 'what should law be?', whereas analytic jurisprudence asks: 'what is law?' In the twentieth century, Hart (1961) argued that law is a system of rules, divided into primary (rules of conduct) and secondary ones (rules addressed to officials to administer primary rules). In this sense, secondary rules are further divided into 'rules of adjudication' (to resolve legal disputes), 'rules of change' (allowing laws to be varied) and 'the rule of recognition' (allowing laws to be identified as valid) (Bayles 1992, p. 21).

When African countries were colonized by the Europeans, the colonial administrators often commissioned studies in an attempt to understand 'their subjects' better in the

D. Kuwali (✉)
Post-Doctoral Fellow, Centre for Human Rights,
Faculty of Law, University of Pretoria, Pretoria, South Africa

Associate Professor of Law, Centre for Security Studies,
Mzuzu University, Malawi
e-mail: dan.kuwali@up.ac.za

O. Onazi (ed.), *African Legal Theory and Contemporary Problems: Critical Essays*, Ius Gentium: Comparative Perspectives on Law and Justice 29,
DOI 10.1007/978-94-007-7537-4_4, © Springer Science+Business Media Dordrecht 2014

exercise of their imperial power. The Europeans transplanted their Western laws to African soil. In so doing, the colonialists did not take any interest in analyzing the received European law's interaction with, and impact on, the indigenous laws and customs which it co-existed within the colonial territories. Instead the European missionaries were of the belief that African customary law was bad for the new religious dispensation and, therefore, should be abolished holus bolus for that sake. The colonialist concluded that native laws were pagan customs which ought to be destroyed and substituted with higher colonial laws (Ayinla 2002, p. 162; Elias 1956, p. 25).

Until recently, scholars of African law were mainly concerned with descriptive discourse and did not focus on the impact of the transplanted colonial laws on the indigenous laws and customs. This gap in the assessment of indigenous African laws has contributed to the predominance of mainstream Anglo-Saxon or Western legal theory and a paucity of knowledge or understanding of the customs and laws in ancient African societies. The hallmark of African legal theory is that is subscribes to natural law as opposed to legal positivism. In contrast to positive law, natural law is universal, binding all people and all States. It is, therefore, a non-consensual law based upon the notion of the prevalence of right and justice. This is most apparent within the field of international law. Natural law was generally displaced by the rise of positivist interpretations of international law (Ticehurst 1997). According to Schachter (1991, p. 36),

> [i]t had become evident to international lawyers as it had to others that the States that made and applied law were not governed by morality or 'natural reason'; they acted for reasons of power and interest. It followed that law could only be ascertained and determined through the actual methods used by the States to give effect to their 'political wills'.

As such, legal theory is viewed through Eurocentric or Americanized lenses. Further, Rajagopal (2006, p. 781) observed that 'it is very important not to equate hegemonic international law with United States unilateralism. Rather, one must pay close attention to how multilateral mechanisms such as the United Nations Security Council are also being used to strengthen hegemonic international law'. An aspect of jurisprudence that has not been adequately pictured in philosophical reflections on the nature of law is the idea of African legal theory. While there are several explanations for this omission, the main culprit is the imperial process of Eurocentrism of international legal discourse. The other reason is that apparent absence of prominence of African voices on the subject matter of jurisprudence in general. This view is confirmed by Rajagopal (1998–1999, p. 2) who laments that '[e]ven the isolated legal academics who study or teach 'Law and Postmodernism in the United States, reveal very little familiarity with any writers from the Third World'. For Slater (1994, p. 113), this vacuum arises from the division of labor in knowledge production that:

> the tendency to erase theory from the history of the non-West can be seen as a pivotal strategy in the West's construction of an international division of intellectual labor, and the turn towards a global agenda has been marked by a continued reflection of the same construction.

The issue of division of labour between the West and the rest is a departure from the initial position of debunking the existence of African philosophy altogether. In any case, there is burgeoning regiment of scholars of African philosophical tradition and Third World Approaches to International Law (TWAIL) Scholars who have quashed the skepticism about non-Western jurisprudence, including African philosophy. Nonetheless, Williams (2006, p. 33) notes that although 'the general denial of African philosophy has died a natural death, the implicit denial of African jurisprudence seems to persist'. Williams (2006) contends that a study of the classical and contemporary texts 'reveals an obvious and conspicuous lacuna and pertinent discovery that presents itself to us is the fact that conspicuously missing in this panoramic canonisation of jurisprudential works is the canonisation of African intellectual resonance and mental disquisition on the idea of law literature'.

For Williams, the dilemma about African jurisprudence raises two important but separate questions. The first is: what is the nature of African jurisprudence? The second relates to what accounts for the dilemma of the canonisation of African jurisprudence in mainstream jurisprudential literature (2006, pp. 34–35). Although both these questions have been addressed by several writers before, this chapter seeks to identify and decode the nuances of Afrocentrism in the mainstream legal theory. Dike and Ajayi (1968, p. 394) assert that 'every people that [do] not want to lose its identity must link up with its past' (cited in Oladosu 2001, p. 22). Therefore, this chapter builds upon the excavation by various African jurists and TWAIL scholars to liberate legal theory from 'the totalizing tendencies of Eurocentric production of knowledge' (Rajagopal 1998–1999, p. 4). The chapter also draws on the oral and visual traditions of ancient African societies since the vast majority of indigenous African laws and customs have not yet been reduced into writing.

4.2 Why an African Legal Theory?

Perhaps before answering the question as to why should there be a concern of African legal theory, the issue that needs to be addressed is the importance of a legal theory. To begin with, law is a system of rules and guidelines which are enforced through social institutions to govern behavior (Hart 1961). The way a society is constituted, including the nature of its laws, is usually reflective of the fundamental values of that society itself. Gluckman (1963, p. 198) opines that legal concepts are more or less ethical imperatives. As such, jurisprudence is basically a human-centred enterprise. Jurisprudence is about humans and thus, law is about humans.

This assumption underlies the contribution of jurisprudence in all cultures (Williams 2006, p. 41). This explains why concepts of law and justice, among others, lie at the heart of the analysis and understanding of contemporary problems faced by humanity in general and communities, in particular. For this reason, legal theory is a useful tool in the search for solutions to problems faced by communities. However, Rajagopal puts a caveat that:

> The prospects for the transformation of international law into a purely counter-hegemonic tool, capable of aiding the weak and the victims, and of holding the powerful accountable, are bleak on its own [further] international law is only a small (though important) part of counter-hegemonic power in the world today. The future of the world–its ability to deal with problems of peace, war, survival, prosperity, planetary health and pluralism–depends

> on a range of factors, including the politics of the 'multitude' [,i.e.,] the governed. The stakes in legal reform between an agenda dictated by elite politics alone and an agenda shaped by mass politics, have never been higher. (Rajagopal 2006, p. 780)

That notwithstanding, African legal theory still has to be emancipated from the Westphalian legal philosophy in order to contextualize contemporary problems faced by Africans in Africa and conceptualize effective tools for solving those problems. As it has been noted in the peace or justice debate obtaining in the Darfur crisis, international law seems to be insufficient to deal with some situations peculiar to Africa. Another example is the inaction of the UN Security Council in the face of genocide Rwanda in 1994. By restricting the authorization of the use of force on the matter of enforcing fundamental rules of international law in the Security Council, the drafters of the UN Charter created an inherently selective and weak system (White 2007, p. 31). This view is strengthened by Oladosu (2001, p. 1) who noted that:

> To the extent that legal positivism claims to be a universally valid and applicable theory, no doubt, its credibility would be substantially diminished, if it can be shown to be either incapable of providing an adequate description of, or of responding adequately to, the peculiar jurisprudential experiences and needs of certain cultures, or, to be peculiarly susceptible to morally undesirable consequences, when put into practice in certain cultural milieu. That legal positivism is defective in both of these ways, when applied in the African socio-political environment, is precisely what these writers are individually out to demonstrate.

It follows, therefore, that African legal theory can play a central role in the quest to find African solutions to African problems by virtue of being tailor-made to the continent. For example (Rajagopal 2006, p. 775) has noted that:

> Current human rights discourse and practice has a choice, a fork in the road [...] it can either insinuate itself within hegemonic international law or it can serve as an important tool in developing and strengthening a counter-hegemonic international law. By ignoring the history of resistance to imperialism, by endorsing wars while opposing their consequences, and by failing to link itself with social movements of resistance to hegemony, the main protagonists of the Western human rights discourse are undermining the future of human rights itself.

It is precisely this very different relation of the personal to the political that makes the Third World texts so alien to the West (Rajagopal 1998–1999, p. 12). Further, discerning African legal theory would help to hear and understand African voices such as appreciating the role of Africa in the United Nations and guide the role of the United Nations in Africa. Furthermore, understanding African legal theory would help the international community to appreciate the concerns by African countries about the 'selective' justice of the International Criminal Court, which is seen as a Western tool used only to persecute Africans. The point made here is that understanding African legal and philosophical thought is useful to understand how they may be relevant to the resolution of these problems. Positive law does not always have answers to problems and it is insufficient to respond to contemporary problems. This explains why Judge Koroma, in his dissenting opinion in the *Nuclear Weapons* Advisory Opinion, challenged the whole notion of searching for specific bans on the use of nuclear weapons, stated that 'the futile quest for specific legal prohibition can only be attributable to an extreme form of positivism' (Judge Koroma 1996, p. 14).

The other point is to highlight the important role of Africa as a contributor to legal theory. For example, with reference to the Advisory Opinion of the International Court of Justice (ICJ) on the legality of the threat or use of nuclear weapons, proponents of the illegality of nuclear weapons emphasized the importance of natural law, urging the ICJ to look beyond the positive norms of international law. The Martens Clause supports this position as it indicates that the laws of armed conflict do not simply provide a positive legal code, they also provide a moral code. For example, this ensures that even the views of smaller States and individual members of the international community can influence the development of the laws of armed conflict. Ticehurst (1997) argues that 'this body of international law should not reflect the views of the powerful military States alone. It is extremely important that the development of the laws of armed conflict reflect the views of the world community at large'.

4.3 Is There an African Legal Theory?

By the end of the nineteenth century, concepts of legal positivism and State sovereignty had become dominant in international legal thinking, leading to extensive codification of legal instruments (Ticehurst 1997). As pointed earlier, critics have doubted the existence of law in ancient Africa due to lack of, *inter alia*, contemporary styled legal institutions, such as the police force, parliaments and courts (Ayinla 2002, p. 148). Even if others agree that African societies have not been lawless per se, the validity and jurisprudential character to the status of indigenous African laws is questioned (Ayinla 2002, p. 148; Williams 2006, p. 35). At the time of colonization of Africa, the Europeans encountered natives with well-established indigenous and religious systems of law and custom. Thus, conquest did not destroy these systems, although it subordinated them to metropolitan Western legal traditions and changed their relationship to political authority and productive relation (Roberts and Mann 1991, p. 8).

Although historical reports indicate that African traditional systems have had a system of rules and governance, there has been no indication whether Africans had or have a theory of law (Williams 2006, p. 35). Taiwo (1998) has noted that often, 'when African scholars answer philosophy's questions, they are called upon to justify their claim to philosophical status. And when this status is grudgingly conferred, their theories are consigned to serving as appendices to the main discussions dominated by the perorations of the Western Tradition'. (Williams and Moses 2008, p. 152).

The question then is: how does a theory come into being? According to Hart (1961, p. 78), the beginning of wisdom in the effort to develop an adequate theory of law is to learn to conceive the law as a form of social rules. There are at least two ways in which a legal theory could be said to have been adopted by a legal system.

The first relates to what may be called a 'predominant position' especially in relation to legal positivism. This may be a situation where jurists and legal scholars of positivist persuasion constitute a significant majority or wield significant or dominant intellectual influence on the practices and discourse in a legal system. The second is where a 'rule of recognition' of a legal system has a lacuna, allowing the satisfaction of some moral standard or another legal rule, – although it may be morally deficient in one way or the other – it would still be considered a valid law of the system (Oladosu 2001, p. 2). Further, according to Obilade (1995, p. 357):

> There cannot be an adequate theory of law without consideration of philosophy. In propounding a theory of law we are philosophising about law. In philosophising about law we may be presenting a theory of law.

Throughout history of mankind, man never existed devoid of laws obeyed by him, although such laws may have existed without articulating them in a sophisticated manner as the modern system of law (Ayinla 2002, p. 148). It is clear that 'African peoples, in the past and at present, are not different from the rest of humanity in the possession and exercise of innate powers of philosophical reflection, and in being endowed with a healthy dose of common sense' (Oladosu 2001, p. 15). This buttresses the fact that even ancient African societies had laws that governed the communities. According to Elegido (2001, p. 127; Elias 1956, p. 1):

> [T]raditional African Societies certainly did have systems of social control which closely resembled modern legal systems. In fact, when those African legal systems are studied in details it is easy to agree [...] that the differentiation between African laws and laws of other people is only superficial.

Therefore, to say that indigenous African societies did not have laws because they lacked formal courts, police and legislatures, is to focus on the form of social arrangements rather than on their function of law. Ayinla (2002, p. 166) states that:

> Certainly, one cannot find in African societies a parliament with all its modern trappings, but there were specific procedures for creating new rules and amending old ones. In societies without Chiefs, like the Igbo or the Kikuyu, new legal rules, when needed, were made by the councils of elders. In societies with Chiefs, like the Tswana in Southern African it was the Chief who made new legal rules in the tribal assembly.

In the same vein, (2002, p. 166) adds that 'on the essence of judges, of course there were no bewigged gentlemen sitting in Oak-panelled rooms, but there certainly were persons or bodies which specialized in deciding disputes concerning legal norms and their implementation'. As regards the police, Ayinla (2002) maintains that there 'existed also in many of these societies' specialized officials whose functions was to help in the enforcement of the rulers' decisions and keep order'. Ayinla (2002), therefore, counsels that:

> The general point is simply that we find arrangement' for the discharge of the essential functions of law-making, adjudication and enforcement, but the forms of these arrangements are different from those prevalent in modem societies for the excellent reason that they had to operate under very different circumstances from those which now obtain. (Elegido 2001, p. 126; Elias 1956, p. 34)

Nevertheless, it remains generally true that the judicial institutions of the more highly organized political societies such as the West, clearly manifest the operation of legal principles than do those of the less politically organized societies, such as the rest. The fact that one justice dispensing machinery is more organized than the other does not mean that the latter does not dispense justice. It is, therefore, incorrect to say that indigenous African law is simply not law because it is different to the kind of law customary to Western societies. The widespread acceptance of the indigenous laws and customs coupled with the 'sincere and deeply held expectations of compliance' by the society tends to assert the normative value of indigenous African customs and laws. The mere fact that such customs and laws are not drafted in the Western tradition does not deprive them of their normative validity (Sheldo 2008, p. 22). Legal theory does not always have to be in black and white. According to Williams (2006, p. 38) below,

> The import is that philosophy essentially deals with the art of wondering. Wonder starts and lubricates the philosophical enterprise. Such inquisitive thought systems are demonstrated by the human mind engaging itself in the search for answers to some fundamental questions and issues of life such as death, the good life, the meaning of life etc. [...] what is of interests is that a system of philosophy does not lie in the mere fact that such system of thought was written down. It is our presumption that [...] philosophy consists not only in its existence in written form but also in substance.

The degree of sophistication attained by the judicial organs of a given community is directly related to the stage and form of its social organization. Western societies with highly developed political system invariably tend to have more advanced body of legal principles and judicial techniques than those with a rudimentary political organization (Ayinla 2002, p. 164). Given the heritage of privilege, in developed legal systems there are usually hierarchically graded courts with well-defined machinery for the enforcement of judicial decisions. Whereas in less developed or developing legal systems, 'rules rather than ruler, functions rather than institutions, characterize the judicial organization of these societies' (2002, p. 164). The apparent informality of the legal process does not mean that the actual situation is chaotic, since the mechanism of choosing the adjudicating elders for the settlement of disputes, as well as that of enforcing their decisions, follows a clearly recognized pattern, even if the means adopted appear casual to the unwary observer (2002). This view is confirmed by Gluckman (1967, p. 28) who has observed that:

> I have studied the work of African courts in Zululand and Rhodesia, and found that they use the same basic doctrines as our courts do African Legal Systems, like all Legal Systems, are founded on principles of the reasonable man, responsibility, negligence, direct and circumstantial and hearsay evidence, etc. African judges and laymen apply those principles skillfully and logically to a variety of situations in order to achieve justice.

In this regard, Murungi (2004, p. 525) has made a persuasive case for the separation of African jurisprudence from the rest of jurisprudence, asserting that:

> Each path of jurisprudence represents an attempt by human beings to tell a story about being human. Unless one discounts the humanity of others, one must admit that one has something in common with all other human beings [...] what African jurisprudence calls

> for is an ongoing dialogue among Africans on being human, a dialogue that of necessity leads to dialogue with other human beings. This dialogue is not an end in itself. It is a dialogue with an existential implication.

It, thus, suffices to say that human society is not necessarily in a 'state of nature' (i.e. lawless) merely because it lacks a sovereign commander, a regiment of uniformed policeman, an imposing penitentiary and courts. The mechanism for securing law and order that the rules of human behaviour may be regarded as law in any given society (Elias 1993, pp. 12–13). Ayinla (2002, p. 151) states that 'the fact that accepted rules though generally unwritten, were observed as binding upon the various members of these different communities'. It cannot be denied that Africa is made up of a diverse set of countries, with varied cultural heritages and different historical experiences (Chimni 2006, p. 4). Yet African societies 'were inferably held together with shared values and their collective responsibility and conscience constituted the reality of society as to what obtains' (Ayinla 2002, p. 151). African law has come to be identified as a term that described the customary laws of the people who have come under a colonial rule (2002). Granted, to decode an African legal theory, there is a need to see what can be salvaged from the legal systems and practices of indigenous people through socio-legal and empirical studies (Holleman 1974, p. 13; Oladosu 2001, p. 15).

4.4 The Nature of African Theory

The dominant philosophy of legal theory is positivist. The choice of a legal theory in the mainstream Western legal theory mainly revolves around two broad considerations – either theoretical or moral advantage; or both (Oladosu 2001, p. 1). Although mainstream legal theory claims to be universal, it has European and Christian origins (Mutua 2000, p. 33). In terms of African legal theory the preference extends to cultural grounds. This cultural orientation has led to an inescapable conclusion that the positivist legal theory is unsuitable for the African legal system. Naturally, proponents of this view have subsequently inclined to natural law theory (Oladosu 2001, p. 1; Gluckman 1967, p. 28). One of the reasons for the decline of natural law was that it was wholly subjective, and contains contradictory norms of natural law (Ticehurst 1997).

However, there are principles, such as the Martens Clause, which provide an objective means of determining natural law: the dictates of the public conscience. 'This makes the laws of armed conflict much richer, and permits the participation of all States in its development' (Ticehurst 1997). Ironically, Ticehurst (1997) has noted that even the opposition of natural law by positivist is not consistent as the 'powerful military States have constantly opposed the influence of natural law on the laws of armed conflict even though these same States relied on natural law for the prosecutions at Nuremberg'. The judgment of the Nuremberg Tribunal, which to a great extent relied on natural law to determine the culpability of the Nazi high command, confirmed the continuing validity of natural law as a basis for international law in the twentieth century. This position is supported by the International Law Commission (1994, p. 317).

There are divergent views as regards the nature of law and its function in every relevant society (Williams 2006, p. 1). Legal positivism posit 'a theory which recognizes as valid laws only such enforceable norms as are enacted or established by the instrument of the state'. The consequence of this conception of law is that for the positivist, 'only statute laws are laws indeed, by the mere fact that they have been posited by an appropriate political authority' (Okafor 1984, p. 157). Okafor contends these conceptual restrictions leads legal positivist to exclude from the province of jurisprudence, 'such fundamental questions as,' what are the essence of law?', 'why is the citizen obliged to obey the law?', 'what is the nature of a just and unjust law?', 'is what is legally wrong also morally wrong?' (Oladosu 2001, p. 7).

It is generally considered that a good law must conform to the spirit of the society because law is a developing social institution which owes its origin not to man's nature but to social convention (Ayinla 2002, p. 147; Lloyd and Freeman 1985, p. 549). Therefore, to understand the nature of African laws one has to dig deeper into the norms and traditions of the society as it permeates the totality of the facet of the life of the society. There are several legal doctrines that have the DNA of African juristic thought – the characteristics of 'African-ness' –in them as outlined below.

4.4.1 Rooted in Custom and Culture

In Africa, law is an integral part of culture (Ayinla 2002, p. 147). This implies that law cannot be separated from the culture of Africans since it is in-built in the life of Africans. Law and custom 'cuts across the totality of the facet of the life of Africans' (Ayinla 2002, p. 167). What this means is that 'juristic thought is embedded in the social relations of the people as obtainable in the society or community' (2002). Williams and Moses (2008, p. 156) have noted that culture has more than one meaning:

> In an intellectual sense, culture is said to be the "act of developing by education, discipline, social experience; the training or refining of the moral and intellectual faculties." In an anthropological sense, culture refers to the "total pattern of human behaviour and its products embodied in thought, speech, action and artifacts, and dependent upon man's capacity for learning and transmitting knowledge to succeeding generations through the use of tools, language and systems of abstract thought.

From these definitions, it is clear that a people's culture embraces a lot of things abstract and real, actual and potential, sometimes perceivable or coded in sets of principles for living.

There are several theoretical approaches to understanding the nature of the relation between law and morality in African jurisprudence (Williams and Moses 2008, p. 156). For example, the 'culturalist thesis' claims that law and morality are both instances of a people's culture or way of life (2008, p. 153). The 'conceptual complementary' thesis, informs that law is incomplete without morality; and morality is equally incomplete without law (Williams and Moses above). In this sense, to violate law is to win the admiration of half the populace, who secretly envy anyone who can outwit this ancient enemy; to violate custom is to incur almost universal hostility. For custom rises out of the people, whereas law is forced upon them from above (Will Durant 1954, p. 26). According to (Williams and Moses 2008, p. 156):

> The highest social value of a given culture is its unity, a holistic construct through which their beliefs and hopes about and experiences of life can be interpreted and understood. A people's culture, therefore, concerns the formation, development and manifestation of the creative essence of man as pictured in that given society. This is often achieved through the regulation of mutual relations of man with nature, society and other peoples.

In Africa, different tradition, belief, custom, practice, religion, value as well as background have always existed in communities or societies. These notions have regulated the affairs of communities and served as the basis of the system of administration of justice. The primary objective of such a system was to promote communal welfare and foster communal well-being by reconciling and harmonizing the divergent interests of different peoples in the society.

However, the drawback to discern an African legal theory on cultural ground is the rich cultural diversity that is the hallmark of the African continent (Oladosu 2001, p. 22). Oladosu (2001, p. 24) contends that where such areas of moral and religious differences are fundamental, as is usually the case in culturally diverse societies. And such moral or religious discrepancies may erode consensus in making and administering laws (2001, p. 24).

However, Nwakeze (1987, pp. 101–105) counsels that 'in the midst of the diversity of African cultures, there is striking cultural uniformity which allows us to talk of "African culture"'. In spite of the complex cultural diversity among African societies, it is possible to focus on the elements of cultural uniformity among these societies Oladosu (2001, p. 24).

To grant that there are elements of cultural uniformity is not in any way to retreat from the observation that there are also elements of cultural diversity among the various ethno-national groups in modern African states. To concede that citizens of African states would agree on many important points of moral values is, likewise, compatible with the rival observation that those same citizens, informed by different religious and ethical beliefs, might disagree on many important points of moral and religious values.

Therefore, in decoding an African legal theory from the various cultures amongst various societies in Africa, one should focus at the cultural practices, values and principles about which there is widespread agreement in the society (Oladosu 2001, p. 24).

4.4.2 *Preserved in Proverbs*

Proverbs played an important role as a vehicle of juristic thought in indigenous African societies. Thus, proverbs have been, and still are, a vital aid to judicial administration in matters of law and justice as well as traditional and socio-political systems in Africa. This view derives from a proverb in Yoruba, which says: *'owe l'esin oro, bi oro ba sonu, owe laa fii wa a'*, implying that: 'proverbs are the vehicle of thought: when the truth is elusive, it is proverbs that we employ to discover it' (Adewoye 1987, p. 1). Proverbs are usually anchored in tradition which is 'a belief or practice transmitted from one generation to another and accepted as authoritative, or deferred to, without argument' (Lord Acton 1952, p. 2). Flesichacker (1994, p. 45) defines tradition as 'a set of customs passed down over the generations, and a set of beliefs and values endorsing those customs'.

A tradition, therefore, is 'anything which is transmitted or handed down from the past to the present' (Shils 1981, p. 12). There is an obvious difference between culture and tradition. According to Gyekye (1997, pp. 218–212), the distinction is highlighted by the fact that people create cultural values but it is not every cultural value created that ends up in the annals of tradition. The difference is that cultural items require time to be transformed into a tradition in every society (Williams and Moses 2008, p. 159).

There are several proverbs that are used as guidelines for law and justice. For example, the English equivalent for *'usi umafuka pomwe payaka moto'* in Chichewa is 'there is no smoke without fire'. This proverb guides adjudicators to determine that there is an arguable case or merit in the allegations proffered in a given case and sometimes the proverb implies reversing the onus of proof of the accused or suspect to exonerate oneself.

Another example is the Chichewa proverb that goes, *'khuyu zodya mwana zipota wamkulu'*. Literally translated as 'berries eaten by a child affect the parent'. The proverb generally implies vicarious liability of a parent or employer for the wrongs of a child or employee, respectively. The proverb is akin to the concept of tertiary perpetrator, where a crime committed by one individual against another extends far beyond the two individuals and has far-reaching implications to the people from among whom the perpetrator of the crime comes. The notion of tertiary perpetrator is extended to the family of the principal perpetrator and the society where the principle perpetrator hails from. In this way, the punishment of the tertiary perpetrator is usually restitution, a fine and a social stigma until the status quo is reversed through manifestation of remorse. The African jurisprudence of vicarious liability, however, tends to support remedies and punishments that tend to bring people together.

4.4.3 Balancing Societal Equilibrium and Stability

The maintenance of equilibrium is one of the cardinal principles that underlie African conception of law (Ayinla 2002, p. 153). Law in African perception is not seen as apportioning of rights but an instrument of social control in terms of the maintenance of social harmony in the society. Rather, law in Africa is seen as an instrument of maintaining social equilibrium (2002, p. 147). In this sense, in Africa, law is basically used for the maintenance of continuous peaceful, harmonious inter-personal relations among the members of the society as a whole (Oladosu 2001, p. 22). According to Ayinla (2002, p. 153):

> Distinction in terms of classification of law into either criminal or civil is meaningless to the Africans and can only aid in misconceiving the idea of law and justice. Law thus "comprises all those rules of conduct which regulate the behaviour of individuals and communities and which by maintaining the equilibrium of society are necessary for its continuance as a corporate whole."

Generally speaking, the idea of the law in African legal theory is not to create offences nor to impose criminality on individuals but rather it directs how individuals and communities should behave towards one another. Its whole object is to maintain societal equilibrium. In this way, the retributive or penal theory does not come into play. Driberg (1934, p. 231) illustrates that:

> An offence of Homicide is not punished from this point of view. What obtained is that when a member of a clan, family or community has been killed, the equilibrium having been disturbed, the law set in to restore it by either execution of the murderer or by payment of compensation. The execution of the murderer or diminishing of the property of his family is incidental to the underlying motive, which is in no sense whatsoever penal but restoration of the social equilibrium.

The kind of philosophy of law subscribes to the view that law and morality are not antagonistic to each other since, by virtue of their inherent origin and development, they both exist to further societal interests, which in the case of African jurisprudence, is the enhancement and maintenance of social cohesion and equilibrium (Williams 2006, p. 45).

4.4.4 Pursuit of Restorative Justice, Not Retributive Justice

In Africa, the concept of law and justice leans towards restorative justice rather than retributive justice as espoused by Western philosophy. The concept of justice in African societies is not retributive in nature but essentially restorative in that it seeks to restore peace, harmony and existing relationship. It is not adversarial. In this view, Elias (1956, p. 287) maintained that the preoccupation with imprisonment as a way of dispensing criminal justice may not sit well with African customary legal practice to the extent that 'punishment of the offender and a corresponding satisfaction of the offended are two distinct questions that must be faced if real justice is to be achieved'. African customary legal practices tend to strike a more useful balance between these two requirements of justice in that they tended to put an equal or greater emphasis on the side of the need for restitution. This is why African jurisprudence is restorative rather than retributive (Wilson 2002).

In situations the offences are gross, African customary legal practices are still not penal or vindictive but aim at making punishment fit the crime committed (Ayinla 2002, p. 158; Oladosu 2001, pp. 13–14). The reconciliation and restorative justice are the primary considerations in African philosophy of law.

(Williams 2006, p. 45). Williams and Moses (2008, p. 153) clearly articulate the process of restorative justice that:

> In his administration of public law, the Chiefs, or whatever the Legal authority may be, sits as a judge and awards the appropriate sentences; but it would be more correct to call the inquiry into a private suit an arbitration rather than a trial, and very often no judgment is pronounced, the general opinion of court being obvious to everyone. (Driberg 1934, p. 242)

A clear example where African concepts of reconciliation and restorative justice prominently feature in providing the foundations for the creation of a legal and political institutions is the emergence of the Truth and Reconciliation Commission in South Africa. As many readers will know, the Commission was created to deal with the violence and human rights abuses of the apartheid era. Proponents of the Commission considered the idea of 'retributive justice' as 'un-African' (Williams 2006, p. 45). For this reason, one of the key objectives of the Commission was the need to promote social stability which was considered a greater good than the individual right to obtain retributive justice and to pursue perpetrators through the courts (Williams 2006, p. 45). Another example of restorative justice mechanisms in Africa are the '*gaçaça* trials' in Rwanda following the 1994 genocide in that country. Similar restorative justice mechanisms – translated as *culo kwor*, *mato oput*, *kayo cuk*, *aciluc* and *tonu ci koka* – are practiced by communities in Northern Uganda (Ocen 2007).

4.4.5 (Re) Conciliation and Compromise

The theory of reconciliation in terms of African legal theory derives from the fact that justice seeks to restore peace, harmony and existing relationship in African societies (Williams and Moses 2008, p. 153). Ordinarily, under the modern judicial process, the court finds, as to with whom lies the legal right. And as a fact finder, decides based on the facts before the court. On the whole, it is a matter of 'winner takes all' and the 'loser loses all'. In African setting it is a zero-sum game, as there is a need for continued fraternity between the parties to ensure a continued harmonious society. With reference to the Barotse of Northern Rhodesia, Gluckman (1967, p. 28) illustrates the framework for accountability and reconciliation in African societies thus:

> When a case came to be argued before the judges, they conceive their task to be not only detecting who was in the wrong and who in the right, but also the readjustment of the generally disturbed social relationships, so that these might be saved and persist. They had to give a judgment on the matter in dispute, but they had also, if possible, to reconcile the parties, while maintaining the general principles of law.

An embodiment of an African concept of reconciliation is again the South Africa Truth and Reconciliation Commission, which was established under the Promotion of National Unity and Reconciliation Act of 1995, *inter alia,* to advance the cause of reconciliation. The idea of reconciliation is to maintain a greater harmony between the parties, which is perpetually undermined by resentment, anger, desire for vengeance in retributive justice (Williams 2006, p. 45; Wilson 2002). The idea of reconciliation of the parties in African societies can be equated to the processes of through mediation, conciliation, arbitration and negotiation in alternative disputes resolution in modern settings. Some like Ayinla (2002, p. 160) have even gone on to claim that alternative dispute resolution owes its origins to the African legal system.

4.4.6 Ubuntu–Interdependence and Collective Responsibility

The concept of 'ubuntu' constitutes the kernel of African traditional jurisprudence as well as leadership and governance. The word 'ubuntu' – the essence of being human – has its origins in the Bantu languages of Southern Africa. 'Actually, 'ubuntu' is a Zulu word, often adapted from the Zulu proverb 'umuntu ngumuntu ngabantu', which speaks particularly about the fact that a person cannot exist as a human being in isolation. It speaks about interconnectedness and interdependence of humanity. This probably helps to explain why Africans tend to see one another as a 'brother from another mother.' 'Ubuntu' is widely believed to be a classical African philosophy or worldview. The import of the word 'ubuntu' is 'I am because we are.' In 1996, the Chairman of the South African Truth and Reconciliation Commission, Archbishop Desmond Tutu, invoked the concept of 'ubuntu' explaining that: 'I am human only because you are human' (Williams 2006, p. 45). 'Ubuntu' is, therefore, regarded as an African communalistic ethic or humanist philosophy focusing on people's allegiances and relations with each other (Gade 2011). The 'ubuntu' philosophy was squarely applied to address injustices which were wrought by the notorious system of racial separation in South Africa, known as apartheid. For purposes of doctrine, 'ubuntu' has been described as:

> The principle of caring for each other's well-being […] and a spirit of mutual support […] Each individual's humanity is ideally expressed through his or her relationship with others and theirs in turn through a recognition of the individual's humanity. Ubuntu means that people are people through other people. It also acknowledges both the rights and responsibilities of every citizen in promoting individual and societal well-being. (South African Government of South Africa 1996, p. 16)

In this sense, 'ubuntu' explains obligation as the moral relationship between the person, the individual and the community. This assertion is confirmed by the Somali proverb which says 'a man who owns one hundred goats but his relatives have nothing is poor'.[1] by a dissection of the 'ubuntu' philosophy further shows that it hinges on respecting human dignity and that the 'human rights' is not an imported concept in Africa. This assertion is fortified by a common Kinganda adage in Uganda that:

> *Ekitiibwa ky'omuntu eky'obutonde; okwenkanankana, wamu n'obuyinza obutayinza kugyibwawo ebyabantu bonna, gwe musingi gw'eddembe; obwenkanya n'emirembe mu nsi.*

[1] Cited in Lindy (2010), p. 28, 73.

What this saying means is that 'the dignity of a human being is fostered by equality and freedom in human rights'.[2] Although the concept of 'ubuntu' traditionally runs counter to the creed of individualism of Western societies, it is clear that the African legal theory is also feeding into the mainstream Western legal theory through concepts such as 'ubuntu.' For example, in the context of United States foreign policy, Bagley (2009) alluded to the concept of 'ubuntu', stating: '[i]n understanding the responsibilities that come with our interconnectedness, we realize that we must rely on each other to lift our World from where it is now to where we want it to be in our lifetime, while casting aside our worn out preconceptions, and our outdated modes of statecraft'. A more candid articulation of 'ubuntu' is international treaty law is the first recital in the Rome statute of the international criminal court of 2002, which states that: 'Conscious that all peoples are united by common bonds, their cultures pieced together in a shared heritage, and concerned that this delicate mosaic may be shattered at anytime'.

More so, 'ubuntu' has traits in principles such as 'humane treatment' in international humanitarian law, or 'mitigation' in criminal law,' 'fair trading practices' in international trade, among others. Examining the reasoning of the ICJ in the *Nuclear Weapons* Advisor Opinion, it is possible to argue that in terms of 'ubuntu' philosophy, the answer to the question of the legality of nuclear weapons is not difficult to find, especially in light of the prohibition of indiscriminate weapons in international humanitarian law.

4.4.7 Brother's Keepers: Societas Humana

The then Secretary-General of the Organization of African Unity (OAU), Salim Ahmed Salim, stated that every African is his brother's keeper, based on the idiom in most African cultures that 'you do not fold your hands and just look on when your neighbour's house is on fire'. This was in response to the accusation of African leaders by the Ugandan President, Yoweli Museveni, that the leaders were condoning the wholesale massacre of Ugandans by Idi Amin under the guise of non-intervention because it was an internal affair of Uganda. President Museveni stated that:

> Over a period of 20 years three quarters of a million Ugandans perished at the hands of governments that should have protected their lives [...] Ugandans felt a deep sense of betrayal that most of Africa kept silent [...] the reason for not condemning such massive crimes had supposedly been a desire not to interfere in the internal affairs of a Member State, in accordance with the Charters of the OAU and the [UN]. We do not accept this reasoning because in the same organs there are explicit laws that enunciate the sanctity and inviolability of human life.[3]

[2] Confirmed by Particia Achani and Christopher Mabazira in an interview with the author at the Centre for Human Rights Pretoria on 9 May 2012 and 10 May 2012, respectively.

[3] President Museveni of Uganda, in his maiden speech to the Ordinary Session of Heads of State and Government of the (OAU), 22nd Ordinary Session of the OAU Assembly of Heads of State and Government, Addis Ababa, Ethiopia, July 1986.

In response, Dr. Ahmed Salim stated that the non-intervention clause in the OAU Charter should not be taken to mean indifference. He contended that there was no clause in the OAU Charter that gave African governments the licence to slaughter its citizens. Dr. Ahmed Salim reasoned thus:

> [The OAU] Charter was created to preserve the humanity, dignity, and the rights of the African. You cannot use a clause of the Charter to oppress the African and say that you are implementing the OAU Charter. What has happened is that people have interpreted the Charter as if to mean that what happens in the next house is not one's concern. This does not accord with the reality of the world.[4]

Consequently, Dr. Salim urged the OAU to play a leading role in transcending the traditional view of sovereignty, invoking African values of kinship and solidarity. He asserted that 'our borders are at best artificial', and that 'we in Africa need to use our own cultural and social relationships to interpret the principle of non-interference in such a way that we are enabled to apply it to our advantage in conflict prevention and resolution'.[5] Dr. Salim's reasoning helps to explain the incorporation of the right to intervene in the Constitutive Act of the African Union (AU) in 2000. The right to intervene in a member state of the AU is rooted in the same school of thought as the notion of 'responsibility to protect' (R2P) endorsed by the UN General Assembly in 2005 (Kuwali 2011). As the cosmopolitan concept of R2P emerged later the AU's right of intervention, R2P emanted 'quite literally, from the soil and soul of Africa' (Luck 2008, p. 1). The former South African President Thabo Mbeki (2003) eloquently expounded that:

> [B]ecause of our interdependence and indeed we share a common destiny, we have to agree that we cannot be ruled by a doctrine of absolute national sovereignty. We should not allow the fact of the independence of each one of our countries to turn us into spectators when crimes against the people are being omitted [...] we will have to proceed from the position that we are each our brothers and sisters keeper.

The African ideology that 'every African is his brother's keeper', can also be juxtaposed with the natural law notion of *societas humana* – the universal community of mankind. In this connection, it can also be argued that the notion of universal jurisdiction is a derivative of the 'brother's keeper' ideology. This view lends credence from the *Zimbabwe Torture case* (*SALC and another* v. *National Director of Public Prosecutions and others* where the South African High Court who ruled that South Africa's legal system can be used to investigate and prosecute Zimbabwean officials suspected of crimes against humanity. According to Judge Hans Fabricius (2012, p. 54):

> The general South African public, who deserved to be served by a public administration that abides by its national and international obligations. It was also in the public interest that South Africa comports itself in a manner befitting this countries' status as a responsible member of the international community, and this would be done by seeking to hold accountable those responsible for crimes that shock the conscience of all human kind. By initiating an investigation into the allegations of torture the Respondents could ensure that the

---

[4] Quoted in Bah (2005), p. 41.

[5] *See* 'Proposals for OAU Mechanisms for Conflict Prevention and Resolution,' Report of the Secretary General on Conflicts in Africa, CM/1710(L.VI), Organization of African Unity, Addis Ababa, 1992, p. 12.

> individual obligations were met in this regard. The decision not to do so is effectively a shirking of these responsibilities, and therefore is of concern to the South African public. The public clearly has an interest to the manner in which public officials discharge their duties under this legislation.

What Justice Fabricus is saying is that as a responsible member of *society humana,* South Africa cannot turn a blind eye to mass atrocity crimes in a neighbouring country where the victims are not protected. This argument is augmented by Hugo Grotius – the father of international law – who stated that 'kings, and those who possess rights equal to those kings, have the right of demanding punishments not only on account of injuries committed against themselves or their subjects, but also on account of injuries which do not directly affect them but excessively violate the law of nature or of nations in regard of any person whatsoever' (Grotius 1925, pp. 472–473). This thesis extrapolates the theory of the 'right of humanitarian intervention' in international law in the responsibilities of sovereignty makes them their 'brother's keeper' (Geldenhuys 2006, p. 2).

4.4.8 Consensus Decision-Making

The golden thread in most treaties on the African continent is the provision of making decisions by consensus. For example, under Article 7 of the AU Constitutive Act, the Assembly of Heads of State and Government are obliged to 'take its decisions by consensus, failing which by two-thirds majority'. Consensus decision-making is a group decision making process that seeks the consent, not necessarily the agreement of participants and the resolution of objections. Allen (1989, p. 157) defines 'consensus' as agreement in opinion; majority view. Consensus can be viewed as, first, general agreement, and second, group solidarity of belief or sentiment (Merriam-Webster 2012). The word consensus is used to describe both the decision and the process of reaching a decision. In African societies, consensus decision-making is thus concerned with the process of reaching a consensus decision, and the social and political effects of using this process.

In traditional African settings, members, especially the elderly, usually engage in 'brainstorming' sessions to solve a problem, make a majority opinion, reach a general agreement or concord. Consensus is usually regarded as the best method to achieve communal goals. Consensus does not necessarily mean unanimity, which – although an ideal result – is not always achievable; nor is it the result of a vote. By doing so, decision-making involves an effort to incorporate all legitimate concerns, while respecting societal norms. What distinguishes consensus decision-making in African societies from other types of group activity is the absence of criticism and negative feedback. If people were worried that their ideas might be ridiculed by the group, the process would fail (Lehrer 2012, p. 22). It can be argued that the consensus decision-making process has given rise to the provisions of consensus in modern international legal instruments. Further, the concepts such as the 'Panel of the Wise', 'Eminent Personalities' and 'Council of Elders; derive from the traditional African decision-making processes and legal doctrines.

4.5 Conclusion

Colonization of African countries by the Europeans did not necessarily destroy the indigenous customs and system of law in Africa but rather obscured these native systems (Roberts and Mann 1991, p. 8). Colonial laws were uprooted in the West and transplanted to the rest. Certainly colonialism transformed the law in the colony and also impacted the relationship between law and morality (Williams and Moses 2008, p. 158). However, there is a lacuna in literature on the effect of colonialism on indigenous African theories of law and customs. It is not farfetched to perceive that the transplanted Western laws were not affected by indigenous African legal theories. As a result of this cross-fertilization of legal systems, the legal theories have been intricately intertwined leaving the hegemonic Western theories to be outstanding. Mainstream legal theories have been outstanding because they have been the focus of Western anthropologists and legal scholars; whereas indigenous African theories were not recorded but instead preserved in proverbs and other oral traditions.

The mere fact that indigenous African customs and laws are not prescribed in the Western sense does not negate their normative value, especially where there exist 'sincere and deeply held expectations of compliance' by the society (Sheldo 2008, p. 22). Such customary norms have proven in several instances to be equally effective as law – properly so called – to address social problems. Granted, African legal thought inclines to natural law whose validity has been doubted because it is highly subjective and contains contradictory concepts. However, principles such as the Martens Clause establishes an objective means of determining natural law. It permits notions of natural law to influence the development of the laws of armed conflict (Ticehurst 1997). In order to decode an African legal theory from the various cultures amongst various societies in Africa, one should focus at the striking uniformity of the practices, values and principles about which there is widespread agreement in the society (Oladosu 2001, p. 24).

The African legal theory has been rendered weak and subjected to hegemonic notions of the Westphalian system (Rajagopal 2006, p. 780). Nonetheless, it is possible to decipher Afrocentric legal theory from the hegemonic legal theory and decode the African contributions to hegemonic legal theory (Rajagopal 1998–1999, 2006). The starting point is to excavate the legal systems and practices of indigenous African societies and salvage legal theories and doctrines employed (Oladosu 2001, p. 15). Many scholars of African law agree that law 'cuts across the totality of the facet of the life of Africans and thus juristic thought is embedded in their social relations of the people as obtainable in the society or community' (Ayinla 2002, p. 167).

Even in pre-Colonial period Africans had set down system for administration of justice in their various localities or communities. Although, the indigenous systems were not as sophisticated as under the Westphalian system, it was designed to ensure stability of society and maintenance of the social equilibrium. The most important objective was to promote communal welfare by reconciling the divergent interests of different people (Tobi 1996, p. 1). In Africa, law is an integral part of culture, seen as an instrument of maintaining social equilibrium with emphasis placed on distributive justice rather that formal justice (Ayinla 2002, p. 147). Ayinla (2002, p. 153) rightly writes that:

> The varied laws and procedure as well as the distinction between civil and criminal law have grown up with the European culture with nothing in common with African cultures. The principles are alien both in growth and sentiment thus cannot be used to explain the bases of primitive legal theory for it will be fallacious to do so.

African societies are based on a collectivist organization while Western traditions tend to be individualistic (Ayinla 2002, p. 153). In an African setting, legal personality is so broad enough that interdependence among the people had imposed collection responsibility on the whole family. The rationale behind this collective responsibility is to ensure a continuous harmonious relationship among the entire members of the community as a corporate whole (Williams and Moses 2008, p. 160).

There are several doctrines that have veritable and pertinent characteristics of indigenous African juristic thought, whose hall mark is reconciliation and restorative – rather than retributive – justice (Williams 2006, p. 45). Further, the non-litigious approach to conflict resolution through mediation, conciliation, arbitration and negotiation is an African heritage in matters of law and justice which must be credited to African legal system (Ayinla 2002, p. 160). It is easy to notice Africanness in the concepts of human dignity and human rights.

The concept of 'ubuntu' is also another philosophy with African roots spreading over to Western theories. For instance, the 'ubuntu' philosophy is embedded in the principle of 'humane treatment' in international humanitarian law, particularly the 'Martens Clause,' which provides authority for looking beyond treaty law and custom to consider principles of humanity and the dictates of the public conscience, when determining the full extent of the laws of armed conflict (Ticehurst 1997). It is possible to argue that the 'ubuntu' philosophy can help address the so called *non-liquet* emanating from the indecision of the ICJ in the *Nuclear Weapons* Advisory Opinion. Other doctrines with characteristics of 'ubuntu' include 'mitigation' in criminal law, 'fair trading practices' in international trade, among others.

Another clear example of African jurisprudence is the traditional consensus decision-making process in African communities whose derivatives are concepts such as the 'Panel of the Wise', 'Eminent Personalities' and 'Council of Elders'. The principle of universal juridiction is also a derivative of the concept of brother's keepers where in *society humana,* one country has the obligation to demand punishment for pertrators of crimes against humanity in another country as noted in the *Zimbabwe Torture* case. The cosmopolitan notion of 'responsibility to protect' is also linked to the right of intervention under thc AU Constitute Act, which is traced from the African ideology of bother's keepers. In view of this rich jurisprudence, Africa should not be perceived as a recipient of, but rather an equal contributor to, the development of legal theory. As an actor on the international scene, the important role of the Africa and African legal scholars in advancing legal theory should not be ignored (Maluwa 2000, p. 201; Muntharika 1995, p. 1706).

References

Acton HB (1952/1953) Tradition and some other forms of order. In: Proceedings of the Aristotelian Order New Series 53, pp. 1–28

Adewoye O (1987) Proverbs as vehicle of juristic thought among the Yoruba. Obafemi Awolowo Univ Law J 3(4), pp. 179–195

Allen RE (ed) (1989) The South African pocket Oxford dictionary. Oxford University Press, Cape Town

Ayinla LA (2002) African philosophy of law: a critique. J Int Comp Law 6:147–168

Bagley EF (2009) United States Department of State special representative for global partnerships, Global Partnership Initiative, Office of the Secretary of State, 18 June

Bah AMS (2005) The intervention dilemma. In: Aboagye FB, Bah AMS (eds) A tortuous road to peace: the dynamics of regional, UN and international humanitarian intervention in Liberia. Institute for Security Studies, Pretoria, pp 29–34

Bayles MD (1992) Hart's legal philosophy. Springer, Dordrecht

Chimni BS (2006) Third world approaches to international law: a manifesto. Int Commun Law Rev 8:3–27

Dike KO, Ajayi JF (1968) African historiography. In: Sills DI (ed) International encyclopedia of social sciences, vol 6. Macmillan, New York

Driberg JH (1934) The African conception of law. J Comp Legis Int Law 16(4):230–245, http://www.newyorker.com/reporting/2012/07/30/120/30fa_fact_leghrer

Durant W (1954) Our oriental heritage. Simon and Schuster, New York

Elegido JM (2001) Jurisprudence. Ibadan: Spectrum Law Publishing

Elias TO (1956) The nature of African customary law. Manchester University Press, Manchester

Elias TO (1993) Legal theory: a Nigerian perspective. In: Jegede MIJ (ed) Nigerian essays in jurisprudence. MIJ Publishers, Lagos

Fleischacker S (1994) The ethics of culture. Cornell University Press, Ithaca

Friedmann WG (1969) Chambers's encyclopaedia new revised edition, vol 8. International Learning Systems Corporation Limited, London

Gade CBN (2011) The historical development of the written discourses on Ubuntu. S Afr J Philos 30(3):303–329

Geldenhuys D (2006) Brothers as keepers: Africa's new sovereignty regime. Strateg Rev South Afr 28(2)

Gluckman M (1963) Order and rebellion in tribal Africa, Chap. 7. Cohen and West, London

Gluckman M (1967) Judicial process among the Barotse. Manchester University Press, Manchester

Grotius H (1925) De Jure Belli ac Pacis. Oxford University Press, Oxford. Book II, Ch. 25, sec. 8, Vol. II

Gyekye K (1997) Tradition and modernity: philosophical reflections on the African experience. Oxford University Press, Oxford

Hans Fabricius (2012) Zimbabwe Torture case (SALC and another v. National Director of Public Prosecutions and others)

Hart HLA (1961) The concept of law. Clarendon Press, Oxford

Holleman JF (1974) Issues in African law. Mouton, The Hague

International Court of Justice, *Legality of the threat or use of nuclear weapons*, Advisory opinion of 8 July 1996, *ICJ Reports 1996 (I)*. (See dissenting opinion of Judge Koroma, p 14)

International Military Tribunal, *The trial of German major war criminals. Proceedings of the international military tribunal sitting at Nuremberg, Germany,* Judgment of 1 Oct 1946

Kuwali D (2011) The responsibility to protect: implementation of article 4(h) intervention. Martinus Nijhoff Publishers, Leiden

Lehrer J (2012) Groupthink: the myth of brainstorming myth. The New Yorker available at: http://www.newyorker.com/reporting/2012/01/30/20130fa_fact_lehrer. Accessed on 28 sept 2013

Lindy A (2010) The early morning phone call: Somali refugees remittances: studies in forced migration, vol 28. Berghahn Books, New York

Lloyd of Hampstead, Freeman MDA (1985) Lloyd's introduction to jurisprudence. Stevens, London
Luck EC (2008) Statement at Arria formula meeting on the responsibility to protect. Working Group on Conflict Prevention and Resolution in Africa United Nations Security Council
Maluwa T (2000) International law making in the organisation of African unity: an overview. RADIC 12:201–225
Mbeki T (2003) Guardian. Lecture of the President of South Africa, Thabo Mbeki, Nigerian Institute of International Affairs, Lagos
Merriam-Webster Dictionary (2012) Available at: http://www.merriamwebster.com/dictionary/consensus. Accessed 7 Apr 2012
Muntharika AP (1995) The role of international law in the twenty-first century: an African perspective. Fordham Int Law J 18:1706–1713
Murungi J (2004) The question of African jurisprudence: some hermeneutic reflections. In: Wiredu K (ed) A companion to African philosophy. Blackwell, Malden, pp 519–526
Mutua M (2000) What is TWAIL?. ASIL Proceedings, April 5–8. Am Soc Int Law. 31–40
Nwakeze PC (1987) A critique of Olufemi Taiwo's criticism of legal positivism and African legal tradition. Int Philos Q 27(1):101–105
Obilade AO (1995) A critique of current trends in legal philosophy. Lagos: University of Lagos Press
Ocen J (2007) Can traditional rituals bring justice to Northern Uganda? Institute for war and peace reporting. Available at. http://iwpr.net/report-news/can-traditional-rituals-bring-justice-northern-uganda. Accessed 7 May 2012
Okafor FU (1984) Legal positivism and the African legal tradition. Int Philos Q 24(2):157–164
Okafor OC (2008) Critical Third World Approaches to International Law (TWAIL): theory, methodology, or both? Int Commun Law Rev 10:371–378
Oladosu J (2001) Choosing a legal theory on cultural grounds: an African case for legal positivism. West Africa Rev 2(2). http://ivr2003.net/Abstracts/documents/OLADOSU-notinAssociations.pdf. Accessed 28 Sept 2013
Rajagopal B (1998–1999) Locating the third world in cultural geography. Third World Legal Stud pp. 1–20
Rajagopal B (2006) Counter-hegemonic international law: rethinking human rights and development as a third world strategy. Third World Q 27(5):767–783
Republic of South Africa (1996) White paper on welfare. Government Gazette of South Africa, No. 16943 of 2 Feb 1996, Pretoria. http://www.greengazette.co.za/dates/20051230. Accessed 9 Nov 2013
Roberts R, Mann K (1991) Law in colonial Africa. In: Roberts R, Mann K (eds) Law in colonial Africa. Heinemann Educational Books, Portsmouth, pp 3–58
Schachter O (1991) International law in theory and practice. Martinus Nijhoff, Dordrecht
Sheldo D (2008) Soft law. In: Armstrong D (ed) Routledge handbook of international law. Routledge, London, pp 66–80
Shils E (1981) Tradition. Chicago University Press, Chicago
Slater D (1994) Contesting occidental visions of the global: the geopolitics of theory and north–south relations, 4 Beyond Law, Mas Alla Del Derecho
Southern African litigation centre and another v. *national director of public prosecutions and others* (77150/09) [2012] ZAGPPHC 61; 2012 (10) BCLR 1089 (GNP); [2012] 3 All SA 198 (GNP) (8 May 2012) (See decision of Judge Hans Fabricius, p 54)
Taiwo O (1998) Exorcising Hegel's ghost: Africa's challenge to philosophy, on the theme: religion and philosophy in Africa. Afr Stud Q 1(4)
Ticehurst R (1997) The Martens clause and the laws of armed conflict international review of the red cross. 317:125–134. Also available at http://www.icrc.org/eng/resources/documents/misc/57jnhy.htm. Accessed 11 May 2012
Tobi N (1996) Sources of Nigerian law. MIJ Professional Publishers, Lagos
United Nations (1994) Report of the International Law Commission on the work of its forty-sixth session, 2 May–22 July, GAOR A/49/10
White ND (2007) Regional organizations and humanitarian intervention. Utrecht J Int Eur Law 24(65):24–33

Williams I (2006) Against the *Skeptical* argument and the *Absence* thesis: African jurisprudence and the challenge of positivist historiography 6. Available at www.miami.edu/ethics/jpsl. Accessed 7 May 2012

Williams I, Moses O (2008) Theories of law and morality: perspectives from contemporary african jurisprudence. In-Spire J f Law Polit Soc 3(2):151–170

Wilson RA, Nesiah V, Zyl P (2002) Challenging restorative justice. Human Rights Dialogue 2(7). http://www.carnegiecouncil.org/publications/archive/dialogue/2_07/articles/246.html. Accessed 29 Sept 2013

Chapter 5
Connecting African Jurisprudence to Universal Jurisprudence Through a Shared Understanding of Contract

Dominic Burbidge

5.1 Introduction

Nabudi kawafi takhamisi kiidiriji *Niidhihirishe izagale kama siraji* *Ili kufuasa ya Liyongo samba wa miji* *Ai mjiwaji naza waji kisiza waji* *ma'a kailiza kisikiliza* *mwanangwa mwema.*	*I begin my five-line verses putting them into rhyme* *so setting them forth that they shine* *like a lamp* *to tell of Liyongo the lion of cities* *Yes, it is a homily that I begin and* *bring to its ending* *How shall I set it out so that I* *may compete (this poem on)* *the good nobleman?*
Napa kwa injili na zaburi ili kiapo *Si mkengeufu pindi shari limbwagazapo* *Nalekeza moyo katokoza shari lilipo* *Mtetea cheo mwenye cheo ateteapo* *hambiwi niawi hata roho na ingatama*	*I swear by the Word and the Psalter* *and it is an oath indeed am no* *waverer when evil overwhelms me* *I direct my heart and scoff at evil* *wherever it is*
Naitenda mja kwa wenzangu *kapata sono* *Wala sina wambo siwenendi kwa* *mavongono* *Bali sikubali lenye dhila na matukano* *Ni mwofu watu nishikwapo naoa mno* *ni muwi wa kondo sikiapo mbi kalmia*	*He who strives for honour is* *is honoured as he strives* *he is not told, You are mine, even* *though his soul is expiring* *I make myself a slave to my friends* *that I may gain friendship* *nor do I slander or run to them* *with complaints* *but I do not* *submit to abuse nor to occasion for humiliation.*

(continued)

D. Burbidge (✉)
Oriel College, University of Oxford, Oxford, UK

Strathmore Governance Centre, Strathmore University, Nairobi, Kenya
e-mail: dominic.burbidge@politics.ox.ac.uk

O. Onazi (ed.), *African Legal Theory and Contemporary Problems: Critical Essays*, Ius Gentium: Comparative Perspectives on Law and Justice 29,
DOI 10.1007/978-94-007-7537-4_5, © Springer Science+Business Media Dordrecht 2014

(continued)

Mbonapo harubu chiugua nawa na afa *Kawa na furaha ja harusi ya mzafafa* *Kaekeza moyo kwa Muungu nisikhilafa* *Ni mwana asadi mtanganya moyo wa kufa* *kwa kucha khazaya na adui kumbona nyuma*	*I am gentle and yield gently* *when people hold me* *but I am a warrior-slayer when I* *hear ill-word's infamy* *When I see the fray even* *though I am ill I become well* *and I become happy like a* *bridegroom in the bridal* *procession* *I turn my heart* *I turn my heart towards God nor* *do I rebel against Him* *I am as a lion proud to die* *fearing only disgrace and that my* *enemy should find me in the* *back-ranks*

The poem is based on a dungeon song, sung by the legendary hero Liyongo while imprisoned by Daud Mringwari on Pate Island, just off Kenya's East coast (Harries 1962, pp. 188–193). The author 'composed a homiletic in order that men may observe the knightly code of a warrior-prince' (Harries 1962, p. 189) and the said hero has been compared to the Arthurian legend and Siegfried saga. Just as with those tales, the point is not merely to recount an entertaining story but to challenge listeners to achieve the same heroism, to display the same level of virtue in the midst of adverse circumstances. The author, probably Saiyid Abdallah, exhorts the listener to be a slave to friends so as to gain friendship, to be 'proud to die' and to strive for honour (Harries 1962, pp. 189–191).

Such commendations are altogether foreign to contemporary understandings of how political institutions function or derive legitimacy. Representing actors often with the simple image of homo economicus, contemporary approaches have encouraged a rationalisation of the incentive structure surrounding the individual such that the role of law and institutions is to guide behaviour towards a more efficient outcome through short-term carrots and sticks. This is an approach utterly alien to republican or deontological approaches, which instead find basis in civic virtue or Kantian integrity.[1]

This chapter outlines a theory of jurisprudence that suggests the social person Africa understands as the basic underpinning to society and law. There is particular need to apply the richness of community, role and reciprocity already present in African social discourse to discussions of legal legitimacy. Theories of African society and politics have so far sought to explain the particularities of the continent

[1] As Philp describes with regard to republicanism: 'I take the appeal of republicanism (so understood) to be that it offers a persuasive account of the interconnection between social, material and normative conditions in the polity, and that it recognizes the importance of a high degree of civic virtue in the state.' (Philp 1996, p. 386)

in terms of institutional misfit with cultural histories. This will always fall prey to criticisms either of culturalism, termed 'ethnocentrism' by Chabal, or 'oversimplification' (Chabal 2009, p. 182). The search for an explanatory model that excuses from analysis a single continent is problematic because any philosophical understandings of social behaviour are either applicable *in potentia* to all members of a species, or are applicable to none. The premise of this chapter is that a true theory of Africa can only exist alongside a theory of the person that has relevance everywhere. The explicandum is not the African but the human, wherever he or she is found. Africa, as one of the most vibrant, beautiful and radical continents of the world, holds evidence that aids this general investigation, and so the point is not to explain the person in Africa but to explain the person with Africa. This view is in agreement with the image of African jurisprudence set out by Murungi where value in African discussions comes not as an 'ethnophilosophy' (2004, p. 520) bearing no relevance for other peoples or contexts, but as a truly human dialogue where the experience of Africa has equal relevance for universal jurisprudential considerations. As Murungi explains:

> Although it may strike one as obvious, an African is an African in the context of other Africans, and, as a human being, he or she is a human being in the context of other human beings. What African jurisprudence calls for is an ongoing dialogue among Africans on being human, a dialogue that of necessity leads to dialogue with other human beings. (2004, p. 525)

In terms of how African jurisprudence is defined, therefore, no theoretical distinction can be made between it and general jurisprudence. In service to the vocation of jurisprudence, the continent of Africa nevertheless provides practical and empirical evidence that is unique and, so far, understudied. In this vein the chapter begins with an introduction to the empirical insights the continent provides in answer to the question of how human solidarity and social norms of cooperation are formed and maintained. How the penetration of the study of Africa by state-centric political science has cut these insights away from contemporary academic discourse on politics, philosophy and jurisprudence, is then outlined. Despite this assailment, the ideals of African community and reciprocity can, in response, be re-worked into a much richer and more universal understanding of the agent and what contract is. Even within jurisprudence, contract has been found to have a far more social and interdependent dimension. A contract is not just a security against free-riding but the affirmation of a pre-existing relationship, a resting point on a journey of cooperation. Given this complexity, the *social* contract fronted by Hobbes and Locke is probably the least *social* a type of contract one could imagine (and so not helpful in the search for a complementary or peaceful state-society relationship). Aligning African concepts of community and reciprocity with a relational approach to the jurisprudence of contract, the final step of the argument presents an agent-centred account of contract and trust creation that is more universally applicable.

Throughout, focus is made on a small phenomenon: the jump from the social norm of reciprocity to the institutionally-guaranteed contract. It is explored how an interpersonal account of the human person makes greater sense of this universally-faced transition than non-relational theories of contract, in turn incorporating the differences found in Africanist studies more seamlessly than institution-based theories have so far managed. This is important for Africa because without such a link the very idea of institutional consolidation is foreign and imposed. It is also important for jurisprudence more generally as the dominant understanding of social contracts – applying leverage and brokering interests – can only be successful insofar as human agents succumb to the carrot and stick.

5.2 African Communalistic Culture

In a daring argument for a bottom-up approach to interpreting African societies, Chabal notes how

> It has often been remarked that in Africa the communal and local dimensions prevail over that of the individual. However, that observation is rarely developed conceptually or analytically. If it is discussed at all, it is either relegated to the question of ethnicity—that is, the influence of what is assumed to be the key marker of individual identity—or it is seen as a leftover from traditions that are fast (even if, in fact, not so fast) disappearing. In both instances, the presumption is that such communal aspects are but staging posts in a universal process of human development that results in converging forms of individualisation. (Chabal 2009, p. 36)

Wiredu provides conceptual clarification for the communal dimensions of African society and sets out, step-by-step, an understanding that cools arguments over the inevitability of 'individualisation'. Defining communalistic society as 'one in which extended kinship linkages play a dominant role in social relations', Wiredu explains how colonialism damaged African statesmanship by disintegrating the political and civil aspects of social life (2001, p. 172). This is a point made by Mamdani too, who shows how the indirect rule of colonials created a 'bifurcated state' able to rent-seek from the population whilst remaining detached from social responsibilities (Mamdani 1996, pp. 300–301). In contrast to Mamdani, however, Wiredu is able to hold on to the abstract uniqueness of African communalism alongside his criticism. 'So strong, in fact, is the sense of communal belonging in the traditional setting', maintains Wiredu, 'that an individual's very sense of self is contextualized not only to the fact of community but also to its values' (2001, p. 172). Similar to Aristotle's considerations of friendship and community, there is in Wiredu's thought a definite expansion of the concept of the self to those around, allowing for a contextualised understanding of the person 'whose settled habits evince sensitivity to the basic values of the community' (2001, p. 172). This is what is also described by Lonsdale as attributable to moral ethnicity, a process of 'ourselves-ing' which 'arises out of internal discourses of social responsibility' (2004, p. 76).

Within this internal discourse there follows an accompanying process of decision-making for overcoming community challenges or social dilemmas. Supporting this process, intense reciprocity and interdependence encourage a convergence of interests between members, especially when the group as a whole is challenged. In addition, the specific roles played by some members seem to demand they be charged with looking towards a solution that suits all concerned even when their personal security is not at stake:

> It is well known that traditional Africans generally, if perhaps not universally, placed such a high value on consensus in deliberations regarding interpersonal projects that their elders would "sit under the big trees and talk until they agree." Agreement here need not be construed as unanimity concerning what is true or false or even about what ought or ought not *to be done*. It only needs to be about what is to be done. (Wiredu 2001, p. 173)

The art of deciding together and reaching compromise is part-and-parcel of what it means to be a community. The agreed end-point of elder discussion is to execute, through an incorporation of all interests, an outcome symmetrical to economists' understanding of the point of optimal provision of public goods. In discussing ideal levels of tax payment, for example, Samuelson calculated an optimal solution by including the level of public goods provision into individual preference assessments. Put simply, assuming money for government is well spent, one would be willing to pay a certain amount of tax in simple receipt of public services if it could be guaranteed that everyone else would pay the same amount. Public goods can be said to be efficiently produced when their cost is proportionate to the aggregation of individual preferences (an equilibrium position only arrived at naturally when all persons *honestly* declare their preferences) (Samuelson 1954, 1955, 1969).[2] This is achieved through the long conversations and the sitting under the tree; by sharing interests and level-shifting perspectives towards the collective, the point of efficiency can be approached.

It is for this reason, although described in far more pleasant language, that Wiredu posits how 'consensual governance in our tradition was essentially democratic', even though it was at the same time also role-entrenched (2001, p. 174). The economist Anthony Downs describes voting in terms of the stating of preferences for social welfare and the identification of the middle, most compromising position – the 'median voter' (1957).[3] Such an approach sees only the most basic signalling of desires, leading to a model that envisages individuals then pulling to the extremes in order to strategically bias the middle point. Compared with the deliberative, communal model, such a voting system looks barely democratic. Rather, Wit is when conversation over the individual *qua* member of a group is made by those whose interests are most intimately bound with others that the outcome will be democratically rich.[4] We eagerly await an economist who can incorporate group preferences into one's own utility curve as well as traditional elders do.

---

[2] In economic terminology, optimal production of public goods occurs where the collective marginal rates of substitution between public and private goods of all individuals concerned equals the marginal rate of transformation between public and private goods.

[3] For the median voter theorem, see Black (1948).

[4] In this sense, indirect democracy can be more democratic than direct democracy because it keeps to the ideals of deliberation.

5.3 Africanist Political Science

Unfortunately, the idealistic account of community outlined above is thought old. According to the current analytical trend, notions of African communalism are more myth than true, or else deemed faulty constructs like Julius Nyerere's *Ujamaa*. The 'idealist and moralist strain' that believed in a conjured-up image of traditional Africa is seen by Freund as a product of the nationalist era which read a sense of ethnic beauty back into the history of the continent but then lost all credibility when independence led to terrible politics (1984, pp. 7, 10–11). With plenty of illiberal aspects and symbolic inventions to find within the examples of 'tradition', the intellectual appeal to tribe and indigenous empire all but fell apart against the rushing wave of theories of underdevelopment, through which 'the new generation of African intellectuals is no longer content to have ancient "civilisations" glorified and African initiatives of whatever stripe and regardless of content, vacuously applauded' (Rodney 1972, p. 13). The work of Frantz Fanon, *The Wretched of the Earth*, strode as vanguard to much of this sudden and enduring trend, viewing colonialism as having caused the African to have become 'an oppressed person whose permanent dream is to become the persecutor' (1963, p. 41). In the words of Jean-Paul Sartre's preface to the book,

> when you domesticate a member of your own species, you reduce his output, and however little you may give him, a farmyard man finishes by costing more than he brings in. For this reason the settlers are obliged to stop the breaking-in half-way; the result, neither man nor animal, is the native. (1963, p. 14)

Due to the enduring poverty in African politics, this image has not been washed away and so urgent solution is demanded by the international community for structural or attitudinal change that may elevate the continent's politics. What the community used to mean is best forgotten as it acts as a weight on the foot, fixing society to the half-way hell of ethnocentrism. Mamdani, for example, describes discussion on Africa as split between modernists and communitarians, whereby modernists are those who believe in rights and locate politics in civil society, and communitarians are those who put age-old communities at the centre (1996, p. 3). In a later piece, Mamdani then pushes the distinction further and argues that political identity should be understood as 'distinct from economic or cultural identities' (2001, p. 662). Here, the political has been ripped away from the communal. How has an understanding so foreign to holistic conceptions of African society come to the fore?

The answer lies not just in the way academia has focused on the negatives of post-independence Africa but also in the institution-based approach that now dominates the interpretation of culture, agency and social norms in general. The penetration this trend has made into African studies is obvious in the recent works of African political science. Nugent, for example, identifies two contemporary groups as diagnosing the African condition. The first those who argue that 'the colonial state was always an alien imposition', and the second those who believe the colonial state to have instead not been strong enough to withstand the sudden absorption by African elites and culture at independence (2004, pp. 8–9). Either culture is damningly different or damning in itself.

Africanist political scientists are responding to the need to integrate studies of the continent with other regional studies of the world, as well as other disciplines. The danger has come in achieving this through an inter-regional integration of structural variables that omits a common understanding of the agent. Bayart, for instance, agrees that 'the study of African societies has yet to be fully integrated into contemporary political studies' (1993, p. 5). His answer, however, is to focus on the structure of the state. Insofar as there is any discussion of culture it is the culture of state actors, not society. Bayart affirms that there is 'no contradiction between the interpretation of the State in terms of social stratification and the analysis of the internal logic of political entrepreneurs' (1993, p. 228). He coins the term 'politics of the belly' to capture how, in Africa, '[a] man of power who is able to amass and redistribute wealth becomes a "man of honour"' (1993, p. 242). The words of the ancient Liyongo have been turned full circle to describe gluttony.

This is a complex state of affairs. Part of the reason political science authors have felt it safe to describe the continent's moral ideals as merely vehicles for moral abuse is because of the move to centre-stage of the problem of corruption: that cause and consequence of poverty. At the same time, no matter its justifications, one cannot help feeling a deeply held loss at the reduction of anthropological and normative studies of African societies to causal variables for the interpretation of state-society incongruence. The sense of loss comes at our inability to now compare African political action to meaningful standards of excellence. Critics wish to limit corruption but avoid saying what non-corrupt politicians should do with their time. Donors want to develop sub-Saharan countries, so fund *non-governmental* organisations. We want a new Africa, so we grow and train the young so they can study elsewhere. All these are examples of trying to solve Africa's problems by avoiding African moral deliberation.

Recent interpretations of African political change have integrated the study of culture with analysis of institutions but the interpretations include no cultural ideals, only a description of how prevalent social norms clash with 'modernity' or bureaucracy (Chabal and Daloz 1999). In similar vein, work on the institutional catastrophe of African administrations explores the brilliant use of state powers by elites for corrupt ends (Bayart et al. 1999), showing how clearly both the domestic and international sources for Africa's troubles have been turned to the advantage of tiny elites at the expense of majorities. Western donors are played off against the Chinese; foreign currencies are hoarded by a few who simultaneously encourage home currency inflation; the degradation of constituencies is maintained so as to ensure citizens can be manipulated at the time of election; instability and violence is managed as leverage over electoral commissions to ensure their conclusions are contested, dangerous and render the country in need of coalition government. In analysing these phenomena, the argument persists that colonialism and its after-effects ensured a weak state that has since been gutted, overturned and manipulated by African cultural residues. As Davidson describes:

> Left with the shells of a fragile and fallible civil society, the majority have sought ways of defending themselves. The principal way they have found of doing this is through "tribalism," perhaps more accurately, clientelism: a kind of Tammany Hall-style patronage,

> dependent on personal, family, and similar networks of local interest. Insofar as it is a "system," clientelism has become the way politics in Africa largely operates. (1992, p. 12)[5]

All such criticisms are valid, but the model used to explain the process renders impossible jurisprudential discussion of African norms and cultures. At base, the model holds that fault lies in African culture's contamination of neutral-bureaucratic institutions. This is a bad argument not because all African culture is good but because there is no such thing as a neutral-bureaucratic institution. The possibility of a neutral-bureaucratic order is the premise behind those who advance the concept of 'neopatrimonialism' to describe how African elites are using administrative institutions to widen the palm of corruption (e.g. Eisenstadt 1973). Whilst the revival of interest in Weber has been applied across disciplines in a new evaluation of administrative-structural evolution (e.g. Evans et al. 1985; North 1981; North and Weingast 1989), when applied to Africa the institutions are seen as mere theoretical pretext to the rational madness of elites (e.g. Bates 2008). Chabal and Daloz argue that, in Africa, 'most important to emphasise is the significance of communities in political practice from the pre- to the post-colonial period' (1999, p. 11) because the weak and cursory development of colonial institutions meant the continent 'never managed to overcome the strongly instrumental and personalized characteristics of "traditional" African administration' (1999, pp. 12–13).

The problem with these analyses is that they are hopeless. That is to say, their pessimism leaves no hope for the human condition. Social scientists will immediately rebuke that whether an investigation leaves a sweet or bitter taste in the mouth is independent to whether it is true and of scientific merit. However, it does matter analytically: an account of any society that makes such assumptions as to eliminate human agency's capacity to formulate new or better social norms, shared strategies and institutions for the development of the societal condition gives only the structuralist point of view, one side of the coin. In this way, such analyses often suffer from an underlying Marxist lens. Persons are treated more as a particular factor of production and 'come to behave politically in consonance with their place in the productive system.' (Chabal 2009, p. 107) The more of them there are and the more exploitative their relations to production, the argument goes, the more dangerous the situation. Under this lens, the social scientist watches for the explosion point in the secret understanding that *then* structure will collapse and a utopia or synthesis will somehow emerge. Whether historically Marxist or neutral-bureaucratic, the structuralist approach is analytically faulty because humans do sometimes act well together and are even known to develop norms that encourage this further; they are capable sources of institutional evolution, not just revolution. As Chesterton remarks in passing, educated men 'only think of a mob as a thing that breaks things – even if they admit it is right to break them. But the mob made these things' (1918, p. 89). Looking at the damage done by colonialism, Mamdani asks, 'How do you address the past without reproducing it?' (2001, p. 659). This is something social scientists need to be quizzed on, because humans seem to have a knack for it.

[5] The phrase 'Tammany Hall' is also used by Weber in his 1919 lecture to refer to 'powerful political clubs of interested persons' (Weber 1948, pp. 103, 110).

The materialisation of cultural values in the study of African society is often a product of the analytical paradigm of authors. In a preface to the 1993 English edition of *The State in Africa: The Politics of the Belly*, Bayart surmises:

> I can admit it now that in the end *The State of Africa* [sic] is less a book on Africa than an essay on the theme of Fullness and Vacuum in politics, a theoretical and comparative essay for which Africa is the pretext and provides the empirical material.... (1993, p. xv)

Indeed, Africanist political science, public policy and jurisprudence are widely acknowledged to be roads on which every ideological carnival dance down. Chabal deftly identifies seven political theories of post-colonial Africa: 'development, Marxist, dependency, socialist, indigenous, neo-patrimonial and democratic' (2009, p. 3). To push debate forward, therefore, what is needed is a change of attention. What contemporary political scientists of Africa share in common is their institutional focus, most often circling on the question of statehood. Nugent writes on the state and social contract in Africa, for example, and identifies three kinds of contract: coercive, productive and permissive. Even the most participatory of these, the productive contract, is state-centric, 'one in which the sovereign authority and the subjects/citizens enter into some form of negotiation over how the rule by the former can contribute to the well-being of the latter' (2010, p. 43). That is not a contract. Indeed, if based on a purely material interaction of give-take, there is no relationship at all (the state being all give and the citizen all take). Analysis is thus presently unable to comment on the kind of relational principles so important for investigating and critiquing African politics. As Chabal points out,

> Although the question of morality is hardly breached explicitly in Africanist political science, it is in fact the elephant in the room. To take but two examples: not only is there constant reference to violence on the continent, much of which is seen by outsiders as peculiarly vicious or 'barbaric', but there is an equal obsession about politicians' lack of moral integrity, which is frequently seen to be at the root of the corruption which undermines development. (2009, p. 67)

Normativity is both an empirical reality and an essential tool for uniting context to comparative, analytical and institutional studies. For it to play this role, however, a refined concept of social norms, consistent with African anthropological findings, needs to meet with an understanding of the human person as capable of cooperation, a *reasoning and social* being.

5.4 From Promises to Contract, from Virtue to Society

At the heart of discussions of African culture and society is the appreciation of the importance of reciprocity. In a continent marked by migration and trade, gift and exchange 'sustain identity, virtue and good relations within a group and between communities' (Chabal 2009, p. 73). Interestingly, the same emphasis on reciprocity is present in some jurisprudence of contract law; it is the argument of this chapter that this is not mere coincidence. The concept of contract forms the foundation for both economic relationships (the business contract) and political relationships (the social contract). Although contract is defined somewhat dully in its formal manifestation as 'an agreement giving rise to obligations which are enforced or recognised by law' (Treitel 1999, p. 1), it is precisely the informal and unyieldingly human aspects of contract that most interest us here. Africanist understandings of interdependence and reciprocity chime with relational theories of contract and so, together, can act as a better foundation for understanding the nature of society. Although the political contract and the economic contract are normally seen as distinct, their conceptual foundations are explored here together because the area under investigation is how humans tip into and formalise basic cooperative relations. In defence of the endeavour, it can be noted that contract law attends to the problem of applying the rule of law generally to particular instances of interpersonal promise-making, and that this is exactly the type of leap from individual relationships to society-wide principles that the social person as understood in African philosophy is capable of.[6]

The basis of contract is offer and acceptance, 'when one party accepts an offer made by the other' (Treitel 1999, p. 8). This is evident in the early contract law of Ancient Rome, from which later legal systems have taken so much. In Roman Law, the *Stipulatio* constituted the formal contract and required an oral promise to be suggested and then accepted by the second party, under the form 'Spondesne? Spondeo' (Hunter 1934, p. 108; see also Buckler 1895, pp. 20–22). Interestingly, appreciation of contract in Roman Law was not a legal invention but a legal response. As Buckler remarks, 'Contract is the handmaid if not actually the child of Trade' and so, '[a]s Roman civilization progresses we find Commerce extending and Contract growing steadily to be more complex and more flexible' (1895, pp. 1–2). That contract merely facilitates and insures social manifestations of reciprocity is its unique selling point. Cohen explains that 'a régime in which contracts are freely made and generally enforced gives greater scope to individual initiative and thus promotes the greatest wealth of a nation' (1933, pp. 562–563). The importance of contracts identify, in turn, the relevance of relational reciprocity for the very foundations of economic and political life.

Law reinforces social norms, the latter being the primary organisers of expected behaviour between citizens. The example of how English contract law came to support executory agreements is a case in point. In Medieval England, a breach of promise was only enforceable if one side of the agreement had completed their terms. The way in which judgement framed the breach of contract was that an unpaid debt remained on the side of the party who had not fulfilled their side of the promise. As Teeven explains, 'the purchaser of a tun of wine was obligated, not because he had agreed to pay for the wine, but because he had received the wine'

[6] As the sociologist James S. Coleman remarks, 'Why use English and American common law as a source for identifying elements of social structure from which a theory might be constructed? Why not use French law, or the Code Napoléon on which it is based? Why not Muslim law, or law as it has developed in Eastern Europe and the Soviet Union? The answer is in part that English and American common law, which develops incrementally through precedent, has a stronger claim to reflect the actual structure of social relations in a society than does a formal code, on which European legal systems are based' (Coleman 1990, p. 146).

(1999, p. 9). This bore numerous problems, such as the fact that prices of goods needed to be fixed at the time a contract was made, and that there was a 'lack of reciprocal remedies in land sales and personal services agreements' (1999, p. 46). The underlying problem was that the framework of the law did not hold persons to account for promises *in futuro* but only for what part of the promise was presently in debit. Resolution came through judgement on *Slade's Case*, which stretched from 1596 to 1602. John Slade had been promised a price for his crops but when he produced them the promisee, Humfrey Morely, did not pay. The courts, after much to-and-fro, found in favour of Slade, and so it was affirmed that '[e]very contract executory imports in itself an assumpsit' (that is to say, the mere promise of future action carries an obligation owed) (Teeven 1990, p. 48).

In contrasting customary law with modern legal systems, Nwabueze complains how customary law lacks this movement towards appreciating executory agreements and comments on how this raises questions as to whether it is capable of supporting industrial society (1971, p. 140). This analysis follows the long line of theorists who argue that the classical writing of discrete law is the only viable guarantor of industrial or urban relations, given the division of labour and property rights the contemporary era of economic growth demands.[7] The most decisive advocate of such an argument was Weber (1978), whose powerful analysis is only genuinely challenged by Durkheim's *Division of Labour in Society* (1933). Durkheim sets out an alternative vision of heterogeneity in professional specialisation leading to 'tightly knit, albeit differentiated, social organisms' (Reiner 1984, p. 177) because of the intense economic interdependence that ensues. The position of Weber is instead supported by modernist understandings of historical trajectory that find evidence for societal progression as won through 'movement from social relations based on status to relations of contract' (Cotterrell 1992, p. 119), and describe how it is 'the *individualism* of Western law and society which has appeared as its hallmark' (Cotterrell 1992, p. 119). This argument would unhinge jurisprudential theories that backed social and informal African norms as holding relevance for universalist jurisprudence, were it not for the recent interest in relational contract theory.

It is possible that the classical understanding of contract is suffering from 'the Wizard of Oz principle of jurisprudence' (Macaulay 1985, p. 478), whereby the magnificently projected image of clarity through written and discrete law is in danger of being knocked over. The alternative, relational theory, has done just that, espoused by Macneil in criticism of discrete contract law's lack of contextual appreciation. Relational theory treats contracts 'more like marriages than like one-night stands' (Gordon 1985, p. 569) by focusing attention on the human relationships and implied understandings alongside what was written down. Epstein notes how, '[t]he set of purely social norms is often regarded as falling in an awkward noman's land between the world of purely subjective preferences (vanilla against chocolate ice cream) and the law of fully enforceable legal norms' (Etzioni 2000, p. 159). By

[7] For a discussion of *neo*-classical contract theory, which compromises this classical position, see Feinman (1990), Campbell (2001, pp. 33, 36).

saying both the subjective and the objective are important, relational contract theory turns scholarly attention on the social norms that unite the two.

Contracts are instruments for providing assurance to endeavours of collective action. Macneil began developing a theory of contracts not through the concept of relation – which has come to categorise his approach – but through the concept of cooperation (Campbell 2001, p. 9).[8] Sifting through the applications of contract law in the courts, and the human relations that lie behind, Macneil took issue with the Hobbesian principles that shore up classical contract theory for failing to appreciate the person as a social being (Macneil 1980). On the philosophical difficulties that underlie contemporary contract law, Gordley unpacks the dilemma. The Aristotelian approach to contract dominated understandings amongst medieval scholastics and reached its peak in the sixteenth and early seventeenth centuries through the synthesis achieved within the natural law school between Roman law and Aristotelian and Thomistic philosophy (Gordley 1991, p. 69). This approach supported the notion of contract through recourse to the capacity of each individual to express one's will through socially interpretable virtues of (1) promise-keeping, (2) liberality (as understood as giving the right amount at the right time) and (3) commutative justice (Gordley 1991, pp. 55, 162). Such a virtue-based approach fell deeply out of favour when Aristotle's methodology and metaphysics were more generally 'thought to have hindered, not promoted, the natural sciences' (Finnis 1998, p. 30), compared with the progress of the Enlightenment era and Hume's affirmations that morality cannot be based on reason. Left without a supportive philosophy for contract law, 'nineteenth-century jurists eliminated the concept of virtue from their discussions and were left with the concept of the will alone' (Gordley 1991, p. 162). It is this emphasis on the will only (which Macneil sources in Hobbes) that is detrimental to understanding the way contracts are actually formed. The will-based, noncooperative principles play themselves out in the courts by assuming that the written contract, a security against reneging, is the entirety of the relationship. The practical problem with classical law of contract is, therefore, that it aims to remedy breaches of trust only by compensation of certain and foreseeable losses. As Campbell explains, '[t]his remedy cannot efficiently govern contracts characterised by complex (*ex ante* unspecifiable) obligations and asset specific (*ex post* non-compensatable) investments' (2001, p. 16).

In opposition to the classical understanding of all contracts being discrete, Macneil offers an alternative perspective whereby contracts are interpreted alongside the relationship of the parties and their original commitment to cooperate. As he argues:

> promises can never encompass more than a fragment of the total situation. At least as fundamental, the amount of information available about the future is always only partial, and promises, however sweeping, can be understood only against the background (Campbell 2001, p. 132).

[8] Indeed, the subtitle of Macneil's first casebook was 'Instruments for Social Co-operation'.

Macneil is doing two things. First, he is acknowledging that humans do not possess full knowledge, and so cannot be expected to consider every possible future scenario when codifying a relationship.[9] Second, he is describing contracts as, at least some of the time, stepping stones for ongoing relationships. Both classical contract theory and neo-classical economics perceive contracts as attempts to constrain the self-seeking tendency to default on a promise. In contrast, Macneil leaves open this other possibility: that participants are writing down a pre-existing unity of purpose. As far as economics goes, the approach puts homo economicus in the bin and the fascinatingly interdependent social person at centre-stage.

How does Macneil justify his attention to the common relationship between the two parties? Apart from the fact that economic exchange produces good feeling by making both parties better off, he observes how a 'commonly held "sense" of the parties may virtually obliterate any present separation as maximisers, thereby making them effectively a single maximiser' (1981, p. 1024). Over the long-term, a relationship can stabilise, such that the behaviour, character and dispositions of the other can come to be expected and relied upon when engaging in decision-making. It is such frequency of interaction that 'gives rise to prescriptive norms, to standards of proper conduct' (Macneil 1980, p. 36). Crucially, the basis of manners and social norms lies not in their actual value but in how they demonstrate solidarity with others (e.g. eating with one's right hand in Muslim countries). Truss, for example, describes manners as 'about imagination, ultimately. They are about imagining being the other person' (Truss 2005, pp. 24–25). Just as a common language is an essential tool for the relation and communication (common imagination) of mutual benefit, so too are common norms essential for grounding contractual behaviour (Macneil 1983). Because of the delicacy of its application, contract law often reflects and guarantees norms; it rarely invents them.

The value of the relational theory of contract comes through its ability to unite understandings of reciprocity with interpretations of promise and social norms. It is interesting that African anthropological studies, which find so much resource in the concepts of reciprocity and social norms, are also built from an understanding of the person that is fundamentally social and interdependent. Whereas Africanist jurisprudence and political science is commonly associated with cultural particularism, the findings of relational contract theory identify an avenue down which African understandings of the social person are of universal merit for the study of society, trust and law.

5.5 Conclusion

Reciprocity is a core finding of studies of African communities and is well known to connect individuals with their social matrix. Indeed, reciprocity, leading to expected behaviour and relationships of trust, is the essence of contract, obvious

[9] See also the concept of bounded rationality (Simon 1997).

throughout the emergence of contract law although only recently appreciated through relational theories. Arguments that describe contract law as a replacement for social norms fail to account for the extent to which promise-making – through offer and acceptance – is a bottom-up process that merely seeks institutional recognition and judicial guarantee some of the time. Contract law is practical and its citizen-led use tends to rely on social norms, in turn consolidating their importance for the judicial system. As Cicero commented long ago: ‘Law springs in its first beginnings from nature: then such standards as are judged to be useful become established by custom: finally reverence and holiness add their sanction to what springs from nature and is established by custom’ (d’Entrèves 1959, p. 115).

The political science penetration of the study of African societies has brought great interest to bear on institutions but has detached concepts of community, reciprocity and norms from discussion of institutional creation and evolution. The steps between interest communication, interpersonal knowledge and behavioural securities are the very fabric of both economic and political exchange. Those who argue, therefore, that culture in Africa is relevant insofar as it explains the institutional degradation of the neutral-bureaucratic model fail to see the importance social norms have for substantiating those very institutions. Defining political achievement as the coordination of human action to solve social questions, we can point out that just as no economic growth is possible without underlying congruence in norms of reciprocity, so too is no political growth possible. The need is not to delete African culture but to realise the extent to which it can contribute to universal debates on how institutions should function and how the rule of law should be applied.

References

Bates RH (2008) When things fell apart: state failure in late-century Africa. Cambridge University Press, Cambridge
Bayart J (1993) The state in Africa: the politics of the belly. Longman, London
Bayart J, Ellis S, Hibou B (1999) The criminalization of the state in Africa. James Currey, Oxford
Black D (1948) On the rationale of group decision-making. J Pol Econ 56(1):23–34
Buckler WH (1895) The origin and history of contract in Roman law: down to the end of the republican period. C. J. Clay and Sons, London
Campbell D (2001) Ian Macneil and the relational theory of contract. In: Campbell D (ed) The relational theory of contract: selected works of Ian Macneil. Thomson Reuters, London
Chabal P (2009) Africa: the politics of suffering and smiling. University of KwaZulu-Natal Press, Pietermaritzburg
Chabal P, Daloz J-P (1999) Africa works: the political instrumentalization of disorder. James Currey, Bloomington
Chesterton GK (1918) A short history of England. Chatto & Windus, London, 6th impression
Cohen M (1933) The basis of contract. Har Law Rev 46(4):553–592
Coleman JS (1990) Foundations of social theory. Harvard University Press, Cambridge
Cotterrell R (1992) The sociology of law, 2nd edn. Butterworths, London
d’Entrèves AP (ed) (1959) Aquinas: selected political writings. Macmillan, New York
Davidson B (1992) The black man’s burden: Africa and the curse of the nation-state. James Currey, Oxford

Downs A (1957) An economic theory of democracy. Harper & Row, New York
Durkheim É (1933) The division of labour in society. Free Press, Glencoe
Eisenstadt SN (1973) Traditional patrimonialism and modern neopatrimonialism. Sage, London
Etzioni A (2000) Social norms: internalization, persuasion, and history. Law Soc Rev 34(1):157–178
Evans PB, Rueschemeyer D, Skocpol T (1985) Bringing the state back in. Cambridge University Press, Cambridge
Fanon F (1963) The wretched of the earth. Penguin, London
Feinman J (1990) The significance of contract theory. Univ Cincinnati Law Rev 58:1283–1318
Finnis J (1998) Aquinas: moral, political, and legal theory. Oxford University Press, Oxford
Freund B (1984) The making of contemporary Africa: the development of African society since 1800. Indiana University Press, Bloomington
Gordley J (1991) The philosophical origins of modern contract doctrine. Oxford University Press, Oxford
Gordon R (1985) Macaulay, Macneil, and the discovery of solidarity and power in contract law. Wisc Law Rev 3:565–579
Harries L (1962) Swahili poetry. Oxford University Press, Oxford
Hunter WA (1934) Introduction to Roman law, 9th edn. Sweet & Maxwell, London
Lonsdale J (2004) Moral & political argument in Kenya. In: Berman B, Eyoh D, Kymlicka W (eds) Ethnicity and democracy in Africa. James Currey, Oxford
Macaulay S (1985) An empirical view of contract. Wisc Law Rev 3:465–482
Macneil I (1980) The new social contract: an inquiry into modern contractual relations. Yale University Press, New Haven
Macneil I (1981) Economic analysis of contractual relations: its shortfalls and the need for a "Rich Classificatory Apparatus". Northwest Univ Law Rev 75(6):1018–1063
Macneil I (1983) Values in contract: internal and external. Northwest Univ Law Rev 78(2):340–418
Mamdani M (1996) Citizen and subject: contemporary Africa and the legacy of late colonialism. Princeton University Press, Princeton
Mamdani M (2001) Beyond settler and native as political identities: overcoming the political legacy of colonialism. Comp Stud Soc Hist 43(4):651–664
Murungi J (2004) The question of an African jurisprudence: some hermeneutic reflections, Ch 43. In: Wiredu K (ed) A companion to African philosophy. Blackwell, Oxford
North DC (1981) Structure and change in economic history. W. W. Norton and Co., New York
North DC, Weingast BR (1989) Constitutions and commitment: the evolution of institutions governing public choice in seventeenth-century England. J Econ Hist 49(4):803–832
Nugent P (2004) Africa since independence: a comparative history. Palgrave MacMillan, Hampshire
Nugent P (2010) States and social contracts in Africa. New Left Rev 63:35–68
Nwabueze BO (1971) Integration of the law of contracts. In: Allott A (ed) Integration of customary and modern legal systems in Africa. University of Ife Press, Ile-Ife
Philp M (1996) Republicanism and liberalism: on leadership and political order – a review. Democratization 3(4):383–419
Reiner R (1984) Crime, law and deviance: the Durkheim legacy. In: Fenton S (ed) Durkheim and modern sociology. Cambridge University Press, Cambridge, Ch 6
Rodney W (1972) How Europe underdeveloped Africa. Tanzania Publishing House, Dar es Salaam
Samuelson PA (1954) The pure theory of public expenditure. Rev Econ Stat 36:387–389
Samuelson PA (1955) Diagrammatic exposition of a theory of public expenditure. Rev Econ Stat 37:350–356
Samuelson PA (1969) Pure theory of public expenditure and taxation. In: Margolis J, Guitton H (eds) Public economics: an analysis of public production and consumption and their relations to the private sectors. MacMillan, London, ch 5
Simon HA (1997) Administrative behaviour, 4th edn. Free Press, New York
Teeven KM (1990) A history of the Anglo-American common law of contract. Greenwood Press, London
Treitel GH (1999) The law of contract, 10th edn. Sweet & Maxwell, London

Truss L (2005) Talk to the hand: the utter bloody rudeness of everyday life (or six good reasons to stay at home and bolt the door). Profile Books, London

Weber M (1948) Politics as a vocation. In: Gerth HH, Wright Mills C (eds) From Max Weber: essays in sociology. Routledge, London, ch 4

Weber M (1978) Economy and society: an outline of interpretive sociology. University of California Press, London

Wiredu K (2001) Society and democracy in Africa. In: Kiros T (ed) Explorations in African political thought: identity, community, ethics. Routledge, London, ch 10

Chapter 6
The Legal Subject in Modern African Law: A Nigerian Report

Olúfẹ́mi Táíwò

6.1 Introduction

Few would deny that all is not well with African judiciaries.[1] Attention is often focused on the behaviour of the executive and of its agents. Additionally, there is evidence that the populace is rarely agitated by widespread abuse of human rights ranging from the, on the surface, benign, e.g., roughing up suspects, to the serious, e.g., extra-judicial killings. Some have tried to explain the failure of African legal systems by exploring the dominant jurisprudence in them usually associated with legal positivism,[2] or arguing that they are animated by principles that are incompatible with various indigenous African cultures and traditions.

In this paper, I explore an aspect of the inadequate performance of an African judiciary that, in my opinion, is rarely addressed even if it is frequently reported: the violation of the rights of the individual.

[1] The latest instances of alleged judges' involvement in corruption have come from Nigeria and Kenya. "N5bn bribery allegation: Interpol quizzes Chief Justice, six others – As ICPC arrests Akwa-Ibom Chief Judge, electoral tribunal members" was the headline in Nigeria's *Vanguard*, Wednesday, April 21, 2004, and the publication of the price list for Kenyan Judges. "'Price list' for Kenya's Judges", BBC News Online, Friday, October 3, 2003 [http://news.bbc.co.uk/2/hi/Africa/3161034.stm].

[2] See in general the debate on this issue by F.U. Okafor, "Legal Positivism and the African Legal Tradition", (1984) 24 International Philosophical Quarterly 157–164; Olúfẹ́mi Táíwò, "Legal Positivism and the African Legal Tradition: A Reply", (1985) 25 *International Philosophical Quarterly* 197–200; P. C. Nwakeze, "A Critique of Olúfẹ́mi Táíwò's Criticism of Legal Positivism and African Legal Tradition", (1987) 27 *International Philosophical Quarterly* 101–105; Jare Oladosu, "Choosing a Legal Theory on Moral Grounds: An African Case for Legal Positivism", (2001) 2 *West Africa Review* [http://westafricareview.com]. See also B. O. Nwabueze, *Judicialism in Commonwealth Africa* (London: C. Hurst Publishers, 1977), Chap. XIV.

O. Táíwò (✉)
Africana Studies and Research Center, Cornell University, Ithaca, NY, USA
e-mail: ot48@cornell.edu

O. Onazi (ed.), *African Legal Theory and Contemporary Problems: Critical Essays*, Ius Gentium: Comparative Perspectives on Law and Justice 29,
DOI 10.1007/978-94-007-7537-4_6, © Springer Science+Business Media Dordrecht 2014

The violation of the rights of the individual is generalized across different areas of African legal systems. In tort, it is instantiated in the lack of enforcement procedures on the part of the state for judgment rendered in favour of individual plaintiffs against individual defendants. The situation is a lot worse when the losing defendant is the state or any of its numerous branches. The same can be said of administrative law remedies especially where executive proclamations are involved. Of most significance to us in this discussion are the exemplifications of individual rights' violations in constitutional law and criminal law. African governments are not noted for losing cases involving them and their citizens, especially when such cases turn on citizens' complaints against the government's violation of their rights. In Zimbabwe, a particularly notorious situation has developed there in recent years that has seen its government levying war on some of its own citizens: white farmers. The problem is most pronounced in the sphere of criminal law. Violations in criminal law range from the abuse, physical and otherwise, of suspects by police and prison officials, to interminable delays in the trial process, to the lack of access to the services of counsel, to extra-judicial killing.

Given the putative centrality of the individual and her rights to the legal systems in African countries, specifically those within the common law tradition, and the additional fact that in those jurisdictions the law and its agencies are charged, theoretically speaking, *primarily* with the protection of the individual, it is meet to ask why the responsibility is shirked so routinely. The centrality of individual rights explains the path that is followed in this essay. I propose to explore the metaphysical template on which rests the modern legal system in a common law country like Nigeria. That is, I wish to explore the notion of the individual whose protection from the predations of the collective power (the state and its agents) and those of her fellows (either as individuals or groups) is the principal raison d'être of the modern state and its pertinent legal system. This individual is the *legal subject*. What implications does this idea of the legal subject have for the operation of the legal system? What follows from the requirement that the modern legal system dedicate itself to the protection of the legal subject?[3] I argue that, generally speaking, operators of African modern legal systems and scholars of African law and legal theory alike have paid too scant attention to the idea of the legal subject in modern African law.[4]

---

[3] Incidentally, once it was agreed that a corporation could be adjudged a 'legal person', it became eligible for many of the privileges and forbearances attached to the human legal subject. This merely serves to underscore the centrality of the legal subject to the modern legal system.

[4] For an exception see, Michael Reisman, "The Individual under African Law in Comprehensive Context", in Dr. Peter Nanyenya Takirambudde, ed., *The Individual under African Law*, Kwaluseni, 1982, pp. 9–27. See also, in general, Thierry G. Verhelst, ed., *Legal Process and the Individual: African Source Materials*, Proceedings of the Economic Commission for Africa Conference of African Jurists, Addis Ababa 1971. It is noteworthy in this respect that in their edited collection of essays, *African Law and Legal Theory* (New York: New York University Press, 1995), Gordon R. Woodman and A.O. Obilade did not consider including the legal subject or the problems attached to the idea of the individual in the law, as one of their subject categories. Nor are they likely to have found too many essays had they chosen to address the issue in their collection. Such is the paucity of writings treating of the theme of the individual in African law and legal theory. I do not mean to

As a result, the legal subject is hardly, if ever, the object of solicitation either on the part of practitioners or that of commentators on African legal theory and practice. By the same token, I would like to argue, if we are to make better sense of why African legal systems fail so often and minimize the disutility to individuals, we must begin to take seriously the metaphysical template from which the key pieces of the legal systems are fabricated.

It is not only in cases involving individual rights and the state that the legal subject is barely existent. The case is just as bad, if not worse, in the administration of criminal justice. Whether it is the police, the prisons, or the courts, we are confronted every day, under *both* military and democratic regimes, with evidence of the near nonexistence of the legal subject. And I shall contend that if many of the egregious instances of the violation of the subject that are standard fare in human rights reports and agitation are to be eradicated, or at least reduced, we must take the legal subject seriously. Indeed we, scholars and practitioners alike, must embark on a far-reaching and widespread programme to educate all who have a role to play in the administration of justice in African countries, be they judges or bailiffs, jailers or police officers.[5]

I work with certain basic assumptions that I do not propose to argue for here. If, as I do in what follows, I continually draw my inspiration from Anglo-American or Euro-American sources, it is because that is where the modern legal system in Commonwealth Africa came from and it is in the relevant Euro-American countries that we have the fullest development yet of the logic of law in its modern incarnation. The reason for this last claim will be clear presently.

The dominant legal system in Nigeria is of alien provenance and no amount of nationalist tergiversations will undermine that historical fact. The fact just stated, from my experience, is apt to be misheard or misconstrued. I do not claim that there were no indigenous legal systems before the alien historical movements of slavery, the Atlantic Slave Trade, Islam, Christianity, and Colonialism, reshaped the African land and mindscapes. But, I submit that in Nigeria and other English-speaking countries of Commonwealth Africa, from the vestments of the personnel to the court architecture, from the rules of legislation to those of adjudication, from the procedures for presenting a case to the legalese in which the case is heard, processed and determined, what I call the modern legal system is the dominant system in their municipal jurisdictions and it does not owe any of its roots to the soils of those countries.

---

suggest that people do not talk about rights. The problem is that they either talk about rights in purely instrumentalist terms or they are too technicist about them in their discussions. For the most part, little attention is paid to the philosophical foundations of our legal system. This is not a job for lawyers, from among whose ranks most commentators in African law come; it is one for legal theorists and philosophers. Unfortunately, few have been the philosophical interventions in African law in the common law countries. This paper is meant to be one such contribution.

[5] To the already extensive judicial education going on in African countries now must be added the input of philosophers and historians of ideas who can inculcate a sense of the enabling philosophical principles of specific legal practices.

In some parts, there is some contestation between the Islamic legal system and the one derived from the British. In such places, for example, Sudan, it will be wrong to say that the modern legal system is dominant without question. Some might point to northern Nigeria as another exception. I think, though, that in Nigeria, the common law system is superior to the Sharia and the latter must yield when there is a conflict. Needless to say, I do not deny that Africans may have varied some of what they have inherited. That is not what is of moment in this discussion. Thanks to its dominance, all other legal systems of indigenous inspiration are bathed in the ether of the modern legal system and enjoy legitimacy only insofar as they do not conflict with its dictates. If what I have just said is true, or at least plausible, it is absolutely vital that scholars engage the historical source-head of the legal system and become better students of its enabling philosophical underpinnings. Such engagement is designed to expand our repertoire of explanatory models for the crucial failures of our judicatures while pointing us in the direction of possible additional remedies to those already afforded by technical discussions in law, sociology and political science.

In similar fashion, we must take the qualifier "modern" very seriously. Whence came the dominant legal system, for example, Britain, they had at various times feudal law, slave law, tribal law and so on. In taking seriously the moniker "modern" we delimit the boundaries of our exemplar in order thereby to separate and distinguish them from those of feudal and other forms of law. It is in this modern legal system that the legal subject is dominant and supreme.

6.2 The Legal Subject: Definition and Significance

Who is the legal subject and why is she central to modern law? Miranda rights have been in the news lately in the United States of America. Scholars of legal theory and practice are familiar with cases up to and including murder in which the accused have been let go on account of the violation of their Miranda rights by the arresting or the investigating police officer.[6] Certainly, some of those cases rile people and offend their moral sensibility. Lawyers or political theorists or philosophers, on the other hand, often wring their hands and bow before the supremacy of process and hope that the cops will do a better job next time around. I have deliberately chosen this rather mundane principle because it typifies the triumph of procedure over outcome that is one of the hallmarks of the modern legal system.[7] It is customary for

[6] For the latest instance of a State Supreme Court tossing out a murder conviction for failure by police to read a suspect his Miranda rights, see Maura Dolan, "Police Are Rebuked on Miranda", *Los Angeles Times*, 15 July, 2003, A1.

[7] Indeed, the present time, when all of these time-honoured principles are under severe attack in the United States of America by pre-modern forces under the generalship of John Ashcroft, the Attorney General, is the best time to come to a deeper appreciation of those principles in their observance.

radical critics of liberal democracy and its twin doctrine of the rule of law to dismiss both as a sham. Only if we grant that they are sometimes genuine and serve, on occasion, to restrain the excesses of the modern state such as are being exemplified by the Patriot Acts in the United States, e.g., detention without trial, can we lament their prospective loss under conditions created by the aftermath of the attacks of 11 September, 2001. I insist that the reason that we lament their possible loss and resist stoutly any despotic inroads into them is because we are confronted with the dismal prospects of living in a world shorn of the robust protections they offer against the rule of arbitrariness or caprice.

Let us turn our attention briefly to Nigeria. I cite the following from a Ford Foundation funded investigation of the administration of criminal justice system in the country. In their study of the role and performance of the police in the criminal justice system, the authors aver:

> The law requires that a police officer should administer the usual caution[8] before taking down an accused person's statement. Six out of every 10 accused persons (64.8 percent) stated that no caution was administered to them. Quite surprisingly, police responses indicate that only in less than one-tenth of the cases (8 percent) would the accused person be cautioned of his right to remain silent. In the other 9 out of 10 cases (90.2 percent) the allegation is merely explained to him without caution. Arrested persons would therefore usually believe that they were obliged to make statements, and the police themselves probably consider it their duty to extract statements from accused persons. This omission to give the caution is a serious breach of the constitutional right (or option) to remain silent and of Rule IIIa of the Judges' Rules which provides for a caution in these terms.
>
> Do you wish to say anything? You are not obliged to say anything unless you wish to do so but whatever you say will be taken down in writing and may be given in evidence.[9]

The fact that the accused persons reported that no caution was administered to them 6 out of 10 times is remarkable enough. The entire book documents in copious, often painful, details the consistency with which various operators of the different divisions of the administration of criminal justice system – the Police, the Courts, the Prisons, the Bar, and the Public – subvert the time-honoured principles designed to serve as safety valves for ordinary citizens against abuse by the state.

The two editors of the volume cited above are very senior members of the Nigerian Bar and both are seasoned and highly regarded scholars. One would have expected some revulsion on their part or at least a measure of righteous indignation at the evidence of malfeasance perpetrated by all sectors of the society in the operation of the criminal justice system. But the following is fairly representative of their reaction from chapter to chapter. Following their indictment of the Police for playing fast and loose with the rule regarding caution, they said:

> That [the omission to give the caution] occurs in so many cases is a sad reflection on police methods. It signifies, at least, that the police are unaware that they have a responsibility to inform an accused person of his right to remain silent after he is charged…

[8] The Nigerian equivalent of the Miranda warning.

[9] M. Ayo Ojomo and I. E. Okagbue, *Human Rights and the Administration of Criminal Justice in Nigeria*, N.I.A.L.S. Research Series No. 1, Lagos:, 1991, pp. 111–112. My emphasis.

> There is obviously urgent need to educate the police properly on their duty to inform an arrested person of his right to remain silent; and that on no account should he be persuaded, urged or compelled to make any kind of statement at all.[10]

In all likelihood, the editors may have taken too seriously the requirement of detachment in their scholarship. Nevertheless, one must protest when it seems as if those who are supposed to chart the path to a more enlightened understanding of the principles that make the modern legal system so appealing adopt what seems at best a lackadaisical attitude towards their flagrant violation by those charged with administering those principles. We are speaking here of a principle the violation of which suffices for acquittal in other jurisdictions animated by the same principles, at least on the surface, as Nigeria's. If the authors are to be believed the problem seems to be one of lack of proper education on the part of the Police. Such an explanation is inconsistent with their other findings that indicate that the problem is not one of lack of education. And if it is, it may have more to do with lack of education respecting the enabling grounds of the requirement that the accused be presumed innocent until proven guilty by a court of law. Police officers do have access to the appropriate information in the course of their training in Police College.

Of course, as is usually the case, many in the criminal justice administration are wont to dismiss as special pleading accused persons' complaints. It is as if they say to themselves: an accused person will say anything to impugn the integrity of the representative of the system. D. O. Adesiyan has observed that although the courts in Nigeria "have stoutly prevented the abuses of power by overzealous public officials," "in some areas, however, the courts have experienced great difficulty in eradicating illegal methods adopted against accused persons. This is so because where the accused persons make allegations, the courts have found it difficult to admit or accept such allegations since such accused persons have had to prove their allegations and this task has never been an easy one for them."[11] The outcome is that the Police have no incentives to clean up their act: they do not stand any chance of losing their cases in the same way that, as we said above, were the same thing to happen in some jurisdictions in the United States or the United Kingdom, the prosecution's case would be in jeopardy. We shall come back to the attitude described by Adesiyan later in this discussion.

What is even more remarkable is that the police would confess to not cautioning accused persons of their rights. Nor is this the only point on which they confess to routine violation of procedure in the study under review. The practice of arresting a suspect's relatives as a way to force the suspect to surrender himself is widespread in Nigeria and the police confess to deploying it. I do not propose to go into recounting the usual diet of gloomy statistics of misbehaviour, often murderous, on the part of those whose responsibility it is to operate the legal system in African countries. What calls for comment is that given the common provenance, at least at the formal level, of the modern legal system in both Africa and Euro-America, in the operation

---

[10] Ojomo and Okagbue, p. 112.

[11] D. O. Adesiyan, *An Accused Person's Rights in Nigerian Criminal Law*, Ibadan, 1996, p. xii.

of the system in Nigeria, the characteristics for the embodiment of which the modern legal system is justly celebrated do not have the same resonance. Why would one culture let go of a murderer on a technicality while another revels in the breach of that same technicality?[12]

One solid answer to the above question must be traced to the philosophical underpinnings, especially the metaphysical template of the modern legal system. The Euro-American legal system is an integral part of modernity. I identify six essential components of modernity: (1) the centrality of reason, (2) autonomy of action, (3) liberal democracy (4) the Rule of Law, (5) the open future, and (6) a near obsession with novelty.[13] There is no time to discuss these components here. However, I can briefly describe the relevant ones.

At the heart of the philosophical discourse of modernity is the human *individual*. But this is not just any individual. There have always been individuals in human society. But modernity is almost alone in making the individual the basic building block of human society. This characteristic of modernity is easily misconstrued. The modern-inflected idea of the individual is radically different from other conceptions of the individual that preceded it. Not only is the modern individual the basic building block of society, she it is whose personal integrity is held inviolate and whose person and other attributes appurtenant thereto may not be acted upon, interfered with, or otherwise bothered except by her permission. The near-absolute walling off of the individual from his fellows and the artificial nature of social bonds that it engenders are what set this idea of the individual apart from other ideas, especially those regarding the priority and superiority of the group. As those who are familiar with the history of Western philosophy know, outside of ideological posturing, there is little resemblance between what is defended now, for example in the United States, as the idea of the person in society and what the leading lights and originary inspiration of the tradition held to be the best way of being human. Neither Plato nor Aristotle would accept any kinship between their views of what it is to be human and what conduces to the best life for humans and those of their so-called successors in the much-vaunted "Western tradition".[14] That is, the current understanding of the nature and attributes of the individual in the western tradition is a recent development.

[12] Answers are not lacking in the literature. In addition to poor education, appeals can be made to endemic corruption, lack of adequate equipment and facilities. What follows is meant to augment existing explanations, not supplant them. What is more, it is rarely canvassed by African scholars.

[13] See in general Jürgen Habermas, *The Philosophical Discourse of Modernity*, trans. Frederick G. Lawrence Cambridge, 1990; Stuart Hall, David Held, Don Hubert and Kenneth Thompson, eds., *Modernity: An Introduction to Modern Societies* Oxford, 1996; Bill Bourne, Udi Eichler and David Herman, eds., *Modernity and Its Discontents* Nottingham, 1987.

[14] This is how Reisman made the same point. "Precisely because so many assume that individuality is an ancient and inherent aspect of Western civilization, it important to mention briefly the constellation of trends in order to appreciate that the West only produced the doctrines and practices of individualism at a comparatively late stage in its own development." "The Individual under African law in Comprehensive Context", 11. For a full historical treatment see Colin Morris, *The Discovery of the Individual: 1050–1200*, New York, 1972.

The individual, in her modern construal, who is endowed with reason, leads the best life not only when she allows Reason to structure her life but is also expected to accept things only when they have been cleared by Reason, not revelation, not tradition. There lies the centrality of Reason. According to the philosophical anthropology that undergirds modernity, human beings who are endowed with Reason are essentially *free* beings. That is, freedom belongs to human beings *qua* human beings. One way in which freedom is manifested is through the capacity of humans to express themselves in the world, that is, *act in and on the world*, in large part to attain their desires and interests. *Autonomy of action* refers to the fact that humans are free and that they should be free to act. Since it is in action that our purposes cross and conflict with one another, it is only post-action, not prior to it, that, properly speaking, *law* becomes relevant. Given what I have just said, it should be obvious that any law that is designed to pre-empt action will be an anomaly, a distortion within this legal system. There is no punishment for thought; nor should there be any.

The freedom of the individual is absolute. Of course, I exaggerate a little. But I do so in order to underscore the point that I make later. The absoluteness of the freedom of the individual is best construed in a presumptive sense. It is similar to what we mean when we say that human beings are essentially free. We do not ask human beings to show why they should be free; we ask those who wish to curb human freedom to show why humans should not be free. By the same token, from the assertion that the freedom of the individual is absolute, it does not follow that this freedom may not be curbed; it merely means that anyone, including governments, seeking to curb it must *discharge* the burden of proof that the interference is warranted and can be justified. I would like to submit that successive Nigerian constitutions do not recognize this kind of freedom. They may be full of high fallutin pronouncements regarding the freedom of the individual.[15] In reality, though, beyond the ritual boring retelling of the genealogy of human rights from the Magna Carta on, which narrative is itself inaccurate,[16] there is no serious engagement with the philosophical anthropology which alone gives the relevant principles regarding the nature of the human person and the dignity that pertain to it their pith.[17]

[15] The usual constitutional provisions have been joined in recent times by pan-African pronouncements concerning human rights. See in general, Chidi Anselm Odinkalu, "The Individual Complaints Procedures of the African Commission on Human and Peoples' Rights: A Preliminary Assessment", (1998) 8 *Transnational Law & Contemporary Problems* 359; Yemi Akinseye-George, "New Trends in African Human Rights Law: Prospects of an African Court of Human Rights", (2001) 10 *University of Miami International & Comparative Law Review* 159–176.

[16] The narrative is inaccurate because at the time of the proclamation of the Magna Carta, England was a feudal society where talk of freedom of serfs would be a contradiction in terms. The freedom that people ascribe to the Magna Carta is more appropriately traced to the Act of Settlement of 1701 and the 1688 Glorious Revolution that prepared the ground for it. It is a sign of the illiteracy that afflicts our understanding of the history of our inherited Euro-American institutions that we think Englishmen, not to talk of women, have been free since 1215.

[17] It is strictly this philosophical dimension that is of moment here. The numerous discussions of human rights and the expanding discourse about them in Africa do not address this element. They take for granted that the idea of the individual is obvious or unproblematic.

What is more, what they give in the main clauses, they render almost nugatory in "clawback" clauses that typify African constitutional rights provisions. "Clawback" clauses refer to those exceptions that are usually attached to constitutional provisions, especially regarding human rights. For example, when it is said in the Nigerian Constitution that "Every person shall be entitled to respect for his private and family life, his home and his correspondence," the clawback clause in the very next provision states: "Nothing in this section shall invalidate any law that is reasonably justifiable in a democratic society – (a) in the interest of defence, public safety, public order, public morality, public health or the economic well-being of the community, or (b) for the purpose of protecting the rights and freedom of other persons." Given that the framers of successive Nigerian constitutions see fit to include in them the clause just cited, one must conclude that such clauses express attitudes that cut across time periods and individual preferences among the framers.

Do Nigeria's constitutional framers mean to suggest that a democratic society, so-called, may interfere with an individual's right to respect for his private and family life, home and correspondence, if such interference is "in the interest of defence, public safety, public order, public morality, public health or the economic well-being of the community?" This is a sure sign that the framers of the constitutions not only did not "take rights seriously"[18] but there is room for doubt that they were aware of the many philosophical conundrums that their proposal might generate. In a sense, they seem to have adopted a crude utilitarian approach in which the rights of an individual may be bartered away for the welfare of the many.[19] I am not aware of much discussion among African scholars of the ethical and political philosophical problems posed by the proliferation of clawback clauses in African rights charters.[20]

In law, the legal subject, possessor of reason, bearer of interest, author of actions, formally inferior to no other, is the object of solicitation. In the modern state, where the state enjoys the monopoly of the legitimate use of violence, the legal subject, such as I have described her, is protected from undue and unnecessary interference from the powers that be. *In the modern state, it is the individual that needs and deserves protection from the state; it is not the state that needs and deserves protection from the individual.* Here is the basis of one of the most important principles of legal operation in the modern state: *the doctrine of the presumption of innocence for the accused until she is proven guilty beyond a reasonable doubt.* The doctrine of

[18] See in general Ronald Dworkin, *Taking Rights Seriously* (Cambridge: Harvard University Press, 1978).

[19] Such an approach was the principal butt of severe criticism by Ronald Dworkin in *Taking Rights Seriously*.

[20] For examples of legal discussion of the problems associated with clawback clauses in the African Charter on Human and Peoples' Rights see, Nsongurua J. Udombana, "Toward the African Court on Human and Peoples' Rights: Better Late Than Never", (2000) 3 *Yale Human Rights and Development Law Journal* 45; Chidi Anselm Odinkalu, "The Individual Complaints Procedures of the African Commission on Human and Peoples' Rights: A Preliminary Assessment", (1998) 8 *Transnational Law & Contemporary Problems* 359. These authors are not exercised by the philosophical issues that rivet our attention.

the presumption of innocence is redolent with philosophical presuppositions that we cannot explore in any detail here.[21] It holds sway in all areas of the law. Although it is remarked upon more in criminal law and allied areas, it is no less required in tort. The defendant in tort does not have to prove that her action does not amount to a tortfeasance; the plaintiff is the one who has to prove that *but for* the action or omission of the defendant, she would not have suffered injury.

In Nigeria, I am doubtful that this presumption is taken seriously. It is very easy to see why this is the case.[22] *The doctrine places the burden on the prosecution to prove the suspect/defendant's guilt; it does not require the defendant to prove her innocence.* The burden is not misplaced. The asymmetry involved is fully intended given the philosophical presuppositions. Again, the doctrine's formulators were well aware that the government has all the resources to thwart justice, plant evidence, and frame the legal subject.[23] The subject does not stand a chance against a state whose personnel are determined to find her guilty. Think of it, the individual does not have the material resources to counter those of the society to which the state and its personnel have unrestricted access. It is not as if all what I just said is unknown to both scholars and ordinary folk in Nigeria. What may be at issue is whether or not we know, and if we do, whether or not we take seriously the philosophical underpinnings beneath the dialectic of the individual-state relationship in the modern context.

6.3 The Philosophical Template

We cannot understand the modern state or the modern legal system without a thorough understanding of its enabling philosophical template. The contractarian tradition[24] that backgrounds the modern legal system works with a metaphysics of diremption in

[21] These include the presupposition that freedom is so important that it has to be supported by a fortress of prohibitions and forbearances; hence, the requirement of proof beyond a reasonable doubt. Another is traceable to the Cartesian foundations of the play of doubt in the quest for and justification of knowledge. When there is doubt, the claim involved is hardly ever accepted; when there is no doubt, it is often accepted. The epistemological foundations of this requirement of proof beyond a reasonable doubt must be located in the skepticism about human nature and its cognitive tools, marked as both are by the possibility of error.

[22] Although I do not discuss it here, a full explanation must include the fact that most participants in the legal profession in Nigeria either do not have any familiarity with the Euro-American philosophical tradition or, when they do, take seriously the implications of the tradition for the legitimacy and justification of the practices they engage in as lawyers, judges, law teachers, court bailiffs, prison officers, police officers, and so on.

[23] The history of the United States of America, especially of the long tenure of J. Edgar Hoover at the head of the Federal Bureau of Investigation, is replete with shenanigans of this sort. And the experience of African Americans also attests to the capacity of the government to derail justice by railroading the legal subject.

[24] Typified by John Locke, Thomas Hobbes, David Hume, and Jean-Jacques Rousseau and revivified in our time by John Rawls.

which the individuals that make up the society did not start out with any organic connections. Rather each is adjudged an independent actor, possessed of reason, capable of associating with his fellows on terms that, ultimately, must subserve his interests and enhance his capacity to achieve his desires, whatever those may be. In forming the state, although the individuals are asked to vacate their right to self-help, they reserve the right to withdraw their consent from the state or its appurtenant institutions if the latter are turned to ends subversive of the individuals' several interests.

Simultaneously, in vacating their right to self-help, the associating individuals yield to the state the monopoly of power which it exercises vicariously in their individual behalf. At the bottom of it all is a view of human nature that is anything but rosy. Left to their own designs, on this thinking, humans cannot be trusted to not take advantage of their fellows, or seek to realize their own desires at the expense of the frustration of their compatriots. A suspicious attitude towards human nature explains the wall of privileges and forbearances built around the individual in the modern state. The basic principle is to leave the individual to his own designs as long as he does not impair the ability of others to achieve theirs. This is what is meant by the absolute freedom of the individual. It is what makes it incumbent on anyone, especially agents of the state, to justify interfering with the exercise by an individual of the prerogative of being whatever she wants to be.

What I have just said should be painfully familiar to Nigerian scholars of the western tradition. Many who work in and debate about issues of human rights and the rule of law have been educated in the tradition from which arose the core ideas summarized above. What should call for comment is why as operators of, and commentators on the modern legal system, we, not unlike Ajomo and Okagbue cited earlier, do not evince a robust sense of the rights and entitlements of the individual in African societies and a sense of outrage, beyond mere humanitarian sympathy, when the humanity of even the least among us is assailed by agents of the modern state.[25]

Why is there no hint of embarrassment when the police confess to subverting time-honoured principles on which rests the legitimacy of the institution in which they operate? Why do judges find it easy to abet the subversion of those same principles and sometimes engage in their subversion themselves, as Adesiyan pointed out above?[26] Why do ordinary folk always react with sympathy and not utter outrage when agents of the state brutalize suspects either in the course of making arrests or when suspects, even convicts, are warehoused in prisons that are manufactories for death and disease?[27]

---

[25] This attitude is manifested in the repeated, often abject appeals to the Executive for relief; visits by Chief Judges of Nigeria's many states to prisons in their jurisdictions to set suspects free who should not have been in the jails in the first place or who may have spent more time awaiting trial than would be merited were they found guilty of the offences for which they have been charged, and so on. Rarely are sanctions imposed on erring officers for violating rights or the procedures that guarantee them.

[26] See note 11 above.

[27] See Ajomo and Okagbue, *Rights and the Administration of Criminal Justice in Nigeria*. Human Rights reports from Nigeria by bodies like the Committee for the Defence of Human Rights are replete with such charges.

I ask these questions in spite of my awareness of the yeoman efforts of human and civil rights groups in African countries and their sterling achievements in advancing the cause of human rights in the continent. That is a welcome development. But the possibility of entrenching the changes that human rights groups strive for as well as reducing the incidence of the abuses that they protest lies in a deeper comprehension and acceptance of the kinds of principles that we have talked about in this section. The problem is that I do not see fundamental engagements with the philosophical principles that I have described, the infusion of which into the population, especially into the ranks of the operators of the modern politico-legal system, will yield the attitudinal orientations requisite for protecting the individual in her singularity and dignity.

Outside of the ranks of the operators of the legal system – police, prisons, the courts, and the bar – and scholars of it, we may not say that the general public has the requisite education in the history and philosophies of the dominant legal system in common law African countries. So we shall not be concerned with why ordinary citizens do not react with outrage at the subversion of the underlying principles of the legal system framed as they are by what we may call Enlightenment humanism. Nor may we say that operators and scholars alike are not schooled in the enabling traditions to kindle in them the appropriate attitudinal responses to the violations endemic to the Nigerian legal system. Indeed it is the burden imposed by their knowledge that warrants their indictment for not responding appropriately. How then do we account for the non-response?

6.4 Making Sense of Failure to Take the Legal Subject Seriously

Here is a possible explanation. The metaphysics that undergirds the modern legal system is one of diremption, of separation between the state and the individual; between one individual and another; between one state institution and another; between the individual and the group; and so on.[28] In the colonial period when the various institutional elements of the modern legal system were implanted in African countries, the colonial authorities made no efforts towards inculcating the relevant temperament in the Africans who ran the system. In fact, many commentators have pointed out that colonial rule was no school for the rule of law.[29] Certainly, there were Africans who sought to acquire the appropriate education and become imbued with the requisite temperament. The colonial authorities and their apologists in the

[28] It is no accident that discussions of human nature in Euro-American philosophy are dominated by the mind-body problem inaugurated by the founder of modern philosophy: René Descartes.

[29] See Omoniyi Adewoye, *The Judicial System in Southern Nigeria 1854–1954*, Atlantic Highlands, N.J., 1977; J. P. W. B. McAuslan and Y. P. Ghai, *Public Law and Political Change in Kenya*, Oxford, 1970.

academy were quick to demonize them.[30] Many Africans were forced to resort to sometimes qualified but often unreasoned enthusiasm for what they frequently mistook for African tradition, personality, or worldview that they identified with communalism or collectivism. The upshot is that ever since then and up till now individualism, both as a principle of social ordering and a model of explanation of social phenomena, has remained anathema to the imagination of modern Africans, be they scholars or operators of the modern forms of social living, especially in law and politics.

This background partly explains why there is a dearth in African law and legal theory literature of discussions of the philosophical dimensions and implications for practice in law of the modern legacy in the legal system. Nigeria is merely an instantiation of a widespread absence in English-speaking Africa. I do not wish to be misunderstood. There are extensive materials regarding individual rights, the place of the individual in different spheres of law, and so on. What is missing is any indication that African legal scholars are deeply aware of or fundamentally exercised by the metaphysics of the self that yields the legal subject in modern law.

Let us consider an illustration. Nigerian judges love to cite the at-its-time-infamous dissent of Lord Atkins in *Liversidge v. Anderson*:

> I view with apprehension the attitude of judges who on a mere question of construction, when face to face with claims involving the liberty of the subject show themselves more executive minded than the executive. In this country, amid the clash of arms, the laws are not silent. They may be changed but they speak the same language in war as in peace. It has always been one of the pillars of freedom, one of the principles of liberty for which on recent authority we are now fighting that Judges are no respecter of person and stand between the subject and any attempted encroachment on his liberty by the executive, alert to see that any coercive action is justified in law.[31]

Kayode Eso, retired JSC, provides the following gloss on the passage:

> In the operation of the rule of law, the role of the judge cannot and <u>must</u> not be less, judges <u>must</u> stand resolutely to prevent <u>any</u> attempted encroachment on the liberty of the subject by the executive. They must be alert, very alert to see that if ever there is a coercion by the executive, that action <u>must be justified in law and not justified on the whims and caprices of man</u>.[32]

It is easy to conclude that both Lord Atkins and Justice Eso have the same attitude regarding the liberty of the subject. Such a conclusion would be unfounded. Although Lord Atkins's fellow law Lords may have taken a dim view of his pronouncements in *Liversidge*, the fact that we do not come across repeated discussions of the British legal system's failure to take seriously the liberty of the subject, while

[30] See, for the Nigerian case, Omoniyi Adewoye, *The Judicial System in Southern Nigeria 1854–1954*, Chap. 6.

[31] (1942) A.C. 206. Cited from I. O. Agbede, "The Rule of Law and the Preservation of Individual Rights", in M. A. Ajomo and Bolaji Owasanoye, eds., *Individual Rights Under the 1989 Constitution*, Lagos, 1993, p. 41.

[32] "Judge-Lawyer Co-operation in the Protection of Human Rights," in Ajomo and Owasanoye, eds., *Individual Rights Under the 1989 Constitution*, 84. Footnote omitted.

the same is not true of the Nigerian legal system of Justice Eso, requires us to consider that the principles enunciated by them may not resonate the same way in the two legal systems, their formal similarities notwithstanding. The difference is that for Lord Atkins the sovereignty of the individual makes legitimate the liberty of the subject and the impermissibility of its abridgment without due process. At all levels of his education, Lord Atkins was never left in any doubt as to the sovereignty of the individual and the sanctity of the individual's space. Even if he were a communist, it is not unlikely that he would be concerned with the perennial problem of resolving the tension between the individual and the community. In all circumstances he must come to terms with issues emanating from and surrounding the metaphysics of the self at the heart of modernity.

Justice Eso's social heritage cannot be said to include individualism as a principle of social ordering or of explaining social phenomena.[33] The metaphysics of the self that informs Lord Atkins's stout defence of the liberty of the subject even in a time of war is not part of Justice Eso's quotidian reality. Yes, he may have studied it in school and imbibed it as part of the operation of the law. But that inheritance is a conflicted one. From the time of the second wave evangelization that inaugurated Nigeria's encounter with modernity in the early nineteenth century, the issue of what to do with the individual in the context of African indigenous cultural heritage has been contested. The debate has not abated. So, it is not unlikely that Justice Eso shares the schizoid attitude that attaches to most ex-colonials.

We experience in a conflicted way the heritage of modernity because of its intimate connection to colonialism. We may, as lawyers, adjudge the individualism consecrated in law a good thing or at least a necessary evil. But, in the rest of our lives we have difficulty extending the same approbation to individualism as a principle of social ordering. Therein lies the rub: whether or not we think individualism is good on the whole or is a principle worth defending in the broader spheres of life may be more important than what we think of it in the cloistered space of our professional commitments. It is where we locate the crucial difference in the respective orientations of Justice Eso and Lord Atkins.[34] I am suggesting that in order for the liberty of the subject to become as dominant in the jurisprudence of African legal systems as it is in Euro-America, legal discourse and legal theory must open up to the philosophical discourse of modernity and African philosophers must overcome their aversion to the metaphysics of the self at the base of modernity. To that philosophical heritage we now turn.

---

[33] According to his biographers, Justice Eso does share the temperament that is consonant with individualism and may even have acquired it from his father. But that it calls for special mention in the biography corroborates my claim that such a viewpoint is not taken for granted in Eso's cultural milieu. See J. F. Ade-Ajayi and Yemi Akinseye-George, *Kayode Eso: The Making of a Judge*, Ibadan, 2002.

[34] Needless to say, Justice Eso may indeed not be conflicted about the modern heritage. We have ex-colonials who are not. I merely use the two justices in my illustration as types, foil for my argument.

The philosophers of the modern state, from Thomas Hobbes through Harold Laski to John Rawls, in their distrust of human nature, articulated designs of the institutions of the state, especially the legal system, that were meant to insulate the individual from the overwhelming power of the state. They sought to put in place a judiciary whose operators are expected to possess a near superhuman capacity for impartiality and disinterestedness that will enable them to perform their roles as arbiters of disputes between the state and the individual as well as bulwarks against the capacity for self-preference and factional advantage of the all-too-human operators of the state's institutions.[35] But judges, in order to perform their functions excellently, must be imbued with a temperament convergent with their institutional roles as impartial arbiters. They cannot afford to see themselves as agents of the state, civil servants or bureaucrats, that is, nor can they assume that their duty is to safeguard the state against the machinations of the individual.

Given what we have already said about the imbalances of power between the puny individual and the mighty state, any judge who does not proceed from a minimal distrust of, or at the least, some diffidence about, the state is a judge who is not likely to be exercised by despotic inroads by the state into the individual's personal space, be that space physical, intellectual, or moral. I argue that in Nigeria, the requisite temperament is rarely found in even our best judges, jurists, legal scholars, philosophers, and political theorists. I take B.O. Nwabueze to be making a similar point in the following passage.

> In relation to the rights and liberties of the individual, Commonwealth judges have exhibited perhaps the most striking difference of attitude from their American counterparts. With the possible exception of Lords Atkins and Denning, a Holmes, Hughes, Brandeis, Black of Douglas is a figure unknown in the Commonwealth. The insight of American decisions on the conflict between liberty and state authority is altogether lacking. There is not even an appreciation of the kind of problem presented by such cases. Commonwealth judges have approached these cases as they do any other legal problem, applying the ordinary methods of logical deductions to a problem that calls for a sensitive balancing of society's most crucial values – the liberty of the individual and the right of the state to preserve itself. As a result there has been a failure to appreciate the question of choice involved, and the vital role of the Court in bringing about an accommodation between the two values such as would secure to both a meaningful and effective scope. The opportunity has thus been lost for informed judicial creativity.[36]

I chose Justice Eso above in juxtaposition with Lord Atkins precisely because he enjoys a well-deserved reputation as a progressive jurist who, when he served on the bench, did not flinch from judicial activism *in favorem libertatis*. So Justice Eso is in no way typical of the orientation that dominates the African bench. Whether or not he harbours the disjuncture discussed above I do not know. I am merely

---

[35] For a discussion of the connection between this view of human nature and the doctrine of the Rule of Law see, Olúfẹ́mi Táíwò, "The Rule of Law: The New Leviathan?" (1999) 12 *Canadian Journal of Law and Jurisprudence*, 151–168.

[36] B.O. Nwabueze, *Judicialism in Commonwealth Africa*, p. 298.

speculating in order to isolate a problem that I think has received little attention, if any, in spite of its importance. For if a progressive jurist like Justice Eso might, in his philosophical predilections away from the law, manifest the disjuncture between his appraisal of individualism in law and in general, how much more can we expect of judges who do not share his robust sense of the liberty of the subject. Individualist explanations are often suspect in Nigerian scholarship and many Nigerians are no less suspicious of individuals, especially those who insist on enjoying the privileges that pertain to individuality.

As G. N. K. Vukor-Quarshie remarks in an analysis of a particularly gruesome rape of justice in Nigeria, the official murder of Ken Saro-Wiwa,

> In contrast, to most Africans only a guilty person would remain silent when accused of a heinous offense, and the existing common law-based rules regarding testimony by an accused must be revised accordingly... Still, we should not jettison the entire criminal law system simply because it is of Anglo-American provenance. Indeed, most of the procedural safeguards and fundamental human rights under the received law have now either become jus cogens under international law or been incorporated in international conventions binding on states parties.[37]

When those who are charged with upholding the presumption of innocence are more suspicious of the suspect than they are of the state, the burden falls on the individual to *prove* his innocence. The fundamental doctrine of the presumption of innocence is subverted if not abandoned. It is as if we are saying to the individual something along the following lines: "How come you are the one arrested out of the many other individuals who could have been arrested, too? The fact that you are here is proof that there is probably something for which you have to answer." This may explain the ease with which Africans collaborate in the subversion of their common humanity by those who are sworn to protect it.

Given the police force's unwillingness to monitor itself and to institute internal mechanisms of accountability, the role of the Nigerian judiciary to act as a check is all the more important. An examination of the justice system's record in dealing with the few cases that have been brought to court is disappointing. The Nigerian judiciary appears unable or unwilling to speedily sanction those officers who have been brought to court, despite overwhelming incriminating evidence. When asked, most Nigerian human rights lawyers can only recall one case in which the courts convicted police officers for the use of excessive force.[38]

After reviewing some of the cases concerning human rights in the post-independence Supreme Court of Nigeria, Justice Karibi-Whyte observed:

> In coming to these decisions the ordinary rules of construction of statutes were applied. The provisions construed were regarded as indeed they were, ordinary statutes of the imperial Parliament or the local legislature as the case may be. <u>No special emphasis was laid on the fact that the liberty of the citizen was involved and that in such cases any benefit of doubt</u>

[37] G. N. K. Vukor-Quarshie, "Criminal Justice Administration in Nigeria: Saro-Wiwa in Review", (1997) 8 *Criminal Law Forum* 87. Footnotes omitted.

[38] Lawyers Committee for Human Rights, *The Nigerian Police Force: A Culture of Impunity*, New York, 1992, p. 10.

> in a decision between the executive and the citizen should be given to the citizen. The court in construing the provisions of such statutes should in all cases, lean towards the liberty of the subject but careful not going beyond the natural construction of the statute. The question that was being asked in all cases was what Parliament meant by the words used? It did not appear that there was at any time any anxiety to safeguard the liberty of the subject.[39]

Many avenues are available to the judge to rationalize his abandonment of the duty of impartiality. He can invoke the doctrine of the presumed constitutionality of legislative acts. He can appeal to the doctrine of political question. However the judge performs the dodge, a failure to appreciate his arbiter role means that the presumption in favour of the citizen is abandoned or attenuated. Karibi-Whyte's lament is instructive because it does not resort to accusing the usual suspects, especially the phenomenon of executive lawlessness, in explaining why the legal subject does not receive the benefit of the doubt premised on what I said earlier about the principle that the primary mode of being of the human individual is freedom and all those who wish to undermine this must prove that their interference is warranted. Karibi-Whyte is saying that Nigerian judges, for the most part, are not possessed of a philosophical temperament that disposes them to rule *in favorem libertatis* in all those situations where there is room, however small, for doubt, especially in cases affecting the liberty of the individual citizen. I am suggesting that if we wish to turn things around, we will need to begin to take seriously the task of creating this orientation and inculcating it in the operators of the modern legal system and ordinary citizens alike.

6.5 Conclusion

One usual way in which people respond to the kind of case at the core of this paper is to suggest that I am trying to turn Nigerians into imitators of the West or that I do not appear to find anything useful in our African heritage. Such a criticism is misaimed. In talking about modern legal system in an African country, we do not need any detours into whether or not we need to embrace any aspect of our heritage.

It is well to remember that none of the rights guaranteed under our Constitution comes as a result of any original thought by Nigerians. Most of those rights had become recognized and enforceable for centuries in some other countries before Nigeria became an independent sovereign State on October 1, 1960. It is only pertinent to say that whilst the inherited English common law had recognized some of those rights, the Universal Declaration of Human Rights in 1948 had put a stamp of universal acceptance to all of them.[40]

---

[39] A. G. Karibi-Whyte, *The Relevance of the Judiciary in the Polity – in Historical Perspective*, Lagos, 1987, pp. 58–59. My emphasis.

[40] T. Akinola Aguda, "Judicial Attitude to Individual Rights in Nigeria," in Ajomo and Owasanoye, eds., *Individual Rights Under the 1989 Constitution*, 68.

For those who advance the rejoinder above, I suggest that they must first dispense with the dominant legal system before they will be persuasive. Until Nigerians decide to rid themselves of the common law inheritance, it is only fair that those of us who find some of its philosophical presuppositions to be promotive, within certain limits, of human dignity should insist that Nigerians join the ranks of the beneficiaries of the best that the modern legal system has to offer. Given that Nigerians have not so decided, what I ask is that we take seriously the fundaments on which that system is built and even if we are going to adjudge the principals inadequate, such a judgment should emanate from a sophisticated understanding of how the system is meant to be, in its best form, in the first place. To do so, the operators of the modern legal system must become ardent students of the philosophical foundations of their system and critically embrace them.

Of course, the question of whether or not this is the legal system we ought to have remains on the table. But that this is the legal system we have and if we want it to work in ways that redeem the commitment to the dignity of the human person on which it is putatively built, we must familiarize ourselves with its enabling philosophies. This is the ultimate charge of my exertion in this paper. Left to me, I'd rather have a legal system in which the legal subject is taken seriously than one in which it is not, irrespective of its provenance.[41]

References

Ade-Ajayi JF, Akinseye-George Y (2002) Kayode Eso: the making of a judge. Spectrum, Ibadan

Adesiyan DO (1996) An accused person's rights in Nigerian criminal law. Heinemann, Ibadan

Adewoye O (1977) The judicial system in Southern Nigeria 1854–1954. Humanities, Atlantic Highlands

Agbede IO (1993) The rule of law and the preservation of individual rights. In: Ajomo MA, Owasanoye B (eds) Individual rights under the 1989 constitution. Nigerian Institute of Advanced Legal Studies, Lagos

Aguda TA (1993) Judicial attitude to individual rights in Nigeria. In: Ajomo MA, Owasanoye B (eds) Individual rights under the 1989 constitution. Nigerian Institute of Advanced Legal Studies, Lagos

Ajomo MA, Okagbue IE (1991) Human rights and the administration of criminal justice in Nigeria, N.I.A.L.S. Research series No. 1. Nigerian Institute of Advanced Legal Studies, Lagos

[41] The original presentation on which this paper is based was made at the 9th Annual Conference of the International Society for African Philosophy and Studies (ISAPS) held at the University of Dar es Salaam, Dar es Salaam, Tanzania, 9–11 April, 2003. An earlier written version was presented at the conference on "Rights in Africa: New Contexts, New Challenges, New Agendas", Program of African Studies, Northwestern University, Evanston, Illinois, U.S.A., 9–10 May, 2003. I would like to thank Seattle University for funding my participation at the ISAPS conference. My appreciation goes to Leni Silverstein for inviting me to participate at the Evanston conference. I would like to thank Kolapo Abimbola for his comments on an earlier version of the paper. My profound gratitude goes to participants at both conferences whose strenuous disagreements with various points in the paper have forced me to rethink some of the earlier formulations and, I hope, present them with less unclarity and extravagance.

Ajomo MA, Owasanoye B (eds) (1993) Individual rights under the 1989 constitution. Nigerian Institute of Advanced Legal Studies, Lagos

Akinseye-George Y (2001) New trends in African human rights law: prospects of an African court of human rights. Univ Miami Int Comp Law Rev 10:159–176

Bourne B, Eichler U, Herman D (eds) (1987) Modernity and its discontents. Spokesman, Nottingham

Dworkin R (1978) Taking rights seriously. Harvard University Press, Cambridge

Eso K (1993) Judge-lawyer co-operation in the protection of human rights. In: Ajomo MA, Owasanoye B (eds) Individual rights under the 1989 constitution. Nigerian Institute of Advanced Legal Studies, Lagos

Habermas J (1990) The philosophical discourse of modernity (trans: Lawrence FG). MIT Press, Cambridge

Hall S, Held D, Hubert D, Thompson K (eds) (1996) Modernity: an introduction to modern societies. Blackwell, Oxford

Karibi-Whyte AG (1987) The relevance of the judiciary in the polity – in historical perspective. Nigerian Institute of Advanced Legal Studies, Lagos

Lawyers Committee for Human Rights (1992) The Nigerian police force: a culture of impunity. Lawyers Committee for Human Rights, New York

McAuslan JPWB, Ghai YP (1970) Public law and political change in Kenya. Oxford University Press, Oxford

Morris C (1972) The discovery of the Individual: 1050–1200. Harper & Row, New York

Nwabueze BO (1977) Judicialism in commonwealth Africa. C. Hurst Publishers, London

Nwakeze PC (1987) A critique of Olúfẹ́mi Táíwò's criticism of legal positivism and African legal tradition. Int Philos Q 27:101–105

Odinkalu CA (1998) The individual complaints procedures of the African commission on human and peoples' rights: a preliminary assessment. Trans Law Contemp Prob 8(2):359–405

Okafor FU (1984) Legal positivism and the African legal tradition. Int Philos Q 24(2):157–164

Oladosu J (2001) Choosing a legal theory on moral grounds: an African case for legal positivism. West Afr Rev 2. http://westafricareview.com

Reisman M (1982) The individual under African law in comprehensive context. In: Dr. Takirambudde PN (ed) The individual under African law. University of Swaziland, Department of Law, Kwaluseni

Táíwò O (1985) Legal positivism and the African legal tradition: a reply. Int Philos Q 25(2):197–200

Táíwò O (1999) The rule of law: the new Leviathan? Can J Law Jurisprud 12(1):151–168

Udombana NJ (2000) Toward the African court on human and peoples' rights: better late than never. Yale Hum Right Dev Law J 3:45–111

Verhelst TG (1971) Legal process and the individual: African source materials. In: Proceedings of the economic commission for Africa conference of African jurists. Economic Commission for Africa, Addis Ababa

Vukor-Quarshie GNK (1997) Criminal justice administration in Nigeria: Saro-Wiwa in review. Crim Law Forum 8(1):87–110

Woodman GR, Obilade AO (1995) African law and legal theory. New York University Press, New York

Part II
Rights

Chapter 7
African Values, Human Rights and Group Rights: A Philosophical Foundation for the Banjul Charter

Thaddeus Metz

7.1 Introduction

Probably the most salient feature of ethical-political-legal thought among indigenous sub-Saharans is the importance accorded to community. Some interpreters of the African tradition maintain that community is itself to be valued for its own sake (e.g., Tutu 1999, pp. 34–35, 212–213), while others hold that living communally has the effect of enhancing some other, more basic value such as people's vitality or well-being (e.g., Magesa 1997; Gyekye 2010).[1] Regardless of the precise relationship between community and morality, there is little doubt that the 'communitarian' label is apt for characterizing sub-Saharan norms (Gyekye 1997, pp. 35–76; Masolo 2004; Wiredu 2008).

There is a *prima facie* tension between communitarianism, on the one hand, and a concern for human rights, on the other. Crudely put, a communitarian perspective accords some kind of normative primacy to a society, whereas human rights are by definition duties that others have to treat individuals in certain ways, regardless of group membership, and even when not doing so would be better for society. Is there any place for human rights in an Afro-communitarian political and legal philosophy, and, if so, what is it?

In this article, I seek to answer these questions, in part by critically exploring one of the most influential theoretical works on human rights in the sub-Saharan region, namely, Claude Ake's 'The African Context of Human Rights' (1987). In this piece Ake famously maintains that a characteristically Western approach to rights is inappropriate for indigenous black peoples, in two major respects. First, Ake contends that although a human rights legal framework might be suitable for an

[1] While still others, such as Bujo (1997, pp. 24–42, 2001, pp. 45–71), contend that communal dialogue is the way that one can reliably come to know how to behave rightly.

T. Metz (✉)
University of Johannesburg, Johannesburg, South Africa
e-mail: tmetz@uj.ac.za

O. Onazi (ed.), *African Legal Theory and Contemporary Problems: Critical Essays*, Ius Gentium: Comparative Perspectives on Law and Justice 29,
DOI 10.1007/978-94-007-7537-4_7,

'individualistic' society, it is not for one of the sort common among traditional sub-Saharan societies, where rights should be ascribed to groups in the first instance. Second, Ake maintains that, insofar as rights are relevant, rights to socio-economic goods are of much more importance in an underdeveloped, African context than rights to civil liberties, due process and the like.

Using Ake's article as a foil,[2] I draw on values salient in sub-Saharan moral worldviews to construct a new, unified philosophy of rights that not only provides reason to doubt his two claims, but also offers a promising way to reconcile a communitarian framework with a robust prizing of human rights. After articulating Ake's position (Sect. 7.2), I spell out in detail the proposition that individuals have a dignity in virtue of being capable of community, and provide evidence for its African credentials (Sect. 7.3). Then, I indicate how a basic requirement to treat our special capacity for community with respect plausibly accounts in a unified manner for a variety of rights, including central human rights (Sect. 7.4) and 'group' ones that intuitively exist (Sect. 7.5). This analysis will, in effect, indicate what all the major articles of the *African (Banjul) Charter on Human and Peoples' Rights* (OAU 1981) morally have in common. Finally, I relate this theory of rights to Ake's two claims above (Sect. 7.6). That is, I show that the idea of individual rights in fact comports well with prominent African judgments of human dignity, viz., that Ake is wrong to think that for rights to 'make any sense at all in the African context' they must be ones of a group (1987, pp. 9–10), and I also argue that Ake is wrong to think that 'liberal' rights are of 'no value to most Africans', as he puts it (1987, p. 10). I conclude by considering objections to the claim that I have effected a genuine reconciliation between Afro-communitarianism and human rights, and by providing reasons to favour my reconciliation over Kwame Gyekye's influential attempt to wed the two perspectives (Sect. 7.7).

7.2 Rights and Ake's Communitarianism

In this section, I first briefly explain what a human right is and how it differs from related concepts such as a group right, after which I present Ake's view that many human rights, particularly those related to civil liberties, due process and political opportunities much prized by those in the West, are unimportant from an African perspective. For Ake, properly valuing community means deeming group rights and rights to socio-economic development to be paramount.

7.2.1 Rights and Types of Them

At the core, one has a *right* to something, by definition, insofar as agents have a stringent duty to treat one a certain way that must be fulfilled even if not doing so

[2] Note that I do not seek to engage with the corpus of Ake's work.

would result in a marginally improved quality of life or in somewhat fewer violations of this same duty in the long run. For example, having a right to property means that others may not steal your things, either in order to make themselves or someone else better off, or even to prevent other thefts elsewhere in society. Note that this definition leaves open the idea that a given right of yours (to property) could be properly overridden by other kinds of considerations, e.g., by another's stronger right (to life).

A human right is of course a particular kind of right, one that, by definition, has three properties, at least one of which is lacking in other kinds of rights. First, inherent to the concept of a human right is that its bearer is an individual, and, specifically, least controversially, a human person. There is debate about whether human rights apply to literally all human beings, including those that are not persons (such as anencephalic infants), and whether they apply to only human beings (or also to, say, chimps). It is therefore wise, when simply defining what I (and what I presume most readers) mean by 'human right', to be neutral among these competing views.

Second, a human right is essentially such that others have a stringent duty to the individual because she has some quality shared by characteristic human beings. Roughly, one has a human right in virtue of one's humanity. That is a rough statement because it suggests that there is in fact some property that every human being has that makes one owed certain duties, where such a claim is controversial and need not be invoked by an adherent to human rights. One might have something fairly called a 'human' right if others must treat you a certain way because you exhibit a feature that *nearly* all, even if not *literally* all, human beings have.

Third, it is part of the meaning of the phrase 'human rights' to be speaking of duties that are so important as to warrant recognition by at least legal institutions. Such recognition usually comes in the forms of: organizing society so that people are not disposed to violate these duties; using defensive force to ward off immediate threats of their violation; censuring, perhaps by punishing, those who have violated them; and facilitating compensation for victims of violations of them. Saying that implicit in human rights discourse is the idea that a political body such as a state ought to recognize them is not to say that they are in fact recognized. I side with those who maintain that human rights are moral categories that in principle offer a vantage point from which to criticize an entire system of enforcement as unjust.

In sum, one essentially has a *human* right to something insofar as agents have a duty to treat an individual a certain way that obtains because of some quality she shares with (nearly) all other human beings, that must be fulfilled even if not doing so would result in a marginally improved quality of life or in somewhat fewer violations of this same duty in the long run, and that is so weighty that it ought to be recognized by legal institutions. I submit that rights other than human rights are well construed as missing at least one of three qualifying features. For instance, a right that does not warrant public recognition is perhaps best called a *merely* 'moral' right. A right that obtains not because of features typical of human beings, but rather of animals, is reasonably called an 'animal' right. And, of most interest to readers of this chapter, a right the bearer of which is not an individual, but instead some kind of collectivity composed of individuals, is aptly called a 'group' right.

7.2.2 Ake on Human Rights

Many sub-Saharan intellectuals are suspicious of the *concept* of human rights, and not merely the *discourse* about it. Human rights discourse has often been criticized for serving ideological purposes, e.g., for legitimating forms of imperial intervention in the affairs of African and other countries. Such criticism does not necessarily reject the claim that there *are* human rights, but instead focuses on the undesirable functions of certain *(mis)representations* of them. However, there are theorists in the African tradition, similar to Jeremy Bentham and Karl Marx in the Western, who reject the existence of human rights as such, or at least the standard Western interpretation of them. The Nigerian political scientist Claude Ake is foremost among them, although there are others.[3]

I read Ake as making two major objections to a human rights-centred approach to development in sub-Saharan Africa. One is that '(t)he idea of human rights, or legal rights in general, presupposes a society which is atomized and individualistic' (Ake 1987, p. 5, see also 9), whereas typical indigenous black societies are not. By terms such as 'atomized' and 'individualistic', Ake means that people tend to think of their own good as distinct from the interests of others. It is only given that kind of orientation, where people are 'conscious of their separateness' (Ake 1987, p. 5), that it can make sense to claim a right, to hold that others have a duty to treat one a certain way even if not doing so would benefit the broader society.

Ake suggests that the values characteristic of black Africans, in contrast, include 'a sense of belonging to an organic whole, be it a family, a clan, a lineage or an ethnic group' (1987, p. 9), such that 'we do not allow that the individual has any claims which may override that of the society' (1987, p. 5). If sub-Saharans tend to 'assume harmony, not divergence of interests' (1987, p. 5), i.e., that the individual's good is compatible with, and indeed *constituted* by, doing whatever would help others, then rights are out of place, for there would not, it appears, be any need to protect individuals from treatment that would benefit the broader society.

Ake's characterization of African values is arguably embodied in maxims that are often taken to encapsulate them, such as 'I am because we are' (e.g., Mbiti 1969, p. 108) and 'A person is a person through other persons' (e.g., Tutu 1999, p. 35). Although these sayings will sound like descriptive banalities to English-speakers unfamiliar with the context, they are in fact primarily evaluative claims. They express the idea that one's highest good is a matter of developing one's personhood or living a genuinely human way of life, which one can do only insofar as one enters into community with other people. The suggestion that African values typically include the idea that the best life is utterly a function of supportive relationships with others seems to jibe with Ake's view that human rights are out of place in sub-Saharan societies; for such rights imply that one's urgent interests can be satisfied only if others forgo well-being that they could have otherwise had.

---

[3] For similar views, see, e.g., Legesse (1980); Gbadegesin (1991, pp. 66–67); Nkondo (2007).

Ake does not reject the concept of rights altogether, but merely individual ones. He maintains that the idea that the individual's good is constituted by what she does for the community is consistent with, and probably even entails, the idea of a group right:

> It is necessary to extend the idea of human rights to include collective human rights for corporate social groups such as the family, the lineage, the ethnic group. Our people still think largely in terms of collective rights and express their commitment to it constantly in their behaviour....If the idea of human rights is to make any sense at all in the African context, it has to incorporate them in a concept of communal human rights. (Ake 1987, pp. 9, 9–10)

Given the way I have defined 'human right' as having an individual bearer, it is a contradiction in terms to speak of a 'communal human right' in the way Ake proposes. However, his underlying point is clear: group rights are apt for an African value system, and not individual ones such as what I and most readers mean by 'human rights'.

Ake has another major reason for rejecting human rights in an African context, at least as normally understood by Western and United Nations advocates of them. The latter tend to believe that rights to freedom of expression and association, to a fair trial and to hold public office are vitally important and worthy of substantial attention from the state. According to Ake, however, if these rights are appropriate, they are only in a society that differs from the sub-Saharan region in not suffering from extreme poverty, for two reasons.

First, Ake claims that what he calls these 'liberal' rights can have value only if there are the resources to make use of them, which Africans by and large lack. Ake provides the example of someone who has the legal right to run for a government position but lacks the time and money to campaign, as he must scramble just to stay alive. For Ake, since this right is 'unrealizable', it is pointless to recognize.

Second, access to socio-economic goods that would help people in 'the struggle for existence in its brutal immediacy' (1987, p. 5) are much more important than rights for those who can 'afford to pursue the more esoteric aspects of self-fulfilment' (1987, p. 5). Supposing one had to choose between food to stave off hunger and medicine to combat disease, on the one hand, or the rights to freedom of speech and thought, on the other, it appears foolish to opt for the latter.

Interestingly, although Ake rejects the applicability of the *concept* of human rights, viz., ones the bearer of which is an individual, he believes that it could be useful to invoke the *phrase* 'human rights' when seeking to foster development in the sub-Saharan region (1987, p. 8). As a rhetorical device, he thinks that *talk* of 'human rights' could be a promising way to unite various constituencies into a coalition that would struggle against fascism, poverty and illness on the African continent.

In sum, Ake maintains that standard Western ideas of rights are not suitable for an African context. For traditional black peoples, the bearer of rights ought to be a group and the objects of them ought above all to be socio-economic goods, whereas, for Westerners, it is suitable for the bearer of rights to be an individual and their objects to include civil liberties, fair trials and similar opportunities. In the rest of this chapter, I provide reason to believe that the concept of human rights is, *contra* Ake, suitable for traditional sub-Saharan societies. I argue that the idea of human (individual) rights is part and parcel of typical African acceptance of a requirement to respect human dignity, and that such respect entails recognition of the so-called 'liberal' rights alongside socio-economic ones.

7.3 Dignity and Community

Ake is correct that African values tend to be communitarian, but they are best interpreted as being only 'moderately' so, as the Ghanaian political philosopher Kwame Gyekye has influentially put it (1997, pp. 35–76), meaning that they are consistent with human rights. My aim in this section is not so much the empirical one of providing evidence that indigenous black peoples actually widely believed in human rights, something an anthropologist would do,[4] but rather the theoretical one of tracing a variety of human and other rights from basic values that many of them have accepted. Whereas Ake argues that fundamental commitments held by many traditional African cultures rule out human rights as fitting for them, my goal is to demonstrate the opposite.

Crucially, Ake neglects the substantial literature indicating that many sub-Saharan societies and their intellectual expositors have believed that individual human beings have a dignity. Kwame Gyekye and Kwasi Wiredu, who have done the most to relate the worldviews of the Ghanaian Akan to an English-speaking philosophical audience, contend that the Akan believe that each human being has a dignity by virtue of being a child of God (Wiredu 1996, p. 158; Gyekye 1997, p. 63). The Nigerian philosopher-theologians Pantaleon Iroegbu and Godfrey Onah each ground their respective Afro-centric moral frameworks on the value of human life, with the former explicitly speaking in terms of 'human dignity' (2005a) and the latter remarking that 'Africans have a sacred reverence for life' (n.d.). Francis Deng, the renowned theorist of human rights in Africa, maintains that the Dinka, a people in the South Sudan, believe in human dignity, grounded on one's having been created by God (2004, p. 501). Mutombo Nkulu N'Sengha, who has written on the Banjul Charter and its bearing on a global ethic, makes it clear that his Luba people, from the central region of Africa, believes in human dignity, as grounded principally on human life (1998), and the influential moral theorist Bénézet Bujo, from the same area, routinely appeals to the concept of human dignity when articulating a characteristically African ethical perspective. Usually, Bujo grounds our dignity on our life-force, as the divine spark in us (2001, pp. 2, 138–139, 142), but on occasion suggests that it inheres in our communal nature (2001, p. 88). Finally, in South Africa one finds members of the Constitutional Court invoking human dignity when articulating what '*ubuntu*' means (1995: para 225, 309–311), the term for

[4] For a brief summary of some of the anthropological research and my judgment about what it shows, see Metz (2012a).

humanness that is often used to capture morality among Zulu, Xhosa and Ndebele speakers and others in the southern African region. South African intellectuals and philosophers also routinely maintain that *ubuntu* involves treating others, who have a dignity, with respect (Ramose 1999, pp. 49–64, 138–145, 163–195; Botman 2000; Mnyaka and Motlhabi 2005).

It would be too strong to say that there is a 'consensus' of those familiar with African ethics that dignity is central to it,[5] but these citations (which could be easily multiplied) indicate that at least one major swathe of sub-Saharan moral thought appeals to the idea. The proposition that typical individual human beings have an equally superlative, essential worth that demands respect is widely taken by ethicists, jurists, activists and the like to entail the appropriateness of the category of human rights. In an African context, our dignity is most often thought to inhere in our souls or life-force (or both), sometimes in our communal nature, and occasionally in our intelligence.

Elsewhere I have argued that dignity *qua* our capacity for community is the most promising idea in sub-Saharan moral thought with which to ground human rights, rejecting the other candidates of divinity, vitality and rationality (Metz 2010, 2011a, 2012b, c). Rather than recount that criticism, I simply here present my findings. That is, I now indicate how our ability to enter into community with others, construed in a certain way, is plausibly what gives us a dignity, and in the next sections demonstrate how that value promises to be the thread sewing together human and other intuitively appealing rights found in the Banjul Charter.

To begin see how our communal nature can make good sense of human dignity and human rights, consider what is plausibly meant by 'community'. I have argued that the ideal of community in characteristic African thought is well construed as the combination of two logically distinct kinds of relationship, what I call 'identity' and 'solidarity'.[6] To identify with each other is largely for people to think of themselves as members of the same group – that is, to conceive of themselves as a 'we', to engage in joint projects, coordinating their behaviour to realize common ends, and to be emotionally invested in the group's doings, e.g., with regard to pride and shame. Identity is a matter of people sharing a way of life, with the opposite of it being instantiated by people defining themselves in opposition to one another and seeking to undermine one another's ends.

To exhibit solidarity with one another is for people to care about each other's quality of life, in two senses. First, it means that they engage in mutual aid, acting in ways that are expected to benefit each other (ideally, repeatedly over time). Second, caring is a matter of people's attitudes such as emotions and motives being positively oriented toward others' good, say, by sympathizing with them and helping them for their sake. For people to fail to exhibit solidarity could be for them to be indifferent to each other's flourishing or to exhibit ill will in the form of hostility and cruelty.

---

[5] For examples of apparently resolutely utilitarian interpretations, see Tangwa (1996); Bewaji (2004).

[6] See Metz (2007), from which next few paragraphs borrow.

Identity and solidarity are different sorts of relationship. One could identify with others but not exhibit solidarity with them – probably workers in relation to management in a capitalist firm. One could also exhibit solidarity with others but not identify with them, e.g., by making anonymous donations to a charity. My proposal, following the intimations of several African thinkers, is that a promising conception of community as worth prizing includes both kinds of relationship. Consider how the two elements are found in these sub-Saharan ethical perspectives: 'Every member is expected to consider him/herself an integral part of the whole and to play an appropriate role towards achieving the good of all' (as per the Yoruba philosopher Segun Gbadegesin 1991, p. 65); '(T)he purpose of our life is community-service and community-belongingness' (according to the Igbo theologian Pantaleon Iroegbu 2005b, p. 442); 'Harmony is achieved through close and sympathetic social relations within the group' (so says the former South African Constitutional Court Justice Yvonne Mokgoro 1998, p. 3); 'If you asked *ubuntu* advocates and philosophers: What principles inform and organise your life?....the answers would express commitment to the good of the community in which their identities were formed, and a need to experience their lives as bound up in that of their community' (sums up the South African intellectual Muxe Nkondo 2007, p. 91).

Some Africans might suggest that we have a dignity by virtue of *actually* being part of a community, as above. For instance, H. Russel Botman remarks that '(t)he dignity of human beings emanates from the network of relationships, from being in community; in an African view, it cannot be reduced to a unique, competitive and free personal ego' (2000; see also Cobbah 1987; Bujo 2001, p. 88). However, this position would counterintuitively entail that individuals who were not in relationships of identity and solidarity, say, those in solitary confinement, would lack a dignity.[7]

In order to be able to conclude that nearly all human beings, including isolated ones, have a dignity on grounds of community, one must hold the view that they have it in virtue of being the sort of individual naturally *capable* of communal relationships with others. If one were driving a bus and had to choose between striking a normal human being and a cat, one should run over the cat, the intuitive explanation for which is that the human being is worth more. On the African-based view I am advocating, the reason the human being is worth more than the cat or indeed anything else in the animal, vegetable and mineral kingdoms is that one has the essential *ability* to commune with others, roughly, the biological capacity to think of oneself as bound up with others and to act for their sake, i.e., *to be friendly or to love*, in a broad sense.

To sum up, I have pointed out that it is common for theorists of African ethics to maintain that human beings have a dignity that demands respect, and have also articulated the view that what confers dignity on us is our capacity for community of a kind that is also influential in sub-Saharan moral thought. In the next section, I explain how a system of human and other important rights characteristic of the Banjul Charter follows from a basic principle requiring us to honour our special capacity for community *qua* identity and solidarity.

---

[7] Setting aside highly contested metaphysical claims to the effect that, say, one is always already in community with spiritual beings such as God and ancestors.

7.4 From the Dignity of Our Communal Nature to Human Rights

African values are well known for being communitarian, on the one hand, but also, as discussed in the previous section, for recognizing the dignity of individuals, on the other. A theoretically promising way to combine these values is in the form of a principle prescribing *respect for persons in virtue of their dignity as beings capable of community*. In this section I demonstrate how this philosophical articulation of salient sub-Saharan values provides a basis for a variety of human rights. The rough idea is that human rights are understood to be duties that the state and other agents have to protect, enable and otherwise express respect for people's ability to commune, where human rights violations are conceived as infringements or other degradations of that ability.[8]

7.4.1 *Socio-Economic Goods*

If what makes us special is our capacity for relationships of identity and solidarity, then the state has a duty to fight poverty, as probably does any other, wealthy agent well placed to do so. Treating people as having the ability to commune and as having a dignity by virtue of that requires fostering community by helping the worst off, for two reasons.

First, if the state did not adopt welfare programmes, it would be failing to respond to the people in its territory as individuals with whom to relate on a communal basis. The state would not be fostering relationships of mutual aid consequent to sympathetic altruism between it and residents, were it to leave them to fend for themselves, and, furthermore, residents would be unlikely to share a sense of togetherness with such a state.

Second, for the state to prize people as capable of community means helping them to develop it amongst themselves, which, in turn, means providing the kinds of resources likely to enable the maintenance and spread of identity and solidarity between residents. Such resources are naturally going to include goods such as money, education, food and healthcare, which will keep people alive and able to engage in joint projects for one another's benefit. However, the relevant resources will also include information, infrastructure, technology, labour and the like that would foster communal relationships and combat anti-social ones, with examples being women's shelters, counselling services, neighbourhood parks and reconciliatory projects.

---

[8] Some of the analysis of human rights is taken from other, recent work (Metz 2010, 2011a, b, 2012b, c), while the discussion of group rights is entirely new; the major contribution of this article is to demonstrate how both human and peoples' rights plausibly have a common, African source in the dignity of our capacity for community.

In sum, if the state did not fight poverty and thereby failed either to exhibit identity and solidarity with its residents or to enable residents to exhibit these relationships with one another, then it would be failing to treat our capacity for such relationships as having the highest value in the world and hence would be violating so-called 'positive' human rights.

7.4.2 Political Power

It is common for African political theorists to point out that traditional sub-Saharan societies are plausibly viewed as recognizing human rights to participation in governance (e.g., Gyekye 1992; Wiredu 1996, pp. 172–190; Bujo 1997, pp. 157–180; Ramose 1999, pp. 135–152; Legesse 2001). Many indigenous black peoples had chiefs or kings who tended to make decisions consequent either to consensus among popularly appointed elders or to anyone speaking her mind about the issue. The legitimacy of political leaders rested on not merely the extent to which they would act for the sake of the common good, but also the consensus-oriented and widely consultative procedures by which they would determine how to act.

These and other democratic orientations, such as one vote for each person, are straightforwardly viewed as ways of respecting people's capacity for community. A state that denied its residents the final authority to make political decisions would particularly degrade their ability to identify with one another, as not only would the state fail to genuinely *share* a way of life with its residents, but also residents themselves would not be sharing a way of life with one another. In addition, a state that accorded people the unequal opportunity to influence political decision-making, say, by giving more votes to the educated, would be failing to treat people as *equally* valuable for being capable of identifying with one another.

7.4.3 Due Process

A basic obligation to respect people's capacity for community means treating them in accordance with the way they have elected to use it. Although one ought in the first instance respond to everyone in a communal way, if another person is acting in an anti-social way, and the only way to make him stop or to assist his victims is to respond in a comparably anti-social way to him, it would not degrade his capacity for community to do so. For example, if someone has stolen an item and refuses to give it back, the state would not be treating his capacity for community disrespectfully if it forced him to do so. Similarly, if a person has foreseeably instilled fear in others because of his violent actions and given them good reason to spend resources protecting themselves, then it would not be degrading to incapacitate him or engage in other punitive actions likely to reduce the likelihood of crime (cf. Holmgren 1983).

Although it would not be degrading to exhibit division and ill will toward another when necessary to counteract her exhibition of these behaviours, it would be degrading to be anti-social in these ways to someone who has not been so herself. Hence, it becomes urgent for a third-party such as a state to resolve disputes between residents, and to do so in a way that is by and large 'fact-finding', i.e., a matter of determining who has been an aggressor and who has not. That, in turn, requires according individuals the rights involved in what is usually called a 'fair trial', e.g., the right not to be punished without guilt having been established, the right to the assistance of an attorney in understanding and making use of the law, the right to mount a defence, the right not to be coerced into confession and so on. All these protections are essential in order to separate the guilty from the innocent, i.e., those who have misused their special capacity to commune with others from those who have not, and to distribute burdens appropriately.

7.4.4 *Civil Liberties*

The last major cluster of human rights that I consider is the collection of 'negative' ones to non-interference. If people have any human rights at all, they have them not to be ethnically cleansed or enslaved for economic advantage, not to be raped for a sense of power, not to be tortured for the fun of it, not to be segregated on a racial basis and not to be assaulted for voicing one's political opinions. I again suggest that violations of these rights are well understood as degradations of people's capacity for community.

In the previous sub-section, I suggested that it is not disrespectful to act in an anti-social way toward someone if that is the only way to rebut his own anti-sociality, but that it would be disrespectful otherwise. Such a principle suggests that what genocide, torture, slavery, systematic rape and other gross infringements of civil liberties have in common is that they are instances of substantial anti-sociality, i.e., division and ill will, directed to those who have not acted this way themselves, thereby denigrating their special capacity to exhibit the opposite traits of identity and solidarity. Concretely, one who engages in such practices treats people, who have not themselves been anti-social or unloving, with great enmity or in an extremely unloving way: The actor treats others as separate and inferior, instead of enjoying a sense of togetherness; the actor undermines others' ends, as opposed to engaging in joint projects with them; the actor harms others for own sake or for an ideology, as opposed to engaging in mutual aid; and the actor evinces negative attitudes toward others' good, rather than acting consequent to a sympathetic reaction to it.

So far, I have explained how the two salient African values of dignity and community, when theoretically united in the principle that agents ought to respect people because of their capacity for community *qua* identity and solidarity, are plausibly at the basis of a wide array of human rights. It would be degrading of individuals, and more specifically their ability to commune with one another, if the state did not fight poverty, were undemocratic, did not guarantee a fair trial, or infringed freedoms of bodily integrity, movement and the like. In the next section, I address the category of rights that Ake believes should be deemed primary in African societies and that famously figures prominently in the Banjul Charter, namely, group rights.

7.5 Individual Dignity, Group Rights and the Value of Community

Group rights are ones in which the bearer is not an individual but rather some kind of assemblage of them. The Banjul Charter is well known for speaking of a 'people' as the relevant group, and there is substantial debate in the literature about what that term is supposed mean, viz., whether it stands for a state or a potentially non-political group such as a nation, and, if the latter, what is involved in the notion of a nation.

Setting the issue of the bearer aside for now, one finds in the Banjul Charter two notable clusters of people's rights, both of which the Ake of 'The African Context of Human Rights' would likely accept, given his clear commitment to fighting what he calls 'fascism' and to meeting basic human needs. First, there are rights of a people not to be dominated and to resist domination (Article 20), and, second, there are rights of a people to natural resources, socio-economic development and an environment necessary for the latter (Articles 21, 22, 24).

A third plausible candidate for a group right is that to culture. *The Charter for African Cultural Renaissance*, recently adopted by the African Union (AU 2006), speaks of: African peoples evolving, being provided resources, and being enriched (Preamble and Articles 3, 5), the rights of minorities to their cultures (Article 5), the cultural advancement of African states (Article 18) and the African diaspora being entitled to consideration (Articles 30, 32, 33). It is natural to think of talk of duties with respect to peoples, minorities, states and a diaspora as being group-based.

Rights to self-determination, socio-economic development and culture do seem to exist, but the question is whether a group is indeed the ultimate bearer of these rights. There are two common ways to conceive of these kinds of rights in the literature, but I reject both in favour of a third alternative.

One way is to accept that groups have an intrinsic value in themselves[9] on the basis of which they are bearers of these and potentially other rights. Working within the community-oriented framework I articulated above, one might suggest that it is not only individuals capable of community that have a dignity, but also actual communities, i.e., networks of identity and solidarity, themselves. If community itself had a superlative, inner value in the way that individuals capable of this relationship do, then it, too, would be good candidate to bear rights.

[9] Or are capable of flourishing, a view that Ake might favour in light of his apparent adherence to an 'interest' theory of rights, as discussed below in Sect. 7.6.

This is not an implausible strategy, and the suggestion that the relevant group is a community *qua* the actualization of identity and solidarity is particularly worthy of exploration. However, I do not take it up, largely on grounds of theoretical parsimony. In seeking to 'codify' rights by appealing to fundamental African values, as I am in this chapter, it would, all things being equal, be more desirable to do so with a fewer rather than greater number of properties. It would therefore be theoretically neatest if I could account for all intuitively relevant rights with the single idea of the dignity of the individual's communal nature.

Another way to put the point is this: in order to know whether one has to appeal both to an individual and a group to account for fairly uncontested rights, one should first see whether it is possible to account for them with only one of these bases. In the following, therefore, I explore the view that all rights are grounded on the dignity of individuals, which dignity they have in virtue of being capable of identifying with others and exhibiting solidarity toward them. If that project turned out to be unsuccessful, then, and only then, would one have sufficient reason to appeal to groups as bearers of rights.

The main rival to the view that groups are valuable in themselves and so are bearers of rights, which the political scientist Chandran Kukathas calls the 'corporate' conception of a group (2006, p. 14), is the view that groups are of merely instrumental value, viz., a 'collective' conception of them (2006, p. 15). On the latter model, a group is nothing but individuals collected in a way that is useful for those individuals, where the collection is not good for its own sake. On this reading, any right that *appears* to be a group right is ultimately not, and is, upon reflection, seen to be merely a right of many individuals. Kukathas favours this view, and consequently deems genocide, for example, to be wrong not because it targets a people or some other group such as humanity, but rather because it kills many individuals (2006, p. 21).

Although I am loathe to maintain that groups have a dignity or other intrinsic value that makes them bearers of rights, I am also resistant to reducing the way to treat a group, particularly a community, to a mere tool to be used for the satisfaction of individual interests. There is instead a third option, one that is a natural companion of the view that individuals have a dignity insofar as they are capable of community. According to this alternate perspective, a community is *expressive* of what makes individuals dignified and so merits some moral protection.

Although a community, *qua* relationships of identity and solidarity, is of course not one and the same thing as the mere capacity for it inherent to the individual human beings who make it up, it is their actualization of that capacity. And it is plausible to suggest that respecting the individual's *capacity* for community requires giving moral consideration to the way he has *actualized* it, or, equivalently, that impairing relationships is to degrade those who have created them. When an agent disrupts communal relationships, say, those of family members, she is doing wrong not merely insofar as the *effects* on individuals will be harmful, but also in that she is *thereby* expressing disrespect of them as individuals who are special because of their ability to commune.

Returning to the specific apparently 'group' rights above, relating to self-determination, development and culture, I am committed to the view that, ultimately, the bearers of them are individuals. However, I need not hold the implausible view that when communal relationships are disrupted, the wrongfulness of it is entirely a matter of the bad *consequences* for individual lives; instead, I suggest that such disruptions are *in themselves* forms of degrading treatment of individuals. For example, overtaking an existent community, as instances of relationships of identity and solidarity, and dominating it for self-regarding ends is to treat disrespectfully the individuals who created it. And by a similar rationale, to fail to protect a group's culture is reasonably deemed to be a human rights violation because it would be a failure to prize individuals who have come to share a way of life.

7.6 Diagnosing Ake's Errors

In the previous two sections, I drew out some of the major implications of a principle of respect for the dignity of persons, where dignity is taken to inhere in the capacity for community *qua* identity and solidarity. I demonstrated how this African-based principle entails and plausibly explains several kinds of human rights and also does a reasonable job of accounting for what Ake and other African theorists have (mis) construed as 'group' rights. In this section, I return to – in order to refute – Ake's two major arguments against the view that a human rights-centred framework is appropriate for an African context.

First, recall Ake's claim that human and individual rights more generally are appropriate only for people who think of themselves as separate, i.e., as those who have a good that can obtain independently of their helping others. If one holds the view that the highest good for oneself is to enter into community with others, then, Ake suggests, individual entitlements that would come at the expense of others' interests are out of place. Recall his view that Africans 'do not allow that the individual has any claims which may override that of the society' (1987, p. 5).

In reply, consider, first, as I have suggested above, that African morality is well interpreted as summed up by the principle that one does the right action and becomes a good person by treating others who are capable of community with respect, where such treatment involves according them individual rights. There is a major difference between simply doing whatever would maximally promote community, on the one hand, and doing what would respect people for their ability to commune, on the other. From the perspective of a moral agent, one seeking to live a genuinely human way of life, one is obligated to respect dignified beings, which means acting in accordance with human rights. In short, thinking of one's own good as bound up with certain supportive relationships with others, which Ake and others rightly deem a communitarian perspective, is perfectly consistent with thinking of those others as having individual rights.

To nail down the point, consider this scenario. In the country where I reside, about only one in four people receives the organs she needs to survive. One way that

I could help prevent many deaths would be to painlessly euthanize healthy, innocent individuals and then redistribute their organs. At the cost of one life, I could save at least three or four more. But it would be mad to suppose that I would be properly valuing community to act in this manner. Instead, to do the right thing and become a real person, I must not do whichever act would maximize community, but instead must respect individuals in virtue of their capacity for it, i.e., deem others to have rights to life that may not be overridden for the sake of benefiting society. Ake formulates his thesis from the vantage point of one *claiming* rights against another, supposing that such an individual must be 'atomized' in her outlook, and he neglects to look at things from the perspective of one *respecting* the rights of another, which need not be 'atomized' or 'separate' at all.

Is Ake correct, however, that for an individual to claim a right against another is for her awareness to be one of 'separateness'? Interestingly, no, not necessarily. When standing up for one's rights, there need not be any implicit judgment that one's good is separate from the flourishing of one's group. Consider cases in which someone aims to kidnap me for a ransom or to rape me to experience a feeling of control. Such actions would not be ones from which the clan or broader society would benefit, and so when I claim that I have human rights not to be treated in these ways, I am not necessarily implying that what is best for me is separate from action for the sake of others.

Now, there will be *some* situations in which claiming individual rights would come at some cost to the society, and, indeed, that is essentially part of what it is to be a right (as defined above in Sect. 7.2). In these situations, I submit, it is not inappropriate to think one's interests as being separate from those of others. Consider the organs case again. If someone were to try to forcibly euthanize you in order to obtain organs necessary to save the lives of three strangers, you would be justified in resisting and doing so on the ground that what would be good for you in this scenario would conflict with the greater good. Here, if your consciousness were indeed 'atomized' or 'individualistic', it would be so in an innocuous sense, and would be neither undesirable, nor 'un-African'. To be sure, duties to aid nuclear and extended family members are weighty in characteristic sub-Saharan moral thought; one is expected to sacrifice quite a lot for others (e.g., Appiah 1998; Gyekye 1997, pp. 70–75). It does not follow, however, that deeply rooted in the African tradition is the view that, say, one lacks an individual right to life. Acknowledging that there can be extreme situations in which individuals are rightly sacrificed, e.g., where the entire community would perish unless an innocent were killed (cf. Gbadegesin 1991, pp. 66–67), shows merely that this right can sometimes be overridden, not that it fails to exist at all, either in fact or in African peoples' characteristic thought.

Recall Ake's second major reason for doubting that human rights are apt for traditional sub-Saharan societies, that civil liberties and political opportunities are not only unrealizable, but also unimportant, in conditions of extreme poverty. If one must choose between the right to free speech and the right to food, where one will go hungry without the right, then the latter takes priority and the former would be empty.

The point seems fair in cases of a stark choice of this sort, as even liberals such as John Rawls acknowledge (1971, pp. 542–543). However, things are very rarely so stark. One way to respond to Ake, here, would be to appeal to empirical evidence indicating that civil liberties and political opportunities in fact are extraordinarily instrumentally useful for obtaining socio-economic goods. That evidence has been around for at least a good 30 years, ranging from the analysis of Rhoda Howard (1983, pp. 467–482) to that of Amartya Sen (1999, esp. pp. 146–188). Indeed, one commentator summarizes Sen's thorough research on food scarcity as having established that 'no substantial famine has ever occurred in an independent and democratic country where government tolerates opposition, accepts the electoral press, and can be publicly criticized' (Vizard 2006, p. 116).

Rather than recount the social scientific data indicating that it is difficult to meet residents' basics needs without so-called 'liberal' rights, I pursue different, more theoretical angles in response to Ake. I point out how the African theoretical foundation above provides reason to doubt that these rights are irrelevant when 'unrealizable' for lack of resources, and also show how it entails that they have an importance comparable to socio-economic rights.

With regard to the conditions under which a right obtains, or is realizable, Ake is well construed as holding what is known as an 'interest theory' of rights, where a right is essentially a protection of an interest (Wenar 2011). Such a conception would make sense of his view that a right is pointless if it is not, in combination with other conditions, sufficient to satisfy the relevant interest. To quote one of Ake's examples,

> Granted, I have the freedom of speech. But where is this freedom, this right? I cannot read, I cannot write. I am too busy trying to survive I have no time to reflect. I am so poor I am constantly at the mercy of others. So where is this right and what is it really? (1987, p. 10)

It is no doubt true that the right to free speech would be of *greater* weight if the individuals who have it had time, education and the like to 'make use of it'. However, given a dignity-based perspective on rights, as articulated above (Sects. 7.3 and 7.4), it is plausible to think that the right to free speech would have *some* importance even under conditions of resource scarcity. In contrast to an interest-based conception of human rights, a dignity-based one construes rights as ways of treating a being with dignity respectfully. The function of a human right, on this latter view, is not necessarily to make anyone better off or to improve his quality of life; instead, at bottom, the point of a right is to avoid another person's degradation (Metz 2011a, pp. 541–543, 545–547).

Specifically, then, consider a state that curtailed people's freedoms of speech and association by forbidding them from criticizing government policies, firing academics who engage in research that the government disapproves of, interfering with the formation and running of trade unions and other civil society organizations, and requiring people of a certain gender or genetic disposition to enter certain professions. And think about a state that impaired people's ability to run for public office, say, by having previous leaders choose the next group of them, or by restricting eligibility to those of a certain lineage.

According to Ake, such policies would not count as rights violations, if people lacked the resources to make use of the legal possibilities. However, I submit that the policies would count as human rights violations, even in such a circumstance, as they would degrade people's capacity for community. In particular, consider the ability to identify with others, and, especially, to engage in joint projects. One's capacity to truly cooperate in an endeavour, or to genuinely share a way of life, would be treated disrespectfully by all the above policies, which would undermine relationships based on voluntary and transparent terms of interaction.

Note that some kind of dignity-based perspective among sub-Saharan leaders probably best explains the substantial growth over the past 10 or 15 years in regional mechanisms designed to protect human rights to civil liberties and political opportunities, such as the *Protocol to the African Charter on Human and Peoples' Rights*, which set up an African Court to enforce them (OAU 1998), and the *African Charter on Democracy, Elections and Governance* (AU 2003), both of which documents explicitly speak of the 'dignity' and 'sanctity' of human beings and of their 'human rights'.

Turning away from whether human rights exist and retain an importance in the absence of resources with which one could take full advantage of them, I address the final issue of whether civil liberties and political opportunities are as important as socio-economic goods. One way to question Ake's claim that they are not would be to appeal to interests that the former would satisfy and to weigh those interests against those satisfied by the latter.[10] Given a dignity-based approach to rights, however, I make a different argument.

Instead, I point out that there are several different respects in which one's capacity for communal relationships can be degraded, and that while there are different degrees of degradations, they are not captured by a civil-political versus economic divide. Above I argued that to treat another's capacity for community with respect plausibly requires observing rights to civil liberties, due process, political power and economic goods (Sect. 7.4). Withholding any of these entitlements would be to degrade the individual. It is true that it would be particularly degrading, say, for a state to withhold food from its residents, but it would appear no less degrading, and probably more, for a state to torture them because of their union activism or to execute them without trial because of their political views.

Such cases, and others, suggest the principle that the more intrusive a policy, the more degrading it is. The more state action impinges on one's survival, or selfhood, or bodily integrity, the more disrespectful, compared to reductions in what one might call 'sociality', e.g., taking money or putting under house arrest. The philosopher and development theorist Martha Nussbaum puts the point by saying that dignity is 'more deeply violated' when 'internal' capabilities are stunted than when 'combined' (or what she perhaps ought to call 'external') ones are (2011, pp. 30–31). Such a view is intuitive and cuts across the civil-political versus economic distinction.

[10] A strategy executed by Howard (1983, pp. 482–490), who invokes the value of moral integrity.

7.7 Conclusion: How to Be a Moderate Afro-Communitarian

In this chapter, I have critically addressed Claude Ake's view that human rights are inappropriate for an African context because of a communal value system shared by many sub-Saharans and because of the economic hardships many of them face. I have argued that although Ake is correct that traditional black peoples below the Sahara tend to think that the ability to live a human way of life is constituted by prizing communal relationships, it does not follow that human rights are inconsistent with such a perspective. Roughly, I pointed out that many of these peoples believe that individual human beings have a dignity, perhaps in virtue of their essential capacity to commune, that demands respect, i.e., that requires a moral agent to observe the human rights of others. I have also argued that awareness of the dignity-based foundation for human rights characteristic of much African moral thought enables one to see the moral significance of rights to civil liberties, due process and political power in comparison with those to socio-economic goods.

I conclude by responding to concerns about whether I have truly reconciled communitarian and human rights frameworks, and by defending the particular way I believe I have done so relative to Kwame Gyekye's influential reconciliation. Regarding the former, some might suggest that I have not in fact demonstrated how individual rights are compatible with a communitarian value system. For one, I have not addressed the concern that sometimes appealing to rights can cause rifts in society.[11] There will be many occasions when observing human rights would not only prevent communal relationships from forming, but also cause discordant ones. For another, I have, in the final analysis, denied that there are any group rights, and instead have sought to reduce peoples' rights to the rights of individuals to respect in virtue of their having actualized their dignified capacity to commune. If a perspective counts as 'communitarian' just insofar as a collective is prioritized, then it appears that I have failed to ground human rights in a communitarian framework.

In reply, I maintain, with much of the field, that there are degrees of communitarianism, ranging from 'moderate' to 'extreme', to use Gyekye's terminology. And I accept that the sort of communitarianism I have advanced here is not extreme. An extreme communitarianism might well either prescribe whichever actions maximize cohesion in the long run, or imply that groups are the ultimate bearers of moral claims. However, these are not the only possible or plausible forms of communitarianism. The moral philosophy I have articulated counts as 'communitarian' insofar as all its elements are based on the single, fundamental value of our communal nature, construed as the capacity to identify with others and to exhibit solidarity with them. I have contended that the best way to respond to the African value of community is not to treat individuals merely as a means to certain social ends, but rather to respect them as dignified because they are capable of community. Surely, to kill one innocent in order to benefit others, perhaps in trivial ways, is not to properly value communal relationships.

[11] An issue that goes beyond Ake's concern that appealing to rights implies an atomized conceptions of oneself.

Gyekye (1997, pp. 35–76) agrees with this conclusion, but provides different grounds for it. He, too, is a moderate communitarian, recognizing human dignity and corresponding individual rights. Gyekye provides three reasons for thinking that African values cohere with human rights, none of which, I now argue, is as compelling as the idea that human rights are well conceived as a matter of respecting beings who have a dignity because they are capable of community *qua* identity and solidarity.

First, Gyekye contends that pretty much whenever individual rights are observed, then the group can expect to flourish (1997, p. 64). A society, he points out, is likely to be better off when its members have the ability to 'do their own thing'. In reply, that might often be true, but will not always be true, as the organs thought experiment discussed in this chapter indicates. Sometimes there are deep conflicts of interest between individuals and the greater good, and in such scenarios, a tough choice must be made.

Second, Gyekye implicitly appears to hold that the appropriate moral framework must reflect the nature of the self, which, combined with the view that the self has both individual and social dimensions, entails that the correct morality must give consideration to a person's autonomy (1997, pp. 52–59). However, nothing morally prescriptive, viz., about how we ought to treat one another, follows merely from descriptive claims about what we are in fact like. The bare fact that individuals can step back and criticize communal norms does not mean that they should be given license to do so, a *non sequitur* that Gyekye appears to make.

Third, and most promising, Gyekye maintains that individuals have a dignity respect for which requires according human rights (1997, p. 63). While I of course am sympathetic to this line, Gyekye fails to flesh it out. He notes that a theorist could seek to ground dignity on either the individual having been created by God or her having the capacity for autonomous reasoning. However, he does not, in the end, provide reason to favour one or the other, and, furthermore, does not derive specific rights from a particular conception of human dignity (cf. Metz 2012c).

In contrast, in this chapter, I have spelled out a theory of human dignity with a clear Afro-communitarian pedigree and demonstrated how it can account for human and other rights that we intuitively have in a unified manner. The 'rational reconstruction' of sub-Saharan values undertaken here gives the reader strong reason to doubt the central claims of Ake's influential work on human rights in an African context, and occasions awareness of what might philosophically unify the human and peoples' rights typical of the Banjul Charter.[12]

References

African Union (AU) (2003) African charter on democracy, elections and governance. http://www.au.int/en/sites/default/files/AFRICAN_CHARTER_ON_DEMOCRACY_ELECTIONS_AND_GOVERNANCE.pdf

[12] For comments on this and related work, I thank Oche Onazi and Oritsegbubemi Tony Oyowe.

African Union (AU) (2006) Charter for African cultural renaissance. http://www.africa-union.org/root/au/documents/treaties/text/Charter%20-%20African%20Cultural%20Renaissance_EN.pdf
Ake C (1987) The African context of human rights. Afr Today 34:5–12
Appiah A (1998) Ethical systems, African. In: Craig E (ed) Routledge encyclopedia of philosophy online. http://www.rep.routledge.com/about
Bewaji J (2004) Ethics and morality in Yoruba culture. In: Wiredu K (ed) A companion to African philosophy. Blackwell, Oxford, pp 396–402
Botman HR (2000) The OIKOS in a global economic era: a South African comment. In: Cochrane JR, Klein B (eds) Sameness and difference: problems and potentials in South African civil society. The Council for Research in Values and Philosophy, Washington, DC. http://www.crvp.org/book/Series02/II-6/chapter_x.htm
Bujo B (1997) The ethical dimension of community (trans: Nganda CN) Paulines Publications, Nairobi
Bujo B (2001) Foundations of an African ethic: beyond the universal claims of western morality (trans: McNeil B) Crossroad Publishers, New York
Cobbah J (1987) African values and the human rights debate: an African perspective. Hum Right Q 9:309–331
Constitutional Court of the Republic of South Africa (1995) The state versus T Makwanyane and M Mchunu, Case No. CCT/3/94, http://www.saflii.org/
Deng F (2004) Human rights in the African context. In: Wiredu K (ed) A companion to African philosophy. Blackwell, Oxford, pp 499–508
Gbadegesin S (1991) African philosophy: traditional Yoruba philosophy and contemporary African realities. Peter Lang, New York
Gyekye K (1992) Traditional political ideas: their relevance to development in contemporary Africa. In: Wiredu K, Gyekye K (eds) Person and community; Ghanaian philosophical studies, I. Council for Research in Values and Philosophy, Washington, DC, pp 243–255
Gyekye K (1997) Tradition and modernity: philosophical reflections on the African experience. Oxford University Press, New York
Gyekye K (2010) African ethics. In: Zalta E (ed) The Stanford encyclopedia of philosophy. http://plato.stanford.edu/archives/fall2010/entries/african-ethics/
Holmgren M (1983) Punishment as restitution: the rights of the community. Crim Just Ethic 2:36–49
Howard R (1983) The full-belly thesis: should economic rights take priority over civil and political rights? Evidence from Sub-Saharan Africa. Hum Right Q 5:467–490
Iroegbu P (2005a) Right to life and the means to life: human dignity. In: Iroegbu P, Echekwube A (eds) Kpim of morality ethics. Heinemann Educational Books, Ibadan, pp 446–449
Iroegbu P (2005b) Beginning, purpose and end of life. In: Iroegbu P, Echekwube A (eds) Kpim of morality ethics. Heinemann Educational Books, Ibadan, pp 440–445
Kukathas C (2006) Genocide and group rights. Unpublished lecture given at the University of Cape Town
Legesse A (1980) Human rights in African political culture. In: Thompson K (ed) The moral imperatives of human rights: a world survey. University Press of America, Washington, DC, pp 123–138
Legesse A (2001) Oromo democracy: an indigenous African political system. Red Sea Press, Trenton
Magesa L (1997) African religion: the moral traditions of abundant life. Orbis Books, Maryknoll
Masolo DA (2004) Western and African communitarianism: a comparison. In: Wiredu K (ed) A companion to African philosophy. Blackwell, Oxford, pp 483–498
Mbiti J (1969) African religions and philosophy. Heinemann Educational Books, Oxford
Metz T (2007) Toward an African moral theory. J Polit Philos 15:321–341
Metz T (2010) Human dignity, capital punishment, and an African moral theory. J Hum Right 9:81–99
Metz T (2011a) *Ubuntu* as a moral theory and human rights in South Africa. Afr Hum Right Law J 11:532–559

Metz T (2011b) An African theory of dignity and a relational conception of poverty. In: de Gruchy J (ed) The humanist imperative in South Africa. African Sun Media, Stellenbosch, pp 233–241
Metz T (2012a) Human rights, African perspectives. In: Chatterjee D (ed) Encyclopedia of global justice. Springer, Dordrecht, pp 501–505
Metz T (2012b) African conceptions of human dignity: vitality and community as the ground of human rights. Hum Right Rev 13:19–37
Metz T (2012c) Developing African political philosophy: moral-theoretic strategies. Philosophia Afr 14:61–83
Mnyaka M, Motlhabi M (2005) The African concept of Ubuntu/Botho and its socio-moral significance. Black Theol 3:215–237
Mokgoro Y (1998) *Ubuntu* and the law in South Africa. Potchefstroom Electron Law J 1:1–11 http://www.ajol.info/index.php/pelj/article/viewFile/43567/27090
N'Sengha MN (1998) The African charter on human and peoples rights: an African contribution to the project of a global ethic. http://globalethic.org/Center/mutombo1.htm
Nkondo GM (2007) *Ubuntu* as a public policy in South Africa: a conceptual framework. Int J Afr Renaissance Stud 2:88–100
Nussbaum M (2011) Creating capabilities: the human development approach. Harvard University Press, Cambridge
Onah G (n.d.) The meaning of peace in African traditional religion and culture. http://www.afrikaworld.net/afrel/goddionah.htm
Organization of African Unity (OAU) (1981) African charter on human and peoples rights. http://www.africa-union.org/root/au/Documents/Treaties/Text/Banjul Charter.pdf
Organization of African Unity (OAU) (1998) Protocol to the African charter on human and peoples' rights on the establishment of an African court on human and peoples rights. http://www.african-court.org/fileadmin/documents/Court/Court Establishment/africancourt-humanrights.pdf
Ramose M (1999) African philosophy through Ubuntu. Mond Publishers, Harare
Rawls J (1971) A theory of justice. Harvard University Press, Cambridge
Sen A (1999) Development as freedom. Oxford University Press, Oxford
Tangwa G (1996) Bioethics: an African perspective. Bioethics 10:183–200
Tutu D (1999) No future without forgiveness. Random House, New York
Vizard P (2006) Poverty and human rights: Sen's 'capability perspective' explored. Oxford University Press, Oxford
Wenar L (2011) Rights. In: Zalta E (ed) The Stanford encyclopedia of philosophy. http://plato.stanford.edu/entries/rights/ – 2.2
Wiredu K (1996) Cultural universals and particulars: an African perspective. Indiana University Press, Bloomington
Wiredu K (2008) Social philosophy in postcolonial Africa: some preliminaries concerning communalism and communitarianism. S Afr J Philos 27:332–339

Chapter 8
Before Rights and Responsibilities: An African Ethos of Citizenship

Oche Onazi

8.1 Introduction

Sunday, 17th of January 2010, stands out as one of the most catastrophic days in the history of the small city of Jos, Nigeria. It marked another round of what has become an endless cycle of violence, destruction and loss of lives, which has come to redefine life within this city. Jos was until recent known as a melting pot for religion, ethnicity, tribe and race. Ironically, the capital city of Nigeria's so-called home of peace has become the home of terror, fear, revenge and death. On this particular day, as I prepared to travel back to Edinburgh to continue my studies, news reached me around noon that fighting had broken out in a certain part of the city. The news was vague; at first, it seemed nothing more than a rumour. It was unclear who was fighting or for what. To avoid taking any chances, it seemed wise to begin my three hour drive to Nigeria's capital Abuja, where I was to fly back to Edinburgh, much earlier than planned.

There was a bit of a hitch as I drove out of my neighbourhood, as some anxious and stern looking young men had mounted a temporary road block, presumably to protect the neighbourhood. As the vehicle I was in, along with another person, halted at the road block, it was surrounded by the men, and the questioning commenced. What is in the trunk of your car? What is in that suitcase? Do you have weapons? Are you Muslims? Are you Hausas? Luckily, we made it through the road block, and indeed, the remainder of the journey passed without any trouble. This is

In memory of Ogaba O. A. Onazi, Adadu I. Onazi, William Walbe, Cecilia Elayo, Yahaya Kanam, Ahmadu Sheidu, Ogaba Onazi, Anthony Pwol and Andrew Ikomi, who all, at one time or the other, touched my life in very special ways. I wish to thank Maksymilian Del Mar, Luke Devlin, and my father, Ochapa C. Onazi, for helpful comments to an earlier version of this chapter.

O. Onazi (✉)
University of Dundee, Dundee, UK
e-mail: o.onazi@dundee.ac.uk

O. Onazi (ed.), *African Legal Theory and Contemporary Problems: Critical Essays*, Ius Gentium: Comparative Perspectives on Law and Justice 29,
DOI 10.1007/978-94-007-7537-4_8,

perhaps because parts of my necklace became visible to one of the men. He exclaimed when he saw it – it's a rosary; they are Christians, let them go! It was only after I had arrived at Edinburgh the next day that I came to terms with the full implications of that encounter. This was indeed after hearing the latest news that what I initially believed to be a skirmish turned out to be an orgy of violence with senseless killing beyond imagination. It could have been worse I thought to myself, if I met a different group, a group not so hospitable to my identity, as has become synonymous with these sorts of conflicts. Fighting between so-called Christians and Muslims spread to other parts of the city and lasted for days. In certain locations, historical neighbours turned upon each other. Hundreds died, including, very tragically, many children.

While different reasons can be given for the various conflicts in Jos (Higazi 2011), and its environs, that encounter at the road block was my personal exposure to arguably the most difficult of factors, one, which also poses problems within different parts of contemporary Nigeria. That was my fortunate encounter with the indigene and settler dichotomy, Nigeria's problematic question of citizenship. This problem stems from local and societal perception of citizenship, which prevents all Nigerians from truly belonging, except in geographical locations where they can trace their tribal or ethnic origins.[1] This is what has led so many in Jos and its environs, especially many children, to their early graves.

The sporadic, but deadly conflicts in Jos, are not only fuelled by this perception of citizenship expressed in law, but also, even more problematically, in the mind-set or consciousness of society (Human Rights Watch 2006). It appears law, in the form of the Nigerian constitution, performs a dual function. It concretises and at the same time preserves this particular societal perception of citizenship. On the one hand, the constitution guarantees a range of legal rights without discrimination to all Nigerians, while, on the other; it creates two classes of citizens – the indigene and settler.[2] The consequence is that a Nigerian can either be a first or second-class citizen depending on if he or she is an indigene or settler to one of Nigeria's constituent states (Alubo 2004, pp. 145–146; Adebanwi 2009, pp. 352–353). The effect is often that an indigene's so-called citizenship rights takes precedence over the rights of settlers. It is this, for the most part, that is at the root of the Jos conflicts and continues to fuel much of the violence.

[1] Jos is the capital of Plateau State-Nigeria. It developed as a city of migrants under British colonial rule; it comprised then, as it does now, of indigenous ethno-religious groups, as well as groups from other parts of the country and parts of the world, particularly the Hausa ethnic group – the group at the centre of these problems. The conflicts are between indigenous (Afizere, Anaguta and Berom) groups on the one hand, and the Hausa ethnic group, a numerically superior group in the wider Nigerian context, but inferior in Jos and neighbouring towns and villages, on the other hand. There are religious dividing lines among these groups. The indigenous groups are predominantly Christian, while the Hausa are predominantly Muslim. This is perhaps an additional reason why the grievances have taken such an extreme dimension. In Jos, as in other parts of Nigeria, there is often a blurry distinction between religious and ethnic identity.

[2] The Constitution of the Federal Republic of Nigeria 1999, s 223(2)(b) and 318(1).

Since that encounter at the road block, I have not only been puzzled by this problem, but more broadly by the idea of citizenship, not only because it is at the heart of the Jos conflicts, but that it is also the key to perhaps a lasting solution to many of Africa's troubles. On deeper reflection, I have come to appreciate that these issues are not unique to Jos or Nigeria, as battle lines have been drawn around a similar question in Kenya (Abdullah 2004), South Africa (Ndlovu-Gatsheni 2007), Congo, Rwanda, Burundi, Uganda, Zimbabwe (Mamdani 2001, 1996),[3] and very recently, Cote d'Ivoire (Marshall-Fratani 2006) to mention a few instances. In researching into this problem I was struck by the fact that although a lot has been written or proposed to address the question, very little consideration has been given to the extent to which the decline of societal or moral values contributes to fuelling such violent disagreements and animosity among people. It seems obvious to me that when citizens brutally kill or maim one another, for whatever reason, or when they fail to empathise with those who have been injured or lost their loved ones; this is indicative of the complete breakdown or decline of the basic moral values of society, values, which remain integral to societal connectedness, collective flourishing, belonging and integration. It is the question of moral values that I take as my point of departure from most of the literature on this question, which instead prioritise the need for clearly defined and universal citizenship rights as the solution to this problem (see, for example, Adejumobi 2001, pp. 148–170).

If, citizenship means more than the rights and responsibilities of the membership of a political community, but also 'individual and group character or virtue' (Burdette 1942, p. 269)[4] achieved through 'understanding, sympathy and practice' (1942), then my argument is that it provides an appropriate context to encourage the kind of moral values necessary for societal connectedness, collective flourishing and belonging. What is being suggested is that there is a type of ethical life (Bankowski 2007) implied in being a citizen, one which embodies a set of moral values to act responsibly in relation to others, something which is taken for granted through a commitment to rights (Carr 2006, pp. 444–446), and responsibilities.

Although the ethical life of a citizen implies a proper understanding of the way of life (Bankowski 2007) associated with the concept (especially how it contributes to individual and collective flourishing), the ethical life, however, is different, but

---

[3] Mamood Mamdani (1996, 2001) has famously described the indigene and settler dichotomy as one of the continuing colonial legacies in Africa. For him, the indigene and settler dichotomy cannot sufficiently be grasped and resolved without historicising it. The binary distinction between citizens – the indigene and settler – is no more than a reproduction, in a slightly different form, of an earlier distinction between native and non-native or that of race and ethnicity under colonial law. Natives had ethnicity whilst non-natives did not. It created a racial hierarchy often comprising of whites, coloureds, Asians, Arabs and Hamites (Tutsi), with the ultimate intent on civilising the natives. Colonial law was the instrument through which such hierarchies and divisions were enforced. Civil law applied only to races (non-natives), whilst customary law applied only the ethnicities (natives). Civil law was the realm of rights, something which was alien to customary law.

[4] The origins of this aspect of citizenship, the virtue of character (discussed in more detail in Sect. 8.3 of this chapter), can be traced to the work of Aristotle (2009).

not unrelated, and cannot be properly appreciated, without a further understanding of the daily moral decisions implicated in that way of life. My anxiety in this chapter is not just about the inadequate understanding of ethical and moral dimensions of citizenship in many practical African contexts, but also the inadequate understanding of the former and latter through rights and responsibilities–talk.

What importantly gets lost in the midst of the dominant rights and responsibilities paradigm is the significance of how people should ethically relate to each other, something which (as I argue in this chapter) can be remedied by a concept of citizenship grounded on African jurisprudential precepts. With an emphasis on human interdependence and interpersonal relationships African jurisprudence provides a better way of encouraging the essential moral values fundamental to societal coexistence. African jurisprudence can help place these relevant values – not legal or residential rights and responsibilities – at the centre of the evaluation of what it ethically and morally means to be, or to live as a citizen. What is attractive about African jurisprudence is that it can provide the impetus for the kind of moral comportment or the ethos among citizens, not to place their values at a threshold above aliens, legal or illegal immigrants. The humanistic basis of the African jurisprudential ethos can help institutionalise a practice among citizens and non-citizens-alike, which encourages them to treat each other with dignity and respect, for no other reason other than for the fact of their humanity.

To provide the groundwork for a concept of citizenship inspired by African jurisprudence, the chapter begins by showing the limitations of the rights-based model, the most influential perception of citizenship. The suggestion here is that a clear or universal delineation of individual citizenship rights does not conclusively guarantee the kind of connectedness required to build more inclusion in society; neither does it provide a harmonious or moral language of interaction among diverse groups who reside in a political community. After this, I consider the significance of citizenship responsibilities, to explore whether it provides sufficient scope to offer the kind of moral values fundamental to societal coexistence. In this instance, I show that while the emphasis on responsibilities may lead to some moral values of concern, it does not, in the end, go far enough. In conclusion, I turn to African jurisprudence to show how it addresses my concerns about the significance of ethical and moral values, something which can potentially and richly contribute to the understanding of how citizenship is widely theorised and practiced.

8.2 Citizenship Rights

Citizenship, among other things, defines terms and conditions tied to the membership of a political community. A citizen, in most dominant accounts, is usually a liberal, autonomous and rational individual. Similarly, a citizen is most often a bearer of rights, which are, but not always, correlative of responsibilities. With the rise and dominance of rights-based liberalism, responsibilities have failed to attract a significant level of emphasis, something which is a departure from the historical and foundational concept of citizenship (Collins 2006, pp. 7–18; Janowitz 1980, pp. 1–3). Citizenship, as a result, has predominantly become rights-based, a property that features among liberal, cosmopolitan and multicultural models of the concept (Shachar 2001–2002). Rights have become both a means and a subset of citizenship (Leary 1999, p. 247). Citizenship is very often reduced to the extension of rights to members of a political community. When commentators clamour for an inclusive concept of citizenship, they are desirable for a rights-based model. Inclusion depends on legal protection through the clear delineation of universal citizenship rights. This is another way of understanding what it means to be equal before the law; in other words, what it means to say everyone should be entitled to citizenship rights independent of ethnic, racial, religious or other group loyalties. Denials of citizenship are often translated as the denials of citizenship rights. Struggles for inclusion in different parts of the world, including different African political communities, have been influenced by this rights-based perception of citizenship.

In terms of its content, citizens' rights often refer to civil, political, economic and social rights (Marshall 1950). The content of citizenship rights is given further meaning by the emergence of the Universal Declaration of Human Rights (UDHR) and other international covenants (Shafir and Brysk 2006, pp. 278–285). These documents have reinforced the relationship between citizenship and rights. They set the standard for the range of rights that should be enjoyed by citizens within various political communities. The documents encourage countries to strive to attain the highest levels of equality, and countries are judged according to their ability to guarantee equal access to these rights. Countries are inclusive to the extent that all their citizens have equal access to these rights. Constitutional and citizenship laws in many domestic contexts have primarily evolved to provide the means to safeguard these rights, especially on behalf of minorities.

In theory, human rights should apply to everyone irrespective of citizenship, something which is synonymous with cosmopolitan models of the concept. In practice, this is not always the case, as rights depend on concrete domestic political settings to apply to concrete people. Membership of a political community through citizenship is essential in determining access to these rights (Benhabib 2005, p. 14). What this means is that access to human rights depend on one's status as a citizen, even though this may not always be the case. For instance, legal residents of political communities are also often entitled to a range of rights. Freedom of speech, religion and conscience, the right to free trial, rights against discrimination or the right to vote, with certain exceptions, do not necessarily depend upon citizenship. The case of illegal immigrants, of course, is quite different as they are unlikely to have access to any state guaranteed rights. The point, however, is that although a range of rights can be obtained through residency, residency rights are not, in any way, the equivalent of citizenship rights. The distinction between citizenship and non-citizenship is an important one. Citizenship offers the potential to include and exclude. It is not surprising, then, that the aspiration for legal residents, especially those who reside in opulent nations, is always to attain the full status of citizenship.

Apart from the protection of the civil and political rights, economic and social rights (Marshall 1950) are also regarded as entitlements of citizenship, and to some extent, legal residency. Questions regarding access to economic and social rights are often contentious, due to the availability of economic resources or simply because of the ideological orientation of the state concerned. Where resources are limited, these rights often are a source of contention regarding how they should be distributed. Citizenship is again an important distributive mechanism. It decisively determines access to these basic rudiments of life, such as healthcare, water, education or other public goods. The inability to access these rights is often equivalent to the loss of citizenship, and this is a primary source of grievance in impoverished parts of the world where resources are often scarce.

There are obvious advantages of the rights-based model of citizenship, especially for political communities divided along ethnic, religious, racial or other lines. Rights can help achieve many things, ranging from the distribution of resources to the resolution of disputes, by providing a neutral framework for negotiation, settlement and agreement (Ghai 2000). However, it is on this point that the strength of rights-based citizenship instantly transforms into a weakness. Although rights may be seen as a neutral framework for reconciling conflicts, or even the basis for securing enduring settlement among disagreeing parties, it is debatable whether rights can sustainably guarantee the difficult task of peacefully living together among people, especially people of great diversity. The point that I am raising is a question mark about the integrative capacity of rights; that is, whether rights can mediate between differences or contribute to a sense of belonging among those who share common boundaries.

What I am asking is that: do rights do more than protect the individual against others? Do rights also encourage reconciliation or relationships between different individuals? Is the bearer of a right obliged to act ethically or responsibly towards others (not only those who are owed duties)? For instance, and to provide an analogy from the conflicts in Jos: should it be assumed that once all residents have access to citizenship rights, all the animosity or hatred between such rival groups would simply disappear? Of course, no one would suggest that rights can exhaustively achieve this, but the point I am trying to make should be obvious, even though it might seem a bit embellished. What I am getting at, nevertheless, is that it is quite possible for individual or collective rights-based claims and counter-claims to become sources of discord, especially in fragile societies, where identities are so fragmented. Paradoxically, rights may themselves become the source of division. In such situations, the rights-based model of citizenship might exacerbate, not reconcile differences. It should not be assumed that once individuals attain equal citizenship rights – civil, political, social and economic rights – then all contestations, conflicts or disagreements would somehow be minimized, if not, disappear altogether. This issue is not unique to divided communities; it is a characteristic inherent in the nature of rights-based claims.

No one helps make this point better than Simone Weil, since one of her main problems with rights was the underlying divisive nature of the claim. For Weil, apart from the inherent hostile nature of rights claims, rights claims can only be effective through force or by the threat to force (Weil 2005). Because of this, she thought rights carried the potential of intensifying rivalry and conflict among individuals, or they simply provided the basis for superficial or mundane claims. A political community that places emphasis on rights, not only becomes composed of disaggregate, but also belligerent individuals. Rights-based claims, according to this view, do not have the capacity to reconcile but instigate rifts between individuals. After all, rights are about liberation or radical autonomy, not community, integration or reconciliation (Selznick 1987). More than this, rights militate against harmonious, empathic and affectionate dialogues and interaction between people (Waldron 1988). To formulate a grievance in terms of rights is to deny the possibility of other more harmonious ways of relating. Rights may be one of the benefits of belonging to a political community, but it is contestable, based on the foregoing argument, whether they adequately and sustainably contribute to processes of belonging. It is questionable, then, whether rights can create an atmosphere for mutual respect, tolerance, reciprocity, care, empathy or other values, which remain essential to any process of belonging. For these reasons, it is important to look – without dismissing rights – towards other ways of constituting the kind of values necessary for societal coexistence.

Of course, there are less individualistic or divisive ways of conceiving rights, which can help promote social cohesion and harmony among different people. However, the problem with rights that I described above does not disappear once they are defined more collectively, as some tend to prefer (Englund and Nyamnjoh 2004, pp. 15–19). Besides, my understanding of the point Weil was making is that something else is required, apart from rights, to encourage the basic values, especially the empathy involved in the processes of societal coexistence. She was questioning the extent to which rights claims have the ability to encourage the proper comportment necessary to recognise and respond to human suffering and vulnerability. Weil illustrated this through analogy of a young girl who has been forced to work in a brothel. For Weil, rights, as a conceptual medium, cannot be relied upon to either grasp or articulate the kind of suffering experienced by the girl. In other words, it would be a misconception of her cry of pain and suffering, if it is simply understood as a breach of contract, property or labour rights. The basic point Weil is making is that rights do not properly encourage the proper values or comportment necessary to understand or empathise with the defilement of her life. This, in my view, is a much stronger indictment on rights than their antagonistic character.

8.3 Responsibilities

If rights, as I have suggested in the previous section, offer a limited scope for the connectedness and integration of citizens, then, what about responsibilities? Intuitively, responsibilities seem to get to the heart of the problem described above with rights, since, in a generic sense, they imply some sort of interpersonal relationships between people, apart from pointing to the importance of virtue and character.

Responsibilities differ in type. Responsibilities to political community can be distinguished from special responsibilities to family members, friends or neighbours. Responsibilities to political community are also different from the kinds of responsibilities that emerge by agreement, or those on account of reparations for a certain kind of legally defined injury suffered (Beever 2008).

Membership of a political community should ideally generate special bonds and relationships among citizens. The political community is often the source of identification, belonging and attachment among citizens. The emphasis on responsibilities is more common with republican and communitarian models of citizenship. Responsibilities generally imply that we are obliged to our political community and to our fellow citizens. Responsibilities to political community, however, are vertical and indirect; they are not horizontal and direct. Responsibilities are institutionalised through different forms of actions performed to show our allegiance to the political community. The social contract is the source of all responsibilities, including (and importantly too) those between citizens.

The obligation to obey the law is a good example of how individual responsibilities are institutionalised through actions performed to the political community. The premise behind all social contract theories is eloquently explained by Mark Tebbit:

> The citizen must obey the laws in everything, because (1) general obedience is the condition for the existence of society, and without it there would be anarchy; (2) the citizen owes the state everything, including his or her life; (3) the citizen has agreed, both explicitly and implicitly, by virtue of receiving benefits from the state and choosing not to emigrate, to obey all the laws; (4) the citizen has the opportunity to persuade the state, through legitimate lobbying, to change the laws, but not the right to disobey them. (2006, p. 94)

Tax is another good example. Citizens pay their taxes not because they always directly benefit from them, even though they might do so sometimes. Among other things, tax is used for different purposes, ranging from wealth redistribution, welfare, healthcare or unemployment schemes, to the provisioning of public goods and services. A citizen's contribution to the lives of others is mediated through the collective institution of tax. Military service is another way of understanding the indirect effect of citizenship responsibilities. The stronger or more able-bodied citizens are conscripted to defend or die for their nation in times of war, or they may be assigned to help the vulnerable in times of natural or unnatural humanitarian disasters. Service to the country by citizens is indirectly addressed to other citizens.

The duty to vote at periodic elections, while not compulsory, is also an important element of understanding the indirect nature or effect of responsibilities. Although it is now quite narrow in its scope, political participation in a more general sense is one of the most important responsibilities of a citizen. Indeed, it is an example of the meeting point between rights and responsibilities, or between liberal and republican or communitarian models of citizenship. Political participation is both a right and responsibility of citizenship. Inclusive citizenship, in this context, is most commonly defined according to the ability to participate politically.

In theory, the purpose of political participation is more than just to provide a yardstick for measuring inclusion or solidarity among citizens. Political participation serves as the hallmark of good citizenship; it is the key to building virtue and character.

The underlying virtuous nature of political participation cannot be fully appreciated outside Aristotle's timeless work on politics. For him, political participation, and thereby citizenship, are both contingent on a background, unmistakably ethical, concept of politics. Starting with citizenship, he saw this as a status derived from the '…participation in giving judgement and holding office' (Aristotle 1992, p. 169). Participation in public (deliberative or judicial) office is the core objective and defining feature of citizenship. Anyone (especially slaves and women in the Aristotelian era) denied the opportunity of political participation is in turn denied citizenship. The nation's constitution often determined the nature of citizenship. Citizenship is most inclusive under a democratic constitution in contrast to authoritarian regimes. Aristotle's concept of democracy is known to be an absolute one, in that it requires all citizens to take part in public decision-making processes. Citizenship is thus another term for active participation. The distinction between participation and representation is, therefore, important for him.

Aristotle's point is that politics is the single most defining process of developing virtue and character. Politics is fundamental to cultivating good citizens or good citizenship. The concept of the good here refers to human good, something which is central to the pursuit of happiness (Aristotle 2009, p. 5). Happiness implies some sort of virtue or excellence; it can be distinguished from the pursuit of wealth, pleasure and honour (2009, p. 6). A human being, according to Aristotle, can only live a good life through the ability to exercise moral virtues (2009, p. 10). Politics thus becomes the habit or *ethos* central to the cultivation of moral virtues (2009, p. 5). Moral virtues, as such, crucially depend on the reciprocal exchanges involved in the practice of politics.

Good citizenship, thus, is formed through the habit of political participation, something which is further dependent on a good constitution. Good citizenship is dependent on the nature of the city and constitution, since excellence or virtue can only be attained through civic function (2009, p. 179). Aristotle is distinguishing between the virtue of a good citizen and that of a good man. He recognised a difference between a good man and good citizen (Keyt 2007, pp. 220–240). The highest standard of goodness, which can be differentiated from the standard of goodness obtained from being ruled, is achieved only through the act of ruling. In other words, there is a superior form of virtue attained through practical wisdom, which Aristotle described as the virtue of rulers.

Through the emphasis on voting at periodic elections, contemporary notions of politics or political participation have since deviated from Aristotle's insights, even though some of his ideas can be found in theories of deliberative democracy. Political participation has today been reduced to electoral participation. It is not clear how through elections; a winner-takes-all phenomenon, that an impetus can be provided to nurture ethical and moral values, especially the basic and necessary empathy among citizens. Although deliberative theories of democracy have not totally deviated from Aristotle, they nevertheless have, with certain exceptions (Krause 2008, pp. 1–26), not given sufficient attention to the significance of values in their vision of politics. They place emphasis on reason and reasonable agreement at the expense of ethical and moral values in deliberative political processes.

Apart from the current emphasis on elections, there is also something generally problematic about the idea of politics, a problem that can be traced to the Aristotelian version of the concept. The problem, on the Aristotelian premise, is that politics is proposed to define how societal and moral values (the type that shape personal and interpersonal relationships) are cultivated. In order words, the premise is that citizens need politics to ethically relate to one another. The difficulty with this is that the private sphere loses its significance to the public sphere in nurturing the most basic set of moral values. Politics de-emphasises or relegates the importance of nurturing moral values through daily non-political activities in the private sphere. Even though it is plausible, I do not think that the answer to this problem lies in the more expansive notion of politics offered by feminist theory, which conceives almost every sphere of life politically (Young 1989). What is being suggested here is that politics should not and cannot underpin our moral values; rather it is our moral values, nurtured through daily ethical exchanges, that should provide the foundations for politics.

A more specific question can be raised regarding the nature or existence of this kind of politics in Africa. Politics, particularly in Africa today, has become corrupt to such an extent that, if it ever had any Aristotelian underpinnings, it is hard to see how it can be recovered. Indeed, it is hard to draw a connection between Aristotle's idea of politics and what currently exists on the African continent. In Africa, politics has hardly been about morals or ethics, and it has also rarely had anything intrinsic about it. It is controlled by tribal (professional) party politicians and their followers, who use it as a means to serve their parochial interests. With this sort of vision of politics, it is no coincidence that problems in places like Jos, for example, took a turn for the worse after they became political. One can make a similar observation about politics in different parts of the world, where the practice has taken a huge detour from its ethical or moral foundations (Agamben 1998, 1996). As such, the practice of immoral politics is not just common among Africans.

Therefore, there seems to be very reasonable justification, as I choose to do, to step outside the realm of politics to cultivate a morally or ethically embedded concept of citizenship. This, for me, is both the prospect and advantage, as I show below, that African jurisprudence provides to citizenship, among other concepts. African jurisprudence can expand and enrich the understanding of both the ethical and moral foundations of citizenship. As will be demonstrated in the next section, much of this depends on how jurisprudence is defined. Indeed, what sets African jurisprudence apart from mainstream notions of jurisprudence is its focus on the human coexistence. African jurisprudence achieves this in such a way that can ground new thinking about what it means to be or to live ethically and morally as a citizen.

Before considering the above in more detail, another more general and important reason why African jurisprudence may be advantageous in this respect is predicated on understanding the limitations of the indirect nature of political responsibilities. Because responsibilities (especially voting and tax) are institutionalised through the state, they do not generate strong enough bonds or attachments among citizens regardless of their diversity. This problem, in Africa, is confounded by the artificial nature of statehood. In the African context, the allegiance to members of ethnic, tribal or religious groups is much stronger than the allegiance to the state. The consequence is that citizens are less responsible or reciprocal to other citizens because of their differences of ethnicity, religion or race.

In a more general sense, and not restricted to Africa, the duties or responsibilities to the state or to political community can lead to the abdication of responsibility to fellow-citizens. The institutionalisation of responsibilities through the state potentially has the effect of encouraging the lack of concern and apathy among citizens regardless of their similarity or diversity. It is difficult, under the auspices of responsibilities, to understand or justify moral and horizontal relationships among individuals in any political community. For instance, it becomes virtuous to pay tax, rather than to directly help the poor, hungry or sick (Bankowski 2001, p. 101). Collective responsibilities tend to undermine our ability to pay attention to particularity or the material conditions of people we encounter on a daily basis. What I am suggesting is that responsibilities to the state militate against the interpersonal responsibilities that citizens should have for each other. For instance, it becomes easier to pay money to some common pool of funds than to directly help a person in need. It becomes easier to vote for a leader at periodic elections, who would take hard decisions for us, rather than take part in reaching those decisions ourselves. In all of these situations, responsibilities fail to have the desired indirect effect. It makes citizens lose sight of the fact that individual acts of responsibility are equally as important as the collective or institutionalised systems of responsibility. The balancing is wrong; inclusive political communities should have both, not one or the other.

8.4 African Jurisprudence

> Start the story with the failure of the African state, and not with the colonial creation of the African state, and you have an entirely different story.
>
> Of course, Africa is a continent full of catastrophes. There are immense ones, such as the horrific rapes in Congo.... But there are other stories that are not about catastrophe. And it is very important, it is just as important, to talk about them.
>
> I've always felt that it is impossible to engage properly with a place or a person without engaging with all of the stories of that place and that person. The consequence of the single story is this: It robs people of dignity. It makes our recognition of our equal humanity difficult. (Adichie 2009)

It should not be controversial to attempt to ground citizenship from the standpoint of African jurisprudence, since there is nothing unusual in arguing that the legal, social and political composition or institutions of any society (especially its concept of citizenship) should be reflective of its traditional moral values. The fact that this is generally lacking in Africa is baffling, but not, at all, surprising. While several reasons can be given to explain this, I discuss at least three. First, it has always been easy to dismiss the existence or potential of African knowledge, given that Africa is usually identified with catastrophic conditions, something which has provided ample justifications to dismiss the existence of anything positive or attractive from Africa, including its traditional forms of thought and knowledge. This is not an attempt to absolve Africans from creating those problems; rather it is an attempt to show that this has in itself often been overlooked as a causal (even though not the only) factor for many contemporary problems in Africa.

The denial of the existence of African knowledge exists in many disciplines, and the field of jurisprudence is no exception. A single story, to use Chimamanda Adichie's words above, prevails in dominant jurisprudential narratives to deny the existence of African jurisprudential knowledge. According to this narrative, African jurisprudential knowledge either does not exist, or where it does exist, it is either inadequate or akin to the knowledge of violence, savagery and barbarity. The conflicts in Jos, which I introduced in the beginning of this chapter, can be used to analogise this point. There is a hidden story obscured by the dominant one. This dominant narrative, with certain exceptions, finds it convenient to leave out stories of the huge expressions of empathy and generosity among residents of the city during the debacles (BBC News 2011). Neighbours and strangers protected, fed, clothed and sheltered other neighbours and strangers caught up in the fighting. Christians were compassionate to Muslims, and Muslims to Christians. Local neighbourhoods in certain parts of the city reinforced their bonds and chose not to join or allow their neighbourhoods to be contaminated by the madness. Like with African jurisprudence, other stories about Jos are non-existent. The story that dominates is simply that of violence and brutality.

The historical denial of the existence of African knowledge, especially since the Enlightenment era, has implanted a strong story in the minds and consciousness of many – non-Africans and Africans alike – that nothing good, including jurisprudential knowledge, can come out of Africa. There is indeed some connection between the denial of the existence of African knowledge and the prevalence of negative stories about Africa. The most urgent, relevant and important task, then, for African jurisprudence is to correct this misleading perception of its perceived non-existence. African jurisprudence must resist this single and negative story, one that not only denies its existence, but also its relevance to issues in the jurisprudential world. A further task that stems from the previous one is the need to tell the real and attractive story of African jurisprudence, a story of a body of work, which can significantly enrich our knowledge of what moral values of community and human interdependence entail. This, for me, not only gets to the substance of what African jurisprudence should entail, but also why the central proposition of this chapter is that it can adequately ground a morally embedded ethos of citizenship.

My point, here, is not that these values exist everywhere across sub-Saharan Africa. There is so much diversity within sub-Saharan Africa to make such a generalisation. Rather, my point is to suggest that our ability to identify, cultivate and define such values cross-culturally remains indispensable to the difficult task of harmonious social coexistence, and furthermore, that citizenship provides the most appropriate context to institutionalise the commitment to them. Not only are these values important to those that belong to the same community, they are also important to how they relate to others who belong to other communities. No political community in any part of the world can be fully inclusive or can have the ability to deal with the kind of problems mentioned at the outset of this chapter without a commitment to these kinds of values.

Second, and following on from the above, is that the widespread acceptance of capitalist modernity in the African continent, whether in the form of development or through other means, has had the effect of encouraging Africans to discard many forms of their traditional moral convictions about coexistence and societal living. What has fallen by the wayside is the significance of traditional moral values and knowledge, which is a necessary ingredient for societal connectedness in any political community. Establishing citizenship from an African jurisprudential standpoint is, therefore, a key to reviving such values, apart from the necessary ethos among people who dwell in the same place.

Third, the invocation of traditional (African) moral values often (and rightly too) invites both suspicion and scepticism. The desire for traditional African moral values can certainly be used to re-invoke or disguise different forms of relativism or forms of tribalism, ethnicity and patriarchy, among other things. These should not be confused as moral values from an African jurisprudential standpoint. Instead, I am referring to commonly held moral convictions about human interdependence and community that can be established cross-culturally across sub-Saharan Africa (see, for example, Greene 1998; Bewaji 2004; Metz 2007; Gyekeye 2010). In particular, I am referring to the values that imply that the quality of our life – especially our moral literacy, development, character, decisions or judgement – is dependent on our interactions or exchanges with others in community.

My understanding of African jurisprudence as an opportunity to tell all stories about Africa, and African moral values can be exposited by reference to John Murungi's (2004) seminal definition of the term. Murungi says, '[E]ach path of jurisprudence represents an attempt by human beings to tell a story about being human' (2004, p. 525), and African jurisprudence provides the opportunity to ground these types of dialogues. This is because African jurisprudence, according to this view, is 'the pursuit and preservation of what is human and what is implicated in being human' (2004, pp. 525–526). African jurisprudence is 'a science of being human as understood by Africans' (2004, p. 523). Not only is this what African jurisprudence entails, it is what the study of jurisprudence in the general sense should entail. Jurisprudence should not be (as commonly the case) reduced to the scientific analysis of the 'nature of law, the validity of law, the nature of legal obligation, the sources of law, the hermeneutics of law, the administration of law, [or] the types of legal regimes' (2004, p. 523); rather it should be an enquiry into and the explication of the nature of being human. African jurisprudence does not take this for granted; it also does not presume that we have a complete understanding of what it means to be human.

Murungi here turns Hegel's often cited denunciation of the existence of African knowledge on its head (Murungi 2013). This is Hegel's exclusion of Africans from membership of the human race on account of their supposed lack of capacity for human consciousness. In Hegel's thinking, human consciousness is equated with legal consciousness. The ability to formulate law is an attribute held only by humans. By denying Africans this specific attribute of humanity, what Hegel ultimately denies is the existence and capacity for African legal and jurisprudential thought. What Hegel unintentionally shows, however, something which seminal thinkers (Austin, Hart and Dworkin, etc.) of jurisprudence have ignored, is that the 'knowledge of law leads to the knowledge of what it is to be a human being' (2013, p. 32). Inspired by these seminal thinkers, the field of jurisprudence widely globalised across the world today, not only overlooks the need to study what it means to be human, but also the need to study what it means, as a human being, to live a good and virtuous life.

Murungi's disagreement with Hegel, then, is not on what the study of jurisprudence should entail; but rather it is on Hegel's mistaken understanding of human ontology. African jurisprudence does not suffer from this shortcoming; it also does not suffer from Hegel's flaw of defining humanity too exclusively. In other words, African jurisprudence 'does not exclude other human beings from the community of human beings' (2013, p. 35). Similarity, it does not prioritise African humanity ahead of non-African humanity. This because being human, in African jurisprudential terms, refers to the social constitution of the person (Murungi 2004, p. 522). It is an enquiry into the nature of being human in relation to other human beings. African jurisprudence, as such, is inherently dialogical (2004, p. 525). Being human entails dialogues between different human beings. Dialogues create the openness necessary for both human being and human dwelling. African jurisprudence takes social cohesion seriously. All laws, legal and political institutions must be constituted in ways that encourage social cohesion.

Social cohesion is intricately linked to justice. And justice is defined according to the desire to give the human being full expression. Justice is defined negatively. Injustice is indicative of what justice is not. After all, we cannot know what justice is until we know what injustice entails (Sklar 1992). Injustice is, first, the negation of the personal responsibility, the responsibility to self, which, in essence, is the responsibility to be a social being (Murungi 2004, p. 523).

The hallmarks of a concept of citizenship with an African character are already becoming obvious from the previous points. But before I say more on this below, I will highlight another important feature of African jurisprudence. While the emphasis is on cohesion and sociability, this does not undermine the importance of individuality or individual rights. The emphasis on the social or community (historically or contemporarily) is not adverse to individual rights. Similarly, community rights do not prevail over individual rights; neither does the former prevail over the latter. There is no hierarchy between community and rights, since they both importantly contribute to the quality of our lives (Onazi 2013, pp. 23–46).

With the emphasis on being human, interdependence, social cohesion and justice, one can clearly envision a concept of citizenship with distinct African characteristics. What follows is an attempt to elaborate on at least five distinctive features or the ethos encouraged by an African inspired concept of citizenship. First, the focus on all dimensions of human relationships by African jurisprudence underscores the importance of societal moral values, something that (as I argued in the previous sections) is not properly achieved through rights and responsibilities. Since being human implies being human in relation to others, this must imply a certain disposition or moral comportment explicably part of the process of living together in society. In another sense, African jurisprudence expands upon our understanding human recognition; that is, it provides another way of appreciating the processes of mutual identification with others based on similarity, specificity, difference and empathy (Douzinas 2000; Honneth 1995; Metz 2012).

Second, the focus on all dimensions of human relationships implies that, all human beings, regardless of territorial boundaries, culture, ethnicity or religion, are morally responsible to each other. Citizenship, from an African jurisprudential standpoint, is primarily focused on being human. What gives the focus on being human a moral advantage over other ways of thinking of citizenship, then, is the cosmopolitan ethos that it implies. Although it is not the only way of achieving this, a concept of citizenship founded on African jurisprudential precepts provides us with another opportunity to understand how to transcend national, local, ethnic, religious and other group loyalties (Kurasawa 2007, p. 127). Human beings are connected to other human beings on the basis of nothing more than the mutual recognition of their humanity.

Third, the African jurisprudential concept of citizenship does not simply focus on being human in all of its glory and perfection as, for instance, with the dominant social contract tradition. Being human also means how we understand human vulnerability and suffering (Metz 2012). Apart from being responsible to all human beings, the ethical life implied by an African concept of citizenship would encourage us to appreciate that all human beings, including the most powerful, are vulnerable to suffering. And there is also a cosmopolitan implication in relation to this point. It is not so much our commonality or perfection that makes us relate to others. Rather, it is the ability of each human being to understand and empathise with the human condition of the other human being. African jurisprudence does not take the need to understand and ameliorate human suffering and vulnerability for granted. While theories of cosmopolitan citizenship (see, for example, Appiah 2006; Sassen 2006; Parekh 2003) emphasise something along these lines, they, with certain exceptions (Benhabib 2004), do not properly address the internal divisions within political communities that demand the same kind of moral responsibility that people owe to individuals in distant communities. In other words, there is so much emphasis on the external at the expense of the internal. The African jurisprudential concept of citizenship does not take this for granted. It does not neglect the internal in favour of the external and vice versa.

Fourth, and building on from the above, the most obvious area in which African jurisprudence contributes to citizenship is on the idea of responsibilities, inclusive of how responsibilities are pivotal to nurturing the kind of moral values that are important for collective flourishing. African jurisprudence assists in renewing our understanding of responsibilities. Responsibilities from an African jurisprudential standpoint simply imply the proper grasp of human responsibilities. African jurisprudence, not only moralises, for lack of a better term, but also socialises citizenship, by bringing it into the realm of human relationships, aligning all human beings within a given community together. On this premise, human responsibilities are horizontal and direct, and furthermore, they do not depend on statehood. Being human in relation to another human being implies a responsibility between one human being for the other. It is a type of responsibility that is not conditional upon anything except the fact of being human. This is what it means to say that our human responsibilities to each other precede the constitution or membership of the state itself. In other words, citizens are not placed at a threshold above aliens, legal or illegal immigrants. The failure to be responsible to the other human being is nothing more than a failure to be responsible to one's self. And this is, in turn, a failure to be a social being (Murungi 2004, p. 523).

The fifth point follows on closely from the previous. It should already be obvious that citizenship from an African jurisprudential standpoint is value-laden, but what has not been emphasised is that moral values are dependent and can only be cultivated through daily relationships, interactions and encounters between human beings. The ethical life implied by being an African citizen is determined by asking the question, what does it mean to be good to others? Being good is dependent and developed through our daily proximate exchanges with other human beings. African citizenship, then, is a form of praxis, to borrow the phrase from Enrique Dussell (1998). Praxis refers to the development of moral comportment through certain types of actions, such as helping, caring, sharing or other ethical exchanges between human beings. Praxis, like African jurisprudence, is a species of a theory of human interdependence. Praxis is about how the presence of one human being is experienced by the other. As a form of praxis, the African jurisprudential approach is also concerned about how people encounter and deal with each other daily. This, and the general arguments of this chapter sets the African approach apart from dominant models of citizenship, which crucially fail to emphasise the importance of moral values.

8.5 Conclusion

In this chapter, I have made a case for a concept of citizenship with distinct African jurisprudential characteristics, the strength of which is the value it gives to human values and relationships. The advantage of an African jurisprudential approach is the emphasis it would place on the development of a type of moral comportment among all human beings to treat each other with empathy, tolerance, dignity and respect. If there is one thing that I have not addressed, it is the practical implications of this argument. As important as this may be, this has not been an objective of this chapter. Instead, the objective has been to question what citizenship means today, and also, to question whether existing understandings of the concept yield to a proper grasp of the ethical life and moral values necessary for societal connectedness, collective flourishing and belonging. A further objective has also been to explore the possibility of establishing citizenship from a different conceptual basis (African jurisprudence), and the extent to which this would provide a better foundation for recommitment to these societal moral values.

Despite this, I conclude by briefly suggesting some ways the insights in this chapter can be translated into practice. In doing so, I am not claiming to be comprehensive; I only seek to suggest at least three possible ways that practice should follow. First, and on general note, the constitution is the most obvious practical proposal towards achieving a concept of citizenship with African characteristics. This is because a constitution is not just a document embodying rules and regulations, but also (to build on arguments from the previous section) an embodiment of the moral values of any given society, which can assist yield to a better understanding of being human. In more specific terms, one way of reflecting the right sort of moral values for purposes of societal intercourse is by drawing up and constitutionalising a covenant of human or moral responsibilities. This would define and set the threshold that would encourage and measure the quality and adherence to these values. The closest approximate to this proposal are 'citizenship tests', or 'good character clauses'; requirements for immigrants seeking citizenship to conduct themselves in a certain ethical or responsible way. Citizenship tests or good character clauses exist in most constitutions around the world, including the Nigerian one, but surprisingly, a similar provision with a related requirement that horizontally binds existing citizens together is missing, one that expects them to show respect and empathy for each other.

To illustrate this point by referring to the Nigerian context again; it should not be too difficult to introduce, through constitutional means, a covenant of moral responsibilities under the Nigerian constitution underscored by moral values. In terms of its content, the specific details of the covenant should be drawn up collectively through debate by all citizens concerned. The advantage of this is the symbolic effect it would have to encourage moral obligations or responsibility rather than to have a legal effect. Apart from the obvious difficulty in pinning down concrete legal concepts from the nebulous nature of the moral values concerned, it would be too naive to expect that inserting a local understanding of values into constitutional or citizenship law on its own will remove the entrenched forms of hatred that already exists in divided communities, such as in Jos and its environs. The conviction that law can provide all the answers to questions that are essentially societal is a claim that is not made here.

In trouble spots like Jos, Nigeria (apart from expunging the indigene and settler dichotomy from the constitution), one may go a step further and propose special citizenship tests for existing citizens. With a focus on the younger generation growing up in Jos, they must be indoctrinated and subjected to tests after a certain age of maturity, and after that, if viable, at certain periods. Another good example can be drawn from a common practice among certain religious sects who subject their followers, to certain tests after a certain age of maturity, to assess whether they properly grasp the central tenets of their beliefs.

Secondly, law certainly has a central role to play in cultivating this kind of behaviour, and it can do so by going beyond constitutional law to orient different forms of action at a societal level. Without being exhaustive, other more practical approaches that can be inspired by law would include a broad based educational strategy, not necessarily restricted to civic, but inclusive of moral education. Moral citizenship, after all (as I prefer to call it) is also a pedagogical agenda. Citizens or aspiring citizens must not only learn or be taught how to be good civic citizens, but also how to be good human beings. It is important, in this regard, to target the younger generation, not only because the future depends on them, but also because they are unlikely to be set in their ways. It does not matter if they attend separate (religious or integrated) schools, traditional African moral values, of the kind discussed in this chapter, must form a central part of the agenda. As part of the educational strategy, a comparative perspective is needed to learn how other countries in different parts of the world have dealt with similar questions. Close to home, the Southern African example, partly because of the consequences of its apartheid history, can provide a model for other African countries. South Africa is perhaps one of the few places in Africa where citizenship is defined by moral values (Swatz 2006, pp. 561–563). Of course, recent violence and intolerance to non-citizens in South Africa may raise question marks about relying on it as a case study. From my point of view, the problems (just as the strengths) of the South African experience need to be studied more closely to decipher what plausible lessons can be learnt from it by other African countries.

Thirdly, and in addition to the above, there is a need also to create non-political deliberative forums within and between local communities, through which individuals can come together for the purposes of developing a better understanding of the human responsibilities they owe to each other. Unlike mainstream ideas about deliberation, the questions for deliberation here should be issues unrelated to politics. The forums should provide the avenue for people to come together to learn, empathise and get to know each other better. It should be a site for reflection, where individuals reflect on both matters of common interest and those of difference. In Jos, for instance, this can serve as a means to anticipate and nip possible conflicts in the bud. As suggested earlier, the specific details of these proposals still have to be worked out in more detail in practical contexts. As mentioned earlier, it has not been an objective of this chapter to provide such specific detail; rather the objective has been to invite further conversation, spark new thinking, indicate or provide the groundwork for these and other possibilities.

References

Abdullah A (2004) Rewriting a new constitution for Kenya: wishing away ethnicity in the constitutional making process. In: Murison J, Griffiths A, King K (eds) Remaking law in Africa: transnationalism persons and rights. Centre of African Studies, University of Edinburgh, Edinburgh, pp 49–70

Adebanwi W (2009) Terror, territoriality and the struggle for indigeneity and citizenship in northern Nigeria. Citizenship Stud 13(4):349–363

Adejumobi S (2001) Citizenship, rights, and the problem of conflicts and civil wars in Africa. Hum Right Q 23:148–170

Adichie C (2009) The danger of a single story. TEDTalks available online at http://www.ted.com/talks/chimamanda_adichie_the_danger_of_a_single_story.html

Agamben G (1996) Means without end: notes on politics (trans: Binnetti V, Casarino C). University of Minnesota Press, Minneapolis

Agamben G (1998) Homo Sacer: sovereign power and bare life. Stanford University Press, California
Alubo O (2004) Citizenship and nation-building in Nigeria: new challenges and contestations. Identity Cult Politics 5(1/2):145–146
Appiah K (2006) Cosmopolitanism: ethics in a world of strangers. Norton and Company, London
Aristotle (1992) The politics (trans: Sinclair T). Penguin Books, London
Aristotle (2009) Nicomachean ethics (trans: Ross D). Oxford University Press, Oxford
Bankowski Z (2001) Living lawfully: law in love and love in law. Kluwer, Dordrecht
Bankowski Z (2007) Bringing the outside in: the ethical life of legal institutions. In: Gitzbert-Studnicki T, Stelmach J (eds) Law and legal cultures in the 21st century: unity and diversity. Wolters Kluwer, Poland, pp 193–217
Beever A (2008) Corrective justice and personal responsibility in tort law. Oxf J Leg Stud 28(3):475–500
Benhabib S (2004) The rights of others: aliens, residents and citizens. Cambridge University Press, Cambridge
Benhabib S (2005) Disaggregation of citizenship rights. Parallax 11(1):10–18
Bewaji I (2004) Ethics and morality in Yoruba culture. In: Wiredu K (ed) A companion of African philosophy. Blackwell, London, pp 396–403
Burdette F (1942) Education for citizenship. Publ Opin Q 6(2):269–279
Carr D (2006) The moral roots of citizenship: reconciling principle and character in citizenship education. J Moral Educ 35(4):443–456
Collins S (2006) Aristotle and the rediscovery of citizenship. Cambridge University Press, Cambridge
Douzinas C (2000) The end of human rights. Hart Publishing, Oxford
Dussell E (1998) Ethics and community (trans: Barr R). Orbis Books, New York
Englund H, Nyamnjoh F (eds) (2004) Rights and the politics of recognition in Africa. Zed Books, London
Ghai Y (2000) Universalism and relativism: human rights as a framework for negotiating interethnic claims. Cardozo Law Rev 21(4):1095
Greene K (1998) Mutumin Kirki: the concept of good man in Hausa. In: Eze E (ed) African philosophy: an anthology. Blackwell, London, pp 121–129
Gyekeye K (2010) African ethics. In: Zalta (ed) The Stanford encyclopaedia of philosophy. http://plato.stanford.edu/entries/african-ethics/
Higazi A (2011) The Jos crisis: a recurrent Nigerian tragedy. Fredrich Ebert Stiftung Discussion Paper 2
Honneth A (1995) The struggle for recognition: the moral grammar of social conflicts. MIT Press, Cambridge, MA
Human Rights Watch (2006) They do not own this place: government discrimination against non-indigenes in Nigeria. Hum Right Watch 18(3/A):17–30
Janowitz M (1980) Observations on the sociology of citizenship: obligations and rights. Soc Forces 59(1):1–24
Keyt D (2007) The good man and the upright citizen in Aristotle's ethics and politics. Soc Philos Pol Found 24:220–240
Krause S (2008) Civil passions: moral sentiment and democratic deliberation. Princeton University Press, Princeton/Oxford
Kurasawa F (2007) The work of global justice: human rights as practices. Cambridge University Press, Cambridge
Leary V (1999) Citizenship, human rights and diversity. In: Cairns A et al (eds) Citizenship, diversity and pluralism: Canadian, and comparative perspectives. McGill-Queens University Press, Canada, pp 247–264
Mamdani M (1996) Citizens and subjects: contemporary Africa and the legacy of late colonialism. Princeton University Press, Princeton
Mamdani M (2001) Beyond settler and native as political identities: overcoming the political legacy of colonialism. Comp Stud Soc Hist 43(4):651–664

Marshall T (1950) Citizenship and social class. Cambridge University Press, Cambridge
Marshall-Fratani R (2006) The war of "Who is Who": autochthony, nationalism, and citizenship in the Ivoirian crisis. Afr Stud Rev 49(2):9–43
Metz T (2007) Towards an African moral theory. J Polit Philos 9:81–95
Metz T (2012) "Giving the world a more humane face" – human suffering in African thought and philosophy. In: Malpas J, Lickiss N (eds) Perspectives on human suffering. Springer, Dordrecht, pp 49–62
Murungi J (2004) The question of African jurisprudence: some hermeneutic reflections. In: Wiredu K (ed) A companion of African philosophy. Blackwell, London, pp 396–403
Murungi J (2013) An introduction to African legal philosophy. Lexington Books, Lanham
Ndlovu-Gatsheni S (2007) Tracking the historical roots of post-apartheid citizenship problems: the native club, restless natives, panicking settlers and the politics of nativism in South Africa. African Studies Centre (ASC) Leiden Working Paper 72
Onazi O (2013) Human rights from community: a rights-based approach to development. Edinburgh University Press, Edinburgh
Parekh B (2003) Cosmopolitanism and global citizenship. Rev Int Stud 29:3–17
Sassen S (2006) Territory, authority, rights: from medieval to global assemblages. Princeton University Press, Princeton
Selznick P (1987) The idea of communitarian morality. Calif Law Rev 75(1):445
Shachar A (2001–2002) Two critiques of multiculturalism. Cardozo Law Rev 23(1):253–297
Shafir G, Brysk A (2006) The globalization of rights: from citizenship to human rights. Citizenship Stud 13(3):275–287
Sklar J (1992) Faces of injustice. Yale University Press, New Haven
Swatz S (2006) A long walk to citizenship: morality, justice and faith in the aftermath of apartheid. J Moral Edu 35(4):551–570
Tebbit M (2006) Philosophy of law. Routledge, Oxford
The Constitution of the Federal Republic of Nigeria (1999)
Waldron J (1988) When justice replaces affection: the need for rights. Har J Law Pub Pol 11:625–642
Walker R (2011) Jos violence: everyone lives in fear of his neighbour. Available online at http://www.bbc.co.uk/news/world-africa-12985289
Weil S (2005) Human personality. In: Miles S (ed) Simone Weil: anthology. Penguin Books, London, pp 69–98
Young I (1989) Polity and group difference: a critique of the ideal of universal citizenship. Ethics 99(2):250–274

Chapter 9
The Practice and the Promise of Making Rights Claims: Lessons from the South African Treatment Access Campaign

Karen Zivi

9.1 Introduction

What does the new South Africa tell us about the state of African legal theory in the twenty-first century? Is this post-apartheid nation a political miracle? Is it evidence of the triumph of the human spirit and a revolution in law and practice? Is it a model to be followed by other African nations? For those who focus on the fact that South Africa has one of the first constitutions to be designed explicitly with international human rights norms in mind, the answer is yes. South Africa's progressive Constitution, exemplary court rulings, and robust civil society, offer a glimpse into what could be the future of the continent. This would be a future in which societies embraced an expansive understanding of human rights and did so both 'from above' and 'from below,' through their founding documents and government agencies as well as through an active citizenry and networks of civil society organizations (e.g., Robins 2008; White and Perelman 2011).[1]

For others, South Africa offers a cautionary tale. A quick scan of the daily news reveals the extraordinary gaps that continue to exist between the rhetoric of rights and the reality of peoples' lives, between the promises of the Constitution and the actions of those in positions of political and economic power. Critics thus argue that the new South Africa may be a liberal democracy in principle, but it is not the revolutionary, social democratic, peoples' state once imagined. It is not a model to which other nations should aspire.[2] Rights rhetoric – and the institutions and policies to

[1] The South African Constitution entitles citizens to traditional political and civil rights as well as to justiciable social, economic, and cultural rights; it also stipulates that court decisions must be consistent with international law.

[2] These critics echo a general concern of many on the political left. This 'left critique' of rights suggests that rights discourse perpetuates certain liberal ideas about individualism and the role of

K. Zivi (✉)
Grand Valley University, Michigan, USA
e-mail: zivik@gvsu.edu

O. Onazi (ed.), *African Legal Theory and Contemporary Problems: Critical Essays*, Ius Gentium: Comparative Perspectives on Law and Justice 29,
DOI 10.1007/978-94-007-7537-4_9, © Springer Science+Business Media Dordrecht 2014

which it has given birth – offer only the illusion of equality, critics argue. The reality is that state institutions and public policies are more committed to protecting property rights and the economic status quo than to advancing real economic and social equality. And even when victories occur in the courtroom the inequities of daily life may remain.[3]

Thus while some praise the nation, and its legal practices and discourses, for illuminating the transformative potential of rights, others suggest that South Africa serves as a reminder of the dangers of rights rhetoric. Champions of South African legal discourse argue that it provides evidence that socioeconomic rights rhetoric, for example, is capable of shedding light on and addressing various forms of injustice, inequality, and oppression (e.g., Heywood 2009; London 2004; Mindry 2008; Pieterse 2008). Critics point out that rights language and the legal structure's association with liberal ideology are inappropriate in the African context, a vestige of colonialism that promises democratic equality while masking and exacerbating the realities of economic inequality (see, e.g., Johnsohn 2006a; Mutua 1997, 2008; Neocosmos 2006).[4]

In this chapter, I argue that neither the celebratory nor the critical perspective adequately captures the complexity of the legal discourse of and lessons to be learned from South Africa. Instead, both perspectives tend to reduce legal discourse, particularly the practice of making rights claims, to "liberalism" and its commitments and thereby miss the important role played by Ubuntu, the African ethical and juridical ideal of human interdependency. To illuminate the role that Ubuntu plays in South African legal theory and practice, I turn my attention to the campaign for the right to HIV treatment access, and in particular, the fight for the right to prevent mother-to-child HIV transmission (PMTCT). This campaign has both its champions and its critics. From some perspectives, it provides irrefutable evidence of the transformative potential of rights discourse and yet, from others, it serves as simply another in a long line of disappointing and dispiriting rights-based political efforts. If, however, we examine this struggle for treatment access as taking place in the courtroom as well as the streets, in the offices of policy makers and in the waiting rooms of community clinics, and we do so from what I call a performative perspective, we come to see the value and the limits of these interpretations.

---

the state and advances neoliberal public policies that ultimately serve the interests of global capital rather than the interests the people. See, for example Brown (2005) and Kennedy (2012).

[3] For example, in the *Grootboom* (2001) case, the plaintiff won a constitutionally recognized right to housing and yet died without a home of her own. *Government of the Republic of South Africa and others v. Grootboom and others*, 2001 (1) SA 46 (CC).

[4] According to Makau Mutua, for example, the black majority in the new South Africa will not be served by rights because 'The deployment of the rights idiom as the principle medium for transformation will in all likelihood fail to reverse the deep-seated legacies of apartheid' (1997, p. 114). Mutua roots the inadequacies of rights-based political practices in their deep intertwinement with capitalism: 'failure of imagination and acquiescence to a free market vision of political democracy has robbed the human rights corpus and the movement of the impetus to think beyond markets and systems of exploitation that produce ugly social structures' (2008, p. 31).

Mention of the fight for HIV treatment access rights in South Africa most readily brings to mind the activities of the Treatment Action Campaign (TAC) and the Constitutional Court ruling in *Minster of Health vs. Treatment Action Campaign* (2002). TAC is both the national and international face of the struggle and the court case, which established a right for HIV-positive pregnant women and newborns to have access to the AIDS drug Nevirapine, is often seen as its high point. However, it is important to recognize that the fight for treatment access was never limited to a single organization, rights argument, or court case. Indeed, it has always been both a legal and a political campaign, one that crosses from the public into the private sector, and engages government agencies, civil society organizations, public officials, elite activists, and ordinary citizens. It has and continues to entail a range of practices that exceed the juridical realm and include, for example, civil disobedience and community health outreach, public media campaigns and treatment literacy programs, publications and demonstrations, policy debate and discussion of the seemingly mundane details of daily life such as access to electricity and clean water.

Taking a closer look at the wide range of practices deployed in the fight for HIV-related health care rights in South Africa, I question the supposition that either its successes or its disappointments can be attributed to the 'liberal' dimensions of their practice alone as both champions and critics often suggest. I do repudiate wholly the concerns raised by critics nor do I offer unqualified praise of the struggle. Instead, I seek to highlight what gets obscured when we reduce the complex practice of rights claiming to the perpetuation of liberal ideas and the reinforcement of neoliberal economics. While I argue that the critique of the struggle offers an extremely important perspective on this and other rights campaigns, it unfortunately obfuscates the varied roots of the rights discourses engaged in South Africa and fails to acknowledge the subversiveness of the new identities and political subjectivities to which the discourse gives rise. At the same time, however, the transformative or subversive nature of these rights-based political efforts can neither be taken for granted nor attributed to a singular legal or political discourse.[5] To bring this complexity to the fore and to show how it is made possible, in part, through the African notion of Ubuntu, I take what I have described elsewhere as a performative perspective on rights claiming (Zivi 2012). A performative perspective on rights claiming allows us to attend not only to what rights claims mean, but also to what they do. In other words, it helps to illuminate the many and varied activities that are done *through* the practice of making rights claims.

[5]I do not mean to suggest that all those who champion a rights-based effort to make change in South Africa do so without qualification. Indeed, many of those at the center of these efforts are acutely aware of the limitations of rights language and the political and economic contexts in which it is deployed. Marius Pieterse, for example, who is a member of Section 27, the public interest law center that includes the former AIDS Law Project, tempers his praise for a rights-based approach to social change by acknowledging that 'the transformative potential of rights is significantly thwarted by the fact that they are typically formulated, interpreted, and enforced by institutions that are embedded in the political, social, and economic status quo' (2007, p. 797).

9.2 A Performative Perspective on Rights Claiming

Before turning more specifically to the fight for access to AIDS treatment, let me say a few more words about a performative perspective on rights claiming and why it is useful in this case. The performative perspective on rights claiming I employ builds on arguments and trends that have been developing in rights scholarship for some time. It is in conversation, for example, with efforts to recognize rights discourse as a political rather than a moral language. Michael Ignatieff (2001) takes up this effort when he calls on human rights activists and lawyers to shift from treating rights as a religious creed or a language of absolute and timeless truths untainted by political realities to recognizing it as a language of politics that involves compromises and tradeoffs, disagreements and even disappointments. Ignatieff urges rights activists to take a more pragmatic approach to understanding the impact of their words and deeds.[6]

To Ignatieff's call, I would add that we must recognize more than just the political conditions under which rights claims are made or the compromises that rights politics may require. We need also to appreciate the fundamentally political character of rights claiming. By that I mean, rights claiming is not just a tool deployed in the game of politics; it is a political practice itself, a practice through which we constitute ourselves and our world.

A performative perspective on rights claiming sheds light on these practices. It reminds us that the activity of making rights entails a set of speech acts – understood expansively to include actions as well as utterances – through which we often bring into existence the very things that we presume or are presumed to reference (e.g., Austin 1975; Derrida 1988; Butler 1993, 1997, 1999; Zivi 2012). Such an approach to the study and understanding of rights is built upon a non-referential theory of language that reminds us that intelligibility and effect is not always a matter of correspondence to facts in the world. Indeed, according to a theory of performativity, what we often take to be natural or given actually comes into being through the repetition of words, gestures, ways of being and thinking. Intelligibility or comprehensibility comes in and through the referencing and repeating of social norms and conventions that are neither static nor always explicitly obvious. Classic examples

[6] I would argue that many in the treatment access movement were always quite cognizant of the 'political' dimensions of rights claiming and approached the discourse pragmatically rather than zealously (e.g., Forbath 2011; Heywood 2009). Of course, taking this pragmatic approach is not necessarily easy given the way rights have been theorized historically, the way international human rights documents are worded, and the cultural expectations that have come to seem commonsensical about rights. For example, the United Nations Office of the High Commissioner for Human Rights states that human rights are 'universal and inalienable', that they are 'inherent to all human beings, whatever our nationality, place of residence, sex, national or ethnic origin, colour, religion, language, or any other status' (http://www.ohchr.org/EN/Issues/Pages/WhatareHumanRights.aspx). Thus it is not surprising that we think, act, and write about rights as if they are and should be clear trump cards because of their implicit legal or moral truth despite the fact that empirical evidence and philosophical argument suggests otherwise.

of performative utterances include 'I bet,' 'I name thee', and "I do." In these utterances the speaking and the doing are equivalent (Austin 1975).

Speech acts work to create relationships, identities, and "facts" through a process of citationality. J. L. Austin (1975) calls those utterances that properly cite conventions – for example, that occur in the correct place at the correct time – felicitous. This felicity or uptake, as Pierre Bourdieu explains, results not from the intention of the speaker but from referencing and repeating 'the combination of a systematic set of interdependent conditions which constitute social rituals' (1994, p. 111). For Judith Butler (1997), however, the process of citationality and the effectiveness of an utterance are more complicated. Citationality is neither a singular nor necessarily intentional event and the intelligibility of a speech act may actually entail mis-citation or subversive repetition. In other words, the effect or force of an utterance, what it makes possible, is not only the result of taken for granted customs, norms, and rituals repeated over time, a process Butler calls 'sedimentation'. It is also the result of using familiar norms and gestures in new contexts, of being misunderstood, and of purposefully misusing a word or gesture in the hopes of being understood anew. Such engagement with the conventions and rituals that make up our shared social rituals means that speech acts can also generate the new, whether these are new norms, new realities, or new subjectivities (Zivi 2008, 2012).

In recent years, theories of performativity have been used to explain the ways in which gender identity comes into being, how hate speech works, and the ways in which one's sense of self and community are constituted through processes of citationality. In this essay, I use a performative perspective to understand what is done in and through the process of claiming rights to treatment access. I thus reconsider a claim such as 'HIV-positive individuals have a right to access AIDS treatment' or 'pregnant women have a right to protect their babies from harm' in terms of both its meaning *and* its force or effects. For example, these rights claims could be read simply as statements of fact, as constative claims in which the speaking subject simply makes reference to an already existing legal or moral reality: that the Constitution, moral norms, or human nature do, in fact, provide these rights. But they can also be read as bringing into being new rights and new subjectivities that did not necessarily exist prior to the process of claims making.

To suggest that the rights and rights-bearing subjectivities which are often presumed to serve as the foundation for legal claims and political activities are actually constituted through the claims-making itself is not to suggest that simply uttering the words or taking a case to court is sufficient to bring either into being. The effects or forces of an utterance, as I suggested above, are neither the result of the intention of the speaker alone nor the product of a singular doing. In fact, they are not solely the result of winning a case in court. As history has proven, neither a written document nor explicit state recognition alone is enough to make a reality of 'having of a right' or being of 'a person with rights'. Both are, instead, the never fixed or assured effects of an ongoing set of activities that occur among individuals who share a complicated social world. A performative perspective on rights claiming suggests, then, that the meaning and power, indeed the very reality of 'having a right', is the effect of rather than the precursor to these utterances and activities. This 'effect', in turn, requires repeated activity that entails the citation of already existing norms, makes possible the creation of new ones, and yet often goes awry.

The practice of making rights claims, on this account, cannot be reduced to engagement with a set of pre-existing legal or moral arguments that succeed or fail to bring about specific social change. It is not simply the case, in other words, those fighting for treatment access rights and the Constitutional Court acknowledged a right that already existed in Section 27 or other parts of the Constitution, nor that the Constitution simply reflected an already existing but often unrecognized moral truth about what human beings are or to what they are entitled by birth. Nor is it the case that one moment in the campaign or one activity made health care rights for HIV-positive individuals a political reality. Instead, rights claiming in the context of the South African AIDS epidemic was, and continues to be, an ongoing, multifaceted, intersubjective, and dynamic activity that has effects that often exceed the intentions of political actors and the gaze of social critics. Claiming a right to treatment is part of the process of 'having' that right, though the latter is, of course, never reducible to the former. And claiming that right occurs in practices beyond legal argumentation or traditional acts of speaking. It is performed, as I show below, through a host of activities, some of which may eschew the language of rights altogether.

To put the point differently, rather than reducing rights to a static ideology or singular vision of justice often identified as liberalism, I treat rights claiming in the context of the fight for treatment access as a varied set of activities that are as generative of new social norms and identities as they are reflective of old ones. Such activities have the capacity to bring something new into existence partly through engagement with and repetition of already existing conventions. This is not to suggest that rights have no existence as legal facts or moral principles. It is, rather, to consider more carefully what it is we do through the making of rights claims and how it is we do this.

A performative perspective on rights thus moves us from a tendency to treat rights as things or instruments we use to bring about a particular end towards a recognition that rights claiming is a complex linguistic practice the outcome of which often exceeds our complete control. It attends to the ways in which our utterances are activities that, when repeated, may do what they say – in this case, bring treatment rights and HIV-positive rights-bearing individuals into existence. And it means appreciating that reference to and reiteration of social conventions and norms is never a simple reflection or reification of those norms. It can entail intended or unintended forms of subversive repetition (e.g., Butler 1997; Chambers and Carver 2008). A performative perspective, then, serves to remind us that the effects of a practice like rights claiming are not necessarily the result of our intention or will. Indeed, it sheds light on the fact that there is always a degree of uncertainty and unpredictability to this practice, particularly since our claims are influenced by, and in turn influence, the context in which we, and the multiple interlocutors to whom we speak, are embedded. The fact is that we always make rights claims in a complicated social context to others who may or may not recognize or understand a claim in precisely the way we expect. This contingency does not make rights claiming any less of an important practice to consider with respect to its democratic implications. Indeed, it is often because rights claiming cannot be perfectly captured in terms of a set of conventions and rules that it is a valuable practice of democratic citizenship.[7]

9.3 The Fight for Treatment Access: A Brief Overview

To understand how rights claiming functioned as a performative practice in the context of the South African AIDS crisis, additional background on the crisis and the treatment access campaign may be helpful. The South African AIDS epidemic is of a scale that is almost unimaginable in other places around the globe. More than five million individuals are living with HIV/AIDS, making it the country with the greatest incidence of the disease in the world. Of those infected, women constitute a majority and some 40 % of these HIV-positive women are of childbearing age. This means that without the use of Antiretroviral drugs (ARVs) taken before and after childbirth and by the newborn, HIV-positive women will transmit the virus to their children in approximately 25 % of cases. Estimates suggest that prior to the implementation of a national prevention program as many as 70,000 babies were infected each year and many died after a short, painful, and illness-filled life.

The South African government knew of the scope of the crisis, and they knew that affordable ARVs were available for quite some time before responding. During what has come to be known as the age of 'AIDS denialism', the South African government, under the leadership of former President Mbeki and former Minister of Health Tshabalala-Msimang, actively prohibited the public distribution of ARVs to pregnant women and newborns, routinely questioned the scientific and medical understandings of the relationship between HIV and AIDS, while enthusiastically promoting alternative therapies that included vitamins and vegetables. Raising concerns about the toxicity of ARVs and, perhaps somewhat rightly suspicions of the intent of Western scientists, the government challenged the mounting evidence detailing ARVs effectiveness in preventing mother-to-child transmission (PMTCT) and balked at the growing global consensus on the long-term benefits of making AIDS drugs available to all (e.g., Cullinan and Thom 2009; Fassin 2007; Geffen 2010; Nattrass 2007; Stephen 2009).

This denialism did not go unnoticed or unchallenged. Begun on International Human Rights Day in 1998 with only a small group of people fasting to protest the government's refusal to distribute ARVs to pregnant women and children, the fight for treatment access has grown into a robust and internationally recognized social movement. The fight for treatment access has brought activists together with members of the medical community and other civil society organizations. And these individuals and groups have mobilized hundreds of thousands of citizens and successfully sued a recalcitrant government to bring into being one of the most

[7] I offer a more extensive discussion of a performative perspective on rights as a democratic practice of citizenship in Zivi 2012.

comprehensive and ambitious national AIDS policies in the world. Spearheaded by the Treatment Action Campaign (TAC), seasoned political activists worked alongside everyday citizens rallying, marching, petitioning, educating, and litigating against a government bent on denying what brought such massive death to its doorstep. They worked at the grassroots, the state, and the international levels, alongside local and international NGOs, enlisting world leaders in their cause, and even persuading global pharmaceutical companies to give AIDS drugs away.[8] And they used the new Constitution's Bill of Rights, particularly the provisions of Section 27 granting citizens a right to access health care and obligating the government to take 'reasonable legislative and other measures…to achieve the progressive realisation of these rights', to press their case in the courtroom and in the public arena.

Individuals and groups fighting for access to AIDS treatment made rights claims to shame and challenge the South African government. Through rights discourse they exposed the government's intent to deny the realities of the AIDS epidemic and block treatment access to HIV-positive individuals, and they achieved much success. They changed AIDS policy at the national level, increased global awareness of HIV/AIDS as a human rights issue, and radically transformed the lives of many (e.g., Forbath 2011; Friedman and Mottiar 2005; Heywood 2009; Heywood and Altman 2000; Kapczyniski and Berger 2009; London 2004).[9] The high points of the campaign include the 2002 Constitutional Court ruling in the case *Minister of Health v. Treatment Action Campaign* (which found that the government's program to prevent mother-to-child HIV transmission, or lack thereof, amounted to a breach of its constitutional obligation to promote citizens' right to access health care services), the many well-attended rallies and demonstrations staged along the way, and, of course, the revision of the National Strategic Plan on HIV/AIDS to include the rollout of ARVs to individuals around the country.[10]

That rights language and the courts were central to the fight for treatment access, interestingly, had a great deal to do with who was leading the struggle and when it was occurring. Indeed, it had much to do with the proximity of the treatment access struggle to the relatively recent anti-apartheid campaigns. As TAC founder Zachie Achmat explained: 'We could not have mounted TAC a generation later…. Everyone would have forgotten the steps. Everyone remembered the songs; the women [HIV-positive, urban, black Africans living in townships] remembered the demonstrations for our rights' (quoted in Forbath 2011, p. 61). Indeed, many involved in the first decade of the struggle for treatment access drew upon their political experiences under the apartheid regime. This meant that they coupled

[8] For illuminating discussions of the role that United States' AIDS organizations such as ACT-UP and the Gay Men's Health Crisis played in shaping the treatment access campaign in South Africa, see Heywood 2009 and Hodes 2010.

[9] The Treatment Action Campaign has produced its own histories of their organization. These include *TAC: An Overview* and *Fight for Our Lives: The History of the Treatment Action Campaign 1998–2010*, both available online at http://www.tac.org.za/community/files/10yearbook/index.html

[10] As of 2012, South Africa has a National Strategic Plan on HIV, STIs, and TB.

faith in the potential of rights claims to engender change in the legal arena with an understanding that making rights a reality would require more than just changes in laws and documents. Past experience had taught treatment rights activists that it would also require active engagement and political responsibility in other arenas. Thus, those seeking treatment access used rights language in the courts to change law as well as in the public realm to shame policy makers, mobilize individuals, and transform daily medical practice.

9.3.1 Liberalism's Discipline?

The fight for HIV-related treatment access rights, particularly as exemplified by activities of TAC, has garnered considerable praise world-wide. It is often portrayed as a model of what human rights norms and rights-based political activism can make possible. And yet, even the successes of the campaign worry some, leading them to caution against too quickly rushing to emulate its values or reproduce its methods in other locations. For these critics, it is essential to identify and understand the power and limits of rights discourse as it has been deployed in the campaign's rhetoric, as well as to draw attention to the unnecessary compromises made and the unwelcome, albeit perhaps unintentional, consequences engendered along the way (e.g., Albertyn and Meer 2009; Johnson 2006b). In this section, I focus my attention on concerns raised by individuals on the political left who worry for example, that TAC has sold out women's rights or gotten into bed with global capitalism. While some critics fault members of the movement itself, others place blame for disappointing outcomes on the larger ideological and socio-economic context in which the treatment access struggle occurred. In these critiques we find an effort to illuminate what Krista Johnson (2006b) describes as the disciplinary dimensions of rights discourse: that is, the power of a set of ideas, values, and practices that we call liberalism to co-opt and often undermine the best of intentions and efforts of those fighting for the rights and health of HIV infected and affected individuals. Critics suggest, in other words, that despite efforts on the part of activists and civil society organizations to address the socio-economic and gendered dimensions of the AIDS epidemic, global economic policy and hegemonic ideas about individual freedom, the importance of property rights, and the role of the state make real social, political, and economic transformation nearly impossible. The vestiges of liberal ideology and political structures or the reach of neoliberal economic policies render even rights victories somewhat empty. For critics, then, the centrality of rights language to the struggle for HIV treatment has a dark side, revealing a series of choices and leading to policies and practices that ultimately serve to reinforce rather than rectify inequality.

This critical perspective on the fight for treatment access, as I suggest below, is not so much incorrect as it is limited and limiting. Though it is attentive, at least implicitly, to the performative nature of rights claiming, it is too narrowly focused on the activities of the Treatment Action Campaign and their battle in the court. It may recognize that rights claiming produces a certain kind of rights-bearing subject rather than presupposing it, and yet it highlights only a small set of the codes, norms, and conventions being cited. According to this perspective, it is a static liberalism, with its commitment to atomistic, property-owning male heads of household, to which advocates for treatment access cannot help but refer and reinforce.

To be fair, those who criticize aspects of the treatment access campaign do acknowledge a number of its successes, just as those who fête the campaign recognize some of its limitations. Critics do not deny, for example, the importance of making ARVs that treat and, in some cases, prevent transmission of HIV/AIDS available to millions of people under South Africa's comprehensive national strategic plan, particularly in the wake of years of government inaction.[11] They share in celebrating the fact that South Africa has almost eradicated mother-to-child HIV transmission, particularly in light of the fact that the country continues to have the highest incidence of HIV/AIDS in their population on the globe.[12] And they appreciate the work that the treatment access movement has done to reduce the stigma associated with HIV/AIDS and to create a community of engaged political subjects.

Yet, they remind us that South Africa continues to have extremely high rates of HIV/AIDS, that women are particularly vulnerable to infection as well as sexual violence, that millions remain without access to ARVs, that quality health care eludes large parts of the country, and that little has changed with respect to the tremendous economic inequalities that contribute to the spread of HIV/AIDS. For critics, the successes of the fight for treatment access cannot fully compensate for such disappointments. And these disappointments must be understood as related, to a large extent, to a reliance on liberal ideas, institutions, and practice. The argument here is that the practice of rights claiming is inextricable from liberal ideology and neoliberal economics – it cites and perpetuates decidedly liberal norms, customs, and codes. It thus cannot help but produce individualistic attitudes toward the epidemic, promote capitalistic gains at the expense of social change, and produce a particular kind of 'entrepreneurial' citizen who ultimately becomes responsible for her own care and treatment. The result is a failure to rectify, indeed even to identify, the real sources of the problems in ways that undermine the radical potential of the struggle for treatment access.

Feminists, for example, argue that the way the treatment access advocates, and TAC in particular, framed the legal issue is symptomatic of and reinforces liberal gender norms that undermine women's equality. By framing a complex issue of gender injustice and inequality – poor black women in South Africa have the highest rates HIV infection among the population and are at greater risk of being infected than men – in terms of the right of mothers to protect their babies from harm or the

---

[11] On the period of South African history now known as 'AIDS denialism', see Geffen (2010) and Nattrass (2007).

[12] Current estimates put mother-to-child transmission rates at 4 %. The National Strategic Plan (2012–2016) seeks to get this rate below 2 % by 2016.

right of children to have access to health care, treatment activists and judges too greatly narrowed the scope of the issue. Absent from this framing, scholars such as Catherine Albertyn and Shamim Meer argue, are larger contextual issues such as violence against women and the fragility of women's autonomous decision-making in the private sphere. And the gendered nature of liberal rights discourse and institutions – the fact that its very ideas are based on the male body and experience, and that its state agencies are populated largely by elites who are often men – is partly to blame for these problems, for forcing the reduction of a clear issue concerning women's reproductive freedom and gender equality to one of protecting and promoting good motherhood. In other words, from the perspective of feminist critics, the emphasis placed by TAC and the Constitutional Court on PMTCT and protecting children's rights reinforces the depiction of women as victims of state inaction and does little either to protect women from infection or to address the culture's deep-seated misogyny that put women at risk of infection in the first place. Positioning women as in need of state protection via a guarantee of their rights also served to undermine women's autonomy with respect to their medical decision-making. While feminist critics acknowledge that a language of choice emphasizing women's autonomous decision-making did play a prominent role in treatment access arguments and activities made in the public arena, they remain concerned that its absence in the courtroom sidelined discussions of the full range of options available to address the epidemic in ways that ultimately devalued and weakened women's autonomy (Albertyn 2003; Albertyn and Meer 2009).[13]

Critics who draw attention to the economic limits of rights discourse direct their critiques less at the actors involved in the fight for treatment access rights and more at the context in which, and history from which, rights claiming arises. For example, Johnson (2006a, b) argues that the South African efforts to expand human rights to include socio-economic ones are marked by only a limited success. At the global level, she argues, 'human rights...continues to be shaped within the hegemonic neo-liberal framework that demands we understand the AIDS pandemic in a particular way – as a health issue rather than as a development or human security issue, as an individual concern rather than as a community or even global concern' (Johnson 2006a, pp. 126–127). Indeed, she contends that because rights discourse is inextricable from a liberal ideology that privileges political and civil rights such as property and individual freedom over socio-economic concerns, it should come as no surprise that policy and practice ends up favoring the interests of global capital at

[13] Biomedical studies of HIV-positive women's experience suggest a less critical but nonetheless complementary description of the way rights have, or have not, influenced women's lives in South Africa. For example, MacGregor and Mills (2011), who studied a small group of HIV-positive women between 2003 and 2008, found that the language of rights and community engagement, so central to the lives of these women in the early years of the treatment access campaign, gave way to the language of personal responsibility and privatized experiences, ultimately individualizing the issue and shifting responsibility away from the state. And see Eyakuze et al. (2008) for another study of the PMTCT programs that suggests such programs do not empower women as much as was expected or is necessary to advance women's equality and autonomy. See Colvin et al. (2010) for a discussion of the production of responsible HIV-positive men.

the expense of the poor and vulnerable (see also Johnson 2006b, p. 664). The simple fact that rights language positions nation-states as either primary violators or guarantors of rights undermines the power of the marginalized and makes it all the more difficult to identify, shame, or transform the global actors and structural forces that contribute to the AIDS crisis (2006b, p. 663).

Evidence suggests that these concerns are not without merit. TAC members, for example, acknowledge that the decision to focus on PMTCT and frame their legal and political case in a particular way was strategic. They chose to highlight the more emotionally persuasive moral and more easily understandable public health and economic arguments, and that meant positioning women as victims of a government failing to protect their rights and the rights of their babies. It meant leaving reasons for why a woman might choose not to take ARVs off to the side. Indeed, as Mark Heywood, a lawyer with Section 27 and a former leader of TAC, explained, 'TAC's first campaign…was intended to be tangible, understandable, emotive, and life saving', to highlight 'the human cost of denial of HIV medication' and to depict it as 'a moral dilemma for society as a whole' (2009, p. 20). TAC specifically chose, in other words, to emphasize the innocence of babies and their mothers' heartbreaking experience of loss, and to pose this as a moral, health, and political tragedy befalling the nation. It was the government, not the individual women, who were the clear culprits in this narrative, violating the rights of citizens and betraying a people (e.g., Zivi 2012, esp. Chap. 5). And it was this focus on a clear enemy that enabled TAC and other players in the treatment access movement to galvanize and mobilize thousands of people (e.g., Hodes 2010).

Just as the feminist critique sheds light on certain problematic aspects of the treatment access fight, so too does the economic critique. Despite efforts to address economic inequality through the protection of rights to treatment access, HIV positive individuals remain economically vulnerable. Even organizations like TAC that were once robust are now experiencing economic and identity crises. For example, as of 2012, the Treatment Action Campaign was struggling financially and existentially despite having garnered international recognition, engendered key legislative and policy changes, and mobilized hundreds of thousands of individuals over the previous decade. Economic crises around the world and shifting priorities of funding organizations, coupled with a growing impression that the AIDS crisis is if not over, then certainly contained, means that there is less money to support the activities of the organization. And as an important employer of South African citizens, particularly women, in an economy where unemployment is extremely high and jobs scarce, these economic constraints take a toll on far more than the organization's ability to function. TAC's current situation seems to reinforce that idea that winning a right in court, even a right that is explicitly tied to socio-economic issues such as health care and requires government action on an issue, often has little impact on the realities of the labor market and the already existing distribution of economic resources.

Additionally, the legal and legislative successes of the organization may actually complicate its message in ways that make it less accessible to a wider public and even to its members. Having won the legal battle on PMTCT, TAC has had to shift its goals and mission. TAC members may still see themselves as fighting for rights, but they acknowledge that their mobilizing and energizing capacities have been diminished now that they no longer have a clear enemy in the government. They recognize that their message is being diluted as they move from an almost singular focus on the demand for treatment rights to the more diffuse job of providing human resources management, that is, moving from fighting the state to making sure that clinics are staffed and supplied adequately so as to meet the health care goals set by the government. With its message unclear to some and its ranks stretched thin by ongoing budget cuts, the future of TAC, and perhaps the treatment rights movement is uncertain.[14]

If for champions of the movement, it is rights rhetoric, understood as a powerful language of morality as well as a set of legal facts and institutions, that was and remains critical for mobilizing people and engendering significant change, it is often this same rights rhetoric, or rather the inextricability of rights from political liberalism and neoliberal economics, that is, for the critics, a part of the problem.[15] The fact that the changes brought about through the practice of claiming health care rights are not as radical or revolutionary as hoped for, in other words, can be attributed, in part, to the liberal ideology inherent in the practice of rights claiming, to that set of ideas, institutions, and practices that individualize social problems, reinforce vast economic inequalities, and depoliticize issues and citizens. On these accounts, the story of the struggle for treatment access appears to be a cautionary tale about the limits, possibly even the dangers, of rights-based political resistance, a warning not to put too much stock in the growing recognition of and struggle to make a human right to health care a reality around the globe. It reinforces the idea that even legal victories may be what Gerald Rosenberg (2009) has called 'much ado about nothing'. Addressing these issues involves, critics argue or imply, the adoption of an alternative language of social justice, an alternative style politics, even a radically different form of governance.[16]

---

[14] This assessment is based on several interviews done with current and past TAC members during May 2012. As one interviewee explained, it is more difficult to mobilize people to protest than it used to be and, ironically, the success of treatment programs might actually kill AIDS activism. Indeed, it is, this person suggested, much easier to mobilize people against a state for actively violating their rights than it is to mobilize the same people to fight for adequately-staffed health clinics. It is also more difficult to mobilize a generation who feel entitled to a set of rights for which they have not had to fight.

[15] I do not mean to deny the nuances of either the more celebratory or critical perspectives on the treatment access campaign. Both recognize aspects of the alternative perspective, and yet clearly place an emphasis on one particular reading of the struggle. Johnson for example, raises concerns about the neoliberal aspects of the struggle while also acknowledging that it 'challenges liberal understandings of rights, promoting a more socialist or nationalist understanding of rights that focuses on equality of access and collective rights and is grounded in the discourse of the liberation struggle' (2006a, p. 126). Still, her conclusion is that 'the dramatic increase in the political franchise and the heightened awareness of one's rights continues to be prejudiced by the priorities of neoliberalism and global markets, as well as internal power struggles and the consolidation of a new political order' (2006a, p. 128).

[16] Mutua, for example, suggests a turn toward African customary law and traditions: 'for rights to make sense in the African context, one has to go beyond the individual and address group identities

9.3.2 Subversive Citations

While both critics and champions of the treatment access campaign offer insights into what rights can and cannot do to address and overcome economic, political, and social inequalities in the context of the South African AIDS epidemic, neither alone nor even once combined do they give us a full picture. Too often, the practice of rights claiming is understood as failing – or succeeding – because of its citation of traditional liberal norms of individual autonomy and state responsibility. However, as I argue in this section, what is being cited in the process of claiming treatment rights is far more than simply a static liberal ideology, and the subject produced through this process is far more complicated than the atomistic individual or even the entrepreneurial, responsible citizen. Rights claiming in the context of the AIDS epidemic, rather than being beholden to liberal ideology or neoliberal economic commitments, actually draws on the hybrid of rights discourses that co-exist in South Africa, a hybrid influenced by African as well as Marxist ideas. In this context, the very intelligibility of rights claiming comes from the citation of or reference to a variety of social codes and this, in turn, makes possible new norms, new ways of thinking, and possibilities for living differently. As I detail below, the African ideas and customs associated with Ubuntu, though not explicitly referenced in either the legal arguments or political practices of the campaign for treatment access rights, are, nonetheless, implicit in both. Ubuntu is embedded in the Constitution and the precedents to which activists and judges refer, and it is there in the spirit and effects of the treatment literacy and community outreach programs that make the right to treatment a meaningful reality for those living with HIV/AIDS.

This reading of the treatment access campaign rests on a theory of performativity that suggests that speech acts 'work', that is, have effects, a force, or an outcome, based, in part, on their intelligibility or comprehensibility. In other words, we have to understand what another says and does through speech and action for it to have an impact on the world. However, this comprehensibility depends less on whether or not an utterance accurately represents or reflects something already existing in the world and more on its reference to or citation of the norms, codes, and customs that form the shared social world in which we are embedded. Of course, given that these codes are neither static nor always identifiable in their original form, and given that they are themselves contested and open to multiple interpretations, the effects of speech act citationality can range quite a bit. As the critical literature on the treatment access movement highlights, the practice of making rights claims in South Africa is comprehensible and powerful to a large extent because it references liberal ideas about state responsibility and individual freedom. As I suggest below, however, rights claiming cited far more than these ideas and the liberal discourse

in the political and economic framework of the state' (2008, p. 34), while Albertyn and Meer (2009) suggest a greater focus on gender inequities is necessary.

with which they are association; it is a practice, then, that has effects that exceed those detailed above.[17]

Indeed, as a theory of performativity reminds us, reiteration and repetition of authorized discourses is less than a clear-cut, intentional, and single event. Not only is it never quite clear which codes are being cited, but also these citations can go awry, be recontextualized, or be purposefully cited in unexpected, unconventional ways. All of these possibilities contribute to what Butler calls the possibilities of 'perverse reiterations', citations and repetitions of social norms and codes that engender something new, excessive, and potentially transformative. As Chambers and Carver explain it, subversive repetition entails 'interventions *enabled* by current cultural constructions even as they *contest* them in political practice' (2008, p. 45). I would suggest that this is what we see in the treatment access movement when we consider the practice of rights claiming more expansively.

Treating rights claims as performative utterances and rights claiming as a performative practice means paying careful attention to what happens in and through the making of rights claims. Treating rights claiming as a performative practice, in other words, means recognizing that in making a claim such as 'I have a right to health care', a speaker does far more than accurately (or perhaps inaccurately) represent a pre-existing moral, legal, or political reality. That is, he or she does more than simply reference the South African Constitution or international human rights norms, and more than simply reference and repeat a static set of liberal ideas and norms. This is made possible, in part, by the fact that rights discourse in South Africa has a number of importantly distinct roots, not all of which reside in the ideas and institutions of a liberal democracy (Dubow 2012). South African rights rhetoric draws on a history of multiple rights traditions, including an Afrikaner and an African tradition. Customary law, Marxism, more republican variations on rights discourse, as well as international discourses on rights all contribute to the background context and conditions in which claims were made for the right to treatment (Church 2005). This results in 'hybrid political discourses that defy…enduring binary categories' of customary versus liberal legal frameworks (Robins 2008, p. 172).

The Treatment Action Campaign and the healthcare rights movement more generally drew upon this more complicated legacy, particularly by referencing the ideas and practices of human rights associated with the anti-apartheid movement and the African National Congress (ANC). TAC's original leaders, for example, had been members of the ANC's Marxist Workers Tendency, and this shaped their vision and mission, leading to a campaign emphasizing treatment rights as part of a larger

[17] In reminding us that rights claiming is an activity embedded in but not fully determined by context, a performative perspective not only offers a more holistic approach to treatment access struggle, it may be more consistent with the perspectives taken by those spearheading the struggle itself. For example, there are important affinities between a performative perspective on rights claiming and TAC's idea of a 'politics-centered approach to ESR advocacy'. For comprehensive discussions of a 'politics-centered approach' to human rights and illustrations of the variety of activities entailed by and importance of context for the meaning of such a politics, see Forbath (2011) and Heywood (2009).

struggle for economic equality and social justice.[18] TAC's first statement of purpose explicitly sets forth this connection between health care rights, economic inequality, and their commitment to advance the interests of the poor:

> The National Association of People Living with AIDS (NAPWA) has initiated the Treatment Action Campaign to draw attention to the unnecessary suffering and AIDS-related deaths of thousands of people in Africa, Asia and South America. These human rights violations are the result of poverty and the unaffordability of HIV/AIDS treatment. (Treatment Action Campaign 2010)

And the PMTCT focus and language was never isolated from these larger socio-economic goals. As Mark Heywood explained early on in the campaign:

> Preventing mother to child HIV transmission has benefits that extend far beyond the life saved and grief prevented. An intervention like this could be used by the government to launch a campaign to encourage much more wide-spread voluntary HIV testing, beginning with pregnant women, but soon extending to fathers. It would create an immediate necessity to train more health workers as counselors and to place them at ante-natal wards. It could also be used as a reason to rapidly improve access and quality of primary health care. (Heywood and Altman 2000)

In addition to recognizing health care rights as part of a larger project of economic justice, TAC also always understood itself to be fighting for gender justice. Members drew on feminist discourses circulating nationally and internationally, for example, as they expanded the claim for a right of access to health care to include claims about the right to know about and have access to various forms of birth control as well as about having children with HIV-infected partners. In these cases, rights claims to health care become larger claims about a woman's right to sexual pleasure and control over her reproductive decisions, and, of course, to her status as a citizen of a democratic nation. TAC has also become involved in advancing 'PMTCT B+', a program that would allow HIV positive women to stay on AIDS drugs even after they give birth as well as in efforts to shape national breastfeeding policy.[19] In this latter case, their Marxist and feminist influences come together once again as TAC activists encourage the state to adopt flexible breastfeeding policies that pay careful attention to the material constraints and differing contexts of women's lives.

In these examples, we can see that claiming a right to health care is not reducible to a traditional claim about an individual right to be free from state interference or a gendered right for vulnerable women and children to be protected by the state. The treatment access campaign, from TAC's perspective, has always been about far more than protecting innocent babies or promoting good mothering; it also involves educating, employing, and empowering women. Indeed, for many women, becoming a part of TAC, whether through political activism, policy

[18] In fact, their original target of criticism was not the government but the pharmaceutical industry and the exorbitant costs it charged for AIDS drugs.

[19] The first generation of PMTCT programs provide AIDS drugs to prevent transmission to the infant, but women are taken off the AIDS drugs once their children are declared HIV-negative, unless, of course, their own CD4 count is at a particular low. Interviews, May 2012.

making, or community outreach, has been life changing. As Lindiwe Mbatha, a TAC member, explains, 'In the past I was abused but now I am a person who can stand up for my rights. Even my husband knows that…. In TAC I learned, for the first time in my life, that we are not nothing, we have rights on this earth. I have learned to make my own decisions and now I can teach other women' (TAC 2010, p. 94). Akona Ntsabula echoes these sentiments when she says that 'through TAC I am where I am today…. Women's leadership training empowered me to fight for women's rights anywhere' (TAC 2010, p. 94). The knowledge individuals gain in TAC is capacitating; it gives men and women the tools, skills, and sense of self to understand and respond to the complexities of disease, the political process, and life in the community.[20]

9.3.3 Citing Ubuntu in the Legal Realm

In addition to feminist and Marxist rhetorics that directly challenge the masculinist and capitalist dimensions of liberal rights, one of the most important, but least acknowledged, discourses being cited is the African discourse of Ubuntu. Part of the cultural heritage of the African majority, Ubuntu conceives of human beings as fundamentally interdependent; one does not become an individual except within and through relationships with others. While one has individual rights, according to this worldview, one also has obligations to the group, and the former are meaningless without the latter. Rights, according to an Ubuntu worldview, do not take precedence over obligations, and yet it is communal solidarity that makes possible the kind of individual dignity and growth associated with having rights. As Cornell and Muvangua explain, 'In Ubuntu human beings are intertwined in a world of ethical relations and obligations from the time they are born…. It is only through the engagement and support of others that we are able to realize a true individuality' (2012, p. 3). Or, as Justice Mokgoro explains, Ubuntu is:

> a philosophy of life, which in its most fundamental sense represents personhood, humanity, humaneness and morality; a metaphor that describes group solidarity where such group solidarity is central to the survival of communities with a scarcity of resources, and the fundamental belief is that '*ubuntu ngumuntu ngabantu, motho ke motho ba batho ba bangwe*,' which, literally translated, means "a human being is a human being because of other human beings." (Mokgoro 1998, pp. 15–16)

To those who would worry that Ubuntu's emphasis on the community would ultimate privilege the group over the individual, Cornell and Marle respond by explaining that Ubuntu is 'not…a simple form of communalism or communitarianism'; it is, instead, a recognition that 'the process of becoming a person, or, more strongly put, how one is given the chance to become a person at all' is something that is never done in isolation from others (2012, p. 353).

[20] Interview, May 2012.

Such African ideas, though they have always been a part of jurisprudence in South Africa, even under colonialism, have come to play a very important role in the new South Africa.[21] Indeed, as a number of prominent judges and scholars have argued, the spirit of Ubuntu has and should continue to shape the legal and moral culture despite the fact that explicit reference to the concept was removed from the Constitution in the transition from its 1994 to its 1996 version (e.g., Bessler 2008; Cornell and Muvangua 2012). The Constitution, particularly in its Bill of Rights, clearly embodies that traditional African concept by promoting social justice and by protecting life, health, human dignity, and the vulnerable. Such provisions and the influence they have had over judicial decisions, provide evidence that Ubuntu is embedded in and infused throughout the new legal system. For example, in *S v Makwanyane and Another* (1995), Justice Langa grounded his position on the unconstitutionality of the death penalty in Ubuntu. Ubuntu, he explained, 'recognises a person's status as a human being, entitled to unconditional respect, dignity, value and acceptance from the members of the community such person happens to be part of,' and the death penalty violates the right to dignity of individuals. It is at odds, he continued, with 'a culture which places some emphasis on communality and on the interdependence of the members of a community' as well as one that imposes 'a corresponding duty to give the same respect, dignity, value and acceptance to each member of that community' and 'regulates the exercise of rights by the emphasis it lays on sharing and co-responsibility and the mutual enjoyment of rights by all' (quoted in Bessler 2008, pp. 88–89).

What then does Ubuntu have to do with the fight for treatment access and health care rights? At first glance it would appear to have little connection because the term is not referenced often in the documents produced by TAC or other treatment access movement organizations, and it is not explicitly mentioned in the Court's decision in *Minister of Health v. TAC*. The absence of the term, however, should not be read as signaling its irrelevance to the claim for a right to treatment access. That is because Ubuntu forms the backdrop, the precedent, indeed a part of the authorized discourse to which the legal case for treatment access continually refers. For example, the *Grootboom* (2001) decision played a key role in the Court's findings in *Minister of Health v. TAC* (2002). In the former case, the Court argues that:

> The Constitution obliges the State to act positively… to provide access to housing, healthcare, sufficient food and water, and social security to those unable to support themselves and their dependents. The State must also foster conditions to enable citizens to gain access to land on an equitable basis. Those in need have a corresponding right to demand that this be done.

---

[21] According to Joan Church, 'Some of the distinctive features that link the various indigenous systems are the communal character of the law and the importance of the group…. Two of the most significant features are that duties as well as rights are stressed and both are shared' (2005, p. 99). And though customary law and ideals such as Ubuntu were never dominant, and were often used in the service of colonial and apartheid aims, its ongoing influence on South African jurisprudence reminds us that rights discourse in South Africa cannot be reduced to liberalism if liberalism is understood as a set of ideas developed solely by Europeans in the seventeenth, eighteenth, and nineteenth centuries.

This idea is then reiterated in *Minister of Health* both through reference to *Grootboom* and through specific identification of the government obligations set forth in Sections 27 and 28 of the Constitution not only to recognize, but also to assist in the realization of women's and children's rights. Moreover, the Court acknowledged that crucial to their findings were the 'poignant account of HIV-positive pregnant women's pleas for access to nevirapine for themselves and their babies', accounts that clearly recognize the interdependency and situatedness of human beings.

It is the multiple legal traditions in South Africa – the legacy of European liberalism, Marxist ideas, international human rights discourse, feminist ideas of gender equality, and the indigenous African Ubuntu – that make it possible for citizens to demand enforcement of socio-economic rights like those identified by treatment access advocates. It is these multiple traditions to which advocates refer, implicitly or explicitly, when they make rights claims. And it is this social context that enables a marked break from traditional liberalism, with its emphasis on civil and political rights, and negative liberties.

9.3.4 Constituting New Political Subjectivities

Ubuntu also plays a role in the practices of treatment access organizations that occur far removed from the legal realm. It is infused in the practices, such as the treatment literacy and community outreach programs, that make implementation of rights and living as a rights-bearing individual possible on a day-to-day basis. This becomes more obvious when we turn our attention away from the campaign's legal discourse to some of its less explicitly rights-based activities, and from an almost exclusive focus on the efforts of TAC to an examination of a more public health focused organization such as mothers2mothers (m2m).[22] As I illustrate below, despite identifying themselves as a public health rather than a rights-based activist organization, m2m runs programs that are critical to making treatment access rights a reality for HIV-positive women and children. Their Mentor Mothers program, for example, is critical to the implementation of the rights set forth in *Minister of Health v. TAC*, and through the women it trains and those it educates via this program, m2m helps to produce individuals who understand themselves as having rights. These individuals are, however, far more complicated than either the individualistic subjects associated with traditional liberalism or the entrepreneurial citizens associated with neoliberalism. Their sense of self is inextricable from their locatedness in a larger community. In other words, through the communities created by the activities of organizations such as m2m, individuals come not only to understand themselves as having a right to treatment access but also as being a part of a community that makes that right a meaningful reality.

[22] On the importance of extra-juridical activities to the construction of political subjectivity in the context of HIV/AIDS see, for example, Forbath 2011; Robins 2008; and Steinberg 2008.

I turn to mothers2mothers in part to recognize that, although the Treatment Action Campaign is the very public face of the treatment access movement, it has never acted alone. Indeed, treatment access and the fight for health care rights has and continues to involve an array of civil society organizations, medical institutions, government agencies, and individual actors. It also involves much more than making claims for health care rights in the judicial realm. As lawyer Fatima Hassan explains, TAC and its allies recognize that 'the law alone cannot fully transform our society, only people can. The most valuable and transformative legal challenges are those that mobilise and educate people so that communities use the law to give effect to their own voices and this own issues' (TAC 2010, p. 29). Or as law professor Heinz Klug put its, 'The effectiveness of [socioeconomic] rights is…as much the product of social mobilisation and civil society engagement as it is the consequence of institutional cultures developed within the realms of the state' (Klug 2010, p. 119). This is particularly evident when one considers the many other activities in which these treatment access organizations and actors engaged, not all of which involved the language of rights, the courts, or taking an adversarial political stance. Indeed, in the context of mothers2mothers' activities, the practice of claiming a right to health care takes the form of living as, and sometimes as if one were already, a subject with rights. This living is done, I suggest, partly through engagement in treatment literacy and community health education programs, both of which are central to the mission and methods of m2m.

Initiated in 2001 by American obstetrician/gynecologist Mitch Besser, mothers2mothers is a non-profit that sees itself as filling a gap in the resource-challenged South African health care system. It does this by training HIV-positive women who have been its clients to educate the next group of HIV-positive women who are confronting the realities of mothering while living with the disease. These educators, known as Mentor Mothers, teach HIV-positive women about their treatment options and drug adherence practices, they discuss family planning as well as breast-feeding methods, explain the science of and the bureaucracy associated with HIV/AIDS, and even role play the process of disclosure. In so doing, they create a community of women who assist each other in confronting the challenges that having HIV adds to being parents. HIV-positive women who are chosen to be Mentor Mothers go through a rigorous training process in which they learn about the biology and science of HIV/AIDS and its treatment, about stigma and discrimination, about laws and policies, and about the resources available to enable women to better care for themselves and their families. Mentor Mothers are then sent into settings, such as community clinics and hospital maternity wards, where pregnant women and new mothers are often learning about their HIV status for the first time (e.g., McColl 2012; Teasdale and Besser 2008).

The presence of Mentor Mothers in clinical settings illustrates both how HIV-positive women, many of whom are poor and black, enact rights bearing subjectivity and how others with whom they interact come to see them anew. HIV-positive South Africans have faced, and continue to face, such significant degrees of stigma that the experience of learning that one is HIV-positive is challenging under even the best circumstances. For HIV-positive women, particularly pregnant ones, it was all the more fraught before and in the early years after the *TAC* court decision. In the late 1990s and early 2000s, doctors and nurses would often berate women for getting pregnant (evidence of not having used condoms) and advise them to have abortions. These encounters left many women feeling an overwhelming sense of guilt and shame, and reinforced tremendous fears of being rejected by family and friends. Though this kind of treatment by medical professionals, and indeed a good deal of the stigma associated with having HIV, has declined in recent years, women are still likely to experience internal forms of stigma, (e.g., shame, anger at self, fear of dying) upon diagnosis. It is in this context that Mentor Mothers do their work, becoming valuable members of the health care teams that support new mothers and change the way nurses and doctors understand the disease and what it means to live with it.

Mentor Mothers are women who were once clients themselves and thus they begin from a place of commonality with newly diagnosed, pregnant women. They know what it is like to learn one's HIV status while pregnant and they know what needs to be done to avoid transmitting HIV to one's child. Additionally, they often share a language as well as specific community experiences with the women they serve while at the same time being able to represent the possibilities of an alternative and bright future. Mentor Mothers thus provide a kind of support and counsel that doctors, nurses, or community health educators of another sort are simply unable to give. Mentor Mothers have the knowledge and the time to answer questions, explain treatment processes, ease fears, encourage disclosure, and listen without judgment. And they know, understand, and live in the communities of which their mentees are a part. These factors enable them to break through a variety of social, emotional, and psychological barriers, and various levels of stigma associated with the complexities that HIV adds to pregnancy and mothering (e.g., Baek et al. 2007; Teasdale and Besser 2008; Thom 2009). They show women that they are not alone, that PMTCT programs work, and that there is a community of support and future opportunities available for HIV-positive women. They tell and show newly diagnosed women that HIV is not a death sentence, that women can live healthy and long lives with the disease, and that they can have healthy babies. Mentor Mothers thus become the support system that enables other women to make their own decisions about how to live with the disease and to parent.[23] In exemplifying what it looks like to be a strong, autonomous, educated citizen living with illness in the context of considerable poverty, Mentor Mothers perform rights-bearing subjectivity even in the absence of that language.

Mentor mothers serve as more than simply role models of individuals living with HIV/AIDS who are accessing treatment options and exercising their rights. They also serve to illustrate the varied kind of political, economic, and social identities available to women with HIV. As paid and knowledgeable employees of m2m, Mentor Mothers often become well-respected members of the community in part because of the education and skills they gain through their training and in part

[23] Interviews with M. Besser, May 18, 2012 and Anonymous, May 2012.

because of their new economic independence.[24] For many, these experiences of communal respect generate a pride in one's self and one's work, a pride and sense of accomplishment not previously felt. While this employment may not qualify as the deep structural change needed and desired by those on the political left, its importance to the survivability of individual women and the health of communities should not be underestimated. Being a part of m2m – whether as a client, a Mentor Mother, or in another capacity – creates a sense of identity and self-worth for the women both because of and in concert with the creation of a community. In fact, one interviewee who had been a client and Mentor Mother returned to the organization after a several year hiatus when she lost her son in a car accident. M2m provided the support she needed, not for being HIV positive, but for being a grieving mother who remained, nonetheless, a valuable and contributing member of the community.[25] And if m2m is a powerful force in the lives of individuals, it is also a powerful force in communities. Through the Mentor Mothers program, communities become more knowledge not only about HIV/AIDS, its treatment, and its complexities, but also about issues such as stigma, gender equality, and legal rights.

This kind of community generation and individual social and economic empowerment has always been central to the mission of mothers2mothers, and it continues today. Women who were Mentor Mothers in the past, now help supervise or train the next generation of Mentor Mothers. In this process, they learn new skills and information while expanding others' understanding of the science and policy of HIV/AIDS, its lifecycle, and available treatment options. As members of m2m report, the education, the work opportunities, and the team and community activities engender great personal growth and serve as keys to their ability to make choices and have control over their lives. Without the knowledge, as well as psycho-social support gained through the m2m groups, HIV-positive women would have a much more difficult time disclosing their status, which is often seen as the first step in addressing internalized stigma, or making decisions about their health and their futures that are at odds with cultural norms or even the advice of doctors and nurses. Here, then, we see in m2m what others have seen in TAC: the ability to 'empower poor South Africans by democratizing…resources and expertise' (Forbath 2011, p. 67).

This does not mean that the language of rights is unimportant to or disregarded by m2m staff. Though an organization like TAC places health care rights at the center of its mission, m2m places the interests and needs of mothers and children at its core while letting the language of rights serve as an acknowledged background. As one Mentor Mother explains, members of different organizations have different roles to play in the political as well as clinical processes: TAC advocates for rights while m2m actors make sure that PMTCT rights are implemented. And

[24] Mentor Mothers who are employed by m2m for a year or two earn a salary. After their mentoring tenure, some go on to work in other capacities for the organization while others become entrepreneurs.

[25] Interviews, May 2012.

though these organizations emphasize slightly different vocabulary or have distinct foci, they clearly work together to make it possible for HIV-positive women to realize their rights and to internalize their status as rights-bearing individuals. As Babalwa Mbono explains, despite their differences, members in these organizations stand in solidarity: 'As women, we need to stand for our rights, our families. Stand together'.[26] The point here is that both mission and context matter to the specificities of language used. Indeed, as Besser explains, he uses rights language much more explicitly when dealing with policy makers involved in the formation of global AIDS policy than in his daily work with m2m. Rights is the common language of policy makers; as a doctor, his is the language of health and medicine.[27] Just as ethnographic research on TAC shows, m2m's work thus contributes to the creation of 'an untidy, uneven, many-layered process of new rights-bearing identities in the making' (Forbath 2011, p. 81). It helps to create new communities and identities for individuals, all of which are part of the practice of claiming rights. And it does this, in part, through an often unacknowledged emphasis on human interdependency and support.

9.4 Conclusion

What, then, are the lessons to be learned from the treatment access campaign about the state of legal discourse in South Africa in the early twenty-first century? It may be both difficult and premature to answer this question too definitively. To move from a case such as the treatment access campaign to predict either that socio-economic rights will be easier (or more difficult) to win in the future or that radical social, economic, and political changes will (or will not) be engendered through rights claiming, is somewhat presumptuous. Nonetheless, South Africa's treatment access campaign does present a unique and important opportunity to consider the benefits and limits, as well as the productive capacity and complex history, of rights-based political language and practices. As Makau Mutua reminds us, the new democratic South Africa 'represents the first deliberate and calculated effort in history to craft a human rights state–a polity that is primarily animated by human rights norms' (1997, p. 65). And as a number of scholars and critics remind us, there is no denying that some of these animating norms are rooted in a traditional liberalism

[26] Interview, May 24, 2012.

[27] Interview with Besser, May 18, 2012. According to Besser, it is m2m's morally compelling and fairly uncontroversial motto of 'helping mothers saving babies', combined with the fact that m2m addresses HIV/AIDS after sex has already occurred, that has allowed it to thrive and grow as an organization. M2m is not set up 'against' anything or anyone. Besser was simply looking for a more effective way to assist women in understanding and responding to the realities of having HIV while being pregnant and he figured that women who have similar backgrounds and experiences would be most effective in communicating messages about treatment as well as in providing emotional support. Interview, May 18, 2012.

with its emphasis on individual autonomy, the protection of private property, and an equality in the public realm that obscures inequalities in the private. Moreover, it is true that human rights norms, particularly those that privilege the negative political and civil rights associated with liberal ideology, often serve to justify, even promote, neoliberal economic policies that privatize large-scale social problems and further entrench inequity. However, as I have argued throughout this chapter, this is only part of the story.

The rights discourse of South Africa is a hybrid one and the treatment access campaign has engaged different strands of this discourse explicitly and implicitly through its legal and extra-legal activities. One of the most important but often overlooked discourses cited along the way is Ubuntu, the African notion that one comes to be an individual with dignity and respect, freedom and rights, through one's membership in a larger community.[28] This embeddeness in community, while essential to the survival of the group itself, in no way diminishes the importance of the individual herself. Indeed, as we can see in the practices of organizations such as mothers2mothers and the Treatment Action Campaign, true individual survival and flourishing is very much an effect of engagement in supportive communities. Whether or not the organizations or actors explicitly reference Ubuntu or the language of rights, whether or not they explicitly connect the two ideas, it is the combination of their practices in the legal realm and outside of it, practices that draw heavily on notions of human interdependence, that make having a right to treatment, health care, reproductive services and seeing one's self as a citizen with those rights a meaning reality.

If the lessons of a performative reading of the South African treatment access campaign are anything, they are lessons of possibility and hope, as well as lessons about the difficult and ongoing engagement of many required to bring about change. Critical perspectives on rights claiming in the legal realm as well as beyond are necessary to remind us that there are hegemonic structures of power that work against both individual and communal well-being. A triumphal narrative, on the other hand, illuminates what has changed in ways that keep us motivated to continue the work. But a robust performative perspective on rights claiming in the context of the AIDS epidemic in South Africa reminds us that the practice of rights claiming, the context in which those claims are made, and the effects they have on individuals and communities are far more complicated than simple the reinforcement of the bad or the bringing to fruition of the good. A performative perspective on the treatment access campaign in South Africa reminds us that what rights mean and how rights discourse shapes and is shaped by shifting relationships between individuals and the state, between individuals and their communities, changes over time and is, even in one particular moment, both multifaceted and potentially contradictory. And therein lies its promise, its democratic potential.

---

[28] Of course, 'liberalism' itself is not a seamless or static set of ideas and institutions, nor are neoliberal economic development policies. To be sure, there are some ideas that take precedence and dominate policy and law making, but even these historically and culturally located ways of thinking and acting have never been without contradiction, or are they completely immune to mis-citation or subversive repetition.

References

Albertyn C (2003) Contesting democracy: HIV/AIDS and the achievement of gender equality in South Africa. Feminist Stud 29(3, Women in Democratic South Africa):595–615

Albertyn C, Meer S (2009) Citizens or mothers? The marginalization of women's reproductive rights in the struggle for access to health care for HIV-positive pregnant women in South Africa. In: Mukhopadhyay M, Meer S (eds) Gender, rights, and development: a global sourcebook. KIT Publishers, Amsterdam, pp 27–55

Austin JL (1975) How to do things with words. Harvard University Press, Cambridge

Baek C, Mathambo V, Mkhize S, Friedman I, Apicella L, Rutenberg N (2007) Key findings from an evaluation of the mothers2mothers program in KwaZulu-Natal, South Africa, Horizons final report. Population Council, Washington, DC

Berger JM, Kapczynski A (2009) The story of the TAC case: the potential and limits of socio-economic rights litigation in South Africa. In: Hurwitz DR, Satterthwaite ML (eds) Human rights advocacy stories. Available at SSRN: http://ssrn.com/abstract=1323522 or http://dx.doi.org/10.2139/ssrn.1323522. doi:10.2139/ssrn.1323522#_blank

Bessler J (2008) In the spirit of Ubuntu: enforcing the rights of orphans and vulnerable children affected by HIV/AIDS in South Africa. Hastings Int Comp Law Rev 31:33–113

Bourdieu P (1994) Language and symbolic power. Harvard University Press, Cambridge

Brown W (2005) Edgework: critical essays on knowledge and politics. Princeton University Press, Princeton

Butler J (1997) Excitable speech: a politics of the performative. Routledge, New York

Butler J (1993) Bodies that matter: on the discursive limits of "sex". Routledge, New York

Butler J (1999) Gender trouble: feminism and the subversion of identity. Routledge, New York

Chambers SA, Carver T (2008) Judith Butler and political theory: troubling politics, 1st edn. Routledge, Hoboken

Church J (2005) The place of indigenous law in a mixed legal system and a society in transformation: a South African experience. Aust N Z Law Hist E-J 94–106

Colvin CJ, Robins S, Leavens J (2010) Grounding "responsibilisation talk": masculinities, citizenship and HIV in Cape Town, South Africa. J Dev Stud 46(7):1179–1195

Cornell D, Muvangua N (2012) Ubuntu and the law: African ideals and postapartheid jurisprudenc. Fordham University Press, New York

Cornell D, van Marle K (2012) Exploring ubuntu: tentative reflections. In: Ubuntu and the law: African ideals and postapartheid jurisprudence. Fordham University Press, New York, pp 344–366

Cullinan K, Thom A (eds) (2009) The virus, vitamins and vegetables: the South African HIV/AIDS mystery. Jacana Media, Auckland Park

Derrida J (1988) Limited Inc. Northwestern University Press, Evanston

Dubow S (2012) South Africa's struggle for human rights. Ohio University Press, Athens

Eyakuze C, Jones DA, Starrs AM, Sorkin N (2008) From PMTCT to a more comprehensive AIDS response for women: a much-needed shift. Dev World Bioeth 8(1):33–42

Fassin D (2007) When bodies remember: experiences and politics of AIDS in South Africa, vol 15. University of California Press, Berkeley

Forbath W (2011) Cultural transformation, deep institutional reform, and ESR practice: South Africa's Treatment Action Campaign. In: White L, Perelman J (eds) Stones of hope: how African activists reclaim human rights to challenge global poverty. Stanford University Press, Stanford, pp 51–90

Friedman S, Mottiar S (2005) A rewarding engagement? The Treatment Action Campaign and the politics of HIV/AIDS. Polit Soc 33(4):511–565

Geffen N (2010) Debunking delusions: the inside story of the Treatment Action Campaign. Jacana Media, Auckland

Heywood M (2009) South Africa's Treatment Action Campaign: combining law and social mobilization to realize the right to health. J Hum Rights Pract 1(1):14

Heywood M, Altman D (2000) Confronting AIDS: human rights, law, and social transformation. Health Hum Rights 5(1):149–179

Hodes R (2010) "It's a beautiful struggle": *Siyayinqoba/Beat it!* and the HIV/AIDS treatment struggle on South African television. In: Beinart W, Dawson M (eds) Popular politics and resistance movements in South Africa. Wits University Press, Johannesburg, pp 161–188
Ignatieff M (2001) In: Gutmann A (ed) Human rights as politics and idolatry. Princeton University Press, Princeton
Johnson K (2006a) AIDS and the politics of rights in South Africa: a contested terrain. Hum Rights Rev 7(2):115
Johnson K (2006b) Framing AIDS mobilization and human rights in post-apartheid South Africa. Perspect Polit 4(4):663–670
Kennedy D (2012) The international human rights regime: still part of the problem? In: Dickinson R, Katselli E, Murray C, Pedersen OW (eds) Examining critical perspectives on human rights. Cambridge University Press, New York, pp 19–34
Klug H (2010) The constitution of South Africa: a contextual analysis. Hart Publishing, Oxford
London L (2004) Health and human rights: what can ten years of democracy in South Africa tell us? Health Hum Rights 8(1):1–25
Macgregor H, Mills E (2011) Framing rights and responsibilities: accounts of women with a history of AIDS activism. BMC Int Health Hum Rights 11(Suppl 3):S7–S7
McColl K (2012) The power of mentor mothers. BMJ: Brit Med J (Int Edn) 344(7849):43
Mindry D (2008) Neoliberalism, activism, and HIV/AIDS in postapartheid South Africa. Soc Text 26(1):75–93
Mokgoro Y (1998) Ubuntu and the law in South Africa. Buffalo Hum Rights Law Rev 4:15–23
Mutua M (2008) Human rights in Africa: the limited promise of liberalism. Afr Stud Rev 51(1):17–39
Mutua M (1997) Hope and despair for a new South Africa: the limits of rights discourse. Harv Hum Rights J 10:63
Nattrass N (2007) Mortal combat: AIDS denialism and the struggle for antiretrovirals in South Africa. University of KwaZulu-Natal Press, Scottsville
Neocosmos M (2006) Re-thinking politics in Southern Africa today: elements of a critique of political liberalism. In: Gibson N (ed) Challenging hegemony: social movements and the quest for a new humanism in post-apartheid South Africa. Africa World Press, Trenton, pp 55–101
Pieterse M (2007) Eating socioeconomic rights: the usefulness of rights talk in alleviating social hardship revisited. Hum Rights Q 29(3):796–822
Pieterse M (2008) Health, social movements, and rights-based litigation in South Africa. J Law Soc 35(3):364–388
Robins SL (2008) From revolution to rights in South Africa: social movements, NGOs & popular politics after apartheid. James Currey, Woodbridge/Rochester
Rosenberg G (2009) 'Much ado about nothing? The emptiness of rights' claims in the twenty-first century United States. Stud Law Polit Soc 48(1):41, Special Issue Revisiting Rights
Steinberg J (2008) Sizwe's test: a young man's journey through Africa's AIDS epidemic. Simon & Schuster, New York
Stephen J (2009) Saints and Sinners: the Treatment Action Campaign. In: Cullinan K, Thom A (eds) The virus, vitamins and vegetables: the South African HIV/AIDS mystery. Jacama, Aukland Park, pp 157–174
Teasdale C, Besser M (2008) Enhancing PMTCT programmes through psychosocial support and empowerment of women: the mothers2mothers model of care. S Afr J HIV Med 9(1):60–64
Thom A (2009) Mothers tackling the AIDS epidemic. Health-e. 12 Jan 2009
Treatment Action Campaign (2010) Fighting for our lives: the history of the Treatment Action Campaign 1998–2010. Treatment Action Campaign, Cape Town
White L, Perelman J (2011) Stones of hope: how African activists reclaim human rights to challenge global poverty, Stanford studies in human rights. Stanford University Press, Stanford
Zivi K (2012) Making rights claims: a practice of democratic citizenship. Oxford University Press, New York
Zivi K (2008) Rights and the politics of performativity. In: Chambers S, Carver T (eds) Judith Butler's precarious politics: critical encounters. Routledge, New York, pp 157–169

Chapter 10
Unpacking the Universal: African Human Rights Philosophy in Chinua Achebe's *Things Fall Apart*

Basil Ugochukwu

10.1 Introduction

Chinua Achebe's *Things Fall Apart* appears to attract significant criticism for its seemingly negative offerings to human rights than for contributions to that cause that could be considered positive (Jeyifo 1993; Cobham 2003, p. 165). My goal in this chapter is to reconstruct this image of that popular novel using the law *and* literature framework. I will do so at two levels. As an initial concern, I will demonstrate that *Things Fall Apart* offered positively to the human rights discourse contrary to persisting criticisms. Secondly, my analyses will add to the debate regarding the existence or otherwise of human rights values in Africa's pre-colonial cultures. Despite having what could be regarded as neo-patriarchal characteristics (Quayson 1994) (in spite of its 'transformative power'), (Gikandi 2001) I will argue that the *Things Fall Apart* narrative is indeed a valid and credible refutation of the view that human rights is not an African value

Ugochukwu is Legal Process Instructor and PhD Candidate at Osgoode Hall Law School, York University, Toronto, Canada. He had his early legal education in Nigeria and received an LLM degree in human rights from Central European University, Budapest, Hungary. Ugochukwu is also a fellow of the Open Society Justice Initiative and winner of the Osgoode Hall Law School Walter Williston Essay Prize in Civil Liberties. An earlier version of this chapter was presented at the Central Michigan University International Conference on Human Rights, Literature, the Arts, and Social Sciences in the fall of 2011. I am very grateful to Professor Maureen Eke and the other organizers for inviting me to that conference and to fellow panelists John Pfeifer, Esther Mulusa, Nigel De Huan Hatton and Eric Njeng. The paper was also presented at the spring 2012 Emerging Scholars Workshop of the Critical Research Laboratory in Law and Society at Osgoode Hall Law School. I extend my gratitude to Sujith Xavier and Igor Gontcharov for inviting me to the workshop and to Patricia Hania, Shanthi Senthe, Faisal Bhabha and Igor Gontcharov for their very helpful comments.

B. Ugochukwu (✉)
Osgoode Hall Law School, York University, Toronto, Canada
e-mail: ugochukwubc@gmail.com

O. Onazi (ed.), *African Legal Theory and Contemporary Problems: Critical Essays*, Ius Gentium: Comparative Perspectives on Law and Justice 29,
DOI 10.1007/978-94-007-7537-4_10, © Springer Science+Business Media Dordrecht 2014

(Donnelly 2003, pp. 77, 79, 1982). Though it is possible to present a human rights content analysis of the book through several themes, I will place special emphasis on its treatment of the right to life, the rights of women and the right to fair hearing and a fair administration of justice.

Western writings often advance the position that human rights were unknown in Africa prior to colonialism or that pre-colonial black Africa had no history at all (Trevor-Roper 1969; Fuglestad 1992). In response, Africans point to certain cultures practiced on the continent that could parallel certain contemporary understandings of human rights (Cobbah 1987). This is granted that Africans may not have used the terms 'human rights' to describe those practices (Ejidike 1999). African scholars also point to how colonialism disrupted the development of those values and how the larger populations of Africans were therefore excluded from the table when some current international human rights norms (now proclaimed in universal terms) were discussed, articulated and formalized (Moyn 2012, p. 159; Anghie 2006; Chimni 2004; Morsink 1999).

Things Fall Apart which is set in the 1800s tells the story of how an Igbo people with a 'complex, vigorous, and self-sufficient way of life' were invaded by a foreign power leading to the eclipsing of their culture (Nnoromele 2000). The people are then thrown in between two conflicting cultures. The one represented the 'traditional way of life... and one man's struggle to maintain that cultural integrity against an overwhelming force of colonial imperialism'. The other was the "European style which, as presented, seems to represent the future, a new community of the so-called 'civilized world.'" Achebe sought, however, to demonstrate how the traditional Igbo society had 'achieved the foundations of what most people seek today...' (Akers Rhoads 1993). These foundations included democratic institutions, tolerance of other cultures, a balance of male and female principles, capacity to change for the better or to meet new circumstances, a means of redistributing wealth, a viable system of morality, support for industriousness, an effective system of justice, striking and memorable poetry and art.

It could still be questioned whether these values sufficiently prove parallels between African philosophy and practices to the more widely recognized universal manifestation of those values either as democratic principles or human rights norms. I wager an answer to this concern in the other parts of this chapter under the umbrella of its governing theme and methodology. In Sect. 10.2 I examine the relationship between artistic, fictional/historical representations of culture and sociocultural reality using *Things Fall Apart* as foil. In Sect. 10.3 I analyze the intersection of law and literature under the particular branch of law *in* literature. The three sections thereafter trace the representation of three distinct universally recognized human rights in *Things Fall Apart*. In Sect. 10.7 I couple together the major strands of analyses from the previous sections and on that basis offer some reflections by way of conclusion.

10.2 Stalemate: Fiction and Reality, History and Imagination

My interest in this subject is animated by my recollections from a discussion on an email list service to which I had been affiliated. A Nigerian professor of an American university who uses *Things Fall Apart* as pedagogical text had provoked the discussion when he posted this question to members of that list service: 'Please is it true that *Things Fall Apart* is a historical novel? Is it based on history and can the representation of women in the novel be said to represent how Igbo women were in the 1800s?' (Ade-Odutola 2010). This simple question produced a slew of responses most of which discussed the relationship between the cultural society and its art forms and in particular the relationship between literature and culture and between law and socio-customary life.

As some of the responses to this question (which I would reproduce presently) demonstrated, there is a challenge on literature to explain its context and to identify its correct role in the production of culture, including legal culture. And as with any effort to analyze the representation of cultural themes in works of art, that engagement defies an easy or simplistic treatment. Literary critics often struggle with the binary of fiction and reality. They contend with history and imagination in developing a coherent understanding of how socio-cultural life informs works of art. They grapple as well with the degree to which that connection explains the production of legal norms and similar social practices in literary materials.

Understanding what is fact and fiction, marking their intersections or sometimes decoupling them is therefore a critical challenge in unraveling the connection that literature has to society. Put differently, deploying literary fiction, particularly of the historical variant, to explain contemporary social reality brings scholars and their critics face to face with the questions of transparency and objectivity. Whose story is the novelist telling and what peculiar personal experiences motivate that narrative? The assumption in most cases is that when a chronicler of fiction whether of the historical or realist variant cannot separate herself from the story but is the protagonist as well as story teller, objectivity could be sacrificed.

Achebe's works, including *Things Fall Apart*, are therefore criticized on this account for setting themselves 'against the construction of the African available within Western fiction' (Quayson 1994, p. 121; Achebe 1975, 1977). I will exemplify this concern by referring to some of the specific responses to the question from the Nigerian professor whose initial anxieties initiated this debate. Chidi Anthony Opara was of the view that to a significant extent *Things Fall Apart* only narrowly reflected the position of Igbo women in the novel's context. He argued that besides one character (the Priestess of Agbala) that was cast in a dominant position, all other female characters in the novel suffered under male chauvinism and had roles limited only to domestic service and the granting of sexual indulgences (Ade-Odutola 2010). Opara believes (to the contrary) that women had stronger roles in the Igbo society of *Things Fall Apart* than the novel acknowledges.

Chinyere Okafor added a voice that seemed to pick up on Opara's views. She asks: 'What real life characters are represented in that superb fiction?' Answering her own question, she said people may regard *Things Fall Apart* as fiction or historical fiction while in fact it is an imaginative work from one person's brain and a man for that matter. She argues that 'If an Igbo woman says that she cannot recognize women of the fictional Umuofia in the world/community of her mother and grandmothers, then the Professor should not dismiss her but try to reconsider his/her reading of the text as history that fits all' (Ade-Odutola 2010).

Whereas Opara and Okafor would interpret *Things Fall Apart* through the lenses of both art and history, Kenneth Harrow was more concerned with picking it out of the mesh of the novel genre. He posits that in *Things Fall Apart*, the genre of historical realism was at play as the novel 'is set in the past [but] attempts to convey realistically what life was like then…' He adds that 'genres are constructs, made of patterns of narratives or story-tellings that structure the way we think about how to tell a story – it isn't simply a reflection of events' (Ade-Odutola 2010).[1] These exchanges are central to this essay to the extent that they more clearly define the binary between plain story-telling and artistic quantity and the fragments of reality that often undergirds the stories.

To create normative standards from literary material presupposes that the context for that normative engagement is real not fictional or imaginary. If, as I will argue, *Things Fall Apart* describes practices from which it is possible to draw out some components of the Igbo human rights philosophy, it will be contradictory to refer to it as only a work of fiction because reality and fiction are two different quantities. In fact a contemporary evaluation of the status of women in the Igbo society would seem to contradict Opara's and Okafor's assertion that *Things Fall Apart* misrepresented the actual situation. The question in reality is whether, and by how much, the status of women in the Igbo society has changed since those pre-colonial days so brilliantly captured in *Things Fall Apart*.

Therefore to maintain balance and objectivity, the status of women in the Igbo society of the *Things Fall Apart* era would warrant some comparison with the status of women in other non-Igbo/African societies of the same period as well. The novel contains substantial information from which it could be argued that while much has changed from the pre-colonial period (many women are now educated, polygamy is no longer as fashionable as in those days, there is secular criminalization of

[1] This approach is similar to the new historicism which draws extensively from critics of the 1920–1950 generation whose works focused on 'historical content [that was] based [on] interpretations [of the] interplay between the text and historical contexts (such as the author's life or intentions in writing the work)'.The new historicism critics are also 'less fact-and-event-oriented than historical critics used to be, perhaps because they have come to wonder whether the truth about what really happened can ever be purely or objectively known. They are less likely to see history as linear and progressive, as something developing toward the present, and they are also less likely to think of it in terms of specific eras, each with definite, persistent, and consistent zeitgeist (spirit of the times). Hence they are unlikely to suggest that a literary text has a single or easily identifiable historical context'. See 'Critical Approaches: Definition of the New Historicism' online: http://bcs.bedfordstmartins.com/virtualit/poetry/critical_define/crit_newhist.html.

violence against women and children), women still struggle for substantive gender equality within the Igbo society of today (Iwobi 2008). Equally, it is a fact too widespread to be contested that there still exist various Igbo customary practices and stereotypes specifically targeting women that are still upheld in the contemporary Igbo society (Ewelukwa 2002).

But rather than diffuse the tension that is present in the effort to connect a cultural society to its literary arts (and especially the novel), the above debate in fact amplifies that connection. As pertinently, dealers in the literary arts such as Obiechina, had long recognized this relationship. He argues that it has not always been fully appreciated how far a particular society both influences the themes and subject matter of its literary types and also profoundly affects their formal development (Obiechina 1973). He notes as well how the changing cultural and social situation in West Africa both gave rise to its novel, and also in far-reaching and crucial ways conditioned the West African novel's content, themes and texture. Obiechina seems to argue that the African novel represented by such works as *Things Fall Apart* is not an imaginary but a product of a dynamic and evolving cultural environment.

While the connection of reality to fiction in constructing the relationship between culture, life and the novel is generally contested in a lot of ways, it is less in doubt that there exists a better and healthier linkage between law and the arts. In the context of Africa and Nigeria in particular, Obiechina's reference to society and culture is especially significant. A generally acknowledged character of the African society is the embeddedness of law within the dominant culture. In a sense therefore, law and culture in many parts of Africa are actually not normatively separate but are bound together (Mokgoro 1997). More significantly, most common social practices become customary law by reason of long, constant usage (see also Asiedu-Akrofi 1989; Oba 2006).[2] Custom in the context of its value in the creation of customary law is therefore taken to be the same as law itself. Examined more closely, what is true of custom and society could be held true as well for law and society. Legal scholarship takes a similar position as confirmed by Hutchinson who states:

> As does life itself, law has a long and intimate relationship with art and literature. Although it is often assumed that there is one-way traffic from law and literature, there is something of a both-ways street between law and art. Most times art relies on and follows law as a source of inspiration…art distils and portrays law and its cast and characters in both flattering and demeaning ways. But on some rare and memorable moments, the trend has reversed – law and life have followed and echoed the styling of art and literature much to the benefit of most concerned. (Hutchinson 2011, p. 13)

Hutchinson's position is important because of its totalizing and generalizing capacity for linking law and the arts even though not from the filter of a specific cultural community. In this case, the marriage of arts, society and law could be viewed as a universal phenomenon and not peculiar to any one particular socio-legal

[2] Notice how the Nigerian Evidence Act, for instance, defines Custom as a 'rule which in a particular district, has from long usage, obtained the force of law'. See C 112, Laws of the Federation of Nigeria 1990, s 291.

system.[3] In the next section, I examine how theoretically grounded is the relationship between law and literature in an interdisciplinary context.

10.3 Things Fall Apart at the Intersection of Law and Literature

Because the study of law and literature is an interdisciplinary endeavor, the field itself defies constraining to a single theory or method from either field that could be successfully extrapolated to the other (Posner 1988). A major challenge therefore (and one similar to that posed by the contestation over reality/imagination, and the historical/fictional narrative) is deciding on the field theory and methodology for studying law and literature. The temptation is for each discipline within the two fields to fall back on the theory and methodology with which they are the most familiar and comfortable as a default position. My approach in this paper is no exception. It is perhaps for this reason that Kenji Yoshino describes law and literature as being a 'schizophrenic discipline' (Yoshino 2005). He supports this description by reference to the two distinct branches of the field that Robert Weisberg identifies: 'law-*in*-literature' and 'law-*as*-literature' (Weisberg 1988).

Law-in-literature (which is the branch with which this paper is concerned for the most part) Weisberg says 'involves the appearance of legal themes or the depiction of legal actors or processes in fiction or drama'. On the other hand, law-as-literature 'involves the parsing of such legal texts as statutes, constitutions, judicial opinions, and certain classic scholarly treatises as if they were literary works'. Yoshino sees, however, a third branch of the field; that which he refers to as law-*of*-literature which deals with 'the regulation of literature through obscenity, defamation, and copyright regimes…' (see also Dawson 1996).

I already have indicated that my discussion of *Things Fall Apart* in this chapter would be from a law-in-literature approach; in which case my interest is narrowed to the novel's representation of legal themes, practices, and actors in the Igbo society within which it was set. I have cut out the human rights field as my area of specific interest and further narrowed this down to the novel's treatment of the right to life, the rights of women and the right to a fair hearing in the administration of justice. Like the novel, some legal writings contain 'fictions' which Posner conceives as a form of metaphor (See also Soifer 1986). Such fictions enable the relationship as well between the novel and the liberal human rights discourse.

[3] See further Morison and Bell (1996, p. 1) ('We share the belief that key legal issues can be not only brought to life in literary texts but explored there in ways that orthodox legal materials cannot rival. Notions of justice or injustice, the social creation and policing of concepts of difference and deviance or even standards of ethical lawyering are not ideas that can be fully explored by looking only at statutes, law reports, official crime figures or even Bar Council reports on standards. The proper mission of the Law and Literature movement is to read literature, not as ('wannabe') literary critics but as lawyers seeking to pursue the legal themes of power, authority, order, adjudication, penalty, justice and so on which occupy us all'.)

In fact Slaughter believes that the 'novel genre and liberal human rights discourse are more than coincidentally or casually interconnected'. Continuing, he states that they are mutually enabling fictions: each projecting an image of the human personality that ratifies the other's idealistic visions of the proper relations between the individual and society and the normative career of free and full human personality development (Slaughter 2007).

Things Fall Apart more than accomplishes the role of placing at the centre the fictionalization of novel and liberal human rights as I would go on to show. It is not by any stretch of the imagination the first African novel written in English 'but it remains one of the most significant and best known'. Confirming its pre-eminent position in the African literary pantheon, Cooper further promotes this significance when asserting that '2 years before Britain granted Nigeria its independence, Achebe's fictionalized critique of cultural imperialism did for colonialism what *Uncle Tom's Cabin* did for American slavery' (Cooper 2008). Irele on his part believes *Things Fall Apart* played up this distinction and significance for two major reasons. The first of those reasons is immediately apt. Irele asserts that the novel provided an image of an African society, reconstituted as living entity and in its historic circumstance: an image of a coherent social structure forming the institutional fabric of a universe of meanings and values. He argues further that because this image of Africa was quite unprecedented in literature, it also carried considerable ideological weight in the specific context of the novel's writing and reception (Irele 2000).

The other reason which he discusses for the significance of the novel is related to the qualitative nature of Chinua Achebe's fictionalization of the African human experience especially in the manner of its presentation. Irele talks about a world 'in which the cultural reference governs not merely the constitution of the novel's fictional universe but also the expressive means by which the collective existence, the very human experience framed within this universe, comes to be conveyed'. He therefore conceives *Things Fall Apart* as being prototypical of Barbara Harlow's 'resistance literature' category 'by reason of its character as a counterfiction of Africa, in specific relation to the discourse of Western colonial domination, and [the novel's] creative deployment of the language of the imperium...'[4]

The 'resistance' description fits the novel greatly especially when viewed alongside Riddell's theory of 'two histories' that serve to highlight differing views of the nature and impact of colonialism (Riddell 1990). Riddell draws two categories of contrasts in this regard. My concern is however limited to the first contrast which balances Joyce Cary's *Mister Johnson* against Achebe's *Things Fall Apart*. The British District Officer who authored *Mister Johnson* viewed 'incorporation as essentially part of the colonial 'apprenticeship' of Africa, when local societies and

[4]Amos Tutuola's *The Palmwine Drinkard* and Chinua Achebe's *Things Fall Apart* though initially appearing as novels have been described as 'authentic culture objects'. To convey this understanding more meaningfully, there are annotated versions of *Things Fall Apart* which 'has transformed the novel by mediating the experience of reading it so that now the reader is no longer free to imagine meanings, but is presented with the informed answers to whatever cultural questions he or she might put to the text. The frame insures that the authenticity of the noel as a cultural artifact is protected [and] safeguarded against deviant understandings' (Harrow 2007, p. 136).

cultures were integrated into a wider world and provided with civilization'. In contrast, *Things Fall Apart* 'describes how the cultural ecology of the [Igbo] was destroyed during the same process'. Riddell summarized the novel in these words:

> In the first half of the novel the completeness of [Igbo] culture as depicted in terms of the integration of political, social, and economic systems; the relationship of individuals to the community, with its vital historical legacy illustrated through proverbs; seasonal festivals and ceremonies; and the association of culture and the environment – the heat and humidity of the rains, the cold of the dry harmattan winds, the use of the leached soils, the unifying force in society of the kola nut, and the vital importance of yam as a foodstuff. (See also Lacayo 2005)

Riddell's contribution apparently foregrounds an issue that is most times front and centre of the African human rights discourse: the position of the individual in the community. The dominant, liberal conception of human rights rests on the idea of an isolated, autonomous individual (Pollis 1982) that is atomistic, disharmonious, confrontational, and often litigious (Henkin 1990). This individual has to be protected from government and society. In Africa, the philosophy is much different. It rests on the understanding that the individual's interest is locked into that of the community. In those famous words of John Mbiti whatever happens to the individual happens to the whole group, and whatever happens to the whole group happens to the individual. 'The individual can only say: "I am, because we are; and since we are, therefore I am". This is a cardinal point in the understanding of the African view of man' (Mbiti 1990, p. 113).

In the African context therefore, it looks more like the community requires protection from the individual. An indication of how this understanding is factored into the African human rights philosophy could be seen in the Preambular and some normative portions of the African Charter on Human and Peoples Rights (Quashigah 2012). In those areas, the Charter broke with the tradition of older international and regional human rights instruments by enshrining not only rights but duties as well, showing that not only does the individual have rights (entitlements); she also is subject to duties (responsibilities). Those duties are owed to others and to the corporate community. So when discussing the particulars of rights as conceived within the African cultural space, it is important to realize that they share similarities with some human rights in their more liberal incarnation. But significantly, that understanding must be forged within the strong communal foundation undergirding that culture. In the next section, I examine how *Things Fall Apart* confirms or denies the existence of the rights that I identified at the beginning as of major concern in this chapter.

10.4 'This Novel Is Sexist': Things Fall Apart and the Rights of Women

I will start with the more contested component of the analysis which is the status of women in *Things Fall Apart* and whether that could even remotely ground a discussion on women's rights. Earlier in this chapter I made reference to an important background material that provides significant insight into the nature of this historical contestation. I reproduced opinions which tended to suggest that *Things Fall Apart* did not accurately reflect the status of the Igbo women of the fictional Umuofia. Not only is the language deployed in the narrative sexist by most accounts, the rights of women within that Igbo community seemed abject and for the most part non-existent. A teacher using the novel as material for her High School class told the story of one particular encounter in one of her classes that went as follows:

> "THIS IS A SEXIST NOVEL!" The (female white) student declared. Her ethnic earnings (sic) jangled in angry assent as she stabbed the pages of her Heinemann paperback for emphasis. As if to distance itself from the offending object, he red-checked imitation Palestine Liberation Organization scarf slipped backward off her shoulders. It was clear that she spoke on behalf of all oppressed humanity. (Cobham 2003, p. 165)

Cobham believes that when the word 'sexist' is used in relation to *Things Fall Apart* it means no more than that Okonkwo, the principal character is misogynistic. Jeyifo saw in the novel as well an Okonkwo whose relationship with his father Unoka and later his son Nwoye are projected over relationships with his nameless mother, his wives, and his daughters (Jeyifo 1993, p. 849). From a feminist perspective, he argues, 'this, more than anything else, reveals the male-centeredness of Achebe in this novel'. He goes on to state that 'While this is incontrovertible, it is only part of the story, and it barely scratches the surface of the complex and ambiguous gender politics of the text of *Things Fall Apart*'.

My goal in this section is not to interrogate the gender politics that Jeyifo identifies but to illustrate the basic criticism that *Things Fall Apart* actually ended up in a neo-patriarchal rat-hole. I will rather show how that fact fits into the theoretical debate about whether human rights values are indeed universal or culturally specific. If the novel is going to be useful for the construction of an African idea of human rights, it must account for the obvious pathetic state of women's rights. It could be argued that if this account cannot be given, then that is a clear indication that human rights were not values within that culture. A careful reading of the novel leaves one in no doubt that though 'its primary concern is woman's place within the larger social and political forces', (Boyce Davies 1986) in doing so, the domineering nature of male power over women was heavily magnified, rendering the subordination of women a virtual *fait accompli*.

The novel commences for example, by identifying its major character as Okonkwo, 'a young man of eighteen' (Achebe 1958). While his father's name was Unoka, who featured prominently in his private apprehensions and fears, Okonkwo's mother was just that, mother. She had no name. To the bargain, she got for herself only a 'single, brief mention' in the entire novel (Jeyifo 1993, p. 848). Quite conveniently, Okonkwo's sisters (much like his mother) were consigned to anonymity as well. Unlike his incipiently lazy father, Okonkwo's mother and sisters worked hard enough, 'but they grew women's crops, like coco-yams, beans and cassava. Yam, the king of crops, was a man's crop'. Okonkwo worried almost his entire life that his daughter Ezinma should have been a boy. Because she was not a boy, she could not carry her father's chair to the village square. That's a boy's job that girls were prohibited from performing. Okonkwo was elated whenever his son, Nwoye grumbled about women but only because it 'showed that in time he would be able to control his women-folk'. He frequently beat his wives and children, and ruled his household overall with a heavy hand.

In spite of criticisms about the sexist qualities of *Things Fall Apart*, its author Chinua Achebe is nevertheless acclaimed for presenting an authentic account of the Igbo society and the position of the traditional Igbo woman (Cobham 2003, p. 167). This is often in contrast to the views I referenced earlier about the novel's unrepresentative quality in this regard and as well those of Buchi Emecheta, whose the *Joys of Motherhood* allegedly painted a distinctly contrary picture. Yet if *Things Fall Apart* presents an authentic portrayal of the status of women in pre-colonial Igbo society, in what sense could the poor treatment of women that is evident in page after page and deemed acceptable within that particular social universe, be considered even remotely significant to the understanding of African human rights philosophy? In fact, would the pathetic representation of the rights of women in Achebe's fictional Umuofia not be evidence of the claim that human rights as currently understood was non-existent in the pre-colonial African society which that community emblematizes? Questions like these make the consideration of the rights of women necessary in the context of this chapter.

Because *Things Fall Apart* is for the most part given a negative evaluation in relation to its handling of the rights of women, a failure to center women's rights concerns in this chapter would be an unpardonable omission indeed. But the significance of this goal owes more to the similarities between the place of women in Umuofia of *Things Fall Apart* and the place of women in the world at that time in history. It is therefore less about just the gender standards of a traditional Igbo society which Umuofia illustrates but more about the prevalent practices of different cultures of that time. If it is argued that human rights did not exist in pre-colonial Africa merely on the basis of how *Things Fall Apart* reflected the lowly status of women, could the same not be said of other non-Igbo and therefore non-African societies where the status of women was no less on the lower level? (Keyssar 2009; Bunch 1994)[5] While women in Umuofia lived under male shadows, that cannot alone be the basis to dismiss the entire culture as lacking human rights credentials if the same standards do not apply to other cultures that placed women in the same difficulties during that period. I turn next to how the novel treated the right to life.

[5] For example Gavigan (1989, p. 336): 'From 1351–1790, English law provided that a woman who murdered her husband was liable to be convicted of "petit treason" and to suffer the fate of female traitors: to be burned at the stake. The official justification for the offence was the duty of subjection and obedience owed by English wives to their husbands; the penalty was defended in the name of the natural modesty of the female sex – it was better to be burned at the stake than to be drawn and quartered, the official penalty for treason'.

10.5 Neither Here Nor There: The Right to Life in Things Fall Apart

As with the rights of women, the right to life in *Things Fall Apart* is given an ambivalent treatment. On the one hand, there seems to be in the novel recognition that human life is sacred and therefore not to be taken lightly without consequences. On the other hand, there are specific instances where human life appears to have the mere short shrift. In both situations, the exemplifier seems to be the cruel fate of the lad Ikemefuna whose own life would literally be a metaphor for this ambivalence. His fate was also emblematic of the opposite directions to which this right was pulled in the novel. In this section I will first examine those instances where the society recognized the importance of the right to life and then look at opposite situations that seem to suggest that the culture did not quite recognize that right.

Our initial introduction to Ikemefuna is as 'a lad of fifteen' (Achebe 1958, p. 8) who along with 'a young virgin' had been offered by the town of Mbaino to Okonkwo's town, Umuofia in return for the life of a daughter of Umuofia taken in cold blood at an Mbaino market. This story indicates that life was important such that when it was taken unlawfully, some form of sanction was triggered. In this particular case the penalty was restitution (Ejidike 1999, p. 76). As it was in the time of the fictional Umuofia of *Things Fall Apart*, so it is today. In contemporary times, states go to great lengths to protect human life and do punish (often severely) those who take the lives of others unlawfully including imposing the death penalty (Hood and Hoyle 2008; Anckar 2004; Smit 2004). The right to life is obviously the most important human right because other rights turn nugatory once the right to life is denied. On a positive note therefore, there was enshrined in the Umuofia culture the practice of respecting and honoring human life.

There is, however, a downside to the Umuofia practice when filtered through the story of Ikemefuna. We are told that only a daughter of Umuofia was killed at Mbaino. How proportionate was it therefore to atone for this offence with two lives (one allowed to live and the other condemned to die) rather than one? Could it not have been sufficient to replace the dead woman with the virgin alone (that is restitutional proportionality)? In any case, was it appropriate that these two individuals were made to pay the price for an offence which they did not commit? If anything, the punishment should be upon the person responsible for the offence not upon someone else in lieu. Furthermore, how necessary was it for Ikemefuna to be later killed (now restitution/death sentence) as permanent atonement for this particular offence even when the dead woman of Umuofia had been replaced by the virgin? These questions and more erode considerably whatever respect may have been accorded the right to life under that culture. Inevitably, the initial recognition that life is inviolable and the reality of how the Ikemefuna episode unraveled seemed to cancel themselves out to the point of negation.

Yet where the above episode may not have proved unequivocal recognition of the respect for life within the Umuofia culture, further evidence of this is supplied in an entirely different context. During funeral ceremonies for one of the greatest men of the clan, Ezeudu, Okonkwo's celebratory gunfire had inadvertently killed one of the dead man's sons (Achebe 1958, p. 109). 'The only course open to Okonkwo was to flee from the clan', Achebe wrote. 'The crime was of two kinds, male and female. Okonkwo had committed the female, because it had been inadvertent'. The distinction between 'male' and 'female' homicide in the Umuofia culture would seem to be similar to the distinction in contemporary criminal law between murder and manslaughter or between murder in the first degree and murder in the second degree. While it remains unclear what the punishment would have been were Okonkwo's action pre-meditated, his punishment for this inadvertence was still not mere banishment from the clan. It was immediately imposed and harshly executed. 'As soon as the day broke', Achebe wrote, 'a large crowd of men from Ezeudu's quarter stormed Okonkwo's compound, dressed in garbs of war. They set fire to his houses, demolished his red walls, killed his animals and destroyed his barn'.

There is enough in the novel to suggest that the people were as zealous in upholding these customary practices as they were anxious and worried about their complexities. After Okonkwo's banishment, for instance, his close friend Obierika having thought long and hard about those events wondered how a man could suffer so grievously for an offense he had committed inadvertently. That moment of introspection also forced his thoughts to a different trajectory and towards a parallel cultural practice that seemed to further undermine the value of human life within that culture. Obierika remembered 'his wife's twin children, whom he had thrown away. What crime had they committed?' But as it turns out -

> The Earth had decreed that they [twins] were an offense on the land and must be destroyed. And if the clan did not exact punishment for an offense against the great goddess, her wrath was loosed on all the land and not just on the offender. As the elders said, if one finger brought oil it soiled the others.[6]

There is a lot that could be said for a culture in which a person could be so harshly punished for taking human life as in Okonkwo's case and at the same time condoned the killing of twins simply for being born twins. This represents at once the best and the worst in terms of the extent to which that culture could claim to place some value on human life. Therefore the recognition of the right to life in the Umuofia culture could be said to have been to the full extent possible. It could also be conceived as being ambivalent or inadequate. But these are not as important as the basic fact that life within that culture did have some recognition and was under the protection of society in those contexts that it was recognized.

---

[6] Ejidike (1999, p. 78) This practice, along with the *Osu* caste system, slavery and human sacrifice, is often supplied as evidence of the 'egregious violations of human rights' by the Igbo society. Yet the writer asks: 'But does the existence of such practices … imply that rights were totally disregarded in the Igbo society to the extent that present-day practices cannot be culturally legitimized?' While not justifying the derogations, he argues further that 'In considering these derogations it is important to differentiate between the spirit of the Igbo culture as distinct from its manifestations. While the former is more or less static, the latter is largely prone to the negative influence of the times'.

10.6 Double Sync: Fair Hearing and the Administration of Justice

The right to a fair hearing when disputes arise between individuals in society has been long recognized as vital to the effective administration of justice. Most national constitutions recognize the right to a fair hearing in some form. All major international and regional human rights instruments recognize and enshrine the right as well. Yet historical accounts indicate that it is a right which has not always existed in the form that it is recognized today. In this section, I intend to show that the Igbo society of *Things Fall Apart* did recognize the right to be heard when disputes arise among members of the community. But as a preliminary point, I will first demonstrate that not all societies had the same accommodation for this right as in Achebe's Umuofia.

For instance, the manner in which the primitive society dealt with serious crimes, like murder, painted a picture of this rather long and difficult developmental process. Uwe Wesel, for example, describes a procedure in which the person accused of crime, already presumed to be the culprit, sought refuge in the hut of a witch doctor. According to this legend, the only right to which the accused was entitled was immunity from harm so long as he remained inside that hut (Trechsel 1997). Bodenhamer, writing about pre-1066 England, said criminal proceedings then were 'oral, personal, accusatory...' (Bodenhamer 1992, p. 11). Trechsel observes that medieval evidentiary rules contained several irrational methods including 'compurgation (oath-taking), ordeal and battle'. Hammurabi of ancient Babylon is credited with the first recorded attempt to lay down fair trial practices by requiring that judges hear at least both sides of a case, thereby '[holding] back the strong from oppressing the weak' (Banaszak 2002).

There is ample evidence in *Things Fall Apart* that fair hearing principles were very much a part of the dispute resolution processes of the pre-colonial Igbo society. This is to the extent that at least parties in dispute were allowed to present their respective cases before some arbitral body. This however should not be taken as conclusive evidence that some of the more irrational or subjective evidentiary methods associated with the primitive society above was not a feature of the traditional Igbo society. Oba states that the supernatural plays an important role in African customary law and that oaths in particular are more extensively used in customary law arbitration among the Igbos than among other ethnic and language groups in Nigeria (Oba 2008; Edu 2004; Ejidike and Izuakor 1992). Yet while these methods were used for purposes of obtaining evidence in that society, there was also room for the right to a fair hearing as currently understood and discussed in domestic and international legal jurisdictions.

The recognition of an adversarial trial process in dispute resolution within the Igbo culture in *Things Fall Apart* is demonstrated in the hearing conducted between Odukwe and Uzowulu before the elders of the Umuofia clan (Achebe 1958, p. 77). It was a matrimonial dispute. The manner in which it was resolved underlines as well both the Igbo psychology of disagreements based on legal rights and the predominant philosophy of assigning innocence or culpability. Uzowulu had been married to Odukwe's sister. Apparently the marriage had been characterized by physical abuse from the husband against his wife. The wife's family, fed up with this situation went to Uzowulu's house and after thoroughly beating him up took their sister and her children away. Uzowulu took his grievance to the elders of the clan to plead for the return of his family. The elders of the clan, also known as *Egwugwu*, therefore assembled for what turns out without a doubt to be a full-blown trial. It commences with the leader of the elders directing the proceedings much in the fashion of a multi-member judicial body with one of the judges presiding.

Four components of this trial make it significant but especially for what it says about the pre-colonial Igbo society's approach to dealing with such disputes and what rights accrue to the parties in dispute. It starts with the leader of the clan elders calling the disputing parties to order. Achebe captures those initial moments:

> The body of Odukwe, I greet you,' he [leader of the clan elders] said, and Odukwe bent down and touched the earth. *The hearing then began* [my emphasis]. Uzowulu [complaining party] stepped forward and presented his case. 'That woman standing there is my wife, Mgbafo. I married her with my money and my yams.

Uzowulu then paints a graphic picture of the pains he endured in the hands of his in-laws and pleaded with the elders of the clan to provide appropriate remedy for his mistreatment. This component of the trial shows that in the Igbo society of the times that Umuofia represents, resolving a dispute involved not just a hearing but one at which the parties in dispute were allowed to plead their cases. It fits the rule of never condemning anyone without a hearing.

The second significant component of this trial is no less crucial from a fair hearing standpoint. The clan elders did not resolve the dispute on the basis of Uzowulu's testimony alone. Upon completion of his evidence, Odukwe as the defending party was also called upon to rebut Uzowulu's testimony which he did in these words:

> My in-law has told you that we went to his house, beat him up and took our sister and her children away. All that is true. He told you that he came to take back her bride-price and we refused to give it to him. That also is true. My in-law, Uzowulu is a beast. My sister lived with him for nine years. During those years no single day passed in the sky without his beating the woman.

After completing his testimony, Odukwe 'called two witnesses [who] were both Uzowulu's neighbors…' They corroborated the evidence of physical violence already mobilized against Uzowulu. This component of the hearing demonstrates the requirement of listening to both parties to a dispute before it is resolved. It also indicates that not only are the disputants able to plead their cases in person, they could also call witnesses to corroborate their testimonies. This equates clearly to the principle of equality of arms in judicial proceedings. In other words, both sides to the dispute have equal chances of success on the basis of the strength of their cases and not the subjective preference of the arbitrators.

After Odukwe's testimony, the third significant component of the hearing was signaled. 'The nine *egwugwu* went away to consult together in their house. They were silent for a long time'. This is similar to the practice of jury trial in some contemporary legal systems where jurors receive oral evidence in the open and then retire behind closed doors to evaluate what they received as a guide towards resolving the dispute. Jury trial is often viewed as a mechanism to secure procedural due process. It is thought to be better for this purpose than one-judge trial courts. Trial by one's peers was integral to the *Magna Carta* as well as the Sixth Amendment to the United States constitution from which the practice established its modern roots (Langbein 1992, p. 123). It could however be argued that the *egwugwu* trial in *Things Fall Apart* fails to meet the requirement of trial by one's peers because the clan elders could hardly be considered peers of the parties in dispute in this case. Further open to question is whether a permanent, all-male adjudicatory body meets relevant standards of gender sensitivity in contrast to an ad hoc one that could have both men and women as members. However, judging that panel by the standards of today misses a crucial point: legal systems of today have come a long way and have evolved over time. Some legal systems (for example the British) adopted jury trials much later in their histories.

The last component of the procedure encapsulates the manner in which the dispute was ultimately resolved. Though the elders could have assigned blame to the party found to be at fault and awarded victory to the other, they rejected that route. Instead, they laid out a model for peace between the parties in a manner that did not sacrifice the relationship of the future for the little gains of the present. The head of the elders had stated: 'We have heard both sides of the case. Our duty is not to blame this man or to praise that, but to settle the dispute'.[7] To Uzowulu who wanted either his wife or the bride price he paid on her head, he said 'Go to your in-laws with a pot of wine and beg your wife to return to you. It is not bravery when a man fights with a woman'. And to Odukwe he admonished 'If your in-law brings wine to you, let your sister go with him. I salute you'.

The adjudicatory temperament underscores the Umuofian and by extension the Igbo philosophy of dispute settlement. According to Ejidike,

> In Igbo juridical principle, social justice precedes the law. Igbo judicial settlement is not adversarial and does not resolve disputes by matching complete guilt against innocence. It does not 'judge' but resolves, involving the compromise to re-establish satisfactory relations between persons, or between a person and ancestors. A good judgment must satisfy both disputants.

The first part of this assertion regarding the adversarial nature of the process does not seem in my view to present a complete account of the Umuofia system of dispute settlement. That system which the Odukwe/Uzowulu dispute symbolizes is adversarial at least in the sense of one party laying accusations to which the other party is obliged to respond. It should, however, be noted that adversariality in this sense does not translate to enmity. The judicial body's approach in the Odukwe/Uzowulu dispute only reinforces the philosophy of compromise and accommodation over

[7] This is, however, a little different than the story of these elders told by Equiano about growing up in a different Igbo society. He states: 'Those Embrenche, or chief men, decided disputes, and punished crimes; for which purpose they always assembled together. The proceedings were generally short; and in most cases the law of retaliation prevailed' (Brooks 2004, p. 7).

plain legal triumph. It is evident that the Umuofia elders delivered a judgment that none of the parties could legitimately describe as unsatisfactory. Rather than a winner takes all situation, there was something in the decision for each of the parties. But above all, it was delivered in an atmosphere of conviviality and of give and take rather than the often bitter, drawn-out procedures of the adversarial system.

In more recent times this philosophy that legal disputes could be solved in a friendly environment has been adopted by domestic and international dispute resolution forums. Different kinds of alternative dispute resolution mechanisms are therefore increasingly being preferred to litigation for a variety of reasons. The multi-door courthouse system for instance gives more options to legal disputants than does the traditional form of litigation that is reliant mostly on judicial coercion for legitimacy and enforcement.[8] Law Schools are becoming aware of the expanding frontiers of the alternative dispute resolution methodology and now integrating its principles into their curriculum (Menkel-Meadow 1992). The claim here is that long before the world realized that alternatives existed for effective dispute resolution different from 'fighting in front of a court' for rights (Grande 1999), Africans had used that process beneficially. The continent's reputation in this regard is not dented by claims that increasing Western appetite for this mechanism is not indicative of any legal transplant from the traditional to modern societies.

As significantly, while the procedure in the Odukwe/Uzowulu trial above may lack in some contemporary fair trial details (there were no lawyers and cross-examination was absent), the very existence of the notion of a trial is still very significant if only from a cross-cultural context for the understanding of human rights values. There are in fact studies produced long after *Things Fall Apart* was written which show a well-developed procedural system in the chieftaincy and politics in centralized Igbo communities that provided for an official prosecutor, cross examination, court fees, oath-taking in support of contentious averments and a well-articulated system against abuses and manipulation (Nzimiro 1972).

10.7 Conclusion

By no means is the main argument of this chapter likely ever going to be the final word on the cultural explanation of human rights values harnessed from an Africa environment. Nor is it entirely possible that the debate on whether historical fiction as an art form could ground any system of normative cultural or legal production. I am persuaded that it is possible for so-called fiction to actually amount to parody of reality and that *Things Fall Apart* is one such grand effort. Scholars from law and literature state clearly that both disciplines are more than casually connected. This

---

[8] See 'Transcript: A Dialogue between Professors Frank Sander and Mariana Hernandez Crespo: Exploring the Evolution of the Multi-Door Courthouse' (2008) 5 *University of St Thomas Law Journal* 665 at 668.

means that law *in* literature in particular provides valid opportunities for isolating legal and cultural norms from artistic representations.

Things Fall Apart is therefore emblematic of this cross-disciplinary possibility and is even more so from a human rights standpoint. It is sitting squarely across the debate on the universality of certain human rights values. In a sense, therefore, it furthers the discourse about the universal quality to the highlighted and analyzed human rights values from a purely African account. While adding to the Universalist dialogue, the novel accomplishes more for the human rights regime and movement than would any effort to deny the existence of these values reinforced within an African space. It does so by demystifying the grand narrative about the peculiarly Western origins of these and other human rights values which in itself would seem to diminish any claim to their universality.

It says a lot about the durability and dynamism of African customary practices that many of these values have survived the effects of colonialism and have in many areas adapted to a changing land and mindscape. For example, even though African women continue to struggle for equality and recognition, their collective situation has improved a lot from the Umuofia period. But a lot still needs to be achieved. Besides, the struggle of women is more a universal phenomenon than an African peculiarity. For this reason the argument in favor of the universality of human rights values could be more usefully organized around a 'wrongs' approach rather than an overly 'rights' one. Except the argument is that the wrongs that manifested in certain cultural practices in Africa, like the subordination of women, were a peculiar African problem? As I have argued elsewhere in this chapter, such an argument cannot stand up to logical scrutiny because those wrongs existed to different levels of intensity in other cultures as well.

There is therefore a lot of work still to do to create a conversation among cultures on human rights values. Marginalizing certain cultures or allocating them to the fringes of a universal debate on rights and values undermines rather than enhances this conversation. Such tendency is also at the core of the challenge posed to a Universalist argument by a more relativist one. Moreover, apart from the specific rights and values discussed in this chapter, many more could still be discovered from not only *Things Fall Apart* but other African cultures as well. There is for example some values specific within the domain of humanitarian law evident in the Umuofia story. This and more could form the thrust of further research and illumination in the future.

References

Achebe C (1958) Things fall apart. Everyman's Library, New York

Achebe C (1975) The novelist as teacher. In: Morning yet on creation day. Heinemann, London

Achebe C (1977) An image of Africa. Mass Rev 18:782

Ade-Odutola O (2010) http://groups.google.com/group/usaafricadialogue/msg/82a2ec732aac816f. Accessed on 23 Nov 2012

Akers Rhoads D (1993) Culture in Chinua Achebe's things fall apart. Afr Stud Rev 36:61

Anckar C (2004) Determinants of the death penalty: a comparative study of the world. Routledge, London
Anghie A (2006) The evolution of international law: colonial and postcolonial realities. Third World Q 27:739
Asiedu-Akrofi D (1989) Judicial recognition of customary law in Nigeria. Am J Comp Law 37:571
Banaszak R (2002) Fair trial rights of the accused: a documentary history. http://www.questia.com/PM.qst?a=101365042. Accessed on 23 Nov 2012
Bodenhamer D (1992) Fair trial: rights of the accused in American history. Oxford University Press, Oxford
Boyce Davies C (1986) Motherhood in the works of male and female Igbo writers: Achebe, Emecheta, Nwapa and Nzekwu. In: Boyce Davies C, Adams Graves A (eds) Ngambika: studies of women in African literature. Africa World Press, Trenton
Brooks J (ed) (2004) The life of Olaudah Equiano: the interesting narrative of the life of Olauda Equiano, or Gustavus Vassa, the African written by himself. RR Donnelley & Sons Company Chicago
Bunch C (1994) An equal voice. In: Reoch R (ed) Human rights: the new consensus. Regency Press, London
Chimni B (2004) International institutions today: an imperial global state in the making. Eur J Int Law 15:1
Cobbah J (1987) African values and the human rights debate: an African perspective. Hum Rights Q 9:309
Cobham R (2003) Problems of gender and history in the teaching of *things fall apart*. In: Okpewho I (ed) Chinua Achebe's things fall apart: a casebook. Oxford University Press, New York
Cooper C (2008) Chinua Achebe's things fall apart turns 50 this year. The Village Voice. http://www.villagevoice.com/2008-02-19/art/things-fall-apart-thinsp-turns-50-this-year/. Accessed on 23 Nov 2012
Dawson N (1996) The law *of* literature: folklore and law. In: Morison J, Bell C (eds) Tall stories? Reading law and literature. Darthmouth, Aldershot
Donnelly J (1982) Human rights and human dignity: an analytic critique of non-western conceptions of human rights. Am Polit Sci Rev 76:303
Donnelly J (2003) Universal human rights: in theory and practice. Cornell University Press, New York
Edu O (2004) The effect of customary arbitral awards on substantive litigation: setting matters straight. J Private Property Law 25:43
Ejidike O (1999) Human rights in the cultural traditions and social practice of the Igbo of South-Eastern Nigeria. J Afr Law 43:71
Ejidike M, Izuakor L (1992) Deity as an instrument of social control: the case of Haaba Agulu. Niger Herit 1:20
Ewelukwa U (2002) Post-colonialism gender, customary injustice: widows in African societies. Hum Rights Q 24:424
Fuglestad F (1992) The Trevor-Roper trap or the imperialism of history: an essay. Hist Afr 19:309
Gavigan S (1989) Petit treason in eighteenth century England: women's inequality before the law. Can J Women Law 3:335
Gikandi S (2001) Chinua Achebe and the invention of African culture. Res Afr Literatures 32:3
Grande E (1999) Alternative dispute resolution, Africa and the structure of law and power: the horn in context. J Afr Law 43:63
Harrow K (2007) Shibboleths: the production of culture. Global S 1:135
Henkin L (1990) The age of rights. Columbia University Press, New York
Hood R, Hoyle C (2008) The death penalty: a worldwide perspective. Oxford University Press, Oxford
Hutchinson A (2011) Is eating people wrong? Great legal cases and how they shaped the world. Cambridge University Press, New York
Irele A (2000) The crisis of cultural memory in Chinua Achebe's *things fall apart*. Afr Stud Q 4:1
Iwobi A (2008) No cause for merriment: the position of widows under Nigerian law. Can J Women Law 20:37

Jeyifo A (1993) Okonkwo and his mother: *things fall apart* and issues of gender in the constitution of African postcolonial discourse. Callaloo 16:847
Keyssar A (2009) The right to vote: the contested history of democracy in the United States. Basic Books, Philadelphia
Lacayo R (2005) http://entertainment.time.com/2005/10/16/all-time-100-novels/slide/things-fall-apart-1959-by-chinua-achebe/#things-fall-apart-1959-by-chinua-achebe. Accessed on 23 Nov 2012
Langbein J (1992) On the myth of written constitutions: the disappearance of the criminal jury trial. Harv J Law Public Pol 15:119
Mbiti J (1990) African religions and philosophy. Heinemann Educational Publishers, Oxford
Menkel-Meadow C (1992) To solve problems, not make them: integrating ADR in the law school curriculum. SMU Law Rev 46:1995
Mokgoro Y (1997) The customary law question in the South African constitution. St Louis Univ Law J 14:1279
Morison J, Bell C (1996) Tall stories? Reading law and literature. Dartmouth, Aldershot
Morsink J (1999) The universal declaration of human rights: origins, drafting and intent. University of Pennsylvania Press, Philadelphia
Moyn S (2012) Imperialism, self-determination, and the rise of human rights. In: Iriye A et al (eds) The human rights revolution: an international history. Oxford University Press, Oxford
Nnoromele P (2000) The plight of a hero in Achebe's *things fall apart*. Coll Lit 27:146
Nzimiro I (1972) Studies in Ibo political systems: chieftaincy and politics in four Niger states. University of California Press, Berkley
Oba A (2006) The administration of customary law in a post-colonial Nigerian state. Cambrian Law Rev 37:95
Oba A (2008) Juju oaths in customary law arbitration and their legal validity in Nigerian courts. J Afr Law 52:139
Obiechina E (1973) Tradition and society in the West African novel. Cambridge University Press, London
Pollis A (1982) Liberal, socialist, and third world perspectives of human rights. In: Schwab P, Pollis A (eds) Towards a human rights framework. Praeger, New York
Posner R (1988) Law and literature: a misunderstood relation. Harvard University Press, Cambridge
Quashigah K (2012) Scope of individual duties in the African charter. In: Ssenyonjo M (ed) The African regional human rights system: 30 years after the African charter on human and peoples' rights. Martinus Nijhoff Publishers, Leiden
Quayson A (1994) Realism, criticism, and the disguises of both: a reading of Chinua Achebe's *things fall apart* with an evaluation of the criticism relating to it. Res Afr Lit 25:117
Riddell B (1990) Let there be light: the voices of West African novels. J Mod Afr Stud 28:473
Sander F, Hernandez C (2008) Transcript: a dialogue between professors Frank Sander and Mariana Hernandez Crespo: exploring the evolution of the multi-door courthouse. Univ St Thomas Law J 5:665
Slaughter J (2007) Human rights Inc.: the world novel, narrative form, and international law. Fordham University Press, New York
Smit D (2004) The death penalty in Africa. Afr Hum Rights Law J 4:1
Soifer A (1986) Reviewing legal fictions. Ga Law Rev 20:871
Trechsel S (1997) Why must trials be fair. Isr Law Rev 31:94
Trevor-Roper H (1969) The past and the present: history and sociology. Past Present 42:3
Weisberg R (1988) The law-literature enterprise. Yale J Law Human 1:1
Yoshino K (2005) The city and the poet. Yale Law J 114:1835

Part III
Society

Chapter 11
Legal Empowerment of the Poor: Does Political Participation Matter?

Oche Onazi

11.1 Introduction

Is it possible to think of political participation outside the human right to vote for representatives at periodic elections? Is political participation also a method of securing non-political goods? Is political participation an intrinsic value, something that should be promoted regardless of consequences, owing to its significance to individual and collective flourishing? Visit any village or city in Sub-Saharan Africa and answers will be found, inclusive of a different notion of political participation. That nearly all essential public goods and services in cities across Africa are provided by one or another form of informal activity supports this. Political participation, therefore, is both intrinsic and instrumental to the poor. It is something upon which their livelihoods depend.

Disillusioned by failed promises of corruptly elected representatives and by the inability to participate in the market, the poor have had no choice but to devise practices, associations, networks and other forms of cooperation to escape these problems, including the limited opportunities to challenge them offered by dominant formal models such as the human right to political participation. The emphasis on formal institutional practices of voting and representation, for instance, has been of little value or use to the struggles of the poor in private, economic, cultural and

This chapter has been published in slightly altered form as part of a special issue on 'Contemporary African Jurisprudence' in 2012 in *The Journal Jurisprudence* 14, 221–224. I thank the publisher, The Elias Clark Group, for permission to reproduce it in this collection of essays.

O. Onazi (✉)
University of Dundee, Dundee, UK
e-mail: o.onazi@dundee.ac.uk

O. Onazi (ed.), *African Legal Theory and Contemporary Problems: Critical Essays*, Ius Gentium: Comparative Perspectives on Law and Justice 29,
DOI 10.1007/978-94-007-7537-4_11,

social domains. This may explain why, although there are exceptions, these informal activities and strategies have barely been pursued under the rubric of human rights. As the informal activities discussed in this chapter attest, the poor are disenchanted by having to rely heavily on a political system that either misrepresents or simply fails to take their interests into account. The human right to vote has functioned as the right to vote for one corrupt representative after another. It can be discerned from the range of informal activities in that the poor want more than the right to vote; they also want autonomy and direct control over important decisions that affect their lives. Collective or self-provisioning of essential public goods and services is used in this chapter to illustrate not only the type of informal political participation articulated by the poor but also the autonomy they derive from it in administering their affairs, apart from the independence this autonomy gives them from formal political institutions.

On the whole, the aim of this chapter is to bring attention to a certain generalisation in recent development thinking about the perceived benefits of formalisation on poverty alleviation. There are different dimensions to this generalisation. It is the reasoning behind claims about the potential benefits of the formalisation of property (Nyamu-Musembi 2007; Barros 2010), business and labour rights (Faundez 2009) on poverty alleviation (Otto 2009). What has also been noted but not sufficiently addressed is the impact that formalisation has had on the value of political participation. Not only is this impact responsible for misunderstandings about that value, it is also to blame for the failure to provide an inclusive model of political participation capable of challenging economic or material inequality. It is this argument that is taken up in this chapter. Thus, it is argued that, apart from firmly grasping the instrumental and intrinsic value of political participation, the expansiveness of diverse forms of activity in the informal sphere provides a significant medium to concretise this value, particularly in ways that can compete with mainstream initiatives aspiring to do the same. They may not have the financial, institutional or intellectual clout of mainstream development initiatives, yet the dispersed, permanent, ad-hoc or unpredictable non-institutional activities command a presence across every city or village in Africa, as indeed in other parts of the third world. It is a reflection of the spirit of Africa, something that extends political participation beyond its actual institutionalisation. Informal political participation, the term given to these activities in this chapter, is embedded in the grassroots and covers grounds that even the best-intentioned, planned and supported formal initiative can only aspire to cover.

The United Nations Development Programme's (UNDP) legal empowerment of the poor initiative is used as a case study for this argument. It is a recent, but also an important, initiative that pursues the logic of formalisation to the fullest at the expense of values such as political participation. Despite emerging in an era in which voice, ownership, participation and good governance serve as institutional mantras, legal empowerment can hardly be said to articulate a model of political participation, let alone one reflective of the voices, struggles and aspirations of the poor. Although it recognises that the lack of political participation can be a factor of poverty, legal empowerment fails to offer a comprehensive policy in response to this problem.

This chapter highlights the misunderstandings around the value of political participation, which has led to the failure of the legal empowerment initiative to adopt a related model; the chapter then discusses the opportunities that such informal strategies may open for social and political transformation. In conclusion, it sketches out certain key features and important lessons that can be drawn from informal political participation, including the advantage the model holds over the human right to political participation.

11.2 Legal Empowerment of the Poor

Legal empowerment of the poor seeks to address the misery of poverty in developing and transitional societies. It unites and generates support from the most influential figures and institutions in international development circles. The initiative has been notable among other things for the calibre of the figures who graced the meetings that led to the report which currently shapes UNDP's legal empowerment work. It is those proposals, encapsulated in the two-volume report *Making the Law Work for Everyone*, that are analysed in the present chapter. Legal empowerment of the poor is simply described as an approach against poverty through law. To date, law has failed to provide comprehensively such a window of opportunity. Addressing exclusion of the poor from law should be at the core of any attempt to liberate the millions around the world who are in the shackles of poverty. As the UNDP report argues, poverty results from the failure of both public policy and markets. Legal protection, particularly the creation of tradeable assets, labour rights, venture capital and intellectual property, is the route to the creation of wealth among the poor. Wealth, on the other hand, is considered a route out of poverty, even though the legal empowerment approach is more nuanced. Wealth creation is not necessarily a ticket out of poverty, and there is some recognition of this in the UNDP report. Despite this, legal empowerment is another term for the legal foundations of entrepreneurship. It relies on law to unlock the wealth-creating potential of the poor.

In addition – and the main subject of concern for the legal empowerment approach – the majority of the poor survive in the informal economy. This excludes them from the type of protections and opportunities that can be gained from the formal system. Informal norms and institutions not only do not protect the poor but also contribute to their oppression (Commission on Legal Empowerment 2008, p. 2). The approach treats informality as a central factor of poverty and exclusion. It sees it as a symptom of poverty that ought to be remedied by the creation of formal and clear regimes of law, economic management and organisation. Informality is equated to illegality and poverty, just as formality is equated to wealth and legality. According to the UNDP report, the advantages of the formal legal system are self-evident. Formality provides certainty and predictability, attributes that cannot be associated with informality. Rights, particularly legally enforceable property, business and labour rights, are therefore the main pillars and building blocks of legal empowerment of the poor.

The report acknowledges, however, that all the permutations regarding the constitutive rights of legal empowerment can succeed only within a thriving democratic environment. It suggests that, in addition to a functional democracy, the poor need those rights that have an effect on the political system. The report thus proposes that 'democracy and legal empowerment are kindred spirits, and are better synchronised than sequenced' (2008, p. 4). This means that, together with the constitutive rights of legal empowerment, the poor must also have access to the rights to vote, freedom of expression and some limited procedural rights. Looked at this way, it would not be wrong to conclude that political participation is implied by the broader objective of legal empowerment. Any doubts about the importance of political participation are quashed when the report states that 'legal empowerment can only be realised through systematic change aimed at unlocking the civic and economic potential of the poor' (2008, p. 5). This not only implies the importance of political participation but also the need for an inclusive concept, one comprising interconnecting political and economic components.

It is disappointing that there are few details as to how this ideal can be realised except through passing references to the right to vote. Surely, political participation, particularly in Sub-Saharan African country contexts, where voting is often corrupt, fraudulent and violent, must have greater meaning than implied by the casual references to voting rights? Political participation must also mean reconstituting polities in such a way that decision-making power can be delegated and dispersed down to the most basic levels and to various facets of society. This is one way of ensuring that everyone, particularly the poor, meaningfully take part in matters that affect their lives. In this context, again, legal empowerment of the poor is disappointing. In contrast, and as demonstrated later in this chapter, this is the strength of informal political participation.

Considering the significance given in this chapter to political participation, attention is paid to the (mis)treatment of this ideal by proposals for legal empowerment. In the following section, I identify and unpack certain themes from the UNDP report that highlight (but fail to deal with) the relational dimension between legal empowerment and political participation. I demonstrate the systemic failure to address sufficiently the political dimensions of economic inequality. In spite of noting that participation is pivotal to attaining legal empowerment, the report does not address political participation in a programmatic way.

11.2.1 Thin Vision of Political Participation

No better words can introduce the significance of political participation than those of the title of chapter three of the first volume of the UNDP report. It boldly claims that legal empowerment is not only good economics but also smart politics. On the surface, this claim appears to appreciate the economic and political dimensions of poverty as part of the broad objective of making law work for the poor. Indeed, the report proceeds from the point of view (and rightly so) that, at present, both law and politics work only for rich, powerful elites. They do not for the poor (2008, p. 44). It notes that political and economic equalities have contributed to the deficiencies of law and related institutions and, furthermore, have impeded access to justice. In instrumental terms, the failure of the legal system impedes economic growth, apart from causing instability and sustaining corruption.

Against this status quo, the report argues that the formalisation of law is central to responding to the needs of the poor, including to politics that would otherwise descend into informal channels. If governments fail to assist the poor, the significance of the formal legal system will lose its legitimacy, leading to further decay of such legal institutions and, ultimately, the fragmentation of society. The failure of law, in this respect, is a precipice for catastrophe. Not only would the economy stagnate, the whole fabric of the state would collapse. Inequality in societies is singled out for making the poor suspicious of the state. According to the UNDP report, the poor have good reason for being suspicious, because institutions of the state arguably determine all the rules, including key ones relating to economic activity.

11.2.2 Participation and Empowerment

The message, then, from legal empowerment is that governance matters, particularly where the poor are vulnerable to crime or corruption or lack meaningful access to courts. Good governance is thus seen as the remedy to such problems; it is defined as the 'form of institutions that establish a predictable, impartial, and consistently enforced set of rules' (2008) that will have a cumulative effect on the creation of just, prosperous and sustainable societies. Good governance unites legal empowerment with the mainstream development orthodoxy that has promoted this mantra since the early 1990s (Gathii 2000; Arrighi 2003). Apart from contributing to good governance, legal empowerment seeks to give voice and identity to the poor. Indeed, identity and voice are preconditions of legal empowerment (Commission on Legal Empowerment 2008, p. 44). Identity simply refers to legal recognition (2008), meaning proof of identity before the law. Lack of such identity, according to the report, facilitates exclusion; identity would make it more difficult to exploit the poor. In a related context, a strong assertion of identity translates into 'civic and economic agency as citizens, asset holders, workers, and businessmen/women' (2008).

On the other hand, voice refers to information and education, organisation and representation. This suggests that the poor need to be informed and educated about their rights and how they can shape decision-making processes. The poor also require representative organisations (cooperatives, trade unions, small-business associations, community and women's associations, etc.) that can demand and negotiate reforms to advance their rights. Voice here seems to mirror (with certain distinctions) Albert Hirschman's (1970) work. There, voice is synonymous with participation in various aspects of public life. Voice, in contrast to what it entails to legal empowerment, means more than traditional forms of electoral and representative participation.

In development discourse there are two generally opposing (but sometimes mutually supporting) views of participation. The first view originates from the emphasis on civil society by neoliberal development initiatives. It is based on an acknowledgment of the limitations of the first-generation neoliberal market reforms and the incursion into institutional and social reforms (Mohan and Kristian 2002). Participation is linked to empowerment, with power conceptualised in harmonious terms. The presupposition is that power is vested in individuals in various communities, who can utilise it to achieve individual and collective goals. To achieve this vision of empowerment, individuals share power and do not necessarily have to dislodge the power of elites. Participation and empowerment are mainstreamed through concepts such as stakeholder participation, local governance and social capital. Organisations like the World Bank (WB) have been the main institutional advocates of such initiatives.

Participation and empowerment often feature as mutually supporting concepts, even though both are rarely clearly defined. Although they appear to emerge from bottom–up processes, a prevailing criticism is that neoliberal participation and empowerment programmes are still determined in the cosy offices of international development institutions, government agencies and non-governmental organisations. Looking at the twin concepts of empowerment and participation in neoliberal development discourse, Mick Moore argues that their emergence has more to do with the organisational needs of the major development institutions than those of the poor. It reflects the recent reluctance and reduction of borrowing by member countries and, as a consequence, the search for new outlets to disburse funds by the WB. The emergence of social funds is a good example. It is one of the most expanding components of the WB's lending portfolios (Moore 2001). In the end, empowerment and participation, concepts with considerable political connotations, appear watered down and too weak to dislodge the social, political and economic power structures that affect the poor. As such, participation and empowerment in dominant neoliberal discourse promise more than they can deliver.

Secondly, and in contrast with the first view, participation and empowerment enjoy a radical interpretation, thanks to critical development scholarship. Power is both relational and antagonistic. It rests on the premise that the transformation of economic and political structures would lead to a radical democratic society, which can in turn be enhanced by participation and empowerment. Empowerment entails the collective participation of the marginalised in civil society to challenge the structures of the state and market. Indeed, the emphasis on civil society sometimes makes it difficult to differentiate between the dominant and the radical view of participation and empowerment. However, it would appear that the main distinguishing feature is that the radical view is vehemently opposed to capitalism and markets and sometimes surfaces as anti-western. Apart from that, participation and empowerment are celebrated as authentic bottom–up processes.

Neither participation nor empowerment is sufficiently defined by the report. In relation to participation, empowerment receives negligible attention in several lines of the report. It is mainly apparent in discussions about the importance of democracy to legal empowerment (Commission on Legal Empowerment of the Poor 2008, pp. 20, 44). To summarise this viewpoint, and to reinforce similar arguments about democracy noted above in Sect. 11.2 'Legal empowerment of the poor', the report suggests that a democratic ethic is a precondition for implementing successful policies, which in turn would increase the inclusion of the poor. No further explanation is given as to how this would be achieved. All that is provided are a few statements that further outline the importance of participation. A good example of this can be seen in what may be the most affirmative statement in favour of participation: '[t]here is no substitute for a truly inclusive, participatory, and deliberative process, where alternative viewpoints are considered and the interests of the poor and marginalised citizens are taken into account' (2008, p. 47). The report then proceeds to recognise (again without specifying) what the requirements for such types of inclusion might entail. It suggests that citizens need to be encouraged to organise and participate effectively in decision-making processes and that centralised forms of government impede such forms of participation. As already noted, it fails to indicate the various policy options for this sort of inclusion, even if it is reluctant to impose a specific policy (2008, p. 26).

Empowerment, like participation, is not defined by the report, but it is clear that it is highly unlikely to subscribe to the radical view of the concept. Not even the definition of 'legal empowerment' given in the report clarifies the underlying concept of empowerment. However, the report does give some indication of what it means by empowerment, as extrapolated from the emphasis on three core rights: property, business and labour. Legal empowerment is defined as 'the process through which the poor become protected and are enabled to use the law to advance' (2008, p. 26) such rights against the state and in (but not against) the market. Rights are compatible with the agenda for markets, particularly the rights prioritised by legal empowerment. According to the report, property, business and labour are the most significant rights that affect the livelihoods of the poor, inclusive of an enabling framework of law and justice. Access to justice and rule of law also become another central tenet of the approach. Read together, these components of legal empowerment would enable the poor to become better citizens, asset holders, workers and business people.

11.2.3 Human Rights

Legal empowerment is couched further in the language of human rights, which implies a wider notion of empowerment. The emphasis on three core rights is justified on the basis of a wider framework of human rights (2008, p. 31). The approach emphasises at length that property, business and labour rights are a species of human rights; as such, they must be developed further through international, regional and national human rights regimes. Here the importance of participation re-emerges in the report. It claims that the poor must be given the opportunity to participate and own the processes leading up to these rights.

A preliminary conclusion that can be drawn from the discussions above is that participation refers to economic participation. Despite these claims, legal empowerment emerges as too narrow in relation to political participation. By focusing on property, business and labour rights, legal empowerment cannot disguise its economic bias. The report appears to repackage older contestable debates about the relationship between law and development, particularly those that conceive economic growth as development. Although it attempts to align itself with more recent development thinking (i.e., the capabilities approach), it fails to do so convincingly. Its selection of human rights makes it appear constricted and even parochial: it places almost total emphasis on realising its narrow vision of rights through the market. The market, it says, not only reflects basic freedoms such as association and movement, but also generates the resources necessary to provide, uphold and enforce the full range of human rights. According to the report, it is these processes that would enable the poor to realise their rights and provide new opportunities for the full realisation of citizenship. Not surprisingly, the report says nothing about market exclusion and how this can also affect the realisation of rights and citizenship.

If empowerment, as the report suggests, means more than realising economic growth, as the capability approach in particular implies, it begs the question: why do property, business and labour rights appear to be more important than water, healthcare or education rights (Nussbaum 2011, pp. 17–45)? In short, why does legal empowerment not promote a more comprehensive human rights approach? From the perspective of this chapter, if we take its claim that legal empowerment is smart politics, why is the right to political participation not among the core rights promoted? These are, of course, rhetorical questions, but the point in raising them is to suggest that the failure to anticipate such issues leaves us with no choice but to conclude that, unlike questions of economic participation, political participation is not taken seriously. With its narrow emphasis on market or economy-related rights, legal empowerment of the poor may be good economics. But by failing to be more specific on political participation, legal empowerment does not live up to its claim that it is smart politics.

11.3 Informal Political Participation

This section makes the case for informal political participation, arguing that it sufficiently grasps and responds to the multiple nature of exclusion, especially exclusion from the formal sphere. In particular, I argue that the vast amount of associational or organisational forms in nearly every village and city of Africa elaborate on the types of political participation that are taken for granted by dominant narratives. These activities point to a notion of political participation that is wider than that available through human rights. While questions relating to human rights are dealt with in more detail in subsequent sections, what follows here is an attempt to clarify what the idea of informal political participation means. In doing so, I also sketch out certain key characteristics and strengths of informal political participation.

Informal political participation means several things, defying neat distinction. Each use of the term tends to reinforce or contradict another. There are also regional differences between its use within and between the global north and global south. Nonetheless, I attempt to distinguish between three different but related meanings of informal political participation. In doing so, I emphasise the last notion. What this preliminary exercise shows is that it is always important to distinguish between the different uses because the term has positive and negative connotations. The point of making this distinction is to try to separate the positive from the negative.

First, informal political participation generally refers to the politics of protest movements, whether this is on the domestic or global sphere. The issues that underpin this sort of politics range from identity, inequality, poverty and war to environmental sustainability, among other forms of political and economic injustice. The old and new social movements or the anti-globalisation and anti-poverty movements of various persuasions adhere to this type of informal political participation. Although the movements are composed of independent groups who differ both in their objectives or in the methods they deploy, they are often united against a common problem: the undemocratic or unaccountable nature of global and domestic formal political and economic institutions of governance. For instance, the unrepresentative nature of global and domestic political systems is the common complaint uniting the recent and diverse Occupy movements. Corporate corruption and greed may have provided the impetus for these movements; however, the grievance is also about the unrepresentative nature of the system of political representation (Hardt and Negri 2011). Participants of such movements are aggrieved because they have lost patience with the system of formal political participation, particularly political parties and politicians who ill-represent their interests. This is a similar theme among participants of the third version of informal political participation described below.

It is impossible to understand the deep-seated nature of the grievances of the protest movements without understanding how they are precipitated by a second dimension of informal political participation. In this context, informal politics means the ability of power actors such as multinational corporations and elites like the Bretton Wood institutions (BWI) to manipulate global and domestic political systems to suit their interests. Through unofficial channels such as corruption, clientelism, lobbying, personal networks and conditionalities, or other carrot-and-stick devices, these transnationals and their local counterparts affect formal political and economic institutions in more effective ways than democratic elections and other formal devices of political participation. There is a clear relationship between the local and global dimensions of informal participation, just as there are distinct local dimensions. Apart from the role of multinational corporations, a good example of how global and local informal political participation interact is the continuing impact of BWI policy initiatives on formulating local government policy. The Structural Adjustment Programmes and now good governance are some well-known examples of policies that have been produced by this form of informal political participation.

The hardships that such policies have created add another layer to the meaning of informal political participation. It is this notion of informal political participation that is emphasised in the remainder of the chapter. By informal political participation, in this context, I refer to the range of survival mechanisms, activities and forms of organisation that transcend social, cultural, legal, economic and political boundaries, which are often generated to respond to or compensate for the inadequacies and exclusions of formal political systems and the forms of participation that they engender (Hetch and Simone 1994, pp. 11–23). They are generated informally since, for various reasons, there are very limited opportunities within the formal political system for such forms of participation. Informal political participation captures the considerable associational life that is symptomatic of most African cities as well as those in other parts of the third world.

Informal political participation also captures the great degree of creativity and inventiveness, apart from the solidarity, reciprocity and cooperation, particularly among those excluded from formal systems, whether these are state or market-based institutions. To give a good example: in both qualitative and quantitative terms, this notion of informal political participation is central to understanding how or in what ways Sub-Saharan African townships and villages work (Simone 2001, 2004). Informal forms of organisations are arguably the most important survival mechanism in African societies for the poor. They react to or attempt to escape the harness and rigidity of formal systems. Varying in shape, size or structure, they range from the network of neighbourhood associations, kinship groups, community-based organisations, cooperatives and trade unions to human delivery systems, thrift associations, women's associations, widows' associations, work-based associations, religious organisations, ethnic-based associations and other organisational forms that cannot be captured conceptually.

Informal political participation arises out of uncertainty, the uncertainty of living in the present and future. Uncertainty is positive and negative, creative and destructive. It points to the advantages and disadvantages of living in the informal world, which is one of resourcefulness and hope on the one hand and on the other of selfishness, exclusion and insecurity. Thus, we must be careful not to overgeneralise about the strengths of this notion of informal political participation. The degree of cooperation that often exists among members of the same group or community can be used to fuel the exclusion of non-members of this group or community. Despite these shortcomings, uncertainty is one of the salient aspects and advantages of informal political participation (2004). There is a correlation between the uncertain futures of those who are excluded from the formal systems and the innovative or emancipatory organisational forms that emerge in response (Colebrook 2002, p. 689). The rather ad-hoc, experimental and uncertain nature of the organisational forms is a result of the uncertain environment in which they are nurtured. Such organisations lack a definitive character; they are often open-ended and flexible. This is why they are quick to adapt to different situations. They are as embryonic as the series of problems that give birth to them. They are resourceful, dispersed and sometimes invisible and spontaneous. As long as there are problems, new collaborative forms between individuals and groups will emerge to address them. This means that, although informal political organisations may be ad-hoc and arise from uncertainty, they are as permanent as the problems that give rise to them. While they may not intentionally be collaborative or mutually supportive, pockets of solidarity, including networks of cooperation, are often built when various groups attempt to expand their range of activity.

Informal political participation is more than the antithesis to formal political participation. Both activities share a complex and ambivalent relationship. Indeed, informal political participation can sometimes be understood as the alter ego of formal political participation. A good analogy is how participants in the informal sphere are not opposed to participating in the formal sphere. For instance, opportunities may be sought in the formal sphere to sustain a variety of activities in the informal sphere, including the support of immediate or extended family members, or religious and ethnic associations, or simply to pay healthcare bills. In another sense, as is often the case in many African cities, workers in the formal political sphere must engage in several informal activities, such as thrift to augment their inadequate wages. Although this is not strictly a political activity, the point is that it is analogous to the way that informal political organisations creatively engage, disengage, embrace, adapt, transform and reinvent formal political forms of participation and organisation. As a more general claim, it shows how informal and formal political participation blur the distinctions and reinforce each other. The boundaries between what is formal and informal, and what is legal and illegal, constantly shifts from one ground to another in space and time (Lindell 2010).

11.3.1 In What Sense Is Informality Political?

It is important to clarify the political dimensions or context of these informal activities. Because they are not always clear, highlighting this is significant to further our understanding of the full dimensions and implications of the notion of informal political participation articulated in this chapter. After all, it is relatively easy, as commonly the case, to describe these activities as merely economic survival strategies that have nothing to do with politics. Although insights from feminist theory on the political nature of the private and social sphere are helpful in dispelling such perceptions, there are other important political implications of informality that need to be brought to attention. The economic sphere is arguably the most important area to have felt the impact of various forms of informal activity. In Sub-Saharan Africa, for instance, it is estimated that 75 % of public goods and services are provided by one form or another of informal activity (Simone 2001, p. 103). An interpretation that can be given to these events is that informality has replaced state (and more recently market) institutions with a type of politics of survival, association, cooperation and solidarity. This is the first sense in which such activities can be described as political. By taking direct responsibility for the provisioning of public goods and services, traditionally a responsibility of the state, the various informal groups are indirectly effecting social change politically. They are not just making demands for better provisioning of public goods and services; rather, they are seizing the type of political power necessary to directly control, allocate and distribute (according to their own rules) public goods and services among themselves. What is arguably the most important lesson that can be drawn from such forms of activity is that the provisioning of public goods and services is sustained politically through, among other things, collective action. Moreover, the informal provisioning of public goods and services points to the limitations and the need to look beyond the inadequacies of the recent policy emphasis on markets and privatisation.

Looking at the purpose behind collective or self-provisioning of public goods and services, we can perceive further political dimensions of such forms of informal activity. First, because most of the activity is driven by the desire of participants to live dignified lives, it is political in the sense that it is irreducibly moral. The means deployed to achieve the essential goods that contribute to dignity do not really matter. In certain situations, illegal squatter settlements, street hawking in public places and siphoning water or electricity would be morally justified from the standpoint of survival. In another sense (and connected to the moral aspect), there is a relational aspect to this politics, a type of politics in which kinship, family, religious and ethnic ties take the centre stage. There is an interaction between the household or extended family network and economic, religious, social and political forms of organisation. This is so confusing that it is difficult to separate one pattern of organisation from another. They all share a degree of interdependence. The externalities generated from one unit of organisation tend to affect the other. When a problem is resolved within one unit of organisation, it has a ripple effect on problems in another unit of organisation. Another way in which this manifests is that, not only do these organisations always offer something new, but they also retain something from the past. Africa's brand of informal political participation is a hybrid of the traditional and modern. It responds to modernity by assimilating it with traditional African values of compassion, care, solidarity, reciprocity, community and collaboration. The amalgamation of the traditional and modern is an example of the creativity and imagination that is borne out of the exclusion, hardship, disorder and impoverishment caused by modern formal political institutions.

In addition to the moral and relational dimension, informal activities are political in the sense that they are distributive. In other words, legal or illegal distribution of public goods and services is arguably the core objective of informal activities. The presupposition is also that distribution will be guaranteed if individuals and groups exercise autonomy over decisions regarding the distribution of public goods and services. Autonomy over decision-making processes points in two directions in which informality takes a political turn (Bayat 1997; Simone 2008). First, it shows that there is an internally democratic element to these activities. Although the groups are as diverse as the activities they carry out (and they vary in the internal quality of democracy), they nonetheless have democratic features such as rules of participation, decision-making, membership, and internal and external dispute-resolution mechanisms. Informality offers individuals and groups the autonomy to make collective decisions as well as conduct other affairs free from the rigid restrictions and rules of the formal sphere. These are not, as commonly regarded, straightforwardly lawless or illegal activities; rather, they are activities sustained by moral economies such as trust, solidarity and cooperation.

Second, distribution through autonomy over decision-making paves the way for the formation and proliferation of legal and illegal problem-solving organisations, something which strikes a family resemblance with theories of associational democracy (Hirst 1994, pp. 49–59). It is indicative of the role that politics ought to play in economic life, among other areas. The share volume of informal activity, as for instance in Africa (Simone 2001, p. 103), is not only an empirical illustration of this, but also shows how the existence of such activity, no matter how minimal the internal level of participation, could (even if this were nominal) deepen the quality of democracy in the societies concerned. The failure to appreciate this is perhaps due to the standard parameters for measuring the quality of democracy. We look to different institutions or a set of institutional practices to measure democracy. What does not count as democratic or political are the vast sets of associational practices of the informal world.

From the perspective of this chapter, a further point can be made about the contribution of informal political participation. It widens commonly held perceptions such as those in human rights of what political participation should mean. It moves the focus beyond its narrow attention to voting, elections and representation. These informal practices point to a wider notion of political participation, even though they do not claim to be the alternative or are unclear as to what this notion should be. Informal political participation reinvigorates the very idea of participating in virtually all aspects of life, with the democratising effect that it has on the economy arguably its single most important contribution. In this context, it works with a background notion of politics that mirrors the Aristotelian concept of politics. It rediscovers, and goes beyond, the Aristotelian ethical notion of politics, to offer a type of politics that encompasses and involves everyone in decision-making over almost all aspects of life (Aristotle 2009, pp. 5–10). It is indeed another way of understanding what Aristotle meant when he asserted that we are all political animals.

This democratising quality may originate from the definitive character of informal political participation. From the foregoing discussions, it appears to be more a combination of moral, social and cultural norms that nurtures a type of political agency, which in turn underpins the highly innovative practices and modalities of organisation. What should be taken from the multiplicity and interaction of various spheres is how they intermingle to produce a distinctive brand of politics, one that is not political (in the traditional formalistic sense of the term) nor authentically cultural, economic and social. Traditional distinctions between economics and politics, public and private, family and society, and religion and secularity are blurred in the context of informal political participation (Hetch and Simone 1994, p. 14). Africa is again a good reference point for this, because there these categories are not separated. What is typical about informal Africa is the porous and interlocking relationships between such spheres. Indeed it is through these sorts of activity that political concepts such as citizenship are realised, not through political institutions or abstract concepts of constitutional rights. The inclusions and exclusions that originate from the assertion of citizenship are better appreciated through local and daily social practices in the informal world.

11.4 The Limit of Political Participation Through Human Rights

Having set out above the rudiments of informal political participation, I explore and consider the options for political participation offered through human rights. Apart from tilting in favour of formal politics (i.e., elections, representation and political party politics), this model of politics fails to offer a comprehensive notion of participation that is capable of capturing the range of informal activities described in the previous section. Moreover, by maintaining strict boundaries between the public and private sphere, human rights contribute to sustaining a similar asymmetry between the political and economic sphere. As such, there is good reason to be sceptical about a dependence on human rights to diffuse the notion of political participation within the legal empowerment agenda. There are two other reasons that human rights should invite scepticism. First, 'participation' is conceived narrowly to mean political participation in the traditional sense of the term. The emphasis is on ways in which individuals can influence the political system through democratic elections or representative forms of government. The human rights doctrine of participation can be found in a combination of the right to self-determination[1] and the right to political participation.[2] Although political participation is further broken down into the right to vote (and to be voted for) in elections and the right to participate in public affairs, the meaning of the latter part of this right is vague. Unlike the right to vote, which remains largely uncontroversial, it is not clear what participation in public affairs is or what sort of activities constitute public affairs. In particular, it is not clear whether the economic sphere should benefit from political participation.

However, doubts over this have been clarified by what is arguably the most inclusive definition in the human rights corpus of the right to participation. This is provided by the Convention on the Elimination of all Forms of Discrimination against Women 1981, which extends participation beyond the traditional and formal political circles mentioned above. It includes participation in various aspects of civil society, from public boards, trade unions and professional associations to community-based organisations. This expands the notion of political participation,

[1] It may not be a coincidence from the point of view of the argument here that the human right to self-determination emerges as a political and not an economic right. On the right to self-determination, see Article 1(1) of the International Covenant on Civil and Political Rights and the International Covenant of Economic, Social and Cultural Rights.

[2] On the right to political participation see, Article 25 of the International Covenant for Civil and Political Rights. See General Comment 25 for an expansion of the right to political participation. Paragraph 1, General Comment No 25: The right to participate in public affairs, voting rights and the right of equal access to public service (Art. 25): 12/07/96 CCPR/C/21/Rev.1/ Add.7. The Universal Declaration of Human rights (UDHR), which preceded the two covenants is also vague on this point when it deals with political participation. Article 21 (a) seems to restrict political participation to the right to take part in government, omitting any form of political and non-political activity unrelated to government. Most of these observations apply to regional human rights agreements like the African Charter on Human and Peoples Rights.

even though it privileges women. In addition, others have argued that the narrow conception of political participation in human rights can be remedied by a more integrated reading of human rights norms by, for instance, interpreting freedom of expression, assembly, speech and anti-discriminatory rights in relation to political participation (see, for example, Secker 2009; Steiner 1988; Franck 1992). While the arguments above are plausible, there is a second and more fundamental reason that raises doubts about whether human rights can provide the foundation for political participation. Because of its significance, it is discussed in detail in the next section.

11.4.1 The Autonomy of the Economic Sphere from Political Participation

The problem is the binary distinction between public and private that is foundational to human rights. Among other consequences, this may reinforce the autonomy of the economic sphere from the political, particularly excluding democratic forms of participation in the economic sphere. This is an old problem, even though it may not often be highlighted. Its antecedents can be traced to the emergence of natural rights. In its historical dimension, natural rights were responsible for insulating politics from society and, thereby, contributing to separating the unity of political and economic forms of domination (Douzinas 2010, pp. 81–100). This was first witnessed in Europe, during the period when feudal society transitioned to bourgeois society. Unlike feudal societies, where there were no clear distinctions between economic wealth, social status and political power, in bourgeois society, politics became confined to the realm of the state, while property and religion, which were previously instruments of class domination, became transformed into private institutions of civil society and protected by natural rights from state intervention.

In the private realm, property became the dominant form of relations. The cumulative effect was that it did not just insulate the (private) economic realm from the (public) state: it was responsible for failing to extend political controls on the economy. Rights, politics and the state existed as abstract and transcendental entities, far removed from social and economic divisions in society. These developments produced tragic consequences for citizens. They ended up living dual lives, one consisting of 'strife in the pursuit of personal economic interest', (2010) and the other 'devoted to political activity and the common good' (2010). Equality and liberty, as such, were at best fictitious concepts, ones that were key to holding the state and rights apart and distanced from the daily sites of oppression and exploitation. Rights, as a consequence, succeeded in making the cleavage in levels of accountability between the economic and political spheres appear natural.

The emergence of the right to vote is another way of understanding how the economy became de-politicised. Universal adult suffrage or the right to vote generated mixed reactions and unintended consequences. This became evident through the prohibition of the requirement of property qualification as a core aspect of the right to vote (Veitch 2007, pp. 64–65). Although this was desirable, it reinforced (without intending to) the insulation of the economic sphere from political accountability. Ideals of equality, freedom and citizenship were distinctive characteristics and rights to be enjoyed from the political sphere. Apart from lacking similar rights and freedoms, the economic sphere became normalised as a regime of domination and exploitation. From then on, there were two different standards of participation and representation in each sphere, apart from the fact that the economic and political spheres became known as distinct and autonomous entities. Regardless of the underlying political undertones in the activities taken by economic actors, these would, under this climate, elide democratic or political standards of accountability. As mentioned in Sect. 11.3 'Informal political participation', the informal role that certain transnational actors play in influencing the content of policies of the formal political system is a good illustration of this problem.

11.4.2 Law

Rights are not the only reason for the minimal levels of political accountability in the economic sphere. Law is also partly a factor, if not a major one, particularly if the close relationship between law, property and capitalism is scrutinised (Hardt and Negri 2009). Different republican constitutional traditions, from the American to the French and the British, and the colonial projects that result from them, place private property as the central 'regulative idea of the constitutional state and the rule of law' (2009, p. 7). Under such republican regimes, law exists as both an abstract and concrete phenomenon. In the abstract sense, law is transcendental, detached or even apathetic to social and material reality. In the concrete sense, on the other hand, law (particularly through the institution of property) concretises the materiality of exploitation and domination. Although property, central to the capitalist economy, possesses its own laws, these exist only to sustain exclusions in society (2009). The economy is insulated from the sovereign political controls of economy, which is in turn to be controlled by 'invisible and internalized' (2009) economic or market-related rules. Private property simultaneously conceals the materiality of human poverty and concretises inequality and exploitation.

11.4.3 Civil Society

At a more basic or societal level, the de-politicisation of the economic sphere is also made possible by the concept of civil society (Meksins 1995, p. 252). This is often defined as a state-free zone, in which citizens exercise their political freedoms. The difficulty with civil society is traced to the premise behind it, particularly simultaneous evolution with capitalism, the market economy and property rights. As discussed earlier, the emergence of capitalism not only led to the separation of the state from civil society, but also united civil society with the market without extending political forms of accountability. This created a different political system than that which had prevailed in history, as it contributed to the preservation of politics and economics as separate spheres. Without the backing of state or political power, civil society is incapable of restraining the economic power of the market. As a political-free zone, civil society is too weak to confront the market, or as is sometimes the case, civil society co-opts or becomes an agent of the harms produced by the market.

All these elements can be discerned from the proposals for legal empowerment of the poor, whether it is through the emphasis on legal formalisation of property rights, markets, human rights or civil society. First, the emphasis of legal formalisation of property rights is consistent with discussions above about the transcendental and abstract nature of law and human rights. Law and rights can be both an abstract and concrete reality in the lives of the poor. This abstraction and concretisation is made possible by property rights. Second, the emphasis on the market, often characterised by the absence of any meaningful political controls, only leaves the poor vulnerable to exploitation. The third point is similar. Civil society is powerless in the face of forms of economic domination and exploitation without any meaningful political mechanisms of accountability. Cumulatively, legal empowerment of the poor neither anticipates nor responds to these problems. The assumption seems to be that answers can be found by creating and formalising opportunities to participate in the economy. What this achieves, on the contrary, is a further reinforcement of the economic sphere, thereby making it autonomous from political controls and political participation.

These historical arguments do not completely explain why human rights have not featured prominently in the informal sphere. It may simply be the importance of cultural, ethnic, religious experiences or other moral economies of groups in the informal sphere. Not only do these influence their version of informal political participation, they simply have nothing to do with human rights. Indeed, some of the activities in the informal sphere would be at odds with human rights. It is also important to add problems recently noted about the way in which human rights can selectively be deployed to make them compatible with free-market initiatives. For instance, civil political rights such as freedom of expression, association and anti-discrimination are deployed in ways that support market activity. Property and contractual rights also have this characteristic, as they are also pivotal to market participation. It is not surprising that property rights, in particular, take centre stage in proposals for legal empowerment of the poor. The wisdom of prioritising property rights so much that they should deserve more protection than healthcare, water or education rights can certainly be questioned. This is apart from the fact that the formalisation of property rights does not necessarily guarantee exclusive rights of the poor. Legal formalisation, as has been noted, also contributes to making the property of the poor vulnerable to capture (Nyamu-Musembi 2007). This is increasingly evident in the privatisation of traditional knowledges, plants or other life forms, the extension of human rights to corporate entities (Baxi 2008; Grear 2007) and, more recently, the phenomenon of land grabbing.

Having said that, the exclusions and vulnerability within the informal sphere make it impossible to totally write off international human rights law. It is also valid to argue that because human rights were exclusive in the past does not necessarily mean they would be exclusive in the future. It would be too naive to suggest this, just as it would also be too naive to suggest that providing a clear regime of human rights can resolve the forms of exclusions in the informal sphere. Given that construction of inclusion and exclusion takes place on a daily basis, informal political participation may provide an avenue to also concretise human rights norms. That way, human rights may cushion the effect of the vast range of collective activity on vulnerable minorities. As such, my argument is not against human rights per se; rather it has been against thinking that the human right to political participation offers a silver bullet. It has shown that there is a case to be made for the politics of the poor, which has been rendered invisible by dominant perceptions of political participation. Answers do not always imply formalising the informal sphere. Solutions may lie in recognising the informal sphere as it is, particularly the scope and opportunity that it can offer for social and political transformation.

11.5 Conclusion

In this chapter, I have attempted to make a case for a broader understanding of political participation that can be appreciated by discursively drawing lessons from the real and everyday struggles of the poor and the marginalised in the informal sector. What should be taken from the informal sector is how such activities yield to a type of politics that is not public or private, economic or political. Not only does informality provide a prism to grasp how to escape the dichotomy between these spheres, informality also provides a basis for the imagination and creation of diverse and new regimes of organisation and ownership. Informal political participation offers a means of comprehending how to conceive new democratic organisations devoted to management of a variety of public-owned goods and services. If there is one distinctive area of contribution that is made by informal political participation, it is to increasing the democratic content of economic activity through the array of rich, dispersed and innovative forms of organisation. As such, my argument has also been to show how informal political participation challenges us to think more carefully about what it means to participate politically.

Given the role that these activities play in securing livelihoods, there is an undeniable instrumental nature to this form of politics. It should be no surprise that the existent forms of collaboration are truly motivated by greed and self-interest. But this is only part of the picture. The desire to cheat is often compensated by the desire to be kind and compassionate. There is often an underlying intrinsic element to informal political participation. It is also characterised by strong outpourings of solidarity, care and compassion among participants. The presence of the family or religious groups throws more weight on its underlying caring element. This makes informal political participation intrinsically moral as much as many other things.

Indeed, whatever anxieties may exist over informal activities more generally, they can be dispelled by widening the scope or the very action of political participation. After all, it is through political participation, in Aristotelian terms, that we learn, nurture or develop as good moral beings.

Informal political participation gives the fullest expression to what feminists in another context called the 'personal is political'. It brings attention, with great distinction, to the political implications and consequences of everyday life. The activities and struggles in the informal sphere blur distinctions between public and private, political and economic. As exclusion and oppression has multiple dimensions, so are the struggles that are waged against them. Informal politics unites against the public and private, political and economic. It demonstrates that the unity of economic and political disadvantage or domination also requires commensurate forms of participation that can confront such forms of exclusion. It shows that political and economic disadvantage often have the same origins. The everyday struggles in the informal world can hardly be described as political or economic; rather they mutually reinforce one another. Thus, my argument has been that we can renew or reinvent, through readings of these struggles against exclusion, the idea of political participation in very inclusive ways. If legal empowerment of the poor is to be true to its word that this requires voice, then there is no better way to achieve this than by paying attention to the politics of those it seeks to assist. Voice not only implies ownership and participation but also authorship, which can be appreciated by close attention to the everyday struggles of inclusion by poor and marginalised communities in the informal world.

References

Aristotle (2009) Nicomachean ethics (trans: Ross D). Oxford University Press, Oxford

Arrighi G (2003) The African crisis: world systemic and regional aspects, New Left Rev 15(5):31–36

Barros B (ed) (2010) Hernando de Soto and property in market economy. Ashgate, Surrey

Baxi U (2008) The future of human rights. Oxford University Press, New Delhi

Bayat A (1997) Uncivil society: the politics of the informal people. Third World Q 18(1):55–58

Colebrook C (2002) The politics and potential of everyday life. New Lit Hist 33(4):689

Commission on the Legal Empowerment of the Poor (2008) Making the law work for the everyone: volume I, United Nations Development Programme

Douzinas C (2010) Adikia: on communism and human rights. In: Douzinas C, Zizek S (eds) The idea of communism. Verso Books, New York, pp 81–100

Faundez J (2009) Empowering workers in the informal economy. Hague J Rule Law 1(1):156–172

Franck T (1992) The emerging right to democratic governance. Am J Int Law 86(1):46–91

Gathii J (2000) Retelling good governance narratives on Africa's economic and political predicaments: continuities and discontinuities in legal outcomes between markets and states. Villanova Law Rev 45:971–1034

Grear A (2007) Challenging corporate humanity: legal disembodiment, embodiment and human rights. Hum Rights Law Rev 7(3):511–543

Hardt M, Negri A (2009) Commonwealth. Harvard University Press, Cambridge

Hardt M, Negri A (2011) The fight for 'real democracy' at the heart of occupy wall street', (2011), Foreign Affairs,. Accessed online at http://www.foreignaffairs.com/articles/136399/michael-hardt-and-antonio-negri/the-fight-for-real-democracy-at-the-heart-of-occupy-wall-street

Hetch D, Simone M (1994) Invisible governance: the art of African micropolitics. Autonomedia, New York

Hirschman A (1970) Exit, voice and loyalty: responses to decline in firms, organizations and states. Harvard University Press, Cambridge

Hirst P (1994) Associative democracy: new forms of economic and social governance. Polity Press, Great Britain

Lindell I (2010) Informality and collective organising: identities, alliances and transnational activism in Africa. Third World Q 25(1):207–222

Meiksins E (1995) Democracy and capitalism: renewing historical materialism. Cambridge University Press, Cambridge

Mohan G, Kristian S (2002) Participatory development and empowerment: the dangers of localism. Third World Q 21(2):247–268

Moore M (2001) Empowerment at last? J Int Dev 13:321–329

Nussbaum M (2011) Creating capabilities: the human development approach. Harvard University Press, Cambridge

Nyamu-Musembi C (2007) De Soto and land relations in rural Africa: breathing life into dead theories about property rights. Third World Q 28(8):1457–1478

Otto J (2009) Rule of law promotion, land tenure and poverty alleviation: questioning the assumptions of Hernando de Soto. Hague J Rule Law 1(1):173–194

Secker M (2009) Expanding the concept of participatory rights. Int J Hum Rights 13(5):657–715

Simone A (2001) Straddling the divides: remaking associational life in the informal African city. Int J Urban Reg Res 25(1):103

Simone A (2004) For the city yet to come: changing life in four African cities. Duke University Press, London/Durham

Simone A (2008) Emergency democracy and the "governing composite". Social Text 26(2):9516

Steiner H (1988) Political participation as a human right. Harv Hum Rights Yearb 1:77–134

Veitch S (2007) Law and irresponsibility: on the legitimation of human suffering. Routledge, London

Chapter 12
The Humanist Basis of African Communitarianism as Viable Third Alternative Theory of Developmentalism

Adebisi Arewa

12.1 Introduction

In this chapter, I argue that the tendency to define developmentalism in Africa in terms of unqualified capitalist or socialist models will not yield to the desiderata of sustainable growth, sustainable development and sustainable human development within the region. For one, the ideological representations and asymmetry embedded in the two opposing world views make them incapable of redressing the most critical issues of the human condition. The chapter argues that adaptation of failed capitalist and socialist models for African developmentalism is bound to fail because they are based on the fallacious premise of developmentalism, something which makes Western ideals of society and modernity the benchmark upon which the development of African nations is founded. Most importantly, I argue that, the adaptation of the two failed models is tantamount to an affliction of their inadequacies, which are visible in all African nations. This outcome is particularly unfortunate, more so because these models are applied without regard to cultural and social realities of Africa. As a response to these problems, the central argument throughout this chapter for a model of development based on African humanist egalitarian principles – the core value animating African socio-economic and political institutions, such as the law, property, capital and so forth. African humanist egalitarianism, so described, can

A. Arewa, BA, LL.B, BL, MBA, Ph.D. (✉)
Fellow Nigerian Institute of Advanced Legal Studies (NAILS), Lagos, Nigeria

Head Editorial & External Linkages Department,
Nigerian Institute of Advanced Legal Studies, Lagos, Nigeria

Executive Director, NIALS Justice E. Ayoola, CON, JSC (Rtd)
Centre for Transnational Legal Practice and Cross-Border Criminality, Lagos, Nigeria
e-mail: bisi_arewa@rocketmail.com

O. Onazi (ed.), *African Legal Theory and Contemporary Problems: Critical Essays*, Ius Gentium: Comparative Perspectives on Law and Justice 29,
DOI 10.1007/978-94-007-7537-4_12,

better guarantee social equity and distributive justice in ways which can never be attained through the refractive ideological prisms of capitalist and socialist development models.

My argument against the corruptions of capitalism and socialism cannot properly be understood outside the context of globalization. Globalization is a reformulation of global capitalism, which seeks to rationalize and justify market fundamentalism and Washington Consensus prescriptions, both of which have failed across the world, especially in the third world. Recent developments in the United States (US) and Europe, underscored by economic depression, huge debt burden, mass unemployment, huge budget deficits, capital market crash and unprecedented corporate governance failure have failed to be addressed through these prescriptions. Rather than cut government spending the affected Western governments are embarking on Keynesian reflationary measures to spend their way out of depression. A high magnitude of public funds has been deployed in the US and Europe to prop up ailing private corporations on the verge of insolvency. These measures clearly run against the grain of capitalist market fundamentalism.

The ongoing global economic and financial crisis has exposed the fundamental flaws of the Washington Consensus and market fundamentalism. The prescriptions have not been applied strictly especially when the subject of application is a core Western economy. This selective practice also exposes the fallacy implied in the gleeful assertion that there is no alternative to market fundamentalism; that is, the Western ideals of capitalism, which gained ascendancy after the collapse of the Soviet Union as well as the diminution of the influence of socialist ideology.

While I am not oblivious of the gains of western capitalism and the innovativeness of its productive processes, it is, however, doubtful whether it is proper for a nascent, developing, or simply any nation, as the US economic crisis clearly attests, to leave its economy to the capricious dictates of market forces or what Hernando de Soto has characterized as the invisible network of laws without reining on them. No nation can afford to embrace such market fundamentalism. Not even the bastion of democracy – that is, the US and the group of industrialized capitalist nations, with their chequered economic history – have left their economies to the vagaries and dictates of market forces. The US pursued what its statesmen and scholars characterize as splendid isolationism after World War I, a euphemism for trade protectionism.

China was a complete enclave at the beginning of the revolution led by Chairman Mao, and it practiced self-sufficiency while carefully growing its economy to a high level of global competitiveness. It was only after achieving this that it embarked on a tolerable level of liberalization. Japan has astutely shielded its industries since the end of World War II, to a high level of global competitiveness and its emergence as the second strongest economy after the US, has only recently been supplanted by China in terms of scale economy and sheer demography. South Korea carefully grew its nascent automobile and electronic industries immediately after the Korean War to a high level of global competitiveness. The path to economic success of several nations, including the nations previously mentioned, illustrate that none of them fully embraced market fundamentalism, which is at the core of globalization.

It is commonplace to state that alleviation and the ultimate eradication of poverty, hunger and starvation is the most critical challenge of governance in Africa and the world. As succinctly put by the 2005 report of the Commission for Africa, African poverty and stagnation are the greatest tragedies of our time. An appreciable understanding of the magnitude of this tragedy requires an examination of statistical analysis of pervading poverty in the group of poor developing nations. In 1970, there were 1.2 billion poor people in the developing world. Of this number, there were 104 million in sub-Saharan Africa, 830 million in East Asia, 208 million in South Asia, 36 million in Latin America, and 27 million in the Middle-East and North Africa. Between 1970 and 2000, there was a tremendous reduction on the number of poor people in the developing world. More specifically, the number fell from 1.2 billion in 1970 to 647 million in 2000. A considerable proportion of the reduction is accounted for by East Asia, where the number of poor people dropped from 830 million in 1970 to 114 million in 2000. Africa, particularly south of the Sahara remains the only sub-region which recorded considerable rise in the number of poor people in the same period.

Will the alternative development model stand *sui generis* in its distinctive characteristics? Will it be a synthesis of the two failed paradigms? Within the context of the ongoing global economic meltdown the chapter seeks to demonstrate the explanatory value of African humanist egalitarianism, which animates every socio-economic and political institution in Africa; that is, institutions of capital, property, and law among other institutions. After the proof of the explanatory value of African humanist egalitarianism, the chapter will demonstrate its potential value in redressing the most critical issues of the human condition, and furthermore, its value as the third alternative model of economic development, which will catalyze real sustainable growth, sustainable development and sustainable human development of Africa and indeed, the world as a whole.

The African region recorded a head-count ratio of 54.8 % in 2000; its proportion of domestic population that is poor remains the highest. There have been abundant efforts to unravel why Africa, especially sub-Saharan Africa has such a disproportionately high number of poor people and, more generally, to determine the causes of poor economic performance in the sub-region. Studies on Africa have found that the lack of high and sustainable economic growth in the sub-region is a critical factor responsible for its inability to make significant progress in the effort to eradicate poverty.

It has also been found that the nature of growth is crucial in terms of facilitating poverty alleviation. Other factors underscored as responsible for lack of growth and resultant poverty, include political instability, corruption and governance failure, macroeconomic volatility, poor investment climate, geographical disadvantage, the colonial legacy, the disproportionate global division of labour and unequal exchange.

A recent study by the Economic Commission for Africa reveals that, if current trends continue, sub-Saharan Africa is unlikely to meet the target of reducing by half the proportion of people whose income is less than $1 a day between 1990 and 2015. The 2006 Millennium Development Goals (MDGs) report also reached the same conclusion. The report shows that between 1990 and 2002, the number of people living in extreme poverty in sub-Saharan Africa increased by 140 million.

In the light of the above, the crucial question is how can poverty be stopped in its track in sub-Saharan Africa? What are the measures needed to meet the objectives in the Millennium Declaration? The potentials of domestic savings to finance required investments are not in doubt, coupled to the fact that savings are less volatile than external finances. This is because unlike the Official Development Assistance (ODA) domestic savings are not subject to 'conditionalities'. Domestic savings, nevertheless, cannot meet the financial resource needs of African nations. Domestic savings cannot be deployed to solve Africa's financing problems because Africa has one of the lowest levels of savings globally relative to its investment requirements.

Between 2000 and 2004, domestic savings as a proportion of gross domestic product (GDP) was 17 % in sub-Saharan Africa and 26 % in the Middle-East and North Africa. It was 35.6 % in East Asia and the Pacific, and finally; it was 21.2 % in Latin America and the Caribbean.

If the MDGs are to be fulfilled, the only way to catalyze sustainable growth in sub-Saharan Africa, it is argued, is to radically increase the level of domestic savings and channel them into productive investments, which must be sustained on a level higher than at the level of domestic savings.

Methodologically, I have elected to explore the entire phenomenon of development through modernization and dependency theory as heuristic devices to unravel and provide plausible explanations for the pervasive poverty that characterizes the group of very poor developing countries. This will provide a basis upon which to argue for a model of development capable of reversing poverty through innovative governance and enlightened economic choices.

12.2 The Theoretical Underpinnings of Developmentalism

Modernization theory evolved at the end of the Second World War, first as the intellectual justification for the promotion of western values and ideals of society in the post-war era, and second, to illumine the attractiveness of such Western notions of society over and above non-Western paradigms. Modernization theory was spearheaded by Talcott Parsons, who propounded a theory of structural-functionalism. Parsons postulated an evolutionary theory of society, which understood development as a process of deterministic and inexorable movements from one state of the evolutionary pedestal to another. He argued that development leads to structural differentiation of social institutions, which will create economic, political and social institutions akin to Western social institutions of capital, market economy, democratic liberalism, the rule of law and due process, freedom of the judiciary, separation of powers, freedom of the press and respect for the fundamental human rights of the citizenry (Huntington 1978, pp. 30–69).

Under the modernization schema, certain conditions must be fulfilled in order to attain the structural differentiation of social institutions pursuant to attaining economic development. The first major condition is rationalization, a concept based upon the works of Emile Durkheim, Max Weber and Talcott Parsons. Rationalization entails the progressive movement from the particular to the universal. In other words, from a society characterized by ascriptive roles to that which is comprised of individual attainment, something which can further be differentiated from the arbitrary ascription of status at birth. The second condition is the significance of the integration of diverse nationalities and nation-building. Democratization is the third condition that must be met pursuant to attaining social differentiation. Democracy according to the modernization theory, underscores social pluralism and transparency. Democracy also eradicates arbitrariness and discretion while fostering constructive engagement by introducing a spirit of sportsmanship to political culture. Finally, the political space must be expanded to be inclusive through mass mobilization of the citizenry to participate in the political process (Hermassi 1978, pp. 239–257).

The abysmal economic performance of post-independence third world developing countries, characterized by the rot and decay of their social, legal and political institutions, the affliction of rapacious and corrupt political elites, restive youths and predatory military, have all combined to engender skepticism about the relevance and efficacy of the modernization theory in the new era (Kadt 1974, p. 65).

In counter-eloquence, the modernization school attributes state failure in the third world to endogenous factors, such as the lack of civic culture necessary to evolve, grow and sustain Western-type political and social institutions. To the modernization theorist, the political culture in third world countries is inorganic; it is characterized by a combination of individual and group solidarity within the clan or ethnic nationality in contrast to solidarity to the national state. What facilitates the lack of organic solidarity is the lack of psychological acceptance of the legitimacy of the national government, democracy, the non-internalization of national laws, the role of the state, and also, the role of political actors vis-à-vis the obligations of the citizenry to the state (Latham 2000, p. 288).

Among many of the foibles of modernization theory elicited by critiques is that it is ethnocentric, deterministic and evolutionist. Its theoretical foundation of structural-functionalism has been subjected to critical appraisal, and characterized as a value-laden paradigm with acute ideological asymmetry (O'Neill 2007).

The pessimism with which the modernization theory was viewed must be considered against the backdrop of the social turmoil which rocked the American society in late 1960s and early 1970s. The cataclysm of this era in the evolution of American society resulted in the call in certain quarters for the curtailment of individual rights in order to impose a greater order. This crisis removed the wind from the modernization sail, and skepticism, was generally expressed in the form of the universality of the so-called core libertarian American values and ethos (Inglehart 2005, pp. 5–25, 26–180).

It was discovered that the modernization theory in itself cannot operate *ex propio vigore*. It cannot yield to any development premium, as its tenets can only impact positively in situations where there is purposive single-mindedness to develop among political elites and the people (Anderson 2005, p. 225).

The law and development movement emerged amidst the throes of the social crisis experienced in the American society between 1965 and 1975; hence it inherited the perceived inadequacies related to its foundations in modernization theory. However, the failing of the modernization theory, and by extension the law and development theory, was completely unconnected to the state of law in developing countries. In other words, the failure of both the modernization theory and law and development movement did not, in any way, negate the centrality of law in society (Brym 2005, p. 214). The law and development movement, however, drew heavily from the fundamental doctrine of the modernization theory, which was predicated on the assertion that law and its institutions will through an evolutionary process progressively attain a level of differentiation similar to Western law and legal institutions (Kiely 1995, pp. 85–143).

Many scholars may not fault the position asserting the centrality of law in development, nor would they fault the evolutionary underpinnings of both the theory of modernization and law and development respectively. What they question is the use of Western institutions as the benchmark for the evolutionary process. They will detect several ideological representations in both models, which establish Western ideals and social/legal institutions as the terminal point on the evolutionary scale. A study of social statics and dynamics involved shows that human society is in a state of flux as well as in constant motion. Human society is unamenable to statics. Thus, it is not improbable that a universalizable ideal misplaces that attribute by yielding to either a variant of itself, which has mutated into a higher form of itself or a completely different form, which supplants and displaces the extant form in the evolutionary process. The central tenet of modernization theory is, therefore, wrong-headed to the extent that it suggests that the evolutionary path to be trodden by the emergent modernizing states of the third world has to be exactly those trodden by Western societies. It shows no understanding of their social-cultural differences.

The foregoing submission is without prejudice to the reality of the gains of Western ideals and values, such as liberal democracy, the rule of law, due process and the respect for individual rights. My point of departure is to disagree with the position that the evolutionary pedestal attained by Western societies is the terminal point on the evolutionary scale in ways Western achievements mark the end of history (Gilman 2004, pp. 1–24, 72–241; Fukuyama 2006, pp. 3–39, 55–131, 143–199, 211–328).

Such wide conclusions can only be made upon the basis of the worst state of intellectual depravity. It is not only pedestrian, but also ahistorical and completely at variance with the dynamics of the dialectic upon which any evolutionary process is predicated. Above every other consideration, it is impossible as it is improbable to contrive and engineer such an end of history, as history moves inexorably in a circle from ages to ages and from epoch to epoch. It is synonymous with the order of the cosmos, which is immutable, constant and not without theoretical foundation. Circularity is not a fallacy in the hermeneutical sciences. The hermeneutic circle breaks the crust of formalism (or pseudo-formalism) which provides the apparent justification for the structural-functionalist conclusion.[1]

[1]According to Fukuyama, history is directional and its end point is capitalist liberal democracy. This view, of course, is not novel. What engages the attention however is the simplicity of

While disagreeing with the central premise of modernization theory and the law and development movement, I submit that the reality in developing countries has, on the contrary, pointed at the lack of political plurality, acute social stratification, wide gaps existing between the classes, the prevalence of absolutist and personalized governments, weak state structures and the total alienation from the people from the national government. Furthermore, citizens have generally shown greater allegiance to their primordial groupings, mainly as a result of the lack of psychological acceptance of the law. In many ways, laws have often been contrived to do the bidding of the dominant political and economic elites. In addition to this, the judiciary is often derelict (Huntington 1996, pp. 8, 32, 59, 109, 344).

While it is commonplace to state that the foregoing limitations are excessive and may limit or constrain the instrumental application of law for social-economic change in developing societies. Those limitations and constraints paradoxically compels (rather than diminishes the centrality of law and its institutions in the development process) the use of law as an instrument capable of catalyzing economic growth and development within this group of countries (Hsiung 2006, pp. 1–3).

The perceived gaps between the structural-functionalist paradigm, the modernization theory and the central tenet of the law and development model, and the reality in the modernizing and developing third world nations, do not in any way diminish the relevance, functionality and applicability of these models to catalyze social/economic change in the third world. Social/economic change only requires the reforming state to accommodate those gaps, and also, to adapt the models to the circumstances of the social and political milieu of the third world.[2]

It is also important to dispel the self-indulgent pessimism of those who have only seen the evil perpetrated in the name of the law. These pessimists fail to see any good that has been wrought through the instrumentality of the law. Not even the limitless potentials of law in advancing economic goals with a view to moving the

---

Fukuyama's reformulation of this view point. It is an apologia by Fukuyama, a former U.S. State Department planner. He identifies two prime factors that supposedly push all societies toward this evolutionary goal.

The first is modern natural science complemented by technology, which creates universal cultures. The second vehicle of history which he derived from Hegel is the desire for recognition, driving innovation and personal achievement. Fukuyama's main concern seems to be whether in the coming of what he considers a capitalist utopia, humans will not become complacently self-absorbed 'last men' or, alternatively, revert to 'first men' embroiled in destructive wars. His argument that western democracies are not hegemonic is a historical in the light of world history and, particularly, the behaviour of the United States and its allies. He first articulated his thesis in the Foreign Policy Journal, National Interest, summer 1989, where he posited that most recent world history is punctuated by the collapse of absolutist regimes, and concomitantly, there is unprecedented ascendancy of liberal forces in these nations.

[2]To create a legal framework for economic development, particularly when considering legal and judicial reforms developing countries should as a matter of priority create substantive and procedurally efficient rules for the husbandry of the economy. A rule could be regarded as substantively efficient if it sets forth a precept that internalizes an externality or compels the efficient allocation of resources. Concomitantly, a rule is procedurally efficient if it eliminates or reduces the cost of or increases the accuracy of using the legal system.

society forward and increasing the well-being of the citizenry are recognized by the pessimists (Davis 2008, pp. 8–14). Having examined the posturing of the modernization theory and its offshoot, the law and development model, I now turn the attention to its antithesis – the dependency theory.

12.3 Dependency Theory

The dependency theory, in contradistinction to the modernization theory holds, among other things, that state failure, underdevelopment and lack of growth in third world countries, is contrary to the position of modernization theorists. Underdevelopment, among other things, is not wholly internal but the result of the political economy of international Western capitalism, which in its evolution had by astute adaptiveness exploited non-Western peoples in Africa, Asia and Latin America by the process of colonization (Ndulu 2008, pp. 5–650).

Through the process above, these regions were forcefully incorporated within the structure of Western international capitalism. Their natural resources and human capital exploited unremittingly for many centuries at first through pillage and slave trade and later through outright colonization (Hubbell 2008, p. 112).

Consequent upon the consolidation of colonialism, an international division of labour was contrived, which structured the economies of the colonies in a manner that would complement the economy of the metropolis. The colonies provided raw materials, which are fed to manufacturing industrial complexes of the metropolis whilst concomitantly turning the colonies into captive markets for the products of such industries. For these purposes, chartered trading companies were commissioned and deployed to such colonies with exclusive rights to engage in the production, trade and evacuation of such raw materials. The plantation economy thrived and white settler enclaves were created (Peet 1999, pp. 3–12, 18–57, 107).

The exploitation remained unabated in the post-independence epoch. New structures that were adaptive to the seeming emergence of a new world order were ingenuously contrived to sustain the stranglehold on the international economic order. Domination was sustained by the agency of transnational corporations, which have operations cutting across international boundaries. These octopi corporations are run as sovereign states and are avid exploiters as well as destabilizers of their host countries (Rahnevia 1997, pp. 3–250).

The unique historical experience of developing countries has is that dependencies have bled these societies of their vitality and zest to develop. They were forcefully conscripted into the international capitalist system with a legion of disabilities. The pillage of their economies during colonialism stunted industrialization, as their economies were deliberately structured to complement that of the metropolis by serving as mere sources of raw materials that were evacuated without added value. Allied to that, and as a consequence of the colonial agenda, the infrastructure they inherited was derelict and run down. The foregoing only results in a vicious circle as these nations slip further and further down the mire of dependence. They require foreign aid, foreign direct investment and loans from both private and public international financial institutions of the West to develop their infrastructure. They remain gross exporters of primary products mainly derived from their extractive sectors, which have no nexus with the other sectors of their economies resulting in lack of diversification and making them prone to price shocks and fluctuation in the commodity exchanges controlled by the West (Desai 2008, p. 150).

According to the dependency school, there is an unbridgeable divide between the Western core and the developing periphery yielding to a structure, which sustains the perpetual exploitation of the periphery by the core (Larrain 1991, pp. 5–215). A key element of the dependency postulate is the identification of the collaboration between economic and political elites in developing nations and Western capitalists, pursuant to the sustenance of the *status quo*. According to dependency theorists, the most vulnerable groups that suffer the tyranny of this unequal world order are the rural poor and the urban poor that are completely untouched by whatever little impact is generated under this economic order (Hettn 1985, pp. 5–150).

The foregoing postulations of dependency theory are not without merit. First, they provide a fresh draught of air against the suffocating impact upon the modernization theory, which many justifiably regard as Eurocentric. Second, they catalyzed the spirit of economic nationalism in a number of developing nations that contrived policies to shield their fledging industries from foreign competition (Ghosh 2001, pp. 3–165).

That said, dependency theory has received its fair share of negative reviews and it has invited critique. To many, its Marxist foundation diminishes the explanatory powers of dependency theory. This became evident after the collapse of the Soviet Union – the subsequent loss of ascendancy by communism and Marxism – coupled with the economic successes recorded by the Asian countries. The phenomenal growth and development of Asian countries like Japan, India, Singapore, South Korea and China, among other countries, has all combined to diminish the influence of dependency theory. The successes of the Asian economies have been achieved without wholesale and unqualified application of modernization model. Similarly, their successes have not been predicated on the dependency model (Tetreault 1986, pp. 5–210). The emergence of China as the world's fastest-growing economy is a testimony to this fact. China's mixed reform agenda of selection but eclecticism has had a profound impact on its economic growth (Leys 1996, pp. 3, 48, 64, 80, 107–188).

Having said that, another criticism that the dependency theory has invited can be attributed to the skeptical and pessimist Marxist perspective of law. That is, the understanding of law as the superstructure of the economic base. To Marxists, law is value-laden, and replete with asymmetry. Law is an ideological representation which is contrived by dominant groups to further their cause. Thus, given the Marxist origins of dependency theory, it is rather hesitant and cautious of annexing law to serve the purpose of development (Brewer 1997, pp. 161, 201–260).

The foregoing is without prejudice to the crucial role played by dependency theory in the evolution of the domain of international law of development. It must be acknowledged that it contributed in bringing the right to development of peoples to the front burner. Though still inchoate and evolving, the concerted and articulate efforts in this regard have generated positive results in terms of trade concessions. Dependency theory has also provided an initiative for the group of highly developed and industrialized nations to partner the group of very poor nations for purposes of economic growth and development. The view is, however, rife in certain quarters that all these incoherent agendas to save the third world are half-hearted and ill-conceived measures that are too little too late. This body of opinion underscores the fact that much more far-reaching measures, the types that surpass the reconstruction agenda contrived to rebuild Europe from the ruins of the World War II, are required to salvage the third world from the mire of poverty (Chilcote 1983, pp. 5–180; Jaffee 1998, pp. 5, 151–199; Willis 2007, pp. 32, 62).

12.4 The Communitarian Basis of African Humanism

In my attempt to elucidate on a distinctively African humanist philosophical basis of all African Institutions, I shall explore the nature of the metaphysical notion of sociability, which is a function of the dependent biological nature of new members of the human species on significant others and matured members of the species for growth, development, security and well-being. Thus, no matter how further we trace the evolution of the human species, man can only be individuated in a society of other humans. He can only attain the total development of the traits that make him human and attain personhood only by being dependent on other significant persons. The individuation of man within community is achieved through the process of socialization (which refers to the entire motion of birth and the forging), something which molds the individual into a functional member of community.

Socialization is, thus, the process of teaching through education and learning. This is achieved through the imitation of significant others, and also, through the development of capacity, vocational skills among other things in a way that enhances the competence of individuals' as functional and non-deviant members of community. Man's capability to develop his capacity to function as a competent unit of development within the community is dependent upon this socialization process.

Unfortunately, since the advent of colonialism this process of socialization has been narrowly construed in terms of Western education; that is, in terms of reading and writing as well as the ability to speak the language of the conquerors. Yet, a Yoruba drummer boy who has been inducted into the vocation of drumming from the age two is no less an educated person than a Harvard trained percussionist. By the time he is 5 years old he would have become quite dexterous in the art of drumming. Through the progressive process of socialization, he is taught the skills of his family trade, which has been passed down from one generation to the other. Aside from the practical skills of drumming, he is taught the mores or lore's of the lineage. In a similar vein, the solitary Fulani herds' boy using a staff to herd hundreds of life stock through wide ranges of pastures is no less educated than the Oxford trained veterinary doctor; he has acquired competencies, which have sustained his people through the ages.

One of the greatest fallacies of developmentalism in Africa is the equation of education to western education. I am by no means understating the methodological value of Western education; rather the point I am trying to make is that it is only one of so many methods of socialization. The widespread acceptance, of socialization through western education, must not be at the expense of the traditional process of socialization, which encapsulates the totality of the world view of the people. The total and un-calibrated embrace of the Western paradigm of socialization will only yield to one outcome; a nation of confused people totally alienated from their primordial and time-tested productive cultural practices of economic sustenance, thrown into the uncertain world of Western global cash economy.

The army of unemployed, underemployed, unemployable youths and adults in African urban centres is a living testimony of this unwholesome outcome highlighted above. This gives a serious cause for concern because of the unremitting rural–urban drift which characterizes the demography of African Nations. In Lagos where I live and work, I am assaulted every day by the spectacles of youths hawking all sorts of inferior products dumped in Nigeria *a la globalization*. This is unacceptable; we certainly do not want to create a nation of street hawkers. This phenomenon is replicated everywhere in Africa. Entire generations are completely removed from their primordial cultural productive base and made to drift in cities totally disenfranchised economically.

African humanist sociability unlike parallel world views in other cultures does not merely underscore sociability as being critical to growth and development of human competencies, its distinctive characteristic is that it is at the core of every African social and political institutions, which are as a rule configured and structured to promote communal interests over and above the promotion of individual interests. The divergence in the concepts of the individual or personhood – adhered to in different cultures and societies – about how the individual stands in relation to others in the social space animate their socio-economic and political institutions, ethos and cosmogony.

Certain cultures are communitarian in orientation and structure, and they tend to emphasize group interest in the promotion of individual interests. The divergence in the concepts of the individual or personhood adhered to in different cultures and societies and about how the individual stands in relation to others in the social space animate their socio-economic and political institutions, ethos and cosmogony. Certain cultures are communitarian in orientation and structure. These communitarian cultures tend to emphasize individuation in terms of overlapping and multi-layered chains of kinship relations, including living-dead relationships, and relationships between the living and the unborn. Individuals are thus linked in this sort of long chain with a sacred duty to contribute to each lived life-time in a way that leads to the continuity of those lineages.

In contradistinction to the above, other cultures emphasize individual rights and liberties as well as conceive the individual more in the light of anonymity, impersonality, individual attributes and competencies. In the former, the individual is an integral constituent of a macro-community who has rights that individualist societies claim they accord everyone. The only difference between the two models is that the individual in communitarian social structure is not anonymous entity, but rather is a stakeholder in society's pursuit of the desiderata of the enhancement of the general well-being of all.

The African worldview does not in any way subsume the personhood of the individual in a deterministic manner under the will of the collective. Rather the African worldview underscores the reciprocity in the mutual dependency of the individual and community for purposes of sustenance and the continuity of all. The rights, liberty, and individuality of the person are thereby not qualified, derogated and or understated by the condition of dependency. Because the two are mutually dependent, it is impracticable to conceive them as mutually exclusive in the social space. The type of 'I' complex which exclusive individualism breeds develops in a society where people fail to see the loftier ideals of the common good. These are ideals are also meant to stricture, circumscribe individual aspirations, including claims on the common patrimony, and also, egoism.

The relation between the individual and community in the communitarian society is not conflictual and at cross purposes. Analogous to human rights, common goods are universalizable ideals of society, which appertain to all and which are *sine qua non* for the attainment of a state of general well-being in which all regardless of their station in life are living a life. Furthermore, these common goods do not devalue or desecrate their shared humanity. Human rights must be situated without their textual locale and made to inhere in the individual as compelled by the African humanist world view. And this is a world which guarantees a full range of rights. These rights, in turn, include full employment and rights to land as a factor of production without which a person is no person in Africa. Every individual is entitled to claim these rights from his community, which is, in turn, under an obligation to guarantee them, not by mere declaration or textually providing for them, but through a lived experience distinct from the mundane plane of practical existence. Instead, it is a sacred bond which holds the strands connecting the individual to his past, present and future. For instance, it is an anathema and indeed, an impossibility to have idle adults in a traditional African social milieu.

In 2003, Hernando de Soto (2000) offered what was then considered in Western circles as a plausible explanation of why, after the fall of the Berlin Wall and the collapse of communism, an unequivocal flowering of capitalism had not been ushered in the developing and post-communist world. The failure of capitalism in these countries was blamed by Western scholars on several factors such as the lack of sellable assets and the non-entrepreneurial culture of their peoples.

Hernando de Soto argued that the real problem for these countries is that they were yet to establish and normalize invisible networks of laws that would turn assets from 'dead' into 'liquid' capital. According to him, standardized laws in the West allow people to mortgage a house to raise money for new ventures. Standardized laws also permit the value of a company to be broken up into so many public tradable stocks, something, which further makes it possible to govern and appraise property, especially with rules agreed-upon that have general application. This invisible infrastructure of 'asset management' which according to him is taken for granted in the West is the missing ingredient for success with capitalism in global north (de Soto 2000).

As convincing as de Soto's argument seems, however, his analysis is rather subterranean and with the benefit of hindsight, his conclusions are at variance with concrete evidence of the inevitable collapse of the capitalist paradigm of production. As a matter of fact, capitalism failed not only 'elsewhere' but most importantly in the West because capitalisms' underlying philosophy of exclusion and profit have failed to address the most critical issue of the human condition – that is, pervasive poverty and the widening gap between the top 5 % of the affluent segment of the population and the poorest among the poor.

Hernando de Soto's invisible networks of laws are mere ideological re-presentations, which only serve, as evidence in the US and the whole of the West have shown, to disenfranchise, exclude and constitute a break on the well-being of the greater proportion of the population. The networks of laws have failed to create employment and redistribute income, but most importantly; the laws have failed to direct the efficient allocation of scarce resources to productive activity that would generate wealth, which can be deployed to serve the common good of all.

Furthermore, capitalism is failing everywhere because its underlying capital asset pricing model is based on fictional assumptions. It holds, for example, that all actors in the capital asset market must have access to the same set of information. In addition to this, transactions must be conducted with transparency without opacity and information asymmetry; that every traded stock has an intrinsic value, from which the market value takes a random walk. Consequently, the market value of capital assets is not a real re-presentation of their intrinsic values and thereby an inaccurate measure of the market worth of quoted firms. In fact, it is impossible to know what this intrinsic value is since the whole system is fraudulent. This is why capitalism will eternally be plagued by market failures. Besides the success of Asian developmental states, such as China, Thailand, Indonesia, and Malaysia, have demonstrated that capitalism can no longer be the unqualified benchmark for developmentalism.

12.5 African Customary Land Law and Theory of Property Rights

I am obliged to dwell considerably on the nature of African customary land law and property rights, first, because in the context of African developmentalism opening up rural Africa is the key to putting the people back to work again, especially after so many years of great dislocation occasioned by a long spell of colonial rule, and now, with globalization. Second, land is the prerequisite to Africa's sustainable economic growth and sustainable development. This is because over 80 % of Africans live in rural areas where they depend on land for their sustenance. Land is also important because these Africans are completely untouched by the version of 'modernity' attained by the post-colonial African state.

I shall endeavour to demonstrate how African humanism is embedded in the African conception of land law and the institution of property. I shall underscore the explanatory value of the African theory of property and show why it is a viable alternative to both capitalism and socialism, which have failed to address the fundamental issue of the human condition – the eradication of poverty and the enhancement of the well-being of human-kind in a sustainable manner.

Africa can achieve full-employment and thereby insulate itself from the adverse effect of the global economic crisis by recourse to its humanist and egalitarian world view, which is the bedrock upon which every social, economic and political institution should be erected in Africa.

Land use and ownership patterns in Africa entail a complex of overlapping claims. The patterns of ownership differ from privately held land by families and lineages to communally held land, all of which are used to guarantee the prosperity, health, general well-being, spiritual and religious practices, livelihood, and full employment of every functional member of community. Still, other huge tracks of land are left unexploited, preserved for future generations. Shifting cultivation is widely practiced in Africa, because of variegated factors such as fluctuation in rainfall, crop rotation and soil fertility, and changes to the requirement for land. Whilst land rights are primarily a function of membership in a group or allegiance to certain political authority, outsiders can acquire property rights through share cropping, customary tenancy, gift and recently, sale. According to Wily:

> Customary domains are territories over which the community possesses jurisdiction and often root title. Within the domain, a range of tenure arrangements typically apply. These include estates owned by individuals or families, and estates owned by special-interest groups within the community such as ritual societies or women's group. This is not to be confused with properties, which are owned by all members of that community in undivided shares, often the larger or remoter pastures, forests, woodlands, swampland and hill tops… these are common properties, defined by virtue of membership to groups, and a group whose composition may change over time. (Wily 2005, p. 6)

African land and resource rights are determined and encrusted within several relationships and units, such as households and networks of kinship. Land and resource rights are also encrusted in overlapping multiple social relationships, such as individual rights within households, households within intricate networks of kinship and networks of kinship within macro communities (Cousins 2007, pp. 281–315).

Property rights emanate from membership of a social unit and can be acquired by 'birth, affiliation or allegiance to a group and its political authority. They also emanate from transactions, such as pledges, purchases, gifts, and customary tenancy (2007). Contrary to the position that individual property rights do not exist at customary law, land and appurtenant resources encompass family and individual rights to arable and residential land. They also entail equal access to collectively owned property resources like forests, waters and grazing land. In other words, land rights are both individual and communal in Africa (2007).

Reflecting on African traditional property law jurisprudence, Ouedraogo posits:

> If the law is seen as no more than a set of norms established by the competent legal authorities, local land tenure practices will be accorded no legal validity and excluded from the judicial

> arena. But if, on the other hand, one sees law from an anthropological perspective as a social phenomenon for regulating individual and collective behaviour, one is obliged to acknowledge that the realm of justice does not necessarily begin with codified law. African societies have shown that they understand this by imposing models of behaviour on their members not on the basis of pre-established rules, but through a complex of social and cultural mechanisms. (2002)

African property rights must therefore be viewed within the context of the humanist and egalitarian world view of Africans, which is embedded in every socio-political institution. It is a worldview which accords proportional socio-economic space to the individual as a link in a long chain of intricate relationships encompassing the living dead, the living and unborn generations. Thus the individual stands in relation to others in the chain of a non-exclusive social structure, which impels equitable allocation of land as a factor of production as well as its appurtenant resources. According to Adam et al.:

> The free transfer of unimproved land could be taken for granted. It was received free and was given free. It was not viewed as a commercial asset. (Adam et al. 2003, pp. 55–74)

Whilst such transfers are done within networks of kinship and family relations, outsiders could also have access to land through gifts, purchase, and customary tenancy and so on.

12.6 Ujamma as a Development Strategy

I am obliged to dwell on previous developmental experiments, which were based on African humanist ethos and egalitarianism. Nyerere's philosophy of Ujamaa is examined as a quintessential African humanist socio-economic developmental experiment in Africa. Over the years, Ujamaa has been subjected to both favourable and adverse critiques. A certain body of opinion suggests that it was fundamentally a legitimate effort to circumvent the post-colonial corruptions of political anarchy, inequity and lack of innovation of the political elite in Africa (Pratt 1976; Boesen et al. 1979). Others, on the other hand, were damning and rather critical of the ideological tincture of Ujamaa as a socialist economic paradigm. According to this view, Ujamaa was at best a misplaced philosophical ideal, which failed to capitalize on several developmental opportunities. In the end, it represented a breach of the compact with the Tanzanian people (Johnson 2000; Scott 1999).

To ideologues, Ujamaa was pseudo-socialism completely bereft of the class struggle which is an antecedent condition for the evolution of a truly socialist state (Shivji 1974). Others saw Ujamaa as a device which the state deployed under Nyerere to circumscribe civil liberty, stifle private innovativeness and enterprise. Ujamaa thereby denied Tanzanians of the gains of individual enterprise, which they considered to be critical to the effort to attain modernity, democracy and economic prosperity (Yeager 1989). Most of these critiques are no doubt *ad hominem* and evaluations through ideological prisms, which lack an empirical basis.

Contrary to the foregoing adverse critiques, I argue that Ujamaa transcends ideology. Ujamaa is a thorough-going conceptualization and articulation of development strategy based on African humanism, which as I earlier argued, is not an ideology in the same sense of Western capitalism and socialism. Capitalism and socialism are different. They are mere ideological representations of existential reality, something which explains why they have abysmally failed in addressing the most critical, fundamental and universal of the issues that affect the human condition, particularly poverty.

Having said that, the major inadequacy of Ujamaa (which incidentally is the pitfall of post-colonial African developmentalism) is that it set Western ideals of development and modernity as the bench-mark of African developmentalism, apart from failing to yield to the desired outcome of sustainable growth, full employment and development for the vast majority of peasants who reside in rural Africa. It alienated them from their time-tested primordial cultural, social and productive reality, which has worked for them in a sustainable manner over the ages. Ujamaa suffered some bouts of the transplant effect, a malady which afflicts efforts at modernity, which is predicated either wholly or partly on the Western paradigm of developmentalism.

12.6.1 Ujamaa: Archetype of African Social Philosophy?

In this segment, I shall seek to provide answers to these related questions. First, is Ujamaa an approximate to African social philosophy? Second, does Ujamaa have any explanatory value as a philosophy? Third, can Ujamaa be deployed for African developmentalism in the light of the spate of adverse critiques, which it has generated since 1999, after the demise of the late Julius Nyerere? (Lane 1999, p. 16)[3] In order to provide answers these questions, I will dwell considerably on the nature of Ujamaa.

The philosophy of Ujamaa, which Nyerere articulated has its origin in traditional African ethos and values, which is underscored by its deep humanistic desideratum of an egalitarian society characterized by social equity and justice. Ujamaa entails a community of humans driven by an acute consciousness of the shared humanity of all its constituents. As contrived by Nyerere, Ujamaa underscores familyhood and communalism of traditional African societies, with a tincture of socialism and Judeo-Christian ideals and world view. Nyerere attempted to fuse Rousseau's contractarian social philosophy and Kantian notions of the ideal liberal society with African communitarian equalitarianism to attain a synthesis of the various strains of philosophy, which could be put to service as a means of unraveling Africa's crisis of developmentalism. Thus, Ujamaa was founded on the three pillars of equality, unity and liberty. As far as Nyerere was concerned, the ideal society must be based on

[3] Lane (1999, p. 16) wrote 'former Tanzanian dictator, Julius Nyerere, was single-handedly responsible for the economic destruction of his potentially wealthy nation'.

these three critical props (Nyerere 1967, p. 16). He argued succinctly that African development must be based on those three features because it is only then that men can work cooperatively. Secondly, there must be freedom, because the individual is not served by society, unless he belongs to that society. Finally, there must be unity, because the individual can only thrive in an environment of peace, security and high well-being. According to him, these three elements of Ujamaa are not alien to Africa. Thus, Ujamaa encompasses the African concept of communalism, which permeates every aspect of African culture, including the communal ownership of the property (land), the pooling of labour and the respect of shared humanity.

The critical question, then, is how to put this concept of African communitarian egalitarianism to service in order to unravel post-colonial Africa's crisis of developmentalism. Nyerere posited that Western capitalism was at variance with the aspirations of post-colonial African states and the third world. Nyerere asserted that the most appropriate path of developmentalism for Africa was socialism. This fallacy, in hind sight, can be forgiven in the light of the bi-polarity of the cold-war era which made the allure of pitching at either end of the ideological divide rather strong for emergent post-colonial states (Nyerere 1961). The distinguishing feature of Ujamaa was the understatement of Marxist notion of class struggle as the foundation of his concept of 'African socialism'. According to him, the basis of African socialism is not the class struggle, but the traditional African institution of the extended family system and communalism.

To him, African socialism is an attitude of the mind, which Africans imbibe through the process of socialization in the extended family. He stressed that African traditional humanist ideals were negatively impacted upon by the African colonial experience, Western education and capitalism. The vortex of economic, social and political power was violently removed from the African socio-political milieu and relocated to the colonial metropolis. The most critical issue in the view of Nyerere, therefore, was how to preserve African humanist attitudes and traditions within the macro-society. He was concerned with the attitudes and traditions, which provided the social security, full employment to all constituents of the community in pre-colonial Africa. And these kinds of social safety nets could only be derived from membership of an extended family (Nyerere 1967, p. 165).

Nyerere drew a sharp, even though to the ideological right, but unconvincing distinction between Ujamaa and Marxist, Fabian, Maoist, Leninist socialism. He also denied an ascription of any general Western influences to his strain of socialism. He argued that Ujamaa was totally intolerant of Western capitalism. Capitalism, according to him, sought to build a happy society on the basis of the exploitation of man by man. Ujamaa, according to him, was not synonymous with Marxist ideology, the ideal society of which can be understood as a function of the inevitable conflict between man and man (Nyerere 1968). He claimed that Ujamaa was a third alternative derived synthetically from the rich and deep African traditional ethos of communalism, something which selectively borrowed from the African colonial experience (Nyerere 1967). With the benefit of hindsight, the implementation of Ujamaa betrayed a Maoist and Fabian socialist leaning. However, what cannot be denied it is Ujamaa's distinct purposiveness to redress the overwhelming dependency of Tanzania by transiting to economic self-reliance. In this regard, Ujamaa seemed to have been influenced by the dependency school of thought, which held sway in the 1960s and 1970s and had many adherents in Latin America and Africa.

Ujamaa was inaugurated in 1967 in the Arusha Declaration. Its set goal was the attainment of self-reliant socialist nation. It was fashionable in the immediate post-independence epoch for African states to pursue self-reliance as a development strategy as dependency and underdevelopment were seen as mutually reinforcing phenomena, which excluded post-independence African nations from the international economic system. Self-reliance was considered as a panacea which would remove African states from their position of peripheral dependencies by transforming them into active players and competitors in the international economic system. To achieve that goal, it was advised that African states must look inwards by fully controlling the factors of economic development through self-conceived policies and policy implementation devoid of external prescriptions. Consequently, it was imperative to mobilize the people from the grassroots and optimize the allocation of limited available resources pursuant to enhancing the well-being of the people (Palmer 1975, pp. 5–6). Nyerere's economic strategy of self-reliance was, however, by no means akin to Mao's isolationism. He made the following distinctions:

> The doctrine of self reliance does not mean isolationism. For us, self-reliance is a positive affirmation that for our own development, we shall depend upon our own resources. (Nyerere 1968, p. 319)

That said, the embrace of self-reliance by Nyerere must also be seen in the light of Tanzania's overwhelming dependence on foreign aid for the implementation of its development plan. Self-reliance became the only plausible way out of the trap of dependency on aid, which often comes with conditionalities that compromise the sovereignty of the recipient state. Therefore, beyond the idealism of Ujamaa, its inauguration in 1967 was the most appropriate response to debilitating economic problems, which characterized the Tanzanian nation at the time.

Ujamaa was therefore conceived to wean Tanzania away from overwhelming reliance on foreign aid and loans whilst concomitantly transiting from peripheral dependency to an agrarian self-reliant economy.

12.6.2 Implementation of Ujamaa

Within the milieu of the economic nationalism of the immediate post-independence Africa, nationalization of the forces of production was considered central to the implementation of Ujamaa. The goal as in most African nations was for citizens to take control of the commanding heights of the economy. Consequent upon the pronouncement of the Arusha declaration, the Nyerere administration expropriated all banks and industrial conglomerates, including large-scale agricultural processing industries. Sixty percent of the dominant sisal industry was taken by the state (Arkaide 1973, p. 37). The state assumed direct control of the 'commanding heights' of the economy by the end of 1967. The spate of nationalization was hailed by the ideological left, and the avowal of self-reliance enamored a host of Scandinavian countries (Coulson 1985, p. 2).

The ideological right was, however, critical of the turn of events in Tanzania, with British banking giants, Standard, National, Gridley's and Barclays generally set on a policy of non-cooperation and sabotage aimed at ensuring that public control of banking failed through the systematic erosion of the confidence of the international investment community in the Tanzanian banking sector and export economy. This stance was ostensibly to stem the tide of nationalizations in Africa (1985, p. 41).

Without prejudice to the nationalization exercise, the state went into all sorts of technical partnerships with transnational corporations who were former owners of nationalized companies. The view, in certain quarters, due to the state's actions was that the 'commanding heights' of the Tanzanian economy was de facto still controlled by foreigners (Shivji 1973). That said, nationalization, however, suffered the inadequacy of creating opportunities for increased corruption, over-bureaucratization, centralization and inefficiency in resource allocation (Bolton 1985 p. 154). Consequently, it dawned rudely on the administration that nationalization was not the panacea after all.

12.6.3 Villagization

The villagization scheme (Ujamaa Vijijini) under Ujamaa was designed to encourage self-reliance, such that would emphasize rural development as a catalyst for sustainable growth and development. It was also designed to assist in the progressive weaning of the Tanzanian economy from overwhelming reliance on foreign aid and loans. The aim of the scheme was to catalyze the metamorphosis of rural Tanzania to create rural economic and social communities where people would live together for the good of all (Nyerere 1968, p. 337). It encouraged the clustering of peasant farmers around common service points rather than dispersed settlements. Peasants were encouraged to work on farm lands formed through cooperative societies rather than on an individual basis. The villagization scheme was rationalized and predicated on traditional African practices of communal living and social equity.

The villagization scheme failed because local peasants were suspicious about the motives behind the state; they were particularly apprehensive of the spectre of nationalization of their lands, hence they refused to cooperate. The scheme was informally abandoned by 1975. The scheme also failed because of other reasons. Firstly, the scheme was top down, and commenced without sufficient ownership or involvement of peasants. The scheme was viewed with skepticism, mistrust, resentment and hostility. Secondly, the state in desperation had recourse to the use of force and coercion to achieve mass villagization. This move further alienated the people. Thirdly, the use of material incentives was counter-productive as villages became overwhelmingly dependent on them and became extremely vulnerable when the paucity of resources led to the withdrawal of such assistance by the state.

On the whole, the scheme failed because it understated the individualism of the African in adapting a similar type of forced collectivization scheme that was conducted in the Soviet Union and Maoist China in the 1930s. On the whole, the way the scheme was implemented was at variance with the social and cultural realities of the rural economy. The planned villages, negated existing rural practice, which included shifting cultivation and pastoralism; poly cropping and dispersed settlement pattern, hence the scheme was resisted by the farmers. The foregoing limitations, however, do not diminish the explanatory value of Ujamaa as a thorough-going paradigm of developmentalism.

It would be a great disservice to the lofty ideals which informed the conceptualization of Ujamaa as a development strategy to evaluate it strictly based on economic indices such as Gross Domestic Product (GDP). Ujamaa must be assessed in the light of human development. And the truth is that Tanzania fared better than most African Nations south of the Sahara in terms of human development during the Ujamaa era. Tanzania enjoyed relative political stability, in a highly anarchic African sub-region during the Nyerere years. In fact, Nyerere's legacy of equity and social justice has made Tanzania to remain one of the most stable nations in Africa. There is a high pervading sense of national identity among Tanzanians because of the considerable advances made in terms of social welfare. Tanzania was insulated from the dangerous ethnic and regionalist politics which have recently rocked the very foundations of Kenya. Generally, Tanzania has also been insulated from the type of bloody and disastrous ethnic conflicts witnessed in Rwanda and Burundi, the types of which that are rather pervasive and recurrent in the entire African continent.

Contrary to the view of some of the adverse critiques, Nyerere does not come across as a typical dictator who ruled repressively. In fact, he persistently sought to institutionalize a modicum of a participatory social and political process in the immediate period after independence. Throughout this period, he institutionalized measures to ensure the movement toward a multi-party system. Thus, the villagization scheme in spite of the shortcomings identified in its implementation was a veritable platform for the dispensation of social welfare and grassroots development.

The villages were important in the highly successful literacy programme. By 1980s, Tanzania had one of the highest literacy rates in Africa in spite of its debilitating state of economy. Every village had at least a primary school, 90 % of the villages had a cooperative store while considerable proportion had access to safe water supply, a health centre or dispensary (Africa Now 1981, p. 58).

12.6.4 The Option of Market Fundamentalism

When compared to some of its peers in the East African sub-region, especially Kenya; Kenya in terms of economic output outstripped Tanzania. Under the period under review, Kenya outstripped Tanzania first by 50 % in 1973, and second by 30 % between 1974 and 1984. In economic terms, it would appear that Kenya fared better, but in terms of human development, as demonstrated earlier, Tanzania indeed fared better.

In fact, by the time we assess the seeming growth advantage of Kenya in terms of the consistent torrents of generous external aid from Western nations and the international financial institutions (which Tanzania rejected on account of its policy of self-reliant development), Tanzania fared better in real terms above and beyond its peers in the East African sub-region. Without prejudice to its recourse to International Monetary Fund (IMF), finance in the 1970s in the face of economic crisis, Nyerere remained critical of neoliberal prescriptions, which according to him leave national economies worse off when embraced.

In hindsight, Nyerere as a statesman was far ahead of his era, as the unfortunate impact of neoliberal prescriptions on third world economies has brought the inadequacies of the neoliberal paradigm to the fore, as a ruinous path to development. Thus, neoliberal economic policies in no way constitute a workable alternative to Ujamaa in the development process in Africa (Sachs 1987; Bienefeld 1998). The explanatory value of African social philosophy, typified by Ujamaa, must be viewed within the context of the ensuing global economic crisis with the attendant abysmal failure of capitalism, something which has been widely regarded as the only alternative after the earlier collapse of Marxist socialism. Ujamaa as African humanist philosophy is relevant, particularly, when cured and purged of its deterministic Marxist-socialism.

12.7 Conclusion

I have thus far shown that both capitalism and socialism have failed to promote humanistic values needed to counter the impersonal and destructive forces of humankind's inhumanity against itself. These have taken the form of wars, tyranny, unjust and oppressive political systems, mass-unemployment, overexploitation of the environment, abysmal economic failures caused by many years of wrong economic choices, diseases, socio-economic hierarchy, suboptimal resource allocation, inhumane treatment of people, adverse policy preferences, misrule, institutional structures, which are generally detrimental to human dignity, integrity and well-being.

At a time when the humankind is at cross-roads about how to attain social justice, equity, sustainable economic growth, sustainable economic development and sustainable human development, I have dwelt considerably on the eternal social and communal embeddedness of human life and existence. That is, I am referring to group solidarity – the benefit to the individual of enjoying the security and the protective umbrella of the group, of conformity to universalizable group customs and norms, which holds society together, of community spirit as overriding forces in human life. The superiority of African humanist paradigm of developmentalism above and beyond the two failed Western economic paradigms lie behind the fact that it emphasizes the well-being of the group, and therefore, the greatest good of the greatest number of the people as the primary purpose of governance and developmentalism. It assumes that what is good for the life of the community or society is or will eventually be good for the individual.

African humanism is neither the impersonal individualistic view of society which capitalism encapsulates, nor the deterministic perspective of human existence, which is at the core of socialist world view and developmentalism. The African humanist world view is to the extent that it underscores the realism that there can be no 'pure' personhood without community and no 'pure' community without constituent individuals. It constitutes a veritable third alternative social philosophy, which animates all human institutions, such as capital, property, law, justice and so forth. I have particularly argued that African humanism would redress the most fundamental and critical issues of the human condition, such as mass unemployment, hunger, scourge of war and conflict, diseases, poverty, inequitable allocation of resources, sub-optimal allocation of resources, environmental degradation and overexploitation, and so on.

Thus, given the developmental deficits which bedevils the world, nay Africa, African Humanist perspective's high explanatory value as, I have succinctly demonstrated brings to the fore its value as a veritable instrument, which if embraced, particularly in Africa will catalyze sustainable economic growth, sustainable economic development, and most importantly, sustainable human development.

It is a single stroke which will open up rural Africa, where over 80 % of the people reside and unleash the latent creative and productive force of the people in a very sustainable and self-reliant manner. For Africa, opening up the rural area will entail investment in rural infrastructure such as rural feeder roads, rural telephony, rural electricity, and mass transportation, such as railways to connect settlements, rural sanitation and clean sources of water, rural health services, rural recreation and so on. Implementation of the foregoing measures will arrest the rural/urban drift and boost agricultural productivity, reduce the level of poverty and diverse the economy away from the unsustainable reliance on the extractive sectors to the sustainable agricultural and manufacturing sectors of the economy.

References

Adams M, Kalabamn F, White R (2003) Land tenure policy practice in Botswana – governance lessons for Southern Africa. Austrian J Dev Stud 19(1):55–74

Anderson ML (2005) Sociology: understanding a diverse society. Wadsworth, New York

Arkaide VB (1973) Planning in Tanzania. In: Cliff L, Saul J (eds) Socialism in Tanzania. East African Publishing House, Dar es Salaam

Bienefeld MA (1998) Structural adjustment and the prospects of democracy in Southern Africa. IDS Bull, June

Boesen J et al (1979) Ujamaa: socialism from above. Scandinavian Institute of African Studies, Uppsala, passim

Bolton D (1985) Nationalization – a road to socialism: the case of Tanzania. Zed Books, London, 154

Brewer A (1997) Marxist theories of imperialism: a critical survey. Routledge, London

Brym RJ (2005) Sociology: your compass for a new world. Wadsworth, New York

Chilcote R (1983) Theories of development: mode of production or dependency? Sage, New York

Coulson A (1985) Tanzania: a political economy. Oxford University Press, Oxford
Cousins B (2007) More than socially embedded: the distinctive character of "communal tenure". J Agrar Change 7(3):281–315
Davis KE (2008) The relationship between law and development: optimist versus skeptics. Am J Comp Law 57:8–14
De Kadt EJ (1974) Sociology and development. Tavistock Publications, New York
de Soto H (2000) The mystery of capital: why capitalism triumphs in the west and fails everywhere. Basic Books, New York
Desai V (2008) The companion to development studies. Oxford University Press, Oxford
Fukuyama F (2006) The end of history and the last man. Free Press, New York
Ghosh BN (2001) Dependency theory revisited. Ashgate, London
Gilman N (2004) Mandarins of the future: modernization theory in cold war America. The John Hopkins University Press, Baltimore
Hermassi E (1978) Changing patterns in research on the third world. Annu Rev Sociol 4:239–257
Hettn B (1985) Development theory in transition: the dependency debate and beyond: third world reponses. Zed Book, New York
Hsiung B (2006) Economic analysis of law: an inquiry of its underlying logic. Erasmus Law Econ Rev 2:1–3
Hubbell L (2008) Rethinking dependency theory: the case of Dominica, the rascal state. J Third World Stud 112
Huntington SP (1978) The change to change: modernization, development, and politics. In: Provizer NW (ed) Analyzing the third world: essays from comparative politics. Schenkman Publishing, Cambridge, pp 30–69
Huntington S (1996) Political order in changing societies. Yale University Press, New Haven
Inglehart R (2005) Modernization, cultural change and democracy: the human development sequence. Cambridge University Press, Cambridge
Jaffee D (1998) Levels of socio-economic development theory. Praeger, Westport
Johnson RW (2000) Nyerere: a flawed hero. The National Interest, 60, passim
Kiely R (1995) Sociology of development: the impasse and beyond. Routledge, London
Lane C (1999) TRB from Washington: gone awry. The New Republic, November 8, p 16
Larrain J (1991) Theories of development: capitalism, colonialism and dependency. Polity, New York
Latham ME (2000) Modernization as ideology: American social science and 'nation building' in the Kennedy era. The University of North Carolina Press, Chapel Hill
Leys C (1996) The rise and fall of development theory. Indiana University Press, Bloomington
Ndulu J (2008) The political economy of economic growth in Africa, 1960–2000. Cambridge University Press, Cambridge
Nyerere J (1961) Scramble for Africa: address to the world assembly of youth. Government Printer, Dar es Salaam
Nyerere J (1967) Freedom and unity. Oxford University Press, London/Oxford
Nyerere J (1968) Freedom and socialism Dar es Salaam. Oxford University Press, Oxford
O'Neill D (2007) A modernization theory: economic growth, income equality and democratization. Paper presented at the annual meeting of the Midwest Political Science Association, Chicago, 12 April 2007. Available at http://www.allacademic.com/meta/p196991_index.html
Ouedrago HMG (2002) Legal conditions for the recognition of local land rights and local land tenure practices. In: Proceedings of the international workshop: making land rights more secure, Ouedrago
Palmer S (1975) Self-reliant development in an interdependent world. In: Erb GF, Kallab V (eds) Beyond dependency: the developing world speaks out. Over Seas Development Council, Washington, DC, pp 5–6
Peet R (1999) Theories of development. The Guilford Press, New York
Pratt C (1976) The critical phase in Tanzania, 1945–67: Nyerere and the emergence of a socialist strategy. Cambridge University Press, Cambridge
Rahnevia M (1997) The post-development reader. Zed Books, New York

Sachs J (1987) Trade and exchange rate policies in growth oriented adjustment policies. In: Corbo V (ed) Growth oriented adjustment programs. International Monetary Fund, Washington, DC
Scott JC (1999) Seeing like a state: how certain schemes to improve the human condition have failed. Yale University Press, New Haven
Shivji I (1973) The silent class struggle. Tanzania Publishing House, Dar es Salam, passim
Shivji I (1974) The silent class struggle. Tanzania Publishing House, Dar es Salaam
Tetreault MA (1986) Dependency theory and the return of high politics. Greenwood Press, New York
Wily L (2005) The commons and customary law in modern times: rethinking the orthodoxies. In: Proceedings of the UNDP-ICC, workshop: land rights for African development: from knowledge to action, Nairobi
Willis K (2007) Theories and practices of development. Routledge, London
Yeager R (1989) Tanzania: an African experiment. Westview Press, Boulder

Chapter 13
Crime Detection and the *Psychic Witness* in America: An Allegory for Re-appraising Indigenous African Criminology

Babafemi Odunsi

13.1 Introduction

> ...Do not believe in anything, merely on the authority of your teachers and elders. Do not believe in traditions because they have been handed down for many generations. But after observation and analysis, when you find that anything agrees with reason and is conducive to the benefit of one and all, then accept it and live up to it. (*Buddha in* Ayorinde 2007, p. 251)

Prior to the advent of colonialism, indigenous people of sub-Saharan Africa had their system of criminology for the prevention or repression of crimes in a broad drive of social control (Ibidapo-Obe 2005, pp. 99–100; Ayo 2002, pp. 193–194). A valuable introduction to the issues discussed throughout this chapter rests on a suitable definition of criminology:

> In its broadest sense, criminology is the entire body of knowledge regarding crime, criminals, and the efforts of society to repress and prevent them. Thus it is composed of knowledge drawn from such fields as law, medicine, religion, science, education, social work, social ethics, and public administration; and it includes within its scope the activities of legislative bodies, law-enforcement agencies, courts, educational and correctional institutions, and private and public social agencies. (Caldwell 1965, p. 3)

With regard to *criminology* inclusively connoting 'the efforts of society to repress and prevent' crime, 'indigenous African criminology' in the context of this chapter would encompass the systems of criminal law, criminal justice, security and law

B. Odunsi, LL.M (Toronto), Ph.D. (Ife) Lecturer (✉)
Faculty of Law, Obafemi Awolowo University, Ile-Ife, Nigeria

MacArthur Fellow, Faculty of Law, University of Toronto, Toronto, Canada
e-mail: sylvanus.odunsi@utoronto.ca; femiodunsi2002@yahoo.com

O. Onazi (ed.), *African Legal Theory and Contemporary Problems: Critical Essays*, Ius Gentium: Comparative Perspectives on Law and Justice 29,
DOI 10.1007/978-94-007-7537-4_13, © Springer Science+Business Media Dordrecht 2014

enforcement, as well other related social control measures adopted by indigenous African societies for the prevention or repression of crime. Along this axis, in subsequent parts of the chapter, as concepts or terminologies dictate, 'criminal law', 'criminal justice', and the other earlier mentioned components will be adopted in referring to criminology.

Principally, indigenous African criminology is entrenched in beliefs, norms and values designed and adopted by the people for themselves, as a result of which the level of respect and compliance is relatively high (Ayo 2002, p. 193; Elechi 2004, pp. 9–10). This can be adduced to several factors. One, law-breakers and their families were prone to shaming or other forms of social chastising in comparatively close-knitted societies. Second and perhaps more compelling, was that crime control among indigenous people, to a very large extent, involved the intervention of supernatural agencies (Oraegbunam 2009). In the prevention, detection and other aspects of crime control, reference is made to supernatural forces for intervention through oath-taking processes and objects of fetishism, charms, magic and some other measures (Ayo 2002, pp. 195–197, 63, 70–73). The supernatural dimension facilitated a socio-legal atmosphere in which the potent elements of mysticism and debilitating fear of terrifying deities helped to keep crimes at relatively manageable levels (Ayo 2002, p. 194).

Colonialism brought about the incursion of foreign norms, values and laws of the colonizing masters. Inherently primed to supplant the ways of the natives (Ayo 2002, pp. 106–107), the colonial *new order* affected and brought about the relegation and suppression of indigenous practices, including those relating to crime control. The suppression took different forms in a purported drive to 'reform' the 'heathen natives'; Western education, religious ministrations and public policies portrayed indigenous African practices as barbaric and abhorrent (Ayo 2002). More directly, as will be discussed later, the colonial masters summarily outlawed some indigenous social control practices or subjected their validity and sustainability to passing some tests. In substitution, Western-styled law social control mechanisms, regarded as scientific, modern and acceptable, were deployed to replace the supposedly archaic and objectionable indigenous structures (Ayo 2002, p. 98; Elechi 2004, p. 20).

To reiterate, and as will be further discussed in greater detail, the supernatural plays a pivotal role in African criminology. The question regarding the legitimacy and/of African criminal law manifestly dovetails into the question of the *acceptability* of the supernatural platform on which it stands. As Ibidapo-Obe notes, '[t]he pervasive misconception about African law can be observed from the initial reluctance to even ascribe the appellation of law to *what was perceived as a collection of superstition, myths and legends'* (Ibidapo-Obe 2005). However, the logic of the criticisms of the supernatural connection and dependency by African criminology becomes doubtful on the face of developments, such as 'Psychic Witness', where crime control agencies in the United States of America, a developed and technologically advanced country, resort to the supernatural in the process of crime detection.

Against this background, using 'Psychic Witness' as an allegory, this chapter discusses and re-echoes the need for a positive view-point of indigenous African criminology. That is, the need to reflect on whether the indigenous system still deserves to be a 'target of relegation, renunciation and scorn' and one 'widely touted as being barbaric, repressive, incoherent, inconsistent and irrational' (Ibidapo-Obe 2005). The need for reappraisal will arise from the positive lessons, which indigenous criminology, offers to modern African states in the daunting fight against crime. The lessons become apparent in the light of the increasing preference by educated and enlightened people to indigenous social control mechanisms because of the manifest inefficiency and failure of states' security and law enforcement organs to prevent or repress the very high and fearful rates of crime affecting citizens' lives and properties (Ayo 2002). Nigeria is adopted to illustrate different aspects of this growing trend.

13.2 Psychic Witness

'Psychic Witness' is a television documentary programme showing how American law crime control agencies use extrasensory means to detect or solve knotty crimes. In the programme, '[i]nterviews and dramatic re-enactments show psychics helping police detectives solve real crimes such as disappearances, kidnappings and murders, at various locations in the United States. Two stories are told in each 1 h episode.[1] It is remarkable that, typically, the crimes solved by the intervention of psychics are the ones in which all the modern hi-tech, scientific gadgets as well as skill and training at the disposal of American detectives have pathetically failed to resolve. 'Psychic Witness' is not the only television documentary programme showing the involvement of psychics in the solving of crimes in America. Another programme in this class is 'Psychic Detectives' (2013).

In the interaction with the supernatural, 'Psychic Witness' in America shares an important common ground of similarity with indigenous African criminology, and this can be used to flag off some significant points. It generally shows that the use of supernatural agencies in criminology in an advanced country indicates that such approach can really assist in social control. The supernatural is, as such, no longer an oddity of uncivilised and barbaric people. Hence, indigenous African style criminology should not be summarily disparaged or discountenanced just because it falls outside the scope of conventional science or empiricism. In a way, indigenous Africans who had for long relied on supernatural forces as the epicentre of social control, perhaps, can rejoice that they have not served 'vain gods'. In some respect, 'Psychic Witness' is a testament to the courage of the American system. It is remarkable that in spite of the high level, technological facilities available for crime control, American detectives can pragmatically 'condescend' to adopt an approach more identified with allegedly uncivilised indigenous African people. This is a reflection of America's realistic willingness to embrace any viable measure that can

[1] 'Psychic Witness' online at http://www.tv.com/psychic-witness/show/61792/summary.html (date accessed 12/2/2011).

benefit the country, regardless of the disrespect or disdain for such measures by other people. Inferably, indigenous African criminology system offers some lessons, which the post-colonial governments in Africa and perhaps, other parts of the world can consider in their battles against crime, especially in the face of the inadequacies of the 'modern' criminological mechanisms. What follows is an attempt to expand on what the African criminology system entails.

13.3 African Criminology System: An Intermix of the Physical and Supernatural

Generally, indigenous African criminology evolved from societal traditions, customs, or native laws, and historical circumstances (Okafo 2007, p. 7). In light of the diversity of these factors the approach to crime control, vis-à-vis strategies and techniques, necessarily differed from one society to another. Nonetheless, the common goal across the divergent indigenous societies, whatever the format of adopted strategies, was the attainment of effective crime control and preservation of collective security (Okafo 2007).

Indigenous African criminology entails an interworking or collaboration of physical and supernatural realms, with a predomination of the supernatural (Oraegbunam 2009; Ayo 2002, pp. 195–197). Though it may be difficult to delineate the boundaries of the physical from the supernatural in traditional criminology, an attempt would be made to discuss the typical approaches or methodologies from the physical and supernatural perspectives.

In the physical realm, community members, individually and collectively, play roles in law enforcement and crime control activities. Various community institutions, groups, and members, at family or personal levels are involved. The activities are coordinated and overseen at structural levels of government such as the Family, the Extended Family as well as the whole community, which, geographically, may be a village or collection of villages, towns and so on (Ayo 2002, pp. 197–204; Okafo 2007, pp. 7–8). At each government and administration level, there are provisions for security maintenance, crime prevention, and general law enforcement by the entire community acting together or as is more often the case, through their elected or appointed representatives as well as by specialized agencies, such as the Age-grade groups (Okafo 2007, p. 8).

The practices in some tribal regions offer illustrations of security and law enforcement operations in the traditional African setting. Among the Yoruba of South Western Nigeria, the local professional hunters played a prominent role in crime control and security maintenance. Relying principally on Dane guns manufactured by the local blacksmiths, the hunters kept watch over the vulnerable parts of the communities, especially at night. Where necessary, the hunters' security activities were complemented by vigilante activities involving other members of the communities that might not be professional hunters (Ayo 2002, pp. 197–204).

Along similar lines, among the Igbo of South-Eastern Nigeria; young men's age-grade groups usually carried the responsibility of security maintenance and general law enforcement. The young men's age-grade groups, used diverse approaches to prevent crimes by identifying, apprehending, and prosecuting persons suspected of committing crimes (Okafo 2007, p. 8). The age-grade group's other responsibilities at times extended to enforcement of judicial decisions by different means. In reflecting on the virtual indivisibility of the physical from the supernatural in indigenous criminology, the hunters and vigilantes customarily used juju medicine as supportive devices as well as charms for individual protection or confidence boosting during security activities (Ayo 2002, p. 199).

13.3.1 Indigenous African Criminology: Different Components of the Supernatural Dimension

The involvement of the supernatural in indigenous African criminology takes different forms. Whatever form of involvement or deployment, the essence was to ensure supernatural protection and security for persons and properties, individually and collectively, through reference to some protecting or adjudicatory deities or juju. Supernatural involvement in crime control can be in the form of prevention, detection, resolution, sanctions or any other aspect. Generally, reference to the supernatural is predicated upon the belief that anyone who defies the adopted medium of supernatural engagement would incur the wrath of the overseeing deity or juju, and face dire other consequences. Some approaches among the Yoruba are discussed below as illustrations of the diverse modes or components of supernatural involvement in traditional criminology.

13.3.2 Indigenous Crime Prevention and Deterrence: The Use of 'Alile'

One popular crime prevention measure among the Yoruba is *alile*. This consists of semiotic tags, charms and other objects used for the protection of properties in households, marketplaces, farms and so on to prevent or deter unauthorized use, entry or taking (Ayo 2002, pp. 195–197). The potency of *alile* is not in the symbolic object used, which can be disused footwear, piece of rag, palm fronds, totems and so on. In design and operation, embedded in *alile* is a curse programmed to harm any person who defies the *alile* to tamper with the property which the *alile* protects. The curse, if activated by defiance in tampering with the property, would instigate protecting supernatural forces to inflict severe sanction on the culprit. In the context of criminology, therefore, underpinning *alile* is an expected deterrence of criminal conducts vis-à-vis fear of the supernatural forces to which the property has been entrusted via the *alile*.

13.3.3 *Another Perspective of Prevention and Deterrence: Deities on Guard*

Somewhat related to the practice of placing *alile* on properties, is the practice of placing households under the protection of some awe-inspiring deities for the security of lives and properties. Customarily, each household in Yoruba is placed under the protection of different deities. Totems of the protecting deities are often placed in conspicuous places to symbolise and publicise their presence (Ayo 2002, pp. 196–197). One of such deities popularly deployed for protection is *Esu.* Though commonly perceived as the biblical devil or Satan, *Esu* is actually regarded by the Yoruba as 'a divinity of mischief who can make things difficult for mankind' (Adelumo and Dopamu 1979, pp. 82–83). In another respect, *Esu* is also regarded as 'a beneficent divinity who is prepared to answer the call of his devotees who give his due' (Adelumo and Dopamu 1979, p. 82). The presence of *Esu* as overseer and protector of a household is normally symbolised by a laterite statue in a human form placed in a slanting position just outside the compound of the household involved (Adelumo and Dopamu 1979, p. 83).

The traditional logic behind using deities as supernatural guards over households is that the fear of incurring the wrath of an implacable god would discourage people from harmful acts, such as stealing from or inordinate attacks on the household. Among the indigenous people, the fear of the deities is potent and real. For example, it is widely appreciated that *Esu* is difficult to placate when provoked, and is so powerful that even his fellow deities are afraid of him. Hence, 'he is held in constant dread, and people at all times seek to be on the right side of him' (Adelumo and Dopamu 1979, p. 82). In underscoring the intimidating ferocity of *Esu* as a protecting deity, the Yoruba believe that once a family or a household has been placed under its protection; Esu 'kills in his typical manner (all) those who injure the buildings or who trespass there with evil intentions' (Ayo 2002, p. 197).

13.3.4 *Crime Resolution and Sanctioning: Invoking the Wraths of the Gods*

Beyond the paranormal prevention of crimes, indigenous African criminology also entails supernatural intervention into processes of detection, apprehension and sanctioning of culprits, or simply the resolution of crimes in some other ways. A number or all of these processes can be aggregated into one event or instance of intervention. One very common mechanism of propelling these processes is oath-taking.

Generally, oath-taking is a widely accepted and practiced measure of resolution of disputes in indigenous African societies. Used very frequently in crime detection, oath-taking is an integral part of the African custom by which the guilty and the innocent involved in dispute resolution and determination (Oraegbunam 2009, p. 70). The resort to the supernatural process of oath-taking is typically made when human efforts to resolve the crime fail or there is a lack of confidence in the human organ in charge. As a direct submission to the supernatural entity, oath-taking entails swearing to a deity or juju (that is a supernatural object) for the resolution of a criminal issue or settlement of other contentious matters. The oaths are worded in such a way that the person swearing invokes a conditional curse on his or herself, invoking the deity or juju to punish them if they lie. Guilt or innocence is established upon the basis of whether the accused dies or not, or if the accused falls ill, encounters some grave misfortune or suffers any other expected consequence as a result of the oath-taking exercise. In some cases, the family of such a person and the whole community may vicariously suffer dire consequences too, depending on the stand of the deity or juju sworn to (Oraegbunam 2009, pp. 7–71).

Among the Yoruba, for example, two deities that are more likely to be engaged with in crime-resolution oath-taking are *Ayelala* and *Sango. Ayelala*, is a goddess worshipped in many places across Yoruba land. Her central functions include dispensation of retributory justice and punishing of evil doers (Awolalu and Dopamu 1979, pp. 90–91). In this light, *Ayelala* is 'always thought of as an anti-wickedness goddess and a guardian of social morality… [and also] known and referred to as the Queen of Justice and ready reckoner who passes judgment when the evil-doer has forgotten' (Awolalu and Dopamu 1979). Where suspects to a crime are brought before the court of *Ayelala* to swear to the deity, there are two possible scenarios. One, a culprit, rather than undergoing the swearing process or 'daring' *Ayelala* may confess to his guilt and receive appropriate sanctions. Alternatively, the culprit, refusing to admit guilt, may opt to swear falsely. *Ayelala*'s wrath and punishment on culprits who are guilty but swear falsely manifest in form of swollen limbs and abdomens with terrible agony. Ultimately, this could result in painful death if they still refuse to confess to the unlawful acts (Awolalu and Dopamu 1979). The effect of the dire punishment of *Ayelala* extends beyond the life of an 'executed' culprit as her victim. Such person cannot be mourned. 'Rather than weeping, the people congratulate the relatives of the victims on the removal of the evil-doers from the society' (Awolalu and Dopamu 1979). Similarly, regarding a crime referred to *Ayelala* for supernatural intervention, suspects can also be made to swear to their innocence before *Sango.* This is the Yoruba god of thunder and lightning, who among others, especially forbids lying, stealing and poisoning. *Sango* represents the 'divine wrath upon the children of disobedience' (Awolalu and Dopamu 1979, p. 84) and is highly dreaded for its thunderous and fiery ferocity. *Sango* characteristically sanctions guilty people who swear falsely before it by striking them to death in a blaze of lightning and roaring of thunder. Reportedly, also in case of stealing, *Sango* would also place, for public display, the stolen items on the bodies of the identified and sanctioned culprits.[2] As a form of posthumous sanctions, a person struck down by *Sango* does not receive normal burial; he can

[2]The writer recalls a widely reported incident that occurred in Bolade-Oshodi, Lagos, Nigeria when he was in primary school in Lagos, Nigeria. Following a rainstorm, a group of persons who allegedly conspired in stealing some items of jewellery were struck and killed by thunderous lightning, their deaths popularly attributed to the supernatural wrath of Sango. Diverse accounts

only be buried by *Sango* priests following the performance of necessary rituals at the spot he or she was struck down. Such a person must also not be mourned based upon the belief that the victim has got his due punishment for his evil deeds as *Sango* does not descend to strike, except to express his displeasure for unwholesome conducts (Awolalu and Dopamu 1979, p. 84). The abhorrence of criminal acts and its other attributes make *Sango* a terrifying icon in the supernatural framework of indigenous African criminology.

13.3.5 When Culprits Are at Large: 'Sending' and Unleashing the Gods

Basically, as an indigenous detective or crime resolution mechanism, oath-taking, is typically undertaken where there are identified suspected culprits that are or can be made to swear an oath to determine their innocence or guilt. However, in some cases, the situation of a crime may be such that perpetrators are unknown, at large and cannot therefore be put through the process of oath-taking. In such a situation, an indigenous criminological practice for detection or other aspects of resolving such crimes is to simply 'send' an avenging deity or juju after the perpetrators. The belief is that the perpetrators, wherever they may be, would be magically located, identified and punished appropriately for the crime committed.

> Among the Yoruba, *Ayelala* and *Sango,* two deities whose enormous criminological powers have been considered above, are more likely to be 'sent' to, or after an unknown or eloping culprit. Once located, the deities would deal with the culprit in their respective characteristic manner of punishing offenders as earlier described.

13.3.6 Arresting Criminals Flagrante Delicto: The Deities Working Through Preventive Charms

Apart from involving the gods in the apprehending and sanctioning of culprits, there are some other means of preventing crimes or apprehending criminals either *flagrante delicto,* or after commission of the crime.[3] A widely known practice among the Yoruba is in the form of placing charmed items, usually brooms, at the thresholds of households as means of supernatural security. The belief is that anyone who comes to steal in such secured households would be enchanted by the item of

---

reported that the allegedly stolen items of jewellery were displayed on the bodies of the dead persons.

[3] The processes described subsequently are based on stories heard over the ages as well as discussions with some elderly people in the course of research for this paper. Generally, they are trite stories that anyone familiar with indigenous criminological practices of the Yoruba can readily relate to.

juju, and would not be able to steal anything. Rather, the criminal-minded person would be supernaturally trapped, sweeping, until his arrest by the householders.

Another similar mechanism is the practice of placing charms with powers to trap, disorientate, drive away or even fatally harm intruders, depending on the coding of the operative charms. In one form, an intruder may simply be hypnotized and left stuck or roaming around the household until he is subsequently apprehended. In another form, if intruders come in a group, based on the working of the charms, while stuck in the scene of crime, discordance would inexplicably arise among them, and they would start and keep quarrelling until they are apprehended. In some cases too, the charms placed in a household may supernaturally unleash bees, wasps or some other dangerous elements on intruders either to drive them away or to inflict fatal injuries on them.[4]

13.3.7 Involvement of Supernatural Forces in Indigenous Criminal Trial Process: Trial by Ordeal

In some cases, suspects in traditional African societies, based on suspicion or apprehension through any of the means, may be put through a trial process whereby the suspect is made to go through some measures to test his innocence. In this aspect, it is not that the suspect is made to swear to a deity or juju to prove his innocence. Rather, the suspect is taken put through a criminal trial by a challenge; proof of his innocence or guilt lies in whether he prevails over or succumbs to the challenge. The popular form of this indigenous criminal trial process is the much vilified *trial by ordeal*, which has been described as 'one of the greatest safeguards of justice' among the people of Southern Nigeria (Oraegbunam 2009, p. 71). As it will be shown is following discussion, supernatural forces are still involved in this seemingly physical process in the indigenous criminal criminal-justice.

Simply put, *trial by ordeal* is a judicial or trial process whereby guilt or innocence of an accused person is determined by subjecting him to painful, unpleasant and dangerous experiences. According to *The Black's Law Dictionary*, *trial by ordeal* is, '[a] primitive form of trial in which an accused was subjected to a dangerous or painful physical test, the result being considered a divine revelation of the person's guilt or innocence. The participants believed that God would reveal a person's culpability by protecting an innocent person from the torture....' (Garner et al. 2004).

The ordeals which an accused can be put through are diverse, depending on the morbid creativity of the people engaged in the implementation of the process. In the context of Nigeria, ordeals which suspects could be put through have

[4]This account was obtained from a leader of one of the prominent vigilante groups operating in Abeokuta, Ogun State, Nigeria. The man affirmed that he has such mechanism set up in his house to complement other indigenous protective measures.

included taking poisonous substances, immersion in water, dipping in boiling oil or exposure to the attacks of crocodiles or other wild animals.[5] Furthermore, according to a commentator:

> [t]he ordeal might take the form of the juice of a tree (e.g. sass wood) mixed with water, or a burnt powder made from it and dissolved in water; a knife or other piece of iron might be heated in a fire; the culprit might be taken to a nearby pond or stream. The guilty one is he who should drink the water and become sick, handle the red hot knife and get burnt, or sink when immersed in water. (Elias 1962, p. 229 in Oraegbunam 2009, p. 72)

Premised on a subjective principle of 'the truth shall set you free'; the process of *trial by ordeal* is underpinned by a belief that through some supernatural intervention, preservation or insulation, a person innocent of an alleged crime shall pass through the ordeal unharmed. Hence, only innocent people would confidently opt to endure a trial while guilty ones are likely to confess to their guilt. *Trial by ordeal* can be a matter of life or death, proof of innocence being survival or escape from death or grievous injuries, and death or injuries being an indication of guilt. For example, in a *trial by ordeal,* the Efik of Southern Nigeria would make an accused consume the poisonous 'esere' bean for the purpose of determining innocence or guilt. An accused that vomits up the bean without suffering harm is innocent while one who becomes ill or dies is considered guilty (Roberts and Vink 1998, p. 92). Among the Igbo, a widow suspected of killing her husband could face diverse forms of *trial by ordeal* to determine her culpability or innocence in the death. Sometimes, the accused would be forced to drink the bath-water used in washing the corpse of the diseased. The belief is that she would die if guilty, while her emerging unharmed would be a proof of her innocence (Oraegbunam 2009, p. 72).

13.4 Colonialism: The Entry of Foreign Norms and Laws into Indigenous Criminology

African countries came under the colonial control of various European powers, with Nigeria falling under the control of Britain. The colonial relationship between Nigeria and England engendered the introduction of English law into Nigeria (Obilade 1979, p. 4).[6] This took different modes; in one vein, Nigeria as a component of the British Empire was subject to laws generally applicable to all parts of the Empire. More specifically, English Law in its different genres was formally introduced and made applicable in Nigeria with the commencement of Ordinance 3 of

[5] See *Criminal Code* Cap. C38, Laws of the Federation of Nigeria 2004, section 207.

[6] Obilade (1979, p. 4): 'One of the notable characteristics of the Nigerian Legal System is the tremendous influence of English Law upon its growth. The historical link of the country with England has left a seemingly indelible mark upon the system: English Law forms a substantive part of Nigerian Law'.

14th March 1863 (Obilade 1979). Colonial rule in Nigeria and other African countries had a general impact of radical alteration of traditional or indigenous legal systems, which manifested in ways that include the following:

(a) Transplantation and imposition of laws and norms made for foreign societies with different ways of life and values.
(b) Making of laws for the African societies by foreign colonial masters who were mainly influenced by their own ways of life while they regarded the African ways of life as primitive and unwholesome.
(c) The subjugation of customary law and traditional values to the laws made under circumstances (a) or (b) above.
(d) Fundamental alteration and illegalization of traditional principles and values formulated and operated for many generations and to which members of the societies have been accustomed.

In the context of Nigeria, the sources of law applicable enlarged from mere customary law, as made and generally accepted by the indigenous people, to the following:

(a) Received English Law
(b) Legislation
(c) Judicial Precedent
(d) Customary Law (Obilade 1979)

It bears noting that customary law as applicable from the colonial era was devoid of the strong unfettered legal potency it enjoyed in the pre-colonial traditional setting. It became subjected to the overriding provisions of the three other sources of Nigerian law. In the first instance, the existence of customary law was relegated to issue of facts to be proved before the English-style court before it can be considered for application in any legal dispute. Except in the exceptional situations where a court has taken *judicial notice* (Asein 2005, pp. 122–124)[7] of a customary law due to previous applications, any person relying on such law must establish or prove its existence as facts in issue by means of cogent evidence. The person proves his or her case by the direct evidence of witnesses knowledgeable in the area of the customary law in question or by some other means such as books (Asein 2005, p. 129). The basis for this procedure is that the judge is regarded as not being aware of the customary laws, even if he comes from the area where the customary law in question applies. However, unlike customary law, there is no need to prove any of the other three English law-based sources of Nigerian law in court as the judge is summarily deemed to have knowledge and awareness of them.

[7]This is a process where, due to previous and frequent applications of a customary law, a court would be deemed to have knowledge and awareness of it such that there is no need to prove its existence afresh before the court where the customary law comes into question. See Asein (2005, pp. 122–124).

Secondly, after proving the existence of any customary law by evidence, such law would be further subjected to legal tests of validity before it can be deemed valid and applicable (Kolajo 2005, pp. 129–138). The tests of validity are:

(i) Repugnancy Test
(ii) Incompatibility Test
(iii) Public Policy Test (Kolajo 2005)

The *repugnancy test* connotes that any customary law 'repugnant to natural justice, equity and good conscience' would be held invalid and unenforceable as law.[8] The *incompatibility test* connotes that any customary law that is 'incompatible with any law for the time being in force' would be invalid and unenforceable as law. In operation, the effect of this test is that any customary law that conflicts or incompatible, directly or indirectly, with any of the other three sources would be invalid and unenforceable.[9] The public policy test connotes that any customary law that is 'contrary to public policy' would be invalid and unenforceable as law.[10] Public policy is flexible and has been described as 'an unruly horse which once one gets astride it no one knows where it would end'.[11] In this respect, 'public policy' has such a dynamic latitude that, based on the inclination of the government at a particular time; it can be invoked or adapted to strike down a customary law that is not caught within the web of the other two tests of validity. A key point of note in the *validity tests* is that the procedure being the legal creation of the colonial masters, naturally was influenced by values of the colonial rulers who were alien to indigenous African societies.

In the web of the legal restrictions on customary law, customary criminal justice system and some criminological mechanisms as previously operating in traditional settings became virtually illegitimate, a situation that still operates in the present times. Section 36 (12) of the Constitution of the Federal Republic of Nigeria, 1999 offers a case-study. The section provides that '…a person shall not be convicted of a criminal offence unless that offence is defined and the penalty therefor prescribed in a written law…' 'Written law' refers to formally promulgated enactments such as Acts of the National Assembly or a law of a state, as contrasted with customary law that is *unwritten* [12] in not being formally made by the conventional legislative process. Thus, it is only crimes set out or written in legislative enactments that would constitute crimes for which someone can be tried and sanctioned. Hence, customary law crimes, which characteristically are unwritten would be null and void and of no legal effect whatsoever.[13]

[8] On this basis, the courts have nullified different customary law rules which were hitherto held sacrosanct and impeccable among the people in the traditional pre-colonial settings. See e.g. the case of *Edet v Essien* (1932) 11 NLR 47.See also the relatively more recent case of *Okonkwo v Okagbue*, (1994) NWLR (368) 301.

[9] See e.g. the case of *Malomo & Ors v Olusola & Ors*, (1955) 15 WACA 12; see also the case of *Okoriko v Otobo* (1962) WNLR, 48.

[10] See e.g. the case of *Re Adadevoh*, (1951) 13 WACA 304; see also the case of latter case of *Meribe v Egbu* (1976) 3 SC 23.

[11] *Enderby Town Football Club v Football Association Ltd* [1971] 1Ch 591 at 606, per Denning M.R.

[12] See the case of *Lewis v Bankole*, (1908) 1NLR 81 AT 100.

[13] See e.g. the case of *Aoko v Fagbemi* (1961) 1 All NLR 400.

Furthermore, some colonial legislative provisions emerged to suppress some components of indigenous criminology in the scope of the *incompatibility* test. For example, with regard to the earlier discussed practice of *trial by ordeal*, section 207 (1) of the *Criminal Code* (Okonkowo 1990, pp. 4–5)[14] provides that:

> The trial by the ordeal of sasswood, esere-bean, or other poison, boiling of oil, fire, immersion in water or exposure to the attacks of crocodiles, or other wild animals, or by any ordeal which is likely to result in the death of or bodily injury to any party to the proceeding is unlawful...

In a related manner, section 208 of the Code further provides that:

> Any person who directs or controls or presides at any trial by ordeal which is unlawful is guilty of felony and is liable, when the trial at which such person directs, controls or presides at results in the death of any party to the proceeding, to the punishment of death, and in every other case to imprisonment for ten years.

Similarly, concerning the securing properties with charms, paranormal forces and so on, section 210 of the *Criminal Code* provides that...Any person who...

> (c) makes or sells or uses, or assists or takes part in making or selling or using, or has in his possession or represents himself to be in possession of any juju, drug or charm...which is alleged or reported to possess the power of causing any natural phenomenon or any disease or epidemic; or
>
> (d) directs or controls or presides at or is present at or takes part in the worship or invocation of any juju which is prohibited by an order of the Minister;... is guilty of a misdemeanour, and is liable to imprisonment for two years.

In effect, the legal system introduced through colonial rule suppressed indigenous criminal law system which the African people were used to and replaced this with alien and incongruous European models of crime control in its different dimensions. Centralised and bureaucratised in nature, the introduced systems had some features. Responsibility for crime control was placed with a formally organised state police who, as components of this central duty, undertake the investigation of crimes, apprehending of law breakers and related activities. Furthermore, imprisonment became a predominant form of criminal sanction. Generally, the complex rules and prescriptions connected with the introduced criminal-justice system inevitably informed the need for lawyers, judicial officers and other professionals to oversee and operate the processes in line with the technicalities. The following commentary offers an apt summation of the incursion of European based criminal law system, and the consequential suppression of indigenous African criminal law practices in Nigeria and other parts of Africa:

> Africa has inherited its approach to the treatment of crime from its colonial era. Some prisons now standing were erected in the nineteenth century and the legal systems followed the colonizers as surely as the Roman Laws went with the Legions. Similarly, treatment systems were European in origin and made few concessions to tribal tradition...[The] importation of foreign treatment measures for offenders was often blind to the better and more effective arrangements locally available. (Clifford 1974, p. 185 in Elechi 2004, p. 20)

[14] Cap. C41, Laws of the Federation of Nigeria 2004. The Criminal Code was enacted in Nigeria on 1st June, 1916, when Nigeria was still under colonial rule; the code was an adaptation of the Criminal Code made for the State of Queensland, Australia in 1899 which in turn emanated from a draft code intended for England in 1878.Okonkwo, *Okonkwo and Naish* (1990, pp. 4–5).

The broad effect of the tests of validity and other interventions in the application of customary law and practices was that customary law, which was supreme in pre-colonial traditional settings, became subordinated to foreign oriented laws. Reflecting on the depth of the subordination, a writer has described the existence of customary law, vis-à-vis its operation in relation to the other sources of law, as a 'legal make-belief' (Oraegbunam 2009, p. 74).

13.5 Indigenous African Criminal Law System and the Imposed Foreign System: Reflecting on Levels of Effectiveness

The use of criminal law, vis-à-vis sanctions as a means of social control, has been predicated on four rationales or expectations. These are *incapacitation*, *rehabilitation*, *deterrence* and *retribution* (Cobley 2005, p. 192). The effectiveness of a criminal law system can thus be measured on how well it succeeds in meeting these expectations in its crime control drive.

The essence of incapacitation is to protect people from deviant conducts by putting away the offender, rendering him unable to cause further harm in the society. Incapacitation can be partial, as in confinement, or total, as in execution of criminals convicted for heinous crimes. Temporary incapacitation under the indigenous African criminal law system can be in form of banishment or affliction with illness by the gods; total incapacitation can be in form where an offender is struck dead by the gods as punishment. With regard to rehabilitation, the aim is that sanctions would reform the offender. Once properly adjusted and compliant with existing norms, the offender would desist from deviant conducts. This aspect is a prominent component of indigenous criminal jurisprudence. Hazardous punishment is typically a last resort in indigenous societies. At different stages, for example, at the point of oath-taking, an offender has an option to admit his guilt and make restitution to the victim or take some other steps to atone for his misconducts. Generally, pursuit of restoration of societal amity and reconciliation is an inherent and important aspect of indigenous practices (Elechi 2004, p. 18). Among other things, this serves the purpose of reforming the culprit who has stepped out of social order. Depending on the context of usage, 'retribution' can connote different concepts such as revenge, denunciation, atonement, or 'just desserts' – that is, the law-breaker gets what he justly deserves. In traditional societies, sanctions as retribution are not primarily for the purpose of vengeance. Essentially, retribution represents the society's collective denunciation or expression of disapproval for the deviant conduct of the offender. In another aspect, it translates to the offender's atonement for his misconducts against the victim and the society as a whole. Retribution also forms a basis for the restoration of societal cordiality. It is in this respect that retribution in the traditional context, at times, would entail the offender, directly or through offender's family, making propitiation to appease deities of the land who have been displeased by the offender's conduct (Elechi 2004, p. 18; Oraegbunam 2009, p. 64; Awolalu and Dopamu 1979, p. 84).

'Deterrence' in its theoretical framework has different perspectives. First, there is the aspect of a standing threat, and the related fear, of supernatural sanctions discouraging people from criminal acts. Where an offender has been actually sanctioned this may serve as deterrence at individual and general levels. Individual offenders would be deterred from future misconducts by their unpleasant experience of sanctions, while others, expectedly, would learn from the situation of the sanctioned offender (Fitzmaurice and Pease 1986, p. 48). Finally, the threat of punishment stands as a form of education and a strong expression of society's disapproval of an act, with the effect of a sanction.

The scenario propels and reinforces the public moral code, creating conscious and unconscious inhibitions against committing crime. Punishment, in form of wraths of the gods or juju, evidently stands as a strong deterrence factor against crime among the indigenous people. With manifest appreciation of the extent of their powers, anger and severity of harm they can inflict, the people reasonably have a strong point to refrain from confronting the gods through criminal acts. A saying among the Yoruba relating to *Sango*, the god of thunder, one of the sanctioning deities earlier discussed, tends to illustrate the capacity of gods to deter deviant acts. The saying goes thus: '*eni Sango ti oju e w'ole, ko ni ba won bu oba koso*' ('He who has seen *Sango* [the god of thunder] striking, would never join in insulting or confronting the *King of Koso*').[15]

Apparently, indigenous crime control mechanisms have functioned effectively in the scope of the four rationales or expectations of criminal law discussed above. Studies have shown that, on the whole, the indigenous systems have contributed to the effective control of crime in the pre-colonial African societies (Okafo 2007, p. 5). Underscoring the level of effectiveness of the indigenous crime control mechanism, concerning Yoruba pre-colonial communities, it has been reported:

> Although the maintenance of security at community level has been an important preoccupation of the Yoruba peoples from time immemorial, the need to pay more serious attention to the issue seems to be mostly felt since independence. In the precolonial era, the strategy adopted against insecurity or threats to life, and property was more preventive than combative. *During this period, the experience with night attacks from marauders, resulting in intracommunal loss of lives and property, was more or less unheard of in the rural communities.* (Ayo 2002, pp. 193–194)

Comparatively, the level of effectiveness of indigenous criminology as described above can hardly be attributed to the English criminal law system imposed on Nigeria through colonial rule. So much has been written about the inadequacies and ineffectiveness of the foreign criminal law system in stemming the tide of criminal conducts in Nigeria and beyond (Ayo 2002, pp. 191–193). While the defects of the

[15] 'King of Koso' is one of the cognomens of Sango. Put differently, the saying can mean that the fear of Sango is a strong basis for caution, as no reasonable person who has seen Sango striking down a wrong doer would want to express such a situation.

foreign system cannot be fully engaged within the restricted scope of this work, it bears noting that the reformative and deterrent impacts of criminal sanctions in preventing crime under the system have particularly been questionable for long. Along this line, it has been observed by a source that,

> …if the wrongdoer calculates at all, it is not upon the probable account of the punishment, but upon the chances of detection – from which it follows that…severe and barbarous punishments are not more effectual than milder ones as deterrents to crime. (Ashworth 1997)

The alarming level of violent and other heinous crimes in Nigeria and other parts of the world, where the foreign system operates, offers an attestation to the limitations of the system. From all indications, there is no longer the fear of criminal sanctions or much reverence for the prescribed social norms and rules.

The relative success and effectiveness of the indigenous criminal law system in the prevention and control of crimes in the pre-colonial societies can be attributed to some factors. Unlike the modern system, which seeks to adopt a 'one size fits all' approach over a cross section of culturally and historically diverse peoples; crime control mechanisms in pre-colonial Africa varied from one community to another. The indigenous strategies of crime control in pre-colonial Africa grew out of each society's traditions, and customs. The strategies also grew out of native laws and the society's historical circumstances and desires.

In the pre-colonial societies, community members, individually and collectively, played roles in each society's law enforcement efforts. This is unlike in the modern system where these tasks are consigned to centrally controlled police and other law enforcement agencies, which largely do not enjoy the trust and confidence of the people. Being home-grown, community members generally accepted and respected the community's methods and procedures for security maintenance and crime control. Members of each community knew the people engaged in the community's security, and crime control machinery, vis-a-vis moral and other credentials. Hence, persons of questionable character were not likely to be entrusted with security or crime control tasks. This is unlike the modern system where security and crime control activities are vested in a relatively detached police force that perennially face questions of incompetence, corruption and other vices.

Furthermore, the intervention of supernatural forces in the dispensation of harsh punishment to wrongdoers serves to instill raw fear in people, offering a strong deterrent force. The level of confidence and beliefs in the capabilities of relatively incorruptible avenging gods, from whom there is virtually no escape, is so high that it is sufficient to dissuade many from wrong doing. In the case of the modern system, the element of fear has been watered down due to different factors. Unscrupulous lawyers, corrupt judicial officers and law enforcement agents and so on tend to offer an avenue of escape for offenders, with a widespread belief that justice is for the highest bidder (Adegunde 2005, pp. 51–52). Besides, the technologically advanced gadgets deployed to crime control, even record failures, due to various limitations – a situation that, perhaps, informs the American detour to the supernatural realm as depicted in *Psychic Witness*.

13.5.1 Clamour for the Past

Despite strenuous efforts at suppressing it by law and other Western influences indigenous criminology and social control system survived and retained its influence in the colonial era and beyond. The prevalence and confidence in indigenous social control mechanisms until the present time is well established. For example, in Nigeria, the indigenous criminological practice of oath-taking remains a popular process of ensuring fidelity or exacting truth. So venerated has been the process that even among political office holders in charge of governance have shown a preference for oath-taking in ensuring performance of pacts entered into with associates instead of relying on conventional courts legally established for such purposes (Okafo 2007, pp. 5–6; Oraegbunam 2009, pp. 69–70).

To reiterate, oath-taking has always been an acceptable practice and a common feature of dispute resolution and crime detection among indigenous Africans. The people's strong belief that it is one of the assured ways of obtaining untainted justice has enabled this practice to survive and remain appealing as a legitimate social control process (Oraegbunam 2009). Along similar lines as oath-taking, there are indications that indigenous criminal law practice of *trial by ordeal* still finds acceptance among the people. An illustration, though a tragic one, was the widely reported 'Okija incident' of 2004 in which police recovered many human skulls and decaying bodies at the site of a shrine in eastern part of Nigeria (Oraegbunam 2009, p. 5).

Preference of supernatural processes of oath-taking or other indigenous practices as dispute-resolution or crime control mechanisms in modern times, above and beyond the conventional legal or judicial mechanisms, raises a central issue of confidence. In one dimension, it signifies the high level of confidence reposed in a long existing indigenous social control apparatus. On the other side, it reflects the lack or low level of confidence in the Western-style conventional mechanism imposed by the colonial masters and sustained by post-colonial governments.

However, the persistent attractiveness of indigenous practices of oath taking, *trial by ordeal* and so on appears to be a paradox. From colonial days till now, some people have unwholesome impression or perception of the practices. For example, in the context of the modern times, a commentator had this to say about oath taking: '[the] practice of oath-taking is not only fetish, barbaric, uncivilized, outdated, anachronistic, criminal, illegal but also contrary to Nigerian jurisprudence as it is superstitious, mysterious, and spiritualistic in a society that is supposed to be dynamic and not static' (Oraegbunam 2009, p. 79). Along similar lines, a judge of the Nigerian Court of Appeal – the next to the highest court in the country – in disagreeing with the position of a lower court on oath taking gave this opinion:

> The belief of the learned trial judge that disputes are decided by swearing "Juju" may be true as a matter of the past. In this century, *that will be a retreat to trial by ordeal which is unthinkable any more than swearing 'Juju' as a method of proof. We cannot now reel back to superstitious fear and foreswear our religious faith.*[16]

[16] *Iwuchukwu v.Anyanwu* (1993) 8NWLR (pt 311) 311 at 323 [emphasis added].

There arises the question of why people persistently find the indigenous social control practices attractive in spite of the uncomplimentary impressions and comments about them, as shown above. Some explanations can be given for the scenario. One is the dissatisfaction and disenchantment with the foreign English criminal-justice system because of its perceived ineffectiveness and inefficiency in crime control and other aspects (Elechi 2004, pp. 20–21). Due to the unceasing increase in the incidence of crimes coupled with the brazen impunities of criminals, as well as criminals escaping sanctions, many tend to view that the foreign English system is ineffective and inefficient for social control in the country. Naturally, there arises a yearning for the 'good old days' when the gods dispensed justice impartially and effectively. This propels an interest and preference of the traditional ways of solving criminal, socio-political and other problems.

It is not only in the area of social control that the colonially imposed system has failed African people. In some places, services, infrastructure and institutions provided by the state justice and other systems are not existent or bare. Consequently, many Africans, especially those in rural communities, feel alienated from the imposed foreign system of social control and services. This, in some ways, has accounted for renewed interest in indigenous systems of social control and service provision, which the people tend to see as more sympathetic and beneficial. Commenting on the persistent and renewed interest in indigenous systems of social regulation and control, it has been observed:

> The renewed interest is based, in part, on the fact that these institutions have proven to be resilient. In addition, they are more effectively institutionalized, and Africans rely upon them to provide required goods and services in the face of the failure of the formal, colonial-based structures. Such goods and services include: security, roads, bridges, schools, post offices, mechanisms for conflict resolution, common-pool resources management and credit provisions, to mention a few. (Elechi 2004, pp. 21–22)

Thirdly, due to fundamental socio-cultural differences, the English-based system of social control in Nigeria lacks the cultural relativity that it enjoys in England, its place of origin. Many Africans, over generations, have simply abided in the traditional ways of operating, disconnected from the foreign system. The ineffectiveness of the foreign system in different areas gives a sense of justification to the adherents of the traditional ways and a stimulus for others to return to the 'old ways of the ancestors'. This situation is well illustrated by a popular refrain among the Yoruba, '*e je ka'se bi won ti nse, ko ba'le ri bi o ti nri*' which, contextually means, 'let's do things the way of our ancestors, so that things would be right or proper'.

Another basis of attraction of the indigenous justice system is the comparatively inexpensive, prompt and relatively uncomplicated nature of the system. By and large, the indigenous justice system appears to satisfy people's yearnings for quicker, less expensive, and culturally relevant justice and social order. The Western-style criminal-justice system is an adversarial contest between the government prosecutors and defence lawyers for the accused in which the victim becomes a mere prosecution witness (Obilade 1979, p. 120).Operating the system entails the operation of a complex set of rules, procedures and technicalities with the involvement of judicial officers, and lawyers on opposing sides for prosecuting and defending the accused. It is trite that the process is cumbersome, expensive, time consuming, and insensitive to the plight of victims in some circumstances. On the contrary, the traditional justice system, being of a restorative and reformative nature, constitutes a prompt, uncomplicated process permitting active involvement and participation by victims, offenders, families and the entire community in arriving at a resolution acceptable to all concerned. Generally, victims of crime under the indigenous justice system are given access to mechanisms of justice and to prompt redress and remedies such as restitution, supported with material and emotional support, unlike the mechanical and impersonal imposed system where victims feel re-victimized by government agencies of social control (Elechi 2004, p. 22). The situation has been summed up this way:

> Essentially, the foreign system contracts poorly with the African criminal justice system... The traditional procedure was simple and devoid of any formality. The approach was more of common sense as opposed to crass legalism or technicality. The natives invariably found it to be convenient and intelligible, being grounded in familiar concepts and notions. They were afforded full participation in this speedy and cheap administration of justice. (Obilade 1979, p. 120)

From the foregoing, it is evident that the continued and increasing embrace of indigenous social control practices in the modern times is not likely to cease any time soon. Diverse reasons and factors will continue to make the traditional ways appealing to Africans, propelling them to further embrace indigenous practices of social control, in disregard of the colonially introduced approaches. The relatively recent resurgence of indigenous security and law enforcement systems and organizations in some African countries highlight this point.

There are diverse forms of unofficial, indigenous security and law enforcement systems and organizations in different parts of Africa. Kick-starting or catalyzing this trend is the general belief that the official, Western-styled systems and organizations are incapable of, or have failed in, providing needed security and law enforcement as effectively as the indigenous systems. The other related reason for the re-emergence of the indigenous styled security and law enforcement organizations is that most citizens consider the official government crime control and law enforcement agencies as imposed, irrelevant, and different in forms and procedures from the citizens' traditional outlooks, convictions, practices, and beliefs.

For example, in Nigeria, where the confidence of citizens in the official government security and law enforcement agencies has seriously waned, if not totally lost, indigenous security and law enforcement organisations have emerged at different times among the dominant tribal groups.

The *'Bakasi Boys'* emerged among the Igbos of the South-Eastern part, while the *Odu'a Peoples Congress (OPC)* emerged among the Yoruba of the South-Western part.[17] In their operations, the *Bakasi Boys* and the *OPC* customarily embrace and rely on supernatural powers, based on indigenous African religious beliefs and practices. Highlighting the *modus operandi,* effectiveness and the related high level

[17] The *Hisha* also emerged among the Hausa/Fulani of the Northern part of Nigeria. "The *Hisha,* is an Islam-based law enforcement organization, officially charged by governments of each of the states where it is operating, with the responsibility of enforcing the state's *shari'a* system". Okafo (13–14).

of public confidence in these indigenous security and law enforcement organisations, a researcher made the following findings concerning the *Bakasi Boys*:

> In the southeastern states of Nigeria where the *Bakasi Boys* operate, the organization is widely regarded as an effective public security and law enforcement group. The organization is, over and above the NPF (the official police), the de facto guarantor of public security, particularly in the Igbo area of the country. The *Bakasi Boys* are reputed to be so good that they are capable of identifying a criminal despite attempts to conceal his or her identity. The *Bakasi Boys* move from one community to another fishing out suspected criminals (mainly perennial thieves, armed robbers, and murderers), arresting, and quickly judging and punishing the criminals. The punishment is typically death, which is applied swiftly by decapitating and burning the adjudged criminal. In my summer 2000–2006 field trips to Nigeria, most of the locals with whom I discussed the *Bakasi Boys*' operations expressed satisfaction with, and enthusiastic support for, the *Bakasi Boys*' crime-fighting activities. Most of the locals expressed confidence that the *Bakasi Boys,* [ostensibly, using indigenous supernatural powers] are able to accurately identify a criminal even among a large group of people, thus avoiding misidentification or punishment of an innocent person. (Okafo 2007, p. 14)

Apart from the large, coordinated, and well-organized indigenous organisations found in African countries, such as the '*Bakasi boys'* and *OPC,* there are other groups operating on principles and ideals of security and law enforcement agencies of pre-colonial African societies. These include neighborhood watch organizations or vigilante groups, found in most African communities, urban and rural. These smaller groups, similarly, arose due to the limitations and inadequacies of the official law enforcement organisations. These security organisations exist to help safeguard security of lives and properties of citizens. In another respect, like the age-grade groups of Igbo land and the hunters association in Yoruba land, as earlier discussed,[18] able bodied young men of each community, acting as vigilantes and supported financially and materially by the other community members undertake tasks of securing the community and enforcing the law. Ordinarily, they operate with the aids of small weapons, and typically as Africans, some reliance on magical powers. In different measures, these organisations contribute significantly to security and law enforcement across Nigeria. With the relative satisfactions of citizens with their services and the persistent shortcomings and loss-of-faith in the government security agencies, there will be a continuous need and recourse to these social control features of pre-colonial Africa.

13.6 Indigenous Social Control Practices in the Framework of the Modern System: Semblances of Official Recognition and Approval

Undeniably, in embracing the services of psychics in crime detection, American law enforcement agencies offer a tacit recognition and appreciation of the legitimacy of supernatural intervention in crime control in the modern times. In diverse ways,

[18] See the section headed, '*African Criminology System: an Intermix of the Physical and Supernatural*'.

official government institutions in Africa too have been lending credence to the legitimacy of the supernatural components of indigenous African criminal and social control practices. The positions and pronouncements of some high level Nigerian courts, including the Supreme Court, the highest court in the country, on oath-taking offer some illustrations.

In the Supreme Court case of *Ume v Okoronkwo & Anor*[19] a case emanating from a native arbitration in respect of title to the land in dispute, Oguegbu J.S.C. while delivering the lead judgment, with a tacit note of approval, *inter alia,* pronounced oath-taking as 'one of the methods of establishing the truth of a matter and was known to customary law and accepted by both parties'. Similarly, in the case of *Ofomata & ors v. Anoka*[20] the question of the legal validity of oath- taking arose for resolution. On the issue the judge, Agbakoba J held,

> Oath-taking is a recognized and accepted form of proof existing in certain customary judicature. Oath may be sworn extra-judicial but as a mode of judicial proof, its esoteric and reverential feature, the solemnity of the choice of an oath by the disputants and imminent evil visitation to the oath breaker if he swore falsely, are the deterrent sanctions of this form of customary judicial process which commends it alike to rural and urban indigenous courts. It is therefore my view that the decision to swear an oath is not illegal although it may be obnoxious to Christian ethics....

Again, in the case of *John Onyenge & Ors v Loveday Ebere & Ors.*,[21] a land dispute case, the question regarding the legitimacy of oath-taking as a component of the customary justice process came up before the Supreme Court. In a unanimous decision, the Court upheld the verdict of a lower court, which was based upon the oath sworn before the '*Ogwugwu Akpu*' of Okija in Anambra State. In the lead judgment, to which other justices concurred, Niki Tobi J.S.C. reaffirmed the Supreme Court's recognition of oath-taking as a valid and legitimate process of customary law arbitration.

Apart from the judicial credence which the indigenous practice of oath-taking has enjoyed in relative measures, as illustrated in the above-noted cases, the process finds some statutory support too. In one respect, there is the range of enactments at federal and state levels, providing for oath taking in respect of public offices or duties, or to ensure fidelity on the part of witnesses in judicial proceedings. True, these may not substantively be the same as the indigenous genre of oath-taking, which entails the invocation of an awe-inspiring deity or juju; nonetheless, the fact that a person may swear on oath to a supernatural entity as, he elects, still has some generic connection with the traditional practice of oath taking. However, in a manner that is significantly similar to the indigenous format of oath-taking, the *Oaths and Affirmation Law* of Kwara State, one of the states constituting the Nigerian federation, provides that an oath may be offered to the other party challenging him to support his allegation by swearing to a traditional form of oath.[22]

[19] *Ume v. Okoronkwo* (1996) 12 SCNJ, 404.

[20] (1974) 3 ECSLR 251 at 254.

[21] (2004) 6 SCNJ 126 at 141–143.

[22] *Oaths and Affirmation Law*, Cap 108, Laws of Kwara State 1994, Sects. 7 and 8.

Beyond the issue of official appreciation of the indigenous practice of oath-taking as earlier discussed, there have been other forms of official appreciation and recognition of the relevance of indigenous criminological practices in the modern times. As a pointer, by means of government policies, laws and logistics in some cases, indigenous security and law enforcement bodies are given legitimate platforms to operate, at times in collaboration with official enforcement bodies.

13.7 Conclusion

The different facets and mechanisms of indigenous African criminology have been considered in previous sections. One factor that runs through and constitutes the bedrock of the indigenous criminology is the inherent, and virtually inevitable, involvement of the supernatural. Even in the essentially physical acts of security and law enforcement entailing patrol, night-watch and related tasks, there is still a reference to the supernatural. The supernatural outlook emanates from the religious, ritualistic or mystic structures in which the traditional criminological practices are grounded.

With the pivotal involvement of the supernatural in indigenous African criminology, it has faced the criticism of being unscientific and concomitant question of acceptability. In a related vein, due to fundamental socio-cultural and religious differences, the colonial masters perceived and disapproved of indigenous social control practices as outdated, barbaric and generally unwholesome. There resulted the suppression of indigenous criminology. The suppression, as earlier noted, took two main approaches. One, foreign criminological systems were imposed, set in the broad structure of introduction of the laws of the colonial masters. Two, there was specific outlawing of indigenous criminological practices by criminal law statutes.

It is true that there can be some cogent grounds to disagree with some aspects of indigenous criminological practices. Being subjective and unscientific, due to reliance on the supernatural, there is the possibility of error and irredeemable miscarriage of justice. For example, there would be a legitimate basis for concern over the way the *Bakasi boys* magically and subjectively identify or detect criminals who were then subjected to summary execution by decapitation and burning. Such manner of dispensing justice may indeed lend credence to the perception of indigenous criminology as 'spiritualistic, barbaric, uncivilized, and criminal'; this would particularly be so, based on the irreversibility of the sanction where an executed accused is later found innocent. Put simply, the possibility of mistakes or mischief on the part of supernatural forces or their human agents makes entrusting crime detection to supernatural forces questionable.

Realistically, the likelihood of miscarriage of justice through reliance on supernatural mechanisms and subjective procedures cannot be trivialized. However, inferring from the range of accuracy in the identification of criminals as shown in different episodes of the programme, the American 'Psychic Witness' seems to be showing, from a somewhat scientific or statistical perspective, that the supernatural forces are not as error-prone as to be out-rightly unreliable. Moreover, in the modern *scientific* and objective criminal systems operated in the technologically advanced countries like America, even in the twenty first century, there are still reports of miscarriage of justice resulting in horrendous suffering, judicial murders or near murders of innocent persons (Grisham 2006). If these *modern* systems are not summarily deemed unacceptable and discarded because of instances or possibility of errors of judgment, then the indigenous system should not be vilified and summarily discarded on the same ground. At any rate, as shown before, indigenous African criminology, in outlook, is not inherently abrasive and blood-lusty. Incidents such as the depicted *Bakasi* scenario, perhaps, should be considered as manifestations of overzealousness catalysed by circumstances in which the *Bakasi Boys* operated.

The charge that indigenous criminological practices are anachronistic and uncivilized is also debatable. It is trite that in the present times, many Africans have acquired high level Western education and values as well as embracing Christianity and other non-indigenous religions. Yet, many Africans, including those in government, still maintain high confidence in indigenous practices, especially oath-taking, for the resolution of disputes, as well as charms and related devices for security, solution to problems and other purposes. In this light, it would be inappropriate to criticize indigenous practices as anachronistic or uncivilized. Furthermore, seemingly, through 'Psychic Witness' and related programmes, America is showcasing the efficacy and desirability of supernatural intervention in modern criminology, or at least as a complement. If America or American security agents are not criticized as uncivilized for reference to the supernatural, then it would be unfair to adjudge the indigenous African approach as such.

Whatever misgivings one may have against the indigenous criminological system, its strength and effectiveness as a social control measure in the modern times should not be overlooked or underrated. 'The wide acceptance that the indigenous models enjoy over their Western-based counterparts strongly attests to the relevance and currency of the indigenous African systems of control, justice, and law even in the modern State' (Okafo 2007, p. 18). The confidence and preference of the indigenous social control mechanisms logically signify the level of effectiveness and compliance the mechanisms would enjoy if deployed by the governments.

Nigeria and other African countries are confronted with disturbing levels of violent and other crimes. The Western-style machineries and institutions for combating the crimes have been found to be ineffective in the battle against crimes. Clearly underlying the impunity with which criminals operate is the lack of reverence or fear of the modern Western-style criminology systems unlike the scenario in the pre-colonial societies. Considering the utility of the indigenous systems in the prevailing circumstances, there is an incontrovertible need in many African countries for the governments to recognize and promote the relevant indigenous systems of security maintenance, crime prevention, and general law enforcement. The first step is to change the perception of indigenous criminology as barbaric, uncivilized and so on, just because of its supernatural or *unscientific* tilt. The American 'Psychic Witness' has shown that there is indeed a need to re-appraise the usefulness of indigenous African criminology. The persistence of indigenous practices in diverse forms also buttresses the need for the re-appraisal.

References

Abegunde B (2005) Corruption the enemy within: legal and institutional panacea. Ibadan Bar J 4, 50–62
Asein JO (2005) Introduction to Nigerian legal system, 2nd edn. Ababa Press, Lagos
Awolalu JO, Dopamu PA (1979) West African traditional religion. Onibonoje Press/Book Industries (Nig.), Ibadan
Ayo SB (2002) Public administration and the conduct of community affairs among the Yoruba in Nigeria. Institute for Contemporary Studies Press, Oakland
Ayonrinde A (2007) Great quotations for all achievers. Bookman Books, Taipei
Caldwell RG (1965) Criminology, 2nd edn. The Ronald Press, New York
Cobley C (2005) Sex offenders, law, policy and practice, 2nd edn. Jordan Publishing, Bristol
Elechi OO (2004) Human rights and the African indigenous justice system. A paper for presentation at the 18th international conference of the International Society for the Reform of Criminal Law, 8–12 Aug, Montreal
Fitzmaurice C, Pease K (1986) The psychology of judicial sentencing. Manchester University Press, Manchester
Garner BA et al (eds) (2004) Black's law dictionary, 8th edn. Thomson West, St. Paul
Grisham J (2006) The innocent man (murder and Injustice in a small town). Bantam Dell, New York
Ibidapo-Obe A (2005) A synthesis of African law. Concept Publications, Lagos
Kolajo AA (2005) Customary law in the Nigeria through the cases. Spectrum Books, Ibadan
Obilade AO (1979) Nigerian legal system. Sweet & Maxwell, London
Okafo N (2007) Law enforcement in postcolonial Africa: interfacing indigenous and English policing in Nigeria. In: International police executive symposium working paper no 7
Okonkwo CO (1990) Okonkwo and Naish on criminal law in Nigeria, 2nd edn. Spectrum Law Publishing, Ibadan
Oraegbunam IK (2009) The principles and practice of justice in traditional Igbo jurisprudence. OGIRISI New J Afr Stud 6:53–85
Psychic Witness (2011) http://www.tv.com/psychic-witness/show/61792/summary.html. Accessed on 12 Feb 2011
Psychic Detectives (2013) http://www.tv.com/shows/psychic-detectives/. Accessed on 30 Jan 2013
Roberts MF, Vink M (1998) Alkaloids: ecology and medicinal applications. Plenum Press, New York

Index

A

African Charter on Human and Peoples Rights, 9, 11, 117, 147, 206, 234
African communitarianism, 241–262
African criminology, 265–287
African culture, 35, 45, 50, 66, 80, 85, 89, 100, 101, 106, 109, 136, 215, 257
African customary law, 6, 32–34, 36, 38, 39, 42–46, 48–51, 53, 54, 56–58, 60, 62, 65, 67, 72, 185, 211
African development, 241, 253, 256, 257
African ethics, 137, 138
African humanism, 6, 35, 37, 38, 44, 50, 52, 53, 63, 250–254, 256, 262
African humanist, 12, 39–50, 53, 67, 241, 243, 250–252, 255, 257, 261, 262
African jurisprudence, 5–8, 10, 73, 77, 79, 81, 82, 89, 93–106, 156, 162–168, 190
African law, 3–5, 7, 8, 19, 22, 33, 39, 42, 44–48, 50, 52, 53, 55, 57, 60, 63–66, 72, 73, 75–79, 88, 109–126, 266
African legal consciousness, 35, 44, 53, 63
African legal systems, 8, 59, 76–78, 84, 89, 109–111, 122
African legal theory, 1–8, 17–29, 72–78, 80, 82, 83, 85, 88, 111, 173, 174
African philosophy, 3, 4, 6, 10, 38, 54, 72, 73, 82, 84, 102, 126, 200
African politics, 36, 98, 99, 101, 140, 157
African values, 9, 86, 131–149, 199, 232
Afrocentrism, 71–89
Afro-communitarianism, 1, 9, 11, 131, 132, 148–149
Anti-formalism, 64–66
Autonomy, 9, 12, 58, 115, 116, 149, 159, 183, 186, 196, 222, 232, 233, 235–236

B

Banjul Charter, 131–149

C

Capitalism, 17–20, 174, 181, 226, 236, 242, 248, 252–254, 256, 257, 261, 262
Centre, 31, 33–35, 37, 50, 61, 64, 66, 85, 98, 99, 105, 154, 156, 205, 206, 232, 237, 251, 260
Character, 9, 20, 48, 54, 75, 105, 155, 159–161, 165, 166, 169, 176, 190, 201–203, 205, 207, 230, 233, 280
Citationality, 177, 186
Civil and political rights, 158, 191, 234
Civil society, 98, 99, 146, 173, 175, 179, 181, 192, 226, 234–238
Codification, 10, 38, 64–66, 75
Collectivity, 133
Colonial, 5–7, 11, 12, 18, 19, 21–23, 25, 31, 33–35, 37–45, 50–52, 55, 56, 58, 59, 61–63, 67, 71, 72, 78, 88, 96, 98, 100, 101, 120, 122, 154, 155, 163, 190, 199, 200, 202, 205, 208, 211, 212, 236, 243, 248, 253, 255–257, 266, 268, 274–282, 284, 286, 287
Colonialism, 17, 19–21, 31, 41, 56, 88, 96, 98–100, 111, 122, 174, 190, 200, 205, 215, 248, 250, 265, 266, 274–278
Colonial law, 7, 34, 51, 55, 72, 88, 155
Common law, 25, 26, 36–38, 48, 60, 61, 64–66, 102, 110, 112, 120, 124–126
Communalism, 8, 28, 96, 98, 121, 189, 256, 257
Communitarianism, 28, 131–136, 148, 189, 241–262

O. Onazi (ed.), *African Legal Theory and Contemporary Problems: Critical Essays*, Ius Gentium: Comparative Perspectives on Law and Justice 29, DOI 10.1007/978-94-007-7537-4, © Springer Science+Business Media Dordrecht 2014

Community, 2, 19, 33, 74, 94, 117, 131, 155, 174, 200, 225, 250, 268
Compassion, 28, 232, 238
Conditionalities, 24, 229, 244, 258
Constitution, 10, 25–28, 40, 116, 117, 121, 125, 136, 138, 154, 157, 161, 166, 168, 169, 173, 175, 177, 178, 180, 183, 186, 187, 190, 191, 204, 205, 211, 213, 233, 236, 276
Contemporary problems, 1–6, 10, 12, 32, 73, 74, 116, 117, 164
Contract law, 101–106
Cooperation, 5, 8, 95, 101, 104, 221, 230, 231, 233, 259
Cosmopolitan, 57, 86, 89, 157, 167
Crime-control, 266–269, 277–284
Criminal law, 12, 13, 25, 48, 85, 89, 110, 114, 118, 124, 210, 265, 266, 277–284, 286
Criminology, 12, 265–287
Culture, 3, 17, 31, 73, 96, 109, 136, 167, 183, 199, 245
Culture's in-between, 17, 18, 22–29
Custom, 3, 7, 10, 34, 39–44, 47, 54, 56–60, 72, 73, 75, 77, 79–81, 88, 89, 106, 177, 182, 186, 203, 261, 268, 270, 280
Customary law, 6, 18, 19, 25, 32–34, 36, 38, 39, 41–51, 53–62, 64, 65, 67, 72, 78, 103, 155, 185, 187, 190, 203, 211, 254, 275, 276, 278, 285

D

Decolonization, 35, 38, 46, 55, 61, 63, 64
Deities, 266, 269–273, 278, 279
Deliberative democracy, 161
Democracy, 25, 26, 97, 101, 113, 115, 117, 140, 146, 147, 149, 161, 173, 174, 178, 179, 187, 188, 224, 226, 227, 229, 232–236, 238, 242, 244–246, 255
Dependency theory, 244, 248–250
Detective, 267, 272
Development, 4, 23, 31, 75, 96, 111, 132, 165, 183, 200, 222, 241, 266
Developmentalism, 241–262
Dialectic, 6, 24, 63, 118, 246
Dignity, 9, 28, 84–86, 89, 116, 120, 126, 132, 136–144, 146–149, 156, 163, 168, 189, 190, 196, 232, 261
Discrimination, 26, 27, 154, 157, 192, 234, 237
Dualism, 31–67
Duties, 2, 9, 11, 51, 87, 131, 133, 139, 142, 145, 158, 163, 190, 206, 285

E

Economic and social rights, 9, 157, 158
Elias, T.O., 6, 33–35, 39, 66
Empathy, 159, 161, 164, 167–169
English law, 6, 33, 34, 36–38, 40, 41, 43, 45, 50, 51, 54, 55, 57–67; 208, 274, 275
Enlightenment, 6, 17, 20–22, 47, 104, 120, 164
Environment, 1, 4, 6, 18, 22, 28, 29, 43, 45, 47, 65, 74, 142, 203, 206, 214, 224, 229, 230, 257, 261, 262
Epistemological, 3, 4, 20, 118
Ethical life, 155, 167, 168
Ethics, 2, 58, 84, 136–138, 162, 227, 265, 285
Ethnic group, 11, 134, 135, 154
Eurocentric, 72, 73, 249

F

Feminism, 36
Feminist, 10, 162, 182–184, 188, 189, 191, 207, 231, 239
Flourishing, 19, 60, 137, 142, 145, 149, 155, 167, 168, 196, 221
Formal, 5, 11, 43, 57, 76, 89, 102, 114, 122, 203, 221–223, 225, 228–232, 234, 236, 282
Formalism, 59, 64–66, 246
Freedom, 8, 9, 25, 26, 33, 45, 60, 85, 116–119, 121, 125, 135, 142, 146, 157, 181, 183, 186, 196, 224, 228, 235–237, 244, 257

G

Globalisation/globalization, 28, 36, 49, 229, 242, 251, 253
Good life, 77, 161
Group rights, 9, 131–149

H

Healthcare rights, 187
Hegemonic, 24, 32, 66, 72–74, 88, 181, 183, 196, 247
HIV/AIDS, 179, 180, 182, 186, 188, 191–195
Homo economicus, 51, 94, 105
Human beings, 12, 21, 28, 77, 78, 84, 85, 95, 116, 133, 136–138, 143, 147, 148, 161, 165–168, 170, 176, 178, 189–191
Human development, 96, 241, 243, 260–262
Human dignity, 9, 28, 84, 89, 126, 132, 136, 137, 149, 190, 261
Humanity, 1, 10, 27, 48, 53, 55, 73, 76, 77, 84, 86, 89, 119, 124, 133, 143, 156, 163, 165–167, 189, 207, 252, 256, 257, 261

Human rights, 6, 24, 33, 74, 131, 154, 173, 199, 221, 244, 265
Hybridity, 6, 24, 31–67

I
Identitarian, 36, 37, 59
Identity, 2, 21, 24, 32, 35, 36, 38, 45–48, 53, 54, 59, 60, 62–64, 66, 67, 73, 96, 98, 101, 137–144, 149, 154, 177, 184, 194, 225, 229, 260, 284
Imperialism, 18, 19, 33, 74, 200, 205
Independence, 35, 38, 45, 50, 52–55, 61, 64, 86, 98, 124, 194, 205, 222, 245, 248, 258, 260, 279
Indigene, 18, 19, 25–28, 154, 155, 169
Indigenous, 3, 4, 6, 7, 12, 26, 27, 31, 33, 34, 36, 37, 39, 41–52, 55, 56, 58–61, 63, 64, 72, 73, 75–78, 80, 88, 89, 98, 101, 109, 111, 112, 122, 131, 134, 136, 140, 154, 190, 191, 265–287
Indigenous knowledge, 4
Individual, 8, 18, 31, 74, 94, 109, 131, 155, 173, 205, 221, 245, 268
Informal political participation, 11, 12, 222–224, 228–234, 236–239
Injustice, 2, 56, 84, 166, 174, 182, 204, 229
Institutions, 1–3, 5, 7, 12, 31, 33, 37, 39, 41, 48, 56, 59, 64, 65, 73, 75, 77, 79, 83, 94, 96, 98–100, 106, 116, 119, 120, 123, 133, 160, 163, 166, 173–175, 182, 183, 185, 187, 192, 196, 200, 222, 223, 225, 226, 229–233, 235, 236, 241, 243–247, 249–251, 254, 255, 257, 261, 262, 265, 268, 282, 285, 287
Integration, 9, 66, 155, 159, 206, 245
Interdependence, 7, 28, 84–86, 89, 96, 102, 103, 156, 164–166, 168, 190, 196, 232
International law, 4, 6, 28, 31–34, 40, 41, 44, 57, 58, 67, 72–75, 79, 87, 124, 173, 249
Interpersonal, 8, 95, 97, 102, 106, 156, 159, 162, 163

J
Judiciary, 47, 55, 56, 61, 65, 67, 109, 123–125, 244, 247
Juridical Negritude, 31–67
Jurisprudence, 2, 5–8, 10, 17, 18, 21, 22, 29, 71–73, 77, 79, 81, 82, 84, 89, 93–106, 109, 122, 123, 156, 162–168, 190, 254, 278, 281
Justice, 2, 23, 31, 72, 104, 109, 138, 166, 174, 199, 225, 242, 265

K
Knowledge, 3, 4, 7, 17–22, 24, 26, 28, 37, 44, 45, 62, 63, 72, 73, 79, 105, 106, 118, 120, 163–166, 189, 193, 194, 237, 265, 275

L
Labour rights, 11, 159, 222, 223, 227, 228
Law and literature, 199, 200, 203–206, 214
Legal consciousness, 34–37, 39, 44, 49, 50, 53, 63, 66, 165
Legal empowerment, 11, 221–239
Legal empowerment of the poor, 11, 221–239
Legal formalisation, 11, 237
Legal philosophy, 2, 5, 36, 43, 67, 71, 74, 131
Legal pluralism, 36
Legal positivism, 72, 74–76, 79, 109
Legal subject, 8, 109–126
Legal system, 8, 25, 40–43, 45, 48, 51, 54, 56–59, 64, 75–78, 84, 86, 88, 89, 102, 103, 109–112, 114–116, 118–123, 125, 126, 190, 213, 223, 225, 247, 274, 275, 277
Legal traditions, 35, 36, 75, 109, 191
Liberal, 25, 26, 56, 57, 113, 115, 132, 135, 136, 146, 156, 157, 160, 173–175, 181–183, 185–187, 189, 196, 204–206, 246, 247, 256
Liberalism, 10, 28, 34, 156, 174, 178, 181, 182, 185, 190, 191, 195, 196, 244
Love, 9, 121, 138, 164

M
Malawi, 17, 19, 25, 27, 71
Market, 2, 57, 59, 174, 184, 209, 221, 226–228, 230, 231, 236, 237, 242, 244, 253, 260
Market fundamentalism, 242, 260–261
Marxism, 10, 187, 249
Metropolis, 32, 248, 257
Modern, 4, 5, 8, 13, 20, 23, 42–44, 48, 51, 52, 54, 55, 58–60, 64, 76, 80, 83, 84, 87, 103, 107, 109–126, 213, 214, 232, 247, 266–268, 280, 281, 283, 285–287
Modernity, 8, 17–22, 24, 28, 46, 50, 51, 54, 57, 59, 60, 95, 115, 116, 122, 165, 232, 241, 253, 255, 256
Modernization theory, 244–249
Modern knowledge, 4, 20

Morality, 26, 27, 56, 58, 72, 79, 82, 88, 101, 104, 117, 131, 137, 144, 149, 185, 189, 200, 271
Moral values, 3, 9, 80, 155, 156, 161–170

N
Nationalism, 38, 51, 53, 59, 249, 253
Natural law, 2, 58, 72, 75, 78, 86, 88, 104
Negritude, 7, 31–67
Nigeria, 33–40, 43, 44, 54, 55, 57, 61, 65, 66, 109–115, 118–121, 123–126, 153–156, 203, 205, 211, 241, 251, 265, 267–269, 271, 273–277, 279–284, 287, 291
Norms, 6, 7, 10, 18, 19, 24–28, 32, 39, 44, 48, 51, 57, 75, 76, 78, 79, 87, 88, 95, 98–106, 139, 149, 173, 176–178, 181, 182, 186, 187, 194–196, 200, 201, 215, 223, 233, 238, 254, 261, 266, 274–278, 280

O
Oath-taking, 13, 211, 214, 266, 270–272, 278, 281, 285–287
Othering, 17, 20
Ownership, 2, 12, 48, 222, 238, 239, 254, 257, 259

P
Pan-Africanism, 8, 53, 57, 63
Performative perspective, 10, 174–179, 187, 196
Performativity, 176, 177, 186, 187
Periphery, 31, 32, 34–37, 61, 63, 66, 249
Person, 2, 7, 8, 25, 26, 28, 52, 84, 87, 94–96, 98, 101, 102, 104, 105, 110, 113–117, 121, 124, 126, 133, 134, 140, 144, 145, 153, 163, 166, 177, 185, 189, 190, 209–213, 250, 252, 269, 271–277, 279, 284, 285
Personhood, 27, 134, 189, 250–252, 262
Philosophy, 2–6, 9–11, 17, 18, 20–22, 27–29, 35, 36, 38, 41, 43, 49, 54, 67, 71–74, 76–78, 82, 84, 85, 95, 102, 104, 107, 115, 120, 126, 131, 132, 148, 189, 199–215, 253, 255–258, 261, 262
Political community, 155–157, 159, 160, 163–165
Political participation, 9, 11, 12, 160, 161, 221–239
Politics, 28, 36, 39, 46, 50–59, 74, 93–95, 98–101, 121, 161, 162, 170, 176, 185, 187, 207, 214, 224, 225, 228, 229, 231–235, 237–239, 260
Postcolonial, 4, 12, 34, 63
Postmodernism, 72
Poverty, 1, 2, 5, 11, 12, 20, 98, 99, 135, 139, 140, 142, 145, 188, 193, 222–224, 229, 236, 243, 244, 250, 253, 254, 256, 262
Privatisation, 232, 237
Property, 2, 11, 12, 27, 43, 57, 59, 82, 103, 133, 157, 159, 174, 181–183, 196, 222, 223, 227, 228, 235–237, 241, 243, 252–255, 257, 262, 269, 279
Property rights, 12, 103, 174, 181, 236, 237, 253–255
Proverbs, 3, 7, 80–81, 88, 206
Public goods, 11, 12, 97, 158, 160, 221, 222, 231, 232
Punishment, 2, 13, 81, 82, 89, 116, 209, 210, 271, 272, 277–280, 284

R
Reason, 4, 8, 20, 35, 38, 44, 51, 56, 72, 73, 76, 83, 85, 97–99, 104, 111, 113, 115–117, 119, 132, 135, 136, 138, 140, 143, 145, 146, 149, 154–156, 161, 162, 188, 203–205, 215, 225, 234–236, 265, 283
Reciprocity, 5, 94–96, 101, 102, 105, 106, 159, 164, 230, 232, 252
Recognition, 23, 26–28, 42–44, 60, 63, 71, 76, 84, 106, 133, 136, 163, 167, 177, 178, 184, 185, 189, 209–211, 215, 223, 225, 247, 284–286
Reconciliation, 13, 52, 82–84, 89, 132, 148, 158, 159, 278
Relational contract theory, 7, 8, 103–105
Republican, 94, 160, 187, 236
Responsibilities, 2, 7, 9, 10, 31, 65, 77, 78, 84–85, 87, 96–89, 110, 113, 114, 153–170, 181, 183, 186, 190, 206, 231, 269, 277, 283
Restitution, 13, 81, 82, 209, 278, 283
Restorative, 7, 54, 82–83, 89, 283
Rights, 2, 24, 33, 71, 98, 109, 131, 153, 173, 199, 222, 244, 265
Rights claiming, 175–179, 181–183, 185–187, 195, 196
Roman law, 102, 104, 106
Rule of law, 102, 103, 113, 115, 119–121, 123, 227, 236, 244, 246

S
Sedimentation, 10, 177
Settler, 154, 155, 169, 248
Social constructionism, 21
Social contract, 49, 95, 101, 102, 107, 160, 167
Social-control, 61, 76, 81, 216, 265–267, 278, 281–287
Socialism, 242, 254–257, 261
Socio-economic goods, 9, 132, 135, 139–140, 146–148
Sociology of law, 2
Solidarity, 5, 8, 28, 35, 52, 60, 86, 87, 95, 105, 137–144, 148, 149, 160, 189, 195, 230–233, 238, 245, 261
South Africa, 10, 25, 26, 40, 71, 83, 84, 86, 87, 131, 136, 155, 170, 173–175, 180, 182, 183, 186, 187, 190, 191, 195, 196, 265
Sovereignty, 24, 33, 41, 66, 75, 86, 87, 122, 258
State, 2, 18, 33, 72, 94, 110, 133, 154, 173, 203, 224, 242, 265
Strategic intersectionality, 36
Structural-functionalism, 244, 245
Subaltern, 41, 48
Subjectivities, 175, 177, 191–195
Sub-Saharan Africa, 1, 21, 134, 164, 165, 221, 231, 243, 244, 265
Supernatural, 12, 13, 25, 211, 266–274, 279–281, 283–287

T
Things Fall Apart, 10, 11, 199–215
Third world, 23, 31–34, 43, 52, 64, 66, 72–74, 222, 230, 242, 245–248, 250, 257, 261
Tradition, 1, 3, 20, 22, 23, 35, 37, 39–51, 56, 57, 59, 60, 73, 75, 77, 80, 81, 97, 98, 109, 110, 115, 116, 118, 119, 121, 131, 134, 145, 167, 187, 206, 277
Transmogrification, 25, 28
Transplantation, 34, 59, 275

U
Ubuntu, 6, 10, 24, 27–28, 84–85, 89, 136–138, 174, 175, 186, 189–191, 196
Ujamaa, 8, 98, 255–261
United Nations, 11, 32, 33, 72, 74, 135, 176, 222
United Nations Development Programme (UNDP), 11, 222–225
Universal, 4, 20, 28, 29, 32, 47, 52, 54, 57, 58, 66, 72, 78, 80, 86, 89, 93–106, 125, 155–157, 176, 199–215, 234, 235, 245, 247, 256
Universal Declaration of Human Rights (UDHR), 125, 157, 234

V
Virtue, 9, 74, 82, 94, 101–105, 132, 133, 136, 138, 139, 143, 145, 148, 155, 159–161, 254

W
Washington Consensus, 242

MIX
Papier aus verantwortungsvollen Quellen
Paper from responsible sources
FSC® C105338

If you have any concerns about our products,
you can contact us on
ProductSafety@springernature.com

In case Publisher is established outside the EU,
the EU authorized representative is:
Springer Nature Customer Service Center GmbH
Europaplatz 3, 69115 Heidelberg, Germany

Printed by Libri Plureos GmbH
in Hamburg, Germany